Neo-Victorian Gothic

Horror, Violence and Degeneration in the Re-Imagined Nineteenth Century

Neo-Victorian Series

The Neo-Victorian Series aims to analyse the complex revival, re-vision and recycling of the long nineteenth century in the cultural imaginary. This contemporary phenomenon will be examined in its diverse British and worldwide, postcolonial and neo-colonial contexts, as well as its manifold forms, including literature, the arts, film, television, and virtual media. To assess such simultaneous artistic regeneration and retrogressive innovation and to tackle the ethical debate and ideological consequences of these re-appropriations will constitute the main challenges of this series.

Series Editors
Marie-Luise Kohlke
Christian Gutleben

Volume 3

Previous Volumes in the Series:

Neo-Victorian Tropes of Trauma: The Politics of Bearing After-Witness to Nineteenth-Century Suffering, vol. 1,
ed. by Marie-Luise Kohlke and Christian Gutleben (2010)

Neo-Victorian Families: Gender, Sexual and Cultural Politics, vol. 2,
ed. by Marie-Luise Kohlke and Christian Gutleben (2011)

Neo-Victorian Gothic

Horror, Violence and Degeneration
in the Re-Imagined Nineteenth Century

Edited by
Marie-Luise Kohlke and Christian Gutleben

Amsterdam - New York, NY 2012

Cover image and design: © Marie-Luise Kohlke

The paper on which this book is printed meets the requirements of "ISO 9706:1994, Information and documentation - Paper for documents - Requirements for permanence".

ISBN: 978-90-420-3625-3
E-Book ISBN: 978-94-012-0896-3
© Editions Rodopi B.V., Amsterdam - New York, NY 2012
Printed in the Netherlands

Printed by Printforce, United Kingdom

Contents

The (Mis)Shapes of Neo-Victorian Gothic:
Continuations, Adaptations, Transformations　　　1
Marie-Luise Kohlke and Christian Gutleben

PART I　　Imperial Impostures and Improprieties

1. The Limits of Neo-Victorian History:
   Elizabeth Kostova's *The Historian* and *The Swan Thieves*　　51
   Andrew Smith

2. Reclaiming Plots: Albert Wendt's 'Prospecting'
   and Victoria Nalani Kneubuhl's *Ola Nā Iwi*
   as Postcolonial Neo-Victorian Gothic　　75
   Cheryl D. Edelson

3. Monsters against Empire: The Politics and Poetics of
   Neo-Victorian Metafiction in *The League of Extraordinary
   Gentlemen*　　97
   Sebastian Domsch

4. A Bodily Metaphorics of Unsettlement: Leora Farber's
   Dis-Location / Re-Location as Neo-Victorian Gothic　　123
   Jeanne Ellis

PART II　　The Horrid and the Sexy

5. Neo-Victorian Gothic and Spectral Sexuality
   in Colm Tóibín's *The Master*　　147
   Patricia Pulham

6. 'Jack the Ripper' as Neo-Victorian Gothic Fiction:
    Twentieth-Century and Contemporary Sallies
    into a Late Victorian Case and Myth   167
    Max Duperray

7. Chasing the Dragon: Bangtails, Toffs,
    Jack and Johnny in Neo-Victorian Fiction   197
    Sarah E. Maier

8. Neo-Victorian Female Gothic:
    Fantasies of Self-Abjection   221
    Marie-Luise Kohlke

PART III   Hybrid Forms

9. Epistemological Rupture and the Gothic Sublime
    in *Slouching Towards Bedlam*   253
    Van Leavenworth

10. Dead Words and Fatal Secrets: Rediscovering
    the Sensational Document in Neo-Victorian Gothic   279
    Kym Brindle

11. 'Fear Is Fun and Fun Is Fear':
    A Reflexion on Humour in Neo-Victorian Gothic   301
    Christian Gutleben

Contributors   327

Index   331

The (Mis)Shapes of Neo-Victorian Gothic: Continuations, Adaptations, Transformations

Marie-Luise Kohlke and Christian Gutleben

Abstract:
Though quintessentially Gothic in its focus on the extended afterlife of the nineteenth-century past within the present, as well as its preferred choice of tropes and themes, neo-Victorianism has not yet been properly situated within either Gothic criticism or Gothic culture, an oversight this chapter seeks to address. Reprising and renovating various motifs of Victorian Gothic and developing later strands like Eco Gothic, Steampunk, Postcolonial and Postmodern Gothic, neo-Victorianism problematises notions of otherness to construct a radically decentred and precarious subjectivity. In spite of its ambiguous identity politics, however, neo-Victorian Gothic also shows itself to be surprisingly politically and ethically resilient, participating in self-conscious cultural reflection and a critique of orthodoxy.

Keywords: ethics, hybridisation, imperialism, neo-Victorian, the other, postmodernism, the sublime, subjectivity, the uncanny, Victorian Gothic.

*****

Today Gothic is omnipresent, diffused through literature, film and other visual media, music, the internet, subcultures, lifestyles, fashion, advertising, tourism and heritage industries – in a seeming frenzy of rendering visible what was once largely relegated to imagination and the arts. This insidious spread of 'the Culture of Gothic' or 'Gothic culture' has been repeatedly remarked upon by critics (Edmundson 1999; Spooner 2006; Botting 2007). Whether read as a signal of obsessive postmodern anxiety about all manners of excess and hybridity (capitalist, technological, sexual, multicultural) or as a sign of a general instability, degeneration or decline of distinct 'Culture(s)', Gothic has permanently emerged from the crepuscular cultural unconscious into the brightly lit mainstream. Perhaps the most remarkable aspect of contemporary Gothic is its hegemonic power to invade all aspects of our consumer society. As Catherine Spooner notes, "[i]t has crossed disciplinary boundaries to be absorbed into all forms of media" (Spooner 2006: 23), suggesting that Gothic, like Dracula, knows no limits. It is not in the least surprising, then, that neo-Victorianism should also reflect the hegemony of Gothic: two fashionable phenomena like neo-Victorianism and (neo) Gothic were doomed to converge, if not to merge, their union almost predestined by their common revivalist premises.

The pervasiveness of Gothic is not only cultural but also commercial, inscribed as it is in a context of incessant globalised consumption and commoditisation. These processes are crucial for they threaten to radically disnature the Gothic. How can the Gothic go on defending marginality once it has become not only trendy but practically run-of-the-mill? How can the Gothic go on celebrating otherness as it becomes increasingly homogenised? Fred Botting forcefully highlights this danger of ontological corruption when he denounces contemporary "candygothic" as the hackneyed merchandisation of fear, which "no longer contain[s] the intensity of a desire for something that satisfyingly disturbs and defines social and moral boundaries" (Botting 2001b: 134). If the new Gothic modes "collude with the norms they once negatively defined", then, "[d]ifference and otherness, too, are absorbed in the serial circulations of the same, a flat plane of indifference, the monstrosity of norms" (Botting 2008a: 10).[1] Furthermore, if contemporary Gothic no longer foregrounds otherness, the question arises: can – or should – it still be considered as Gothic? One of the purposes of this volume is to examine just what kind of answers neo-Victorianism might bring to these questions and how it deals with Gothic's generic mutations and transformations. Arguably, it is precisely by exploring the Gothic in relation to the nineteenth-century past and the period's specific cultural field that neo-Victorianism endeavours to circumvent the hypermodern, globalised and uniform presentation of the Gothic, in the process re-kindling an intensely disturbing desire that unsettles norms and redefines boundaries once more.

---

[1] Elsewhere Botting confirms his analysis of contemporary Gothic: "Domesticated, welcomed, assimilated, 'normal monstrosity' eclipses the possibility of difference and otherness" (Botting 2007: 200).

Yet neo-Victorian Gothic is not (or at least not only) a product of postmodernity's joint processes of digitalisation and globalisation, as is evident from its historical emergence as both a literary genre and wider cultural phenomenon. Admittedly, neo-Victorianism's exact 'date of birth' remains a contentious issue, with critics variously situating its origins immediately after the death of Queen Victoria, after the Second World War and the end of high Modernism, or even later still, most commonly in the 1960s with the publication of Jean Rhys's *Wide Sargasso Sea* (1966) and John Fowles's *The French Lieutenant's Woman* (1969). In all of these cases, however, it predates the advent of Gothic's globalisation and tyranny of standardisation. Therefore, neo-Victorianism cannot be read simply as a product of Gothic culture, but must also be understood as the *purveyor* of said culture. For in effect, neo-Victorian fiction enacts Gothic principles and, as such, takes part in the constant reactivation of the Gothic.

Surveying the various studies of Gothic, it is striking to notice how their analyses of the Gothic might similarly apply to neo-Victorianism. Thus when Julian Wolfreys writes that in the Gothic "what returns is never simply a repetition […] but is always an iterable supplement: repetition with a difference", adding that in Gothic, "the dead continue to live on, to survive beyond life, in the afterlife that we call reading" (Wolfreys 2002: 19, 141), he might as well be formulating a resonant description of the dense intertextuality of neo-Victorian fiction. When Andrew Smith analyses never-dying ghosts as "a persistent reminder of what a culture can only express in oblique terms", describing the "[m]aking visible [of] what it is that haunts the ghosts" as "the crucial challenge for contemporary Gothic" (A. Smith 2007b: 153), he seems to evoke neo-Victorianism's comparable struggle with historical elision and unrepresentability, as well as its recurrent tropes of haunting and spectrality. When Markman Ellis claims that Gothic "hosts a contest between different versions of history", its fictions "indulg[ing] a kind of creative anachronism, proposing untoward, perverse connections between the deep past and contemporary life and politics" (Ellis 2000: 14), he might instead be affirming neo-Victorianism's deconstructionist tendencies and its claims for political relevance as opposed to entertaining escapism. When Christine Berthin notes apropos Gothic hauntings that "[i]n the recesses of each of us lurks a past that is not ours but that, nonetheless, conditions our every move" (Berthin 2010:

67), she inadvertently focalises the psychological and ideological links between Victorianism and neo-Victorianism also. When Botting defines the Gothic uncanny as "a return from the past", combined with "an effect of a disturbed present, a present affected by massive upheaval and transformation" (Botting 2008a: 7), could he not be describing the neo-Victorian spirit instead? Finally, when Carol Margaret Davison insists on the "Gothic lesson that only by confronting the ghosts of the past is progress possible" (Davison 2009: 211), she could as readily be highlighting the neo-Victorian's ethical imperative of 'working through' unresolved traumas of the period.

What we are asserting, then, is that *neo-Victorianism is by nature quintessentially Gothic*: resurrecting the ghost(s) of the past, searching out its dark secrets and shameful mysteries, insisting obsessively on the lurid details of Victorian life, reliving the period's nightmares and traumas. At the same time, neo-Victorianism also tries to understand the nineteenth-century as the contemporary self's uncanny *Doppelgänger*, exploring the uncertain limits between what is vanished (dead) and surviving (still living), celebrating the persistence of the bygone even while lauding the demise of some of the period's most oppressive aspects, like institutionalised slavery and legally sanctioned sexism and racism. Such are the very Gothic constitutive features of neo-Victorianism. Clearly there exists a generic and ontological kinship between Gothic and the neo-Victorian phenomenon, and this kinship is independent from – albeit reinforced by and in turn reinforcing – the neo-Gothic cultural craze.

1. The Gothic 'Underbelly' of Past Time, or Self-as-Other

Neo-Victorianism's frequent resort to Gothic, a genre and a mode emphatically concerned with otherness in its manifold shapes and monstrous misshapes, might be best understood in terms of Western culture's relentless future-orientated self-differentiation from what we are purportedly no longer, not least our Victorian others teetering on the cusp of our own self-conscious (post)modernity. As Spooner points out, "it is the Victorian era which appears to figure most prominently as a new version of [Robert] Miles' 'Gothic cusp'", with the nineteenth century "newly revealed as the site of struggle between incipient modernity and an unenlightened past" (Spooner 2007: 44). On psychological and ideological levels, the Victorians function as our threatening doubles and distorted freak-show/funhouse mirror images, disclosing something akin to rejected atavistic or archetypal selves, our superseded progenitors who are nonetheless still with us, if only as an evolutionary vestige. Accordingly, the Victorians, the material traces of their art, industry, and architecture and the more surreptitious legacies of their thought insistently remind us that the postmodern condition, in spite of early (now superseded) claims asserting the flattening out or loss of history altogether, equates to occupying an *historically* stratified and saturated haunted space. Yet although theoretical debates on neo-Victorianism often focus on self-evidently Gothic tropes – of spectrality, monstrosity, the double, madness, spiritualism, incarceration, and the trace (of lost manuscripts/documents, histories and voices) – the widespread gothicisation of this genre has gone largely unmentioned or has been noted only with regards to individual texts.[2] As practitioners of the 'serious' business of cultural memory work and excavation, critics seem intent on minimising their own implication in Gothic culture.

The equally serious-minded Victorians, of course, also invested heavily in excavation, imaginatively and intellectually as well as physically. In temporal terms, this included the progressive institutionalisation of history, natural history/anthropology, and archaeology as separate disciplines; archaism through the cultural celebration of Celticism, medievalism, classical and Egyptian

---

[2] Cora Kaplan's *Victoriana*, for instance, includes a single reference to Gothic relating to the rise of the Gothic novel, while Ann Heilmann and Mark Llewellyn's *Neo-Victorianism: The Victorians in the Twenty-First Century, 1999-2009* makes only four references to Gothic: two to Victorian and earlier Gothic literature, one to Sarah Blake's *Grange House* (2000), and another to John Harwood's *The Ghost Writer* (2004). Yet actually, the vast majority of fictions and films discussed in their study could be readily categorised as Gothic texts. As might be expected from its gothically inflected title, Rosario Arias and Patricia Pulham's edited collection *Spectrality and Haunting in Neo-Victorian Fiction: Possessing the Past* mentions Gothic somewhat more frequently (on 10 pages in total); again, however, all these references relate to Gothic generally in terms of genre, sub-genres (like the tale or contemporary London Gothic) and generic tropes (like the double), to pre-twentieth-century Gothic fictions or individual neo-Victorian novels, to the inclusion of 'Gothic' in critical titles, and to Gothic architecture and settings. Kate Mitchell's *History and Cultural Memory in Neo-Victorian Fiction: Victorian Afterimages* displays a similar trend; while she perceptively stresses "the centrality of the figure of the ghost […] as a metaphor for both the persistence of the past and our relation to it today" (Mitchell 2010: 180), she does not explicitly or consistently relate it to the centricity of the Gothic in neo-Victorianism.

antiquity; and the development of historical fiction as a distinct genre. Simultaneously, the Victorians were busy excavating spatially, not only via archaeological sites and the building of railway and canal tunnels, but also in their construction of whole 'underworlds' of new water supply systems and sewers for the effluviums of modern metropolises. Analogously, neo-Victorianism is commonly held to expose the metaphorical dark underbelly of nineteenth-century life and society, the period's social, economic, and colonial injustices, as well as concomitant acts of gendered, class-linked and racialised oppression and violence. As Rosario Arias has pointed out, neo-Victorian novels such as Mathew Kneale's *Sweet Thames* (1992) and Clare Clark's *The Great Stink* (2005) literalise this metaphor in their focus on the underground sewers constructed during London's mid-nineteenth century sanitation programmes:

> Beneath the metropolis lie encrypted symptoms and traces of its physical and spiritual 'sickness', which come to the surface in the portrayal of the Victorian underworld, as well as in the persistent presence of disease and waste in the world above. (Arias 2010: 136)

The depiction of lurking threats beneath the surface of civilised order, of the breaking out of repressed vileness that is both constituent and product of the infected, monstrous social body, has clear Gothic overtones. Arias connects these to neo-Victorianism's aim to "lay bare, debunk, and destabilize" romanticised notions of the Victorians and their achievements in "sanctioned versions of a sanitized past" (Arias 2010: 138, 154), so as to offer a much darker picture of the period as, above all, pathological.[3] Arguably, neo-Victorian Gothic

---

[3] Even a celebratory text such as A.S. Byatt's *Possession: A Romance* (1990), which depicts the artistic and intellectual spirit of the age as much more vibrant than that of our own, still ends up pathologising the Victorians for their despicably hypocritical and oppressive gender relations. Not coincidentally, the Victorian poetess Christabel LaMotte's first name recalls Coleridge's Gothic poem of the same title, while her greatest surviving work centres on the female monster Melusina; aptly, LaMotte ends her days as the doubly quintessential Gothic female, both innocent victim, falsely accused (of child murder), and fallen woman, punished for her sexual transgression and symbolically 'incarcerated' in a tower.

utilises the inherent doubleness of nineteenth-century society with its extremes of wealth and abject poverty, high morality and widespread vice, celebrations of purity and excessive filth, philanthropy and inhuman exploitation for Gothic effects of dis-identification, sensationalism and outraged horror as, indeed, did the Victorians themselves. As such, neo-Victorian Gothic also participates in an implicit critique of the metanarratives of civilisation and progress, on which the Victorians prided themselves and for which they are still stereotypically celebrated today.[4]

One of the main nineteenth-century developments in the Gothic, as noted by Andrew Smith, was a shift from external forms of (often supernatural) threat to "the progressive internalisation of 'evil'", resulting in more nuanced psychological treatments but also "predominantly secularised version[s] of 'monstrosity'" (A. Smith 2007a: 87). The incorporation of corrupting otherness into the individual and the social body blurred distinct categories to the point where any 'purity' of classification seemed unsustainable since always already compromised and adulterated. As Wolfreys remarks, in parallel with Gothic's diffusion from manifestations in specific locales (Catholic countries and other foreign lands in distant times) to "anywhere" – and, one might add, any*time* also – "[t]he Victorians may be read as embracing the gothic, taking it into themselves in intimate and disconcerting ways" via "an inward turn" that does not merely bring the other home to stay but "find[s] it already at home" (Wolfreys 2000a: xiv, 2000b: 31, 37), in prior and permanent residency, so to speak.[5] This produces an inescapable proximity to perennial otherness, since the other can no longer be safely confined or relegated to an elsewhere, accounting for what Wolfreys terms Victorian Gothic's increasing "sense of the alterity of subjectivity […] which undoes any sense of the subject's own comprehension of

---

[4] A typical case in point is the 2001 BBC documentary *What the Victorians Did for Us*, focusing on the period's advances in science, engineering and social reform.
[5] According to Wolfreys, in the final decades of the nineteenth century, "the Victorian gothic turned once again to the foreigner, to the outsider, to the otherness of colonized lands and imperial subjectivities" (Wolfreys 2000b: 32). Yet arguably, this complemented rather than reversed the trend of interiorisation, since these decades also coincided with the rise of decadence and the publication of classics like *The Picture of Dorian Gray* (1890-91) and *Dracula* (1897), which continued to warn of degeneration at home and corruption that stemmed as much from within as without.

coherence, presence or meaning", uncanny manifestations deriving "from the other *within* that identity we name as Victorian" (Wolfreys 2000a: xviii, xx, original emphasis). It seems no coincidence that the aesthetically hybrid and assimilatory genre of the middle-class novel should undergo a decidedly Gothic turn and proliferation during the Victorian age, with the Gothic not merely competing with but also *infiltrating* realist fiction, nowhere more obviously so than in the works of Charles Dickens. Indeed, one might speculate that neo-Victorian writers' and filmmakers' preference for adapting Dickens's work in particular may stem as much from his writings' decidedly Gothic strains and effects, *soliciting* uncanny returns and persistent re-visitations, as from the author's iconic status. Like the blacking-factory boy turned celebrity novelist, the Victorian novel's main producers and consumers among the self-consolidating middle classes were perched precariously in-between their society's extremes, conscious that even a single act of economic imprudence or twist of fate might spell disaster for their aspirations of progressive self-improvement and cast them back into the vile undifferentiated social sump. At least in part, the rise of Victorian Gothic must be attributed to attendant anxieties about the potential collapse of only seemingly secure identities into ineradicable otherness. Victorian Gothic, in other words, both reflected and contributed to the evolution of the radically unstable, unpredictable and untrustworthy modern subject, which at best *performs* rather than constitutes a unified, rational, and defensibly self-secure ego. If in the still more materialistic present age of global capitalism we are perhaps more concerned with money than class status, a comparable anxiety remains discernible as regards the insidious threat of both individual and collective identities' othering and infiltration – be it in the projected exponential rise of mental health issues, the alarm at 'home-grown' terrorism, the Islamophobic response to a perceived creeping Muslimisation of the Christian Occident, or the fear of the secret paedophile 'monster' lurking behind the kindly mask of neighbour, teacher, and priest.

A parallel might be drawn here with one of the classics of Victorian Female Gothic, Charlotte Brontë's *Jane Eyre* (1847). Sandra M. Gilbert and Susan Gubar famously described the novel as focused on the protagonist's crucial "confrontation, not with Rochester but with Rochester's mad wife Bertha", an emblem of Jane's transgressive impulses, a manifestation of her "truest and darkest double [...], the ferocious secret self' Jane repeatedly tries to repress (Gilbert and Gubar 1979: 339, 360). Jane's encounter with the other literalises Franco Moretti's argument that the *Bildungsroman* – a term first coined and theorised in the nineteenth century – constitutes "the *most contradictory* of modern symbolic forms", portraying personal development and socialisation as "consist[ing] first of all in the *interiorization of contradiction*. The next step being not to 'solve' the contradiction, but rather to learn to live with it" (Moretti 2000: 10 original emphases) – that is, to learn to live with oneself as intrinsically other. Similarly, at the heart of the antithetical union of 'neo' and 'Victorian' lies not the confrontation between (post)modernity and the actual Victorian(s), but rather between postmodern subjectivity and its own dark double projected back in time in a desperate attempt to learn to live with irresolvable contradiction. The appropriated Victorian formation story of modern subjectivity, then, is inherently Gothic, with the fragmented self eventually evolving into "the omnipresent traumatised and (self-) alienated subject of postmodernity – a subject radically 'othered' and 'other' even to itself" (Kohlke and Gutleben 2010b: 2).

Neo-Victorian Gothic, we want to propose, constitutes one means of re-negotiating enduring anxieties about such a relativistic precarious sense of subjectivity and its cultural history through the exploration of temporal convergence/difference and even collapse into the Victorians as ourselves-as-other.[6] While continuing the Victorian trend of rendering Gothic otherness everywhere and nowhere, however, the neo-Victorian also *reacts against* it by re-instituting a temporal distancing effect and, to a lesser extent, a spatial displacement also via the evocation of 'exotic' colonial settings (as did Imperial Gothic at the end of the Victorian age). With specific reference to the later nineteenth century, Kenneth Womack asserts that "the Victorian gothic manifests itself [...] both as a subversive supernatural force and as a mechanism for social critique" of prevailing moral and spiritual ideologies, thus constituting the genre

---

[6] The 'other' in this construction, it should be noted, indicates not a singular alter-ego, but a fragmented *plurality* of versions of otherness, just as the madwoman in the attic stands for a range of unacceptable and inassimilable others vis-à-vis Brontë's protagonist and the English social body (the rebellious devil-child, the illicitly desiring woman, the embodiment of irrationality, the feminist revolutionary, the racially marked foreigner, the un-Christian spirit of anger and vengeance).

as a potentially "ethical construct" (Womack 2000: 168, 172). Yet it arguably does so exactly because Victorian writers were commenting on their own here-and-now,[7] whereas neo-Victorian commentary on contemporary affairs and anxieties is much more obliquely encoded, if decipherable at all, in imagery of the past.

Whereas in the main Victorian Gothic's temporal settings coincided with the writers'/readers' present, or else with the recent, often familial past of the immediately preceding generation, for modern-day writers/readers the Victorian itself assumes the quality of the antiquated and archaic, which Gothic originally assigned to the medieval and Renaissance periods.[8] In neo-Victorianism, Gothic is not so much "a language, often an a-historicising language, which provides writers with the critical means of transferring an idea of the otherness of the past into the present" (Sage and Smith 1996b: 1), as it allows them to transfer an idea of the (self-)otherness of the *present* into the *past*. This is particularly so in the case of temporally dual texts, which directly juxtapose the Victorian with a present-day timeframe, sometimes even employing the trope of literal time-travel.[9] The dual time-frame approach, of course, ironically duplicates and performs modern subjectivity's Gothic fragmentation and alterity at the level of textual structure. Meanwhile the neo-Victorian Gothic's frequent reprising of the typical Gothic inter-generational plot surrounding genealogy, inheritance, contested legacies and family secrets, as in Charles Palliser's *The Quincunx* (1989), A.S. Byatt's

---

[7] "The revival of Gothic, the point at which it could be said to be 'Victorian', is the moment at which it is being used explicitly to articulate the questions of the present, and setting them in that same recognisable present" (Warwick 2007: 33).

[8] Warwick pertinently remarks that nowadays "in the popular imagination the Victorian is in many ways *the* Gothic period" (Warwick 2007: 29, original emphasis).

[9] Invariably associated with gothically inflected plots, the neo-Victorian time-travel trope can relate to movement both ways through time, involving twentieth-/twenty-first-century protagonists travelling back to the earlier century, as in Marghanita Laski's *The Victorian Chaise-longue* (1953), Octavia Butler's *Kindred* (1979), and Fred Saberhagen's *After the Fact* (1988), or precipitating nineteenth-century protagonists forward in time, as in Karl Alexander's *Time After Time* (1979), Liz Jensen's *My Dirty Little Book of Stolen Time* (2006) and Miranda Miller's *Mina in Utopia* (2010). (Note, however, that Butler's neo-slavery narrative and Saberhagen's novel about an attempt to avert President Lincoln's assassination are only 'neo-Victorian' if the term is employed as an umbrella term for all fiction self-consciously engaging with the nineteenth century regardless of evoked national and geographical contexts, which is the sense in which we employ it here.)

Possession: A Romance (1990) and Michael Cox's *The Meaning of Night* (2006), as well as the latter's Jane Eyresque sequel *The Glass of Time* (2008), thematically underlines the past's continuing afterlife even when seemingly superseded, the way it gothically extends, disseminates, and transmutes into the very fabric of subsequent *being*.

2. Uncanny Becomings: Modern Subjectivity and the Child

The figuration of self-as-other also has a direct impact on related themes of deviance and aberration that dominate both Victorian and neo-Victorian Gothic – only that in the latter, it is the Victorian itself that becomes pathologised. Clearly Moretti's claim that "[a] large part of twentieth-century thought […] defined normality against *its opposite*: against pathology, emargination, repression" – all strikingly Gothic tropes – applies equally to the previous and following centuries. Hence, "normality", which the gothic traditionally both subverts and reaffirms, accounting for its simultaneous radical and reactionary potentials, is "seen not as a meaning-ful, but rather as an unmarked entity", a "self-defensive result of a 'negation' process", which ensures that "normality's meaning is to be found *outside itself*: in what it excludes, not in what it includes" (Moretti 2000: 11, original emphasis). In much the same way, our desired 'normality' as socially and self-consciously ethical twentieth/twenty-first-century subjects is founded on the Victorian others we rigorously seek to exclude from the liberal and 'liberated' ideal of postmodern identity. Put differently, the Victorians often become 'the damned', whom we must confront in the underworld of the re-imagined nineteenth century, a purgatory to burn away their unexpiated sins so as to allow present-day subjects to re-emerge from the text, if not exactly purified of historical guilt and association, at least reconfirmed in our own comparatively more liberal-ethical subjecthood.[10]

This is not to say that neo-Victorianism does not value 'heritage' or 'historical roots' (as the opposite is patently the case), but

---

[10] Admittedly, such an analogy begs the question what purposes neo-Victorianism may serve for supercilious racist or sexist readers/viewers, who might be indulging much more dubious prurient impulses analogous to those the Gothic genre has been held to pander to, impulses in which even 'ideal' neo-Victorian consumers remain problematically implicated. In other words, our particular readings of re-imagined nineteenth-century violence and perversity may be not so much an index of Victorian values as of our own proclivities.

rather that it elegiacally validates 'the Victorian' exactly because it *wants* to view it as already dead, past and superseded, as *other-than* the present. The period's appeal lies in its (would-be) *transcended otherness*, alternately gothically horrid and cheerfully quaint, as when National Trust visitors wander through Victorian kitchens where the only 'servant' is a cheerful adult volunteer in fancy dress rather than a half-starved and exhausted child-skivvy worn out by hard labour to a pale wraith of self (though, of course, not all servants were so ill-used). Similarly, the popularity of Victoriana, say an ornately decorated piece of china enthusiastically bid for at auction or bargained over at an antique fair, is ghosted by the horrific working conditions under which that object was produced, again often including dangerous child labour, as described in both Sheri Holman's darkly disturbing *The Dress Lodger* (1999) and A.S. Byatt's equally Gothic *The Children's Book* (2009), which respectively reference the Sunderland and Burslem potteries. Just as much Victorian Gothic tends to unleash terror and/or horror only to eventually re-contain or vanquish it (at least seemingly, partly, or provisionally), neo-Victorian Gothic constitutes a funereal song that implicitly *celebrates* rather than laments the period's passing, even while inviting/enabling the recurrent return of its excesses and abuses in the cultural imaginary. In both the cited novels, this move is replicated by the working-class child protagonist's escape from the body and soul destroying pottery environs. In *The Children's Book* this is further underlined by the literal transition from the Victorian age to the twentieth century and the growth into post-Victorian adulthood of the texts' various child protagonists. All, that is, apart from the Peter Pan-like (middle-class) Tom Wellwood, whose suicide stands as a stark reminder of the lingering inimical influence of the past and the way historical traumas, individual as well as collective, cannot be conclusively vanquished.[11]

---

[11] Tom's suicide indicates a failure to come to terms with the modern riven self-as-other. His terrifying and degrading sexual abuse by older boys at boarding school takes place in an appropriately Gothic setting, namely the institution's underground boiler-room, which also uncannily echoes the dark grim fairytale locales of his mother Olive's children's fantasy 'Tom Underground'. (Indeed, it is Tom's retreat underground to read his story's latest instalment, sent him by Olive, that precipitates the abuse.) Repeatedly, Tom feels as though his 'real' life is the one imagined for him in fiction by another, until the Gothic fantasy consumes his actual existence.

If as James R. Kincaid notes, the child is redefined as a peculiarly gothicised figure in nineteenth-century literature (Kincaid 2000), from Dickens's *Oliver Twist* (1838) and Brontë's *Jane Eyre* to Henry James's *The Turn of the Screw* (1898), the uncanny or monstrous child becomes if anything still more prevalent in neo-Victorian fiction. It does so both as the after-image of horrific historical traumas (for example of slavery, child prostitution, and racism) as in the case of the ghost-children in Toni Morrison's *Beloved* (1987), Joanne Harris's *Sleep, Pale Sister* (1993), and Carol Goodman's *The Ghost Orchid* (2007), and as the trope of loss (of innocence, faith in goodness, life's sanctity, civilisation's progress) through the non-spectral figuration of imperilled, abused or murdered children, as in Caleb Carr's *The Angel of Darkness* (1997), Michel Faber's *The Crimson Petal and the White* (2002), Sarah Waters's *Fingersmith* (2002), A. N. Wilson's *A Jealous Ghost* (2006), Belinda Starling's *The Journal of Dora Damage* (2007), Laura Fish's *Strange Music* (2008), and Kate Williams's *The Pleasures of Men* (2012).[12] To a lesser extent – but herein lies a crucial difference to Victorian Gothic – the neo-Victorian child also functions as the embodiment of (albeit relative) evil in the form of the victim-perpetrator, the abused viciously lashing out at her/his perceived abusers, even to the extreme of murder, as in Margaret Atwood's *Alias Grace* (1996) and Peter Behrens's *The Law of Dreams* (2006). Children in Victorian Gothic, even when violently angry (like Jane Eyre) or suspected of possession by evil spirits (as in the case of Florence and Miles in James's novella) are more sinned against than sinning. In neo-Victorian texts, however, children themselves may become the actual or suspected *pro*generate source of potential corruption and wrong-doing, via which they assert a dubious and dangerous agency otherwise denied them.[13]

---

[12] Lucie Armitt reads such "cultural morbidity" as one way "in which our collective response to dead or 'disappeared' children carries Gothic resonances", often linked to actual child murders in the present, such as that of Sarah Payne in England in 2000, and to fears concerning the prevalence of paedophilia (Armitt 2011: 18).

[13] *Alias Grace*, for instance, suspends judgement as to the teenage Grace Marks's guilt in the murders of her employer and his housekeeper-mistress, providing competing possible interpretive frameworks, including literal spirit possession, multiple personality disorder or PTSD (possibly in part on account of incestuous abuse), violent coercion, and willing participation motivated by sexual jealousy and material greed.

Yet who, we might ask, do these haunted/haunting children stand for? Perhaps, to some extent at least, they represent ourselves as the 'offspring' of the Victorians, struggling to assert ourselves against our predecessors' influence and remaining implicated in the perpetuation of the earlier period's iniquities, not least as regards paedophilia, child abuse and child murder, all of which remain common today and occur on a regular basis even in 'First World' countries. The neo-Victorian child's extreme vulnerability to violation, juxtaposed with its own capacity for destructive fury, also instantiates our own deeply conflicted response to the Victorians and how to relate to their heritage. Like its Victorian child precursors – and the Victorians as they appear to us today – the neo-Victorian Gothic child "is mysterious and capable of actions and responses that are both endearing and horrifying" (Kincaid 2000: 4). It figures sheer unknowable otherness, both within the Victorians and ourselves.

Fittingly, then, in *The Children's Book*, the Gothic continues to haunt the liberated child's life. Philip Warren first finds refuge in the subterranean vaults of the South Kensington (later the V&A) Museum and then in the artistic middle-class surroundings of the bohemian Wellwoods' home and that of the potter Benedict Fludd, whose apprentice he becomes. Yet the Gothic implications of his first sanctuary as a symbolic "crypt" of the Victorians' assailed collective cultural unconscious (Byatt 2009: 6), as well as the gothically freighted name of the second, Todefright, already hint at the dark secrets underlying the seemingly idyllic families and communities in which, socially and psychologically, Philip remains an outsider until shortly before the novel's end. Intermittent flashbacks to the intolerable existence Philip and his sister Elsie fled, characterised by grinding poverty, backbreaking labour, premature death, and overcrowded conditions in which incest was rife, foreshadow the revelation of one of the Gothic's founding and most abiding of motifs: the father's tyrannical victimisation and incestuous assault on his daughters. Indeed, *The Children's Book* displays a proliferation of Gothic motifs, from frightening underground settings, ghostly lost children, doublings (both in characters and situations),[14] and the

---

[14] Each of the Wellwood children has a fictional double in their mother's stories; the revelation of Fludd's incest is foreshadowed in Humphrey Wellwood's attempted seduction of his daughter Dorothy (though in typically Gothic fashion, he turns out not to be her real father); and Tom's suicide repeats that of Fludd. Doubling here

abused young Pamona's nude somnambulism, to the locked Bluebeard's chamber where Benedict Fludd conceals the pornographic artworks inspired by his transgressions. Eventually these are 're-buried', this time literally, by Pamona and Philip following her father's apparent suicide in pique at his thwarted desire when his elder daughter, Imogen, escapes his clutches in marriage to a 'good' father figure. Yet although a freely elected union, Imogen's apparently happy marriage to Prosper Cain retains Gothic overtones of traumatic repetition/re-enactment, their age differential ghosted by the spectres of child abuse, incest, and Imogen's symbolic 'father murder'.

Through such uncanny echoes and repetitions, neo-Victorian Gothic questions the extent to which, whether as traumatised Victorian characters or post-Victorian 'liberated' selves, individuals are ever truly autonomous subjects, free to pursue their own fates or rid themselves of burdensome pasts. For the formation story of Victorian to (post)modern subjectivity also involves what Moretti, in gothicised Foucauldian terms, describes as the interiorisation and fusion of "external compulsion and internal impulses into a new unity until the former is no longer distinguishable from the latter. This fusion is what we usually call 'consent' or 'legitimation'" (Moretti 2000: 562). The self-disciplining subject thereby produced embodies the necessity "that, as a 'free individual', not as a fearful subject but as a convinced citizen, one perceives the social norms as *one's own*" (Moretti 2000: 16, original emphasis), that is, one becomes unknowingly 'inhabited' by them. Normalising interpellation actually undermines the unified autonomous subject it only *seems* to produce, by effecting the permanent absorption of otherness into the self. Only the nature of the internalised otherness may differ in kind for Victorian and postmodern subjects – with the latter's sense of monstrous alterity constituted by the ghostly Victorian.

In either case, the resulting 'freely' consenting or ideologically interpellated subject evinces an uncanny resemblance to Victorian Gothic victims of mesmerism or hypnotic trance, which become possessed or remotely controlled by an external agency, undoing the ego and suspending the discourse of inalienable rights

---

constitutes a form of reiteration, which Victor Sage and Allan Lloyd Smith appropriately describe as "the modern form of haunting; reiteration of narrative manoeuvres and motifs, unholy reanimation of the deadness of the past" (Sage and Smith 1996b: 4).

interwoven with the republican and revolutionary sentiments of early Gothic.[15] At once extraneous and internal, this agency fuses instilled subject and manipulated object, parasitic guest and unknowing host as *mutually and deterministically constitutive* of self-as-other/other-as-self. This seems radically at odds with the neo-Victorian's purported "re-assertion of the themes of emotional authenticity and sincerity within individual human relationships" underlining the re-entry of "feeling and the affective" into both literary re-visions and "critical discourse on this period" (Heilmann and Llewellyn 2010: 26). For in one sense, the interpellated self becomes a priori *in*authentic, no longer capable of sincere autonomous (as opposed to ideologically determined/ infused/replicated) feelings, a quasi automaton or un-self, manipulated by mysterious and ungraspable forces of which the subject gains only shadowy, hence all the more terrifying intimations.

The Gothic's traditional incitement to over-stimulation and excess affect constitutes the other side of the neo-Victorian coin, as if to over-compensate for the suspicion that its shock effects and persons subjected to them, whether victims or violators, are essentially hollow selves. This tendency reflects a move within neo-Victorianism more widely to capitalise on intense somatic sensations and affect so as to produce a virtual immersion of readers/viewers within the Victorian scene in all its sensual immediacy. Drawing on David Price's *History Made, History Imagined: Contemporary Literature, Poiesis and the Past*, Silvana Collela asserts that "[t]he reader is repeatedly invited to sense the past in order to make sense of it" (Collela 2010: 87). Yet the kind of sensual import and affect produced, and therefore the 'sense' characters and readers are invited to make of the period, will vary according to particular Gothic sub-genres and settings employed, not least as regards evocations of the Gothic sublime and abjection, perhaps the mode's ultimate intensifications of affect.

3. Neo-Victorian Imperial, Eco and Steampunk Gothic

Most commonly the Gothic sublime arises in contemplations of nature in the midst of existential extremity, as the imperilled individual

---

[15] Roger Luckhurst read Gothic's periodic resurgence in relation to "the cyclical history of trance-states as they have been theorized within modernity", particularly mesmerism/magnetism, the backlash against it, and the eventual sanction of hypnotism (via Jean-Martin Charcot) as a legitimate tool of scientific enquiry (Luckhurst 2000: 148).

confronts the possibility of her/his own annihilation by an arbitrary inimical (often human) power and seeks solace in the intimation of a still greater power that exceeds human agency, manipulation, and apprehension. Though this immensity diminishes the self to the point of insignificance, it also serves as a refuge, temporarily lifting the (sacrificial) subject out of its precarious condition by projection into unbounded otherness. The wilderness as source and site of sublime terror, largely relegated to the Imperial and American Gothic or else replaced with the urban cityscape in nineteenth-century texts, only regains some of its mysterious power in neo-Victorian versions of the same (and combinations/adaptations thereof). Or else the neo-Victorian sublime arises in the context of advanced scientific or technological breakthroughs projected back in time, in an inversion of the futuristic visions of nineteenth-century writers such as Jules Verne and H. G. Wells, which developed into modern science fiction. Applied to neo-Victorian contexts, particularly as regards steampunk, these later instances of the sublime relate to what Botting terms the overwhelming spectacles and "artificial sublimity of computer-generated worlds" (Botting 2002: 278) or what John Mullan describes as "the dizzying reaches of interplanetary space or the vertiginous spirals of the human genome" (Mullan qtd. Zylinska 2001: 1).

The more traditional version of the sublime is exemplified by Matthew Kneale's *English Passengers* (2000). Lost in the Tasmanian wilds, the titular white explorers resort to self-destructive infighting, undergoing a vicious degeneration from their civilised selves while hunted by the Anglicised mixed-race Peevay, who reverts to 'native' habits as he seeks retribution for the colonisers' wholesale destruction of his people, assuming the Gothic role of an unseen persecutory spirit of vengeance and 'natural' justice. Yet "this terrible place", as Dr Thomas Potter describes it, is ironically viewed by the Reverend Geoffrey Wilson as a divinely imbued "dizzying" vista, "variously hidden and revealed by the dark clouds, […] a jagged sea of cliffs and peaks, of tumbling rocks and desperately clinging greenery, extending to the horizon" (Kneale 2001: 368, 362-363), recalling the Romantic sublime found in foundational Gothic texts like Ann Radcliffe's *The Italian, or the Confessional of the Black Penitents* (1797). Here Wilson expects to discover the Garden of Eden and foolishly deems his prayers for guidance answered by a powerful lightning strike that only leads the travellers further astray. In the colonial context,

Kneale's neo-Victorian Gothic makes clear, the sublime functions as a Western imposition analogous to Orientalism, by which the invaders seek to penetrate something they can never understand in and of itself, apart from their exploitative relation to it. The imperialists are othered as violators of the natural world and its rightful inhabitants.[16]

Novels like Carol Birch's *Jamrach's Menagerie* (2011) develop this theme still further in a neo-Victorian variant of Imperial Gothic that might usefully be termed 'Eco Gothic'. The latter explores man's terrifying will to power through violence against 'Nature', linking imperialism to the horrors of excess materialist greed that leads to irreversible legacies of environmental destruction. Very much part of neo-Victorianism's ethical agenda, this innovation clearly engages present-day concerns by historicising our world's accelerating ecological crises as haunted/precipitated by the Industrial Revolution, as traumatic re-enactments of the earlier period's increasingly globalised competition and strife for territory, resources and markets. Birch's text dramatises the intertwined predatory politics of imperialist and capitalist consumption via the narrator Jaffy Brown's participation in a bloody whaling expedition cum monster hunt to the ends of the empire, so as to procure an 'ora' (or Komodo dragon) for a rich collector of exotic species. Face to face with the beast, Jaffy experiences an instant of self-alienating sublime terror, echoing his earlier response to a whale's fierce death throes: "The awe, as if I'd come to the edge of a big hole in the earth and peered in and seen something wild and unspeakable looking back" (Birch 2011: 168). That unspeakable otherness, however, rebounds on the sailors as, analogous to the Ancient Mariner's slaying of the albatross, their 'crimes against nature' condemn them to disaster and shipwreck, as well as – that most Gothic of tropes – cannibalism, by which the abjected other is literally assimilated into the self. Ironically, cast adrift in one-time rich whaling grounds, the mariners fail to be rescued because the monsters of the deep have been hunted to near-extinction, obviating regular ship traffic, so that eventually the men are reduced to consuming one another in an extreme parody of capitalism's boundless dehumanising consumption. The human self at the mercy of

---

[16] As Peevay remarks, "Truly it was a mystery to confuse how they ever could kill all my ones and steal the world, or even why they wanted it, as it was no place they could endure" (Kneale 2001: 354).

its appetites becomes the true source of monstrous horror, but unlike Dr Jekyll or Dorian Gray released through self-destruction, Jaffy sentences himself to living with abjection. Returned to London as one of only two survivors, he eventually settles down to sell exotic birds and aviaries, creating a splendid enclosed "bird garden" at the back of his business premises (Birch 2011: 343). Yet his simulated self-contained "wilderness" (Birch 2011: 336), a would-be new Garden of Eden, signals a fantasised impossible return to a time before the fall into the base materiality he wishes to flee, the permanent Gothic prison-house of his cannibal otherness.

Similarly, Tom Holland's *The Bone Hunter* (2001) evokes the sublime in the context of gothicised human depredation of another ecosystem. Conflating American Gothic, via the hunt for dinosaur fossils in the Wild West, with Urban Gothic set in New York City, figured as a hotbed of crime and professional corruption, the novel chronicles the competitive murderous quest for prehistoric monsters, which only reveals the real monsters to be wholly human. Lily Prescott and her fellow travellers are amazed to come upon a literal Gothic castle in the midst of the Wyoming prairie that the castle's owner, the Marquis de Halles, is violently clearing of both buffalos and Native Americans to enable profitable investment by cattle ranchers:

> From beyond the crest of the hill coyotes yapped and there came the shrieking of the carrion birds, but nothing so dreadful as the droning of flies, nor so awful a sight, black across the plain below the ridge where Lily stopped, bolt upright in her saddle, staring down through the shroud of the gyring swarms. She clasped a hand across her mouth, but although she tried she couldn't turn away her gaze, and so still she looked out at the corpses in their hundreds, their thousands, and she thought how even in its extinction there seemed something of the infinite about the buffalo herd. (Holland 2001: 263)

Sublime and abjected nature collapse into one. Edmundson appropriately remarks that "apocalyptic Gothic often comes in an ecological mode", with the reader "ecounter[ing] the fear that, as a punishment for human excess, especially of the technological sort, the world is doomed to become a flyblown waste" (Edmundson 1999: 27). The protagonist's terrifying vision evokes an artificially emptied wilderness, a scene of man-made apocalypse resonant of a post-nuclear nightmare. As the buffalo flesh is burnt so the bones can be ground down for saleable fertiliser in what the Marquis intends to expand into an industrial scale operation, assisted by future railroad building, "freight cars loaded with refrigerators" and "[p]acking plants filled with machines", "[t]he corpses of the buffalo [...] stretched so unbroken that in the mist it looked as though all the prairie had been scorched and wasted to black" (Holland 2001: 264, 269). The trope of species extinction thus doubles as the uncanny harbinger of what Steven Bruhm identifies as one of the main present-day anxieties which contemporary Gothic simultaneously aims to "arouse and assuage": the fear of accelerated technological change begun in the latter part of the Victorian age, including "[a]dvances in weaponry – both military and medical – [that] have rendered our culture vulnerable to almost total destruction" (Bruhm 2002: 260).[17] Neo-Victorian Eco Gothic suggests that the sublime has become permanently displaced or haunted by the postmodern horror of abjection. Put differently, in postmodernism's state of radical disillusion the numinous, the sacred, or the (super)natural may only be conceivable and, indeed, representable through its absolute negation.

Fear of technologically driven violence, destructive materialism, and imperialist excess are also evident in steampunk, the fictional and filmic products of which are overwhelmingly Gothic.[18]

---

[17] This trope also appears in other neo-Victorian fictions, often with steampunk elements and linked outright to the military or industrial complex, focusing on the production of a terrifying 'ultimate' weapon. See, for example, the megalomaniacal industrialist Alex Bellman's steam machine gun in Philip Pullman's second volume in the Gothic Sally Lockhart series, *The Shadow in the North* (1986), or Ronald W. Clark's much earlier *Queen Victoria's Bomb* (1967), which imagines the development of a nineteenth-century nuclear bomb to be deployed in the service of empire.

[18] Not least, "[f]ew phrases are more aptly descriptive of the steampunk oeuvre than 'an irreverent attitude towards boundaries'" (Bowser and Croxall 2010: 28, citing Jay Clayton's *Dickens in Cyberspace*) – which equally describes the Gothic. In so far as science fiction grew out of Victorian Gothic (Warwick 2007: 34), it is unsurprising that steampunk, also focused on technology and the scientific imagination, should constitute an important strand of neo-Victorian Gothic. Yet we would stress that most steampunk writers/practitioners do not tend to describe themselves as 'neo-Victorian'.

This seems to contribute to their often ambiguous politics, interpretable as reactionary as well as subversive, particularly as much steampunk, including its subcultures and fashion, seems to revel stylistically, even nostalgically in imperial aesthetics from Victorian pith helmets to elaborate weaponry evidently intended for brutal conquest.[19] Nonetheless Rachel A. Bowser and Brian Croxall suggest that steampunk can be read in terms of neo-Victorianism's ethical cultural memory work, in which "our projections and fantasies about the Victorian era meet the tropes and techniques of science fiction" – and one should add, science fiction's socio-cultural critique – "to produce a genre that revels in anachronism while exposing history's overlapping layers" (Bowser and Croxall 2010: 1) – a Gothic description of 'interstitiality', though they do not discuss steampunk as such as a Gothic genre. Arguably, steampunk's potential politico-ethical contradictoriness should be read as an uncanny reflection of the West's conflicted legacies of Empire, underwritten by anxiety about new forms of economic and military neo-imperialism, currently perhaps most conspicuous in the Middle Eastern arena, which simultaneously act as sources of nationalist pride/kudos and new national traumas of defeat and cultural decline.

Steampunk texts overtly problematise the fall 'into' modern technology that not only becomes a de-naturing but a source of an alternative sublime, evoking awe and terror in the face of complex, marvellous machines, their terrible beauty and their inestimable power for effecting good or evil. As Rebecca Onion proposes, to some extent steam-based and other nineteenth-century technologies, "once so reviled, enter back into the cultural lexicon as icons of a new utopian landscape", revivifying human creativity and uniqueness via a democratising hands-on 'tinkering' and individualised processes of production and consumption reminiscent of the Arts and Crafts movement, as well as "the perceived innocence of technological and scientific knowledge" (Onion 2008: 139, 142). Yet the celebration of the machine almost invariably has a Gothic dark side of potential abuse via its facilitation of authoritarian control and/or tyranny, more often than not related to imperial power and politics. Thus Robert

---

[19] See, for instance, Jude Cavale's '24 Cool Steampunk Weapons from Another Era' (Cavale 2010). A similar ambiguity pervades Steampunk's depiction of gender relations.

Rankin's comic *The Japanese Devil Fish Girl and Other Unnatural Attractions: A Novel* (2010) envisages a Victorian space-age where, following a Wellsian Martian invasion, Britain has conquered and colonised the Red Planet, using the aliens' own "back-engineered" spaceships to brutally exterminate the indigenous population via a form of primitive biological warfare (Rankin 2010: 13). Unknown to Queen or country, Her Majesty's conspirators, led by Winston Churchill, rounded up some 1500 civilians "in the advanced stages of any sexually or otherwise transmitted or transmittable diseases" and sacrificed the unfortunate "incurables" by dispatching them to Mars aboard three converted "plague ships" (Rankin 2010: 12), thereafter concocting a heroic battle by the Queen's Own Electric Fusiliers as cover-story for the genocide. Devoided of life, the red planet is duly assimilated into the imperial domains, and supremacist Britain henceforth exercises exclusive control over human spaceflight and interplanetary trade with other alien species. Tongue-in-cheek Rankin highlights the selectivity of British cultural memory, which prefers to foreground Britain's resistance to Nazi totalitarianism responsible for the genocide against the Jewish people – not least by the canonisation of Churchill, here transformed from national hero to villain – while too conveniently glossing over (or forgetting altogether) its own colonial massacres and historical abuses in 'defence' of Empire.

Not coincidentally, later in the novel, a British dirigible, carrying the protagonists, engages in a spectacular display of violence parodying notions of the 'evil Empire' and the 'War of Terror', while evoking echoes of 9/11 (for instance, in images of panicked passengers jumping to their deaths from the burning airship). Parked above New York's Central Park, the British (rather than the US) suffer an attack by fundamentalist Christian (rather than Islamist) terrorists, which they repel via the airship's "heat ray" defence system (Rankin 2010: 148), devastating the park and large parts of the city. In this sense, steampunk cannot simply be read as a nostalgic celebration of empire; rather, analogous to other subgenres of neo-Victorian Gothic, it deconstructs metanarratives of Western progress, enlightenment and humanitarian liberalism. Like the other texts discussed in this section, it does so through a pathologisation of imperialist/capitalist enterprise as monstrously insatiable and over-reaching. Indeed, Rankin's main storyline revolves around the ingénue protagonist George Fox and his mercenary master, the aptly (and gothically) named entrepreneur

Professor Cagliostro Coffin. The latter has no compunction about making his living by callously displaying a dead Martian as part of his travelling cabinet of curiosities and later profiteering from exhibiting a stolen, 'excavated' religious artefact, claimed by various species, precipitating an intergalactic conflict. Hence Coffin's callous, not to say fiendish self-interest uncannily duplicates the imperial politics of Rankin's alternative Britain.

Other steampunk novels, as in George Mann's Newbury and Hobbes detective series,[20] go further still, re-vamping Queen Victoria from maternal national figurehead to Gothic mastermind of a project of imperial expansion and world domination. In Mann's *The Affinity Bridge* (2008), set in 1901, Victoria's reign is perpetuated indefinitely, the monarch's life being artificially extended through the use of ominous medical technology. Living a secretive life in half-light and utter seclusion from public view, confined to a mechanised wheelchair and connected to a variety of apparatuses and tubes, Mann's Victoria seems a mash-up of a plotting Miss Havisham, the megalomaniac Dr Arliss Loveless of *Wild Wild West* (Warner Brothers 1999), and cyborg characters from *Doctor Who* (1963-89, 2005-present). Threats to Empire relate directly to Victoria's cyborg status. For if the monstrous other in neo-Victorian Imperial and Eco Gothic is prevailingly *human*, steampunk readily reprises Victorian Gothic's resort to what Kelly Hurley terms the "abhuman" (Hurley 1996: 3-20, 2002: 190), troubling ontological boundaries between animate and inanimate, organic and inorganic, 'natural' and fabricated humanity. In an instance of the mechanical sublime, Mann's protagonists gaze wonder-struck into an automaton's "mechanical brain": "It was like seeing human thought processes in action, like some sort of bizarre window into the human soul", causing them to speculate that "the human brain was the same as this incredible device, a series of clockwork switches and cogs rendered flesh and blood. [...] they were looking deep into the very fabric of its being" (Mann 2008: 102-103). Human 'nature' is at once sublimely ennobled and mechanistically abjected, figured as precariously interstitial and hybrid, no longer definitely one thing or another.[21]

---

[20] To date, Mann's series includes *The Affinity Bridge* (2008), *The Osiris Ritual* (2009), and *The Immortality Engine* (2011).
[21] In this scene, Steampunk's "exteriorisation of interiority", instead of "shore[ing] up psychological interiority" (Bowser and Croxall 2010: 27), calls it radically into doubt.

In the case of the new 'creations' in Mann's novel there is no redeeming intimation of a beneficent intelligent (that is, divine) designer in the background analogous to William Paley's 1802 watchmaker argument, rather the opposite. Initially the degenerative plague of cannibalistic zombies or "walking cadavers" terrorising London (Mann 2008: 27), combined with serial strangulations in Whitechapel, suggest the supernatural at work. The crisis, however, is eventually traced back to inimical human agents linked to the profitable business of mass produced "artificial intelligence" (Mann 2008: 88),[22] as automatons increasingly service ordinary citizens, corporations and government as anything from butlers and airship pilots to assassins. With cinematic Frankensteinean overtones also evident in Victoria's representation, the eponymous 'affinity bridge' interconnects stolen (unbeknownst to the perpetrators, virally infected) human brains with clockwork circuitry, as Mann recycles current fears regarding the ethics and (un)foreseeable ends of scientific research into means of life-extension and/or immortality, bioengineering, nanotechnology, and artificially modified/expanded human cognition and capabilities (so-called 'cyberception' and 'technopathy'), as well as non-human artificial 'life'. In this respect, Joanna Zylinska's comments on femininity's relation to the cyborg have much wider relevance for the neo-Victorian's use of this trope; "rather than "represent[ing] a triumphal overcoming of [...] body and self", she suggests, cyborgs are better understood as representing "an intrinsic queerness – even uncanniness – of identity and the problematic boundedness of embodiment" (Zylinska 2001: 130). This links back to the hollow self and the concomitant fear of depthlessness discussed earlier: the subject's manipulation by a combination of external control and internal regulatory mechanisms/engineered adaptations relegates (self-)consciousness to a disposable "by-product of the human organism" (Mann 2008: 302).

Hence the cyborg in neo-Victorian as well as wider Gothic is inextricably connected to issues concerning the limits of subjects' power, self-control and self-knowledge, as well as their complete

---

[22] In contrast, Gail Carriger's Parasol Protectorate series does introduce supernatural elements, by employing a 'soulless' heroine and vampire and werewolf protagonists and villains. Carriger's series stretches to five volumes so far: *Soulless* (2009), *Changeless* (2010), *Blameless* (2011), *Heartless* (2011) and *Timeless* (2012). *Soulless* also came out in a Manga version in 2012.

loss/appropriation – a theme Mann underlines by his use of more traditionalist Gothic tropes of possession/self-surrender, such as madness, mediumistic visions, and the occult.[23] Newbury's friend Sir Charles Bainbridge, Chief Inspector of Scotland Yard, fittingly remarks of the 'mad' scientist Villiers that his self-styled philanthropist's investment in progress is "not about changing the world" but rather "about wielding power" (Mann 2008: 291). Almost invariably in neo-Victorian Gothic, the villainous or dangerous (self-)others turn out to be those individuals who dedicate their lives unreservedly to so-called 'progress': nationalistic, capitalistic or scientific. Accordingly, the sinister final twist of Mann's novel comes as no surprise: Queen Victoria pragmatically instructs Veronica Hobbes to retain "at least a handful" of the affinity bridges "in working order", concluding, "One never knows when the technology may prove useful" (Mann 2008: 350), presumably as a weapon. Sebastian Domsch's pertinent observation in his chapter on *The League of Extraordinary Gentlemen* (1999-2009) as regards the graphic novel's re-contextualisation of "Gothic monstrosity into larger social and political frameworks", in and by which even 'good' characters become implicated and controlled, clearly has relevance for Imperial Gothic and steampunk more generally, calling into question the belief in "the rightfulness of the 'bigger cause'" supposedly being pursued (this volume: 114).

Victor Sage and Allan Lloyd Smith have suggested that "[t]he literary declension of terror is an inevitable response to the atrocity exhibition of the twentieth century" (Sage and Smith 1996b: 5), while Lucie Armitt argues similarly that an identifying element of twentieth-century Gothic is "the manner in which the real-life horror of two world wars takes over from the imagined horrors of the supernatural and/or superstition" (Armitt 2011: 2). Both readings may be usefully

---

[23] While Amelia, the sister of Veronica, is confined to an asylum on account of the seizures accompanying her inexplicable second sight, the special agent and anthropologist Sir Maurice Newbury proves an opium-addicted explorer of the occult, leading Victoria to fear that he might succumb to possession by the "dark arts" (Mann 2008: 349). Van Leavenworth's chapter in this volume fittingly reads the asylum setting of the interactive fiction *Slouching Towards Bedlam* as "foreground[ing] the ideological boundary between classifiable and unclassifiable knowledge", the breakdown of which via "[d]iagnostic [f]ailure[s]" precipitates the Gothic sublime (this volume: 261, 260).

extended to twenty-first-century Gothic also, since the "atrocity exhibition" and "real-life horror" have been repeated in various forms from Bosnia to Rwanda to Iraq to Afghanistan and Syria right up to the present-day. Steampunk cynicism regarding the responsible exercise of political/corporate/scientific power relates as much to its duplicitous occluded operations today as to the nineteenth century re-imagined with futuristic technologies that have by now become disturbingly feasible or already real. This legitimate paranoia towards inimical impersonal, hence unlocatable and virtually incontestable power revivifies Gothic terror, in part reversing its declension.

4. Neo-Victorian Urban Gothic, Crime and Sensation Fiction

As evinced by the foregone examples, much neo-Victorian Imperial, Eco, and steampunk Gothic intersects with further prominent and intertwined genres: Urban Gothic and/or crime/detective fiction. Unsurprisingly, many neo-Victorian crime fictions and films are described as 'Dickensian', for as Alexandra Warwick notes, "[i]t is Dickens who makes use of, and indeed establishes, a metropolitan sensibility that distinguishes a new Victorian Gothic (Warwick 2007: 32), facilitating the focus on criminality and degeneration in urban settings. Unsurprisingly, Dickens himself and/or his works are regularly reprised in neo-Victorian Urban Gothic, from Peter Carey's *Jack Maggs* (1997), Sarah Waters's *Fingersmith* (2002), Louis Bayard's *Mr. Timothy* (2003), and Matthew Pearl's *The Last Dickens* (2009) to Dan Simmon's *Drood* (2009). As does Victorian Urban Gothic, its neo-Victorian counterparts employ the impenetrable sprawling labyrinthine cityscape, rather than nature, as source and/or catalyst for experiences of radical alienation, intense horror and sublime terror, with potential threats lurking around every corner. Imbued with paranoia, the city takes on a hallucinatory quality, itself becoming a monstrous living entity, a multitudinous other, a living phantasmagoria. The killer and serial killer, who feature prominently,[24] merge indistinguishably into the urban anonymous masses, becoming, as it were, emanations of the city itself. As Sarah E. Maier proposes in her chapter, the profuse reprisings of the Whitechapel killings, for instance, "rely upon the shadowy figure of

---

[24] Another favourite bogeyman offender of neo-Victorianism is the resurrectionist and/or deranged doctor, as in Villier's case in *The Affinity Bridge*.

the Ripper as a touchstone of unknowable historical fact"; hence the threat can no longer be localised within a specific monstrous other or integrated into any "one subjectivity" (this volume: 199, 203). Evil becomes less of a function of individual characters' psychopathology; instead psychopathologies become functions of a more general societal evil. Whereas the Victorian city provided the stage for acts of Gothic villainy, like Dracula's bloodletting or Hyde's vicious attacks, and their detection, the neo-Victorian city becomes a stage for the villains themselves, as well as a performative space for the evil-doers' pursuers to engage with the psychology of evil and otherness within – even as they hold it at bay – in an interminable play of deferral. As the killer in *The Pleasures of Men* reflects on the newspapers and their reading public, "They want me to continue. I am like a play to them, and they wish for more crime" (Williams 2012: 361).

The killers' minds rather than the process of bringing them to justice moves into the foreground. Put differently, the Gothic obscurity surrounding the crime is transferred onto the perpetrator. Accordingly Ackroyd's *Dan Leno and the Lime House Golem* (1994) focuses on the female serial killer's self-narration, as she forges a diary to implicate her husband and stages her crimes for dramatic effect, in a displaced rage at oppressive social institutions like the family and marriage that failed her. Caleb Carr's *The Angel of Darkness* (1997) also adds a different frisson to the traditional Gothic notion of the *femme fatale* by opting for a female serial killer, yet most of the book is given over not to her identification, which occurs quite early on, but to the meticulous background research into her childhood and upbringing and attempts by the alienist Laszlo Kreizler and his team to unravel the convoluted workings of her disturbed mind. Repeatedly, as in the case of Atwood's Grace Marks, the criminal, especially if a woman, is not depicted as degenerate so much as a trauma victim of socio-economic iniquities and double moral standards, a conduit for (or medium acting out) the malevolent influence of a diseased society.

The neo-Victorian's blood spattered spectacles of violence, often lovingly lingered over, must be read in part as attempts to re-whet jaded appetites glutted by graphic gore and bodily violations depicted on television and cinema screens, so as to enable literature to compete on a more level playing field.[25] An evident motif of Gothic excess, such ploys for exaggerated appeals to the nerves and productions of affect, within both characters and readers, also links neo-Victorian Urban Gothic to the legacies of nineteenth-century sensation fiction. The latter, of course, in part constituted a reinvigoration of Female Gothic, drawing on a range of typical tropes from the earlier subgenre: women's victimisation and domestic entrapment, false imprisonment, madness, transgressive (female) sexual desire, seduction and abuse. All of these recur regularly in neo-Victorian Urban Gothic and crime fiction, including the previously referenced *Sleep, Pale Sister*, *Fingersmith*, and *The Journal of Dora Damage*, as well as Valerie Martin's *Mary Reilly* (1990), Sarah Waters's *Affinity* (1999), and Carina Burman's *The Streets of Babylon: A London Mystery* (2008). Underlining the neo-Victorian's prevalent focus on gender politics, crime fiction presents itself as a means of exploring wider patriarchal and societal 'crimes against women', from incest and domestic violence to sexual slavery, many of them still rife today,[26] and thence offences against other marginalised subjects. Urban Gothic's obsessive engagement with such 'historical' abuses may be read as a cynical commentary on how (too) little has changed in real terms since the Victorians. In this context, murder may ironically become a form of social critique.[27]

The murdering other becomes a figure of the 'ordinary' individual or collective subject's evil propensities through what Max Duperray, in his chapter on the multitudinous literary after-lives of Jack the Ripper, terms the "relationship between individual secret pathology and indiscernible monstrosity" (this volume: 177). So too in Alan Moore and Eddie Campbell's graphic novel series *From Hell*

---

[25] Allan Lloyd Smith pertinently notes that postmodernism's "culture of the spectacle, whipping on a culture of 'waning' affect, produces close parallels to the sensationalism of the Gothic" (A.L. Smith 1996: 15).

[26] Even the most ingenious of writers would be hard-put to conceive a more Gothic story than the real-life Fritzl case in Austria, where the father imprisoned and sexually enslaved his own daughter for 24 years in the dungeon-basement of the family home, secured by a series of locked doors, incestuously assaulting her and fathering eight children with her, including a miscarriage, until finally exposed in 2008.

[27] Neo-Victorian Female Gothic thus develops a trend already incipient in some Victorian sensation fictions such as Wilkie Collins's *The Woman in White* (1859-60) and (with regards to the attempted murder of her husband by the titular protagonist) Elizabeth Mary Braddon's *Lady Audley's Secret* (1862).

(1991-1996) and its 2001 film adaptation of the same name by the Hughes brothers discussed in Maier's chapter, which imagine a royal conspiracy and cover-up surrounding the actual Ripper killings. The graphic novels, more so than the film, afford an in-depth psychological study of the murderous Royal physician Sir William Gull, whose dying visions intimate historical twentieth-century horrors to come, not least the ascendancy of Hitler, born during the time of the killings. Unlike the ultimately contained/containable guilt of notorious criminal characters from Victorian fiction, like Dorian Gray or Jekyll/Hyde – expellable with their deaths – Gull's evil is figured not as his own but that of the pathologically unbalanced spirit of his age. This is mirrored in the narrative's fraudulent spirit medium, Robert James Lees, and in the film's drug addicted, psychic, and finally suicidal investigator, Inspector Frederick Abberline, disturbing clear demarcations between good and evil, self and other. Hence questions as to the nature of evil conflate with what Andrew Smith, referring to Stevenson's novella, terms central "[q]uestions about the ownership of the self" (A. Smith 2007a: 97). So too in Williams's gothically introspective *The Pleasures of Men*, whose mentally unstable protagonist Catherine Sorgeiul projects herself into the mind of the 'Man of Crows' killing young women on the streets of Spitalfields, London, albeit in the 1840s, decades before the Ripper. As Marie-Luise Kohlke discusses in her chapter on neo-Victorian Female Gothic, Williams's novel never makes clear whether Catherine, trance-like, fantasises herself as the killer as she traces his steps to visit the sites of his killings, or whether, conversely, the killer infiltrates her mind, possibly even directing her movements, suggested by the disclosure of his invasion of her home to read (and write in) her diary. *The Pleasures of Men* thus resurrects the spectre of the other's interiorisation by the self, but leaves unresolved who exactly is the 'ghost' in which machine.

Comparable ontological questions about protagonists' receptivity to evil and its seductions arise in Tom Holland's *Supping with Panthers* (1996, published as *Slave of My Thirst* in the USA), a cross between Imperial and Urban Gothic. Fairly unusually for neo-Victorian Gothic, the novel employs a genuinely supernatural evil that follows the explorer, Doctor John Eliot, home from Kalikshutra on the

Empire's remote Indian frontier to London,[28] staging a "reverse colonization" (Arata 1990), which vitiates Englishness through psychological obsession, literal infection and outright mutation in a potent mix of zombies, vampirism, human sacrifice, and virulent blood disease. Not least, the demon woman Lilah, a combination of the mythical Lilith and Circe, transforms Eliot's friend George Mowberley, the Queen's own Minister for India, into a "*bloody wog girl*" as he writes Eliot in a terrified letter, recounting his desperate failed attempts at escape during which he is violated by prowling London "gentlemen" in a parodic repetition of the empire's 'rape' of colonial territories (Holland 1996: 323 original emphasis). As in the case of the racial supremacist Dr Potter in *English Passengers* and his final grotesque transformation into absolute other as an exhibited 'aboriginal' specimen, in *Supping with Panthers* too the Western subject is as likely to be consumed or co-opted by otherness as triumph over it. The Gothic threat prevails, rather than being vanquished, reflecting an implicit (if not always consistent) post-imperial critique, as Eliot too wanders the capital's night time streets in his obsessive search for Lilah and the cause of the 'alien' imported disease.[29]

The densely palimpsestic narrative plays complex postmodern games with its readers, as Victorian Gothic and cultural intertexts proliferate in Holland' veritable 'discursive imperialism' of appropriation. Besides a vampiric Lord Byron, the novel features John William Polidori and Bram Stoker.[30] Mary Kelly, Eliot's one-time

---

[28] Otherness is embodied by an Orientalised, preternaturally beautiful, immortal female power identified with "Kali the Terrible", a name Professor Huree Jyoti Navalkar fittingly explains in similar terms to the Gothic sublime: "terror in our Hindu philosophy is but an opening on to the absolute" (Holland 1996: 11). She also has intertextual links with H. Rider Haggard's titular *She* (1887); indeed, tongue-in-cheek, Holland includes a Private Haggard in the British expeditionary party.

[29] Written at the tail end of the West's first AIDS epidemic in the 1980-90s, the novel's focus on infection, linked to a highly sexualised terror, can be seen to mimic the general panic about the hitherto unknown disease and its manner of transmission, as well as the fear that medical science would prove powerless to control it. Edmundson coincidentally describes "the discourse of AIDS" as "surely our major public occasion for indulgence in apocalyptic Gothic", going on to note how the disease "lends itself readily to Gothic depictions" in terms of inhabiting or haunting its victims like a curse for past 'unnatural' transgressions (Edmundson 1999: 28).

[30] Stoker assists Eliot's investigations, part of the narration takes the form of Stoker's journal, and he adapts the events for his classic novel, apparently accepting Professor

patient, is rescued by him from Lilah only at the cost of his own transformation into a blood-thirsty fiend in the guise of Jack the Ripper, eventually slaying the woman he saved – as Lilah renders literal what Maier calls the Gothic "seduction to become the monster to catch the monster" (this volume: 211). Eliot becomes "the slave of all [he] had sought to repress" (Holland 1996: 377), vacillating between utter contempt for his one-time efforts to preserve vile life and periods of tormented guilt and abject horror when he intermittently regains a sense of his former selfhood. Notions of (self)presence and ontology are further problematised by the novel's repeated references to Lilah's and her servants' elaborate 'games' and the incessant, terrifying spatial and visual hallucinatory experiences and shape-shifting transformations – or perhaps more accurately, *simulations* – to which Lilah subjects her victims. Two twentieth-century developments, closely linked to Gothic concerns, seems to infuse Holland's text: on the one hand, conspiracy theories regarding government mind control experiments; on the other, the rise of computer games and virtual worlds, where the self becomes an avatar, an artificially generated, othering 'embodiment' or personification. Appropriately, an opium den is used as one of the entry points to Lilah's realm, while the maniacal killing need implanted in Eliot is reminiscent of Adrian Lyne's psychological horror film *Jacob's Ladder* (1990), in which the titular Vietnam veteran discovers that his terrifying visions/memories are the after-effects of secret trials of a military drug aimed at maximising primal aggression. Eliot has, in effect, been brainwashed and genetically (re-)programmed: "the rhythms of my transformed state had been written into my very cells: murder, euphoria, disgust, then pain; and in the end, inexorably, murder once again" (Holland 1996: 393).

Moreover, Lilah's handmaiden Suzette describes setting up "a wholly novel type of game" for Eliot and thereafter "follow[ing] each turn you took through our maze", except that in this game plan the non-human intelligence inevitably wins. In this sense Holland's text resembles the computer-based interactive fiction *Slouching Towards Bedlam* (2003) discussed in Van Leavenworth's contribution to this

---

Huree Yhoti Navalkar's advice against using him as a model – "if you can make of me the hero of a romance, then I am a Dutchman" (Holland 1996: 356) – to create Van Helsing instead.

collection, where the monstrous Logos, infecting avatar-characters (and thence, metaphorically, players also), cannot be definitively categorised as either "(super)natural phenomenon or technologically manifested entity" (this volume: 260). For the sublime Lilah exists in an alternative reality that she "recreates" wherever she may be – "here, where we live, is infinity", Suzette warns Eliot (Holland 1996: 385). Crucially, in her final confrontation with Lord Byron, Lilah threatens in effect to 're-wind' the sequence of events to Kalikshutra and 'replay' the action – just as one might begin a 'virtual reality' game anew – this time allowing Eliot to fall rather than survive the assault of her zombified devotees. Either way, as proves the case in *Slouching*, when the player is invited "to replay the work in an attempt to contain the Logos" only to discover her/himself incapable of ever succeeding in doing so (this volume: 272), it is always the other – Lilah or Logos – who determines the outcome. Relieved of his Ripper cravings only to be vampirised instead, feeding on Lucy, the wife of a former murdered friend, and charged by Byron to find an (impossible) materialist scientific cure for vampirism through the study of Lilah's supernatural blood, Eliot remains inextricably enmeshed in Lilah's interminable game, her virtual reality, his 'Second Life' made real. Like the monstrous characters of *The League of Extraordinary Gentlemen*, Liliah's corrupted victims "live on in a way that denies them the narrative closure that their source texts had deemed important to contain the anxieties that they or their stories provoked" (Domsch, this volume: 103), with Holland's readers also denied the reassuring sense of an ending. The neo-Victorian uncanny desire for narrative afterlives, repetition and endless continuity issues in the terror of an infinity of existing 'caught' in an other's story. The labyrinthine urban setting thus mirrors the sublime on a number of levels: standing for the impenetrable convolutions of the gene code, the vertiginous postmodern web of interminable (inter)textuality, and the unknowability/inescapability of Lilah's virtual 'Great Game' with humanity. For all its occasional resort to ironic comedy and sometimes outright farce, neo-Victorian Gothic is haunted by the fatalistic possibility that progress, quest for knowledge, and change for the better may never be achievable, that advancement through time may simply produce eternal stasis in an abject, morally debased condition.

5. Neo-Victorian Postmodern and Postcolonial Gothics

"The Gothic and the postcolonial", as Tabish Khair emphatically stresses, "are obviously linked by a common preoccupation with the Other and aspects of Otherness" (Khair 2009: 3). Clearly, though, in Gothic's case generally and the Victorian Gothic's case in particular, the other – as a frightening site of the unfamiliar or the unintelligible – is not considered from the colonised point of view. It is this "negativised unknowability" of the indigene (Khair 2009: 4) – obvious in the negative prefixes – which postcolonialism rejects and endeavours to revise. Hence, otherness is either perceived from inside-out by the indigenous subject (with the coloniser/imperialist re-figured as the monstrous threat), or else in the coloniser/imperialist's dialectic relation to the indigenous other as self-same (with otherness revealed as a projection of something already inherent in the perceiving subject). Fundamentally, then, the question of otherness becomes the locus of an ethical struggle according to which the other *of* the self is always an other *in* the self, a recognition representing the postcolonial writer's main responsibility. Either way, however, Gothic abjection rebounds upon the colonial subjects rather than constituting those subjected by Empire.

If the postcolonial approach of the Gothic is meant to be ethical, it is certainly also political. How, indeed, could the representation and empowering of the colonised other avoid following a political agenda? As Gayatri Spivak has shown in her seminal essay, 'Can the subaltern speak?', the whole point of postcolonial literature is to give voice to the subaltern, to allow the colonised other to finally speak for her/himself and no longer be spoken by the colonial masters. This oppositional and retributional stance can also be found in postcolonial Gothic where the other, the monster or the revenant speaks out against her/his oppression and annihilation. What is at stake in the exploration of these forms of otherness – and this is a major difference from the postmodernist approach to Gothic – is not, or at least not primarily, ontological but essentially political, insisting on individual resurrections which always possess a collective or national dimension.

Jane Eyre's Bertha Mason is often considered as an archetype of the Victorian Gothic character, the epitome of the fearful unknown and threatening monster; hence neo-Victorian revisions of this archetype constitute a fruitful example to illustrate the difference between the postmodern and postcolonial programmes. When Rhys rewrites the story of the mad woman in the attic in *Wide Sargasso Sea*, she adopts Bertha's point of view and speaks in the first person, because the sense of exile is experienced at first hand, intimately and personally. The scandal of dis-location and the suffering of ostracism are thus voiced from the inside with intensity and urgency, like a desperate cry and a political allegation testifying to the injustice of the other's rejection and setting apart. In Rhys's postcolonial version, the Gothic monster becomes a political mouthpiece, from both colonial and feminist perspective. Similarly, the postmodernist reprise of *Jane Eyre* by the English novelist D.M. Thomas is certainly not devoid of an ideological purpose, since *Charlotte* (2000) is structured so as to show that the only source of happiness in the novel comes from a union between the coloniser and the colonised, the foreign and the native, the other and the same.[31] But the political vigour is entirely lost because of Thomas's systematic recourse to an aesthetics of simulation. Plagiarising, imitating or parodying *Jane Eyre*, Thomas cynically plays with Gothic modes and tropes, a playfulness which becomes blatant in the final section of the novel, consisting of Bertha's self-proclaimed "Negro" son's testimony (Thomas 2000: 160). This document represents a wonderful instance of pastiche in which Thomas strives to recreate the subaltern voice. To a certain extent pastiche, which has been described as "the official style of the postmodernist camp" (Foster 1985: 127), stands for the *opposite* of the postcolonial cries of revolt and idiosyncratic language of indignation. Thomas's recreation of a West Indian voice partakes of a linguistic game and a stylistic exercise in mimicry; this element of ludism distinguishes the postmodernist ironic revisitation of the Gothic from the postcolonial political re-appropriation.

This does not mean, however, that neo-Victorian Postcolonial and Postmodernist Gothic cannot coalesce successfully. For instance, Peter Carey's *Jack Maggs* (1997), a 'mash-up' of Dickens's *Great Expectations* (1860-61), *Oliver Twist* (1838), and biographical

---

[31] The Gothic dimension of Thomas's novel is nowhere more evident than in the conception of the contemporary protagonist who constantly presents herself not only as a Doppelgänger but as a revenant of Jane Eyre and/or of Charlotte Brontë in an ontological confusion representative of her unstable subjectivity. Her repetitive perception of the spirits of dead slave children similarly contributes to the novel's Gothic insistence on the reverberating presence of past affliction.

fragments of the canonical author's life, "repeats and re-cognises Britain's repressed criminalised and criminalising past" (Sadoff 2010: 176), quite literally bringing otherness 'home' – though not as might be expected. For while Carey too depicts the clandestine return of the transported convict to the empire's metropolis to make himself known to his (in this case literal) son, the novel's Gothic other proves to be not the traumatised convict, here re-figured as witness to British barbarism, but rather the exploitative magazine hack and author, Tobias Oates, who steals and manipulates Maggs's story with an eye for the main chance, becoming obsessed with his tale to the point of hallucinating scenes from the convict's life in a Gothic process of self-othering. Their relationship becomes a struggle over possession of the story – which implicitly stands for the construction of (post)colonial history also – with Maggs eventually forcing the writer to burn the manuscript, only for Oates to resurrect/rewrite it after Maggs's return to Australia. In this evident metafictional commentary on 'vampiric' appropriation of subaltern experience/identity that merges into plagiaristic consumption, postmodernist pastiche and irreverent playfulness with canonical texts re-affirm the subaltern, critiquing his symbolic re-victimisation.

Postmodernism and postcolonialism, then, share a prevalent anxiety with the relativities and lack of certitude regarding (self) possession and dispossession – of histories, metanarratives, intellectual property and material/territorial wealth. Arguably, the emptied-out self-as-other, defined, constructed, and controlled by inimical 'master' ideologies is, at least in part, a Gothic product (and function) of the advent of globalised capitalism and its intricate mysterious networks of power, which also underlie the continued threats to autonomy experienced by postcolonial nations in the face of neo-imperialist strategies enacted on international economic and military fronts. Theo D'Haen's discussion of Postmodern Gothic is revealing in this context:

> Poststructuralist and aesthetic postmodernism could then be two ways of relating to late capitalism from within. The latter directly translates late capitalism's commodifying influence into an "aesthetic" experience, reduplicating as it were the very personality (or non-personality) make-up

multinational capitalism needs: functional man, broken up in disparate units, without any essence to him, man as malleable putty[.] (D'Haen 1995: 286)[32]

Postcolonial Gothic with its postmodern tendencies, then, is intrinsically double: in creating space for self-consciously other voices speaking from elsewhere than the centre, "counter-writ[ing] the dominant order's discourse" and "redress[ing] the balance of history as unfinished business" (D'Haen 1995: 292), it both resurrects the uneasy spectres of historical atrocities and injustices and, paradoxically, seeks to lay them to rest. In doing so, however, it renders embattled history increasingly indeterminate, a potentially relative and depthless construct, which may be counter-productive, not to say de(con)structive to the autonomous identity politics postcolonialism relies on. Yet that same depthlessness simultaneously affords opportunities for subversions through what Allan Lloyd Smith calls the Gothic's "ransacking [of] an imaginary museum of pastness, or rifling a Baedeker of 'foreignness' to deck out its touristic exoticism" (A.L. Smith 1996: 11). For that museum is democratically open to all, so that postcolonial nations can ransack imperial motifs and themes, radically estranging and 'monstrifying' them in the process.

This inversion of the process of monstrification, along with the political agenda of Postcolonial Gothic, are well illustrated in Cheryl D. Edelson's chapter in this volume. Using the work of two Oceanic writers, Albert Wendt and Victoria Nalani Kneubuhl, Edelson shows how the colonial obsession with grave digging, excavations and plunder represents a monstrous interference in the process of historical and familial continuity for indigenous populations. So viewed from a postcolonial perspective, the Victorians' Gothic fascination with the other and the traces of life in death become the catalysts for an act of resistance and an art of re-memory, a politics of condemnation and of commemoration. In her own contribution to this collection, Jeanne

---

[32] Though not mentioning capitalism or postcolonialism, Allan Lloyd Smith's comparative analysis of 'Postmodernism/Gothicism' takes a similar view of self-declension: "[i]n both we confront the embattled, deconstructed self, without sureties of religion and social place, or any coherent psychology of the kind observable in both the Enlightenment or modernist traditions" (A.L. Smith 1996: 7). In contrast, postcolonialism aims at a viable *re*constructed coherent self.

Ellis similarly insists on the political implications of the Gothic in the postcolonial appropriation of neo-Victorianism. As an example Ellis takes the South African artist Leora Farber and her work on photographic stills and video footage featuring hybrid constructions in which the contemporary artist tries to graft herself unto the body and identity of her Victorian ancestor. The endeavour is one of empathy – rather than simulation – trying to recover a silenced history, to express the undying nature of the dead, and to display the inextricable hybridity of the postcolonial self. Systematically, then, the postcolonial relation to neo-Victorian Gothic is one of an uneasy confrontation, as if the Gothic itself were alien or foreign, as if the Gothic stood for a colonial concept and conception that have necessarily to be revised, contested and integrated in a political programme of self-assertion and self-definition.

For postmodernism, on the contrary, the Gothic seems more kindred. If we accept Jacqueline Howard's contention that Gothic fiction has never been "a 'pure' genre, but a combination of styles", a medley of "disparate discursive structures" (Howard 1994: 12, 2), then this generic hybridity is a first element which links the Gothic to postmodernism and its aesthetic synthetism and syncreticism.[33] The idea of impurity which is central to the Gothic, both in the formal and in ideological fields, is also exploited in postmodernism, famously defined by Salman Rushdie as the art of "mongrelisation": "*Mélange*, hotch-potch, a bit of this and a bit of that is how *newness enters the world*" (Rushdie 1991: 394, original emphases).

Another fundamental common point can be distinguished in the relation to the past and its haunting nature. Just as Gothic novels are fond of retrieving lost documents from the past and of showing the inevitable, lurking, undying presence of the past in the present, just so postmodernist novels play with historical archives and bear witness to the spectral persistence of the past in society and in fiction. Francis Fukuyama's 1989 essay 'The End of History?' has done much harm in the understanding of postmodernism. In effect, if early forms of postmodernism may have pursued the modernists' radical quest for innovation obsessed with contemporaneity and severed from historical

---

[33] To further substantiate her claim of hybridity, Howard also mentions that Gothic novels "draw on folklore, fairy-tale, myth, legend, superstition" so as to form "an intentional hybrid" (Howard 1994: 43, 47).

continuity, Fukuyama's aphoristic title can in no way reflect the principles of the actual postmodernist productions from the 1980s onwards. It is indeed quite striking that, at the same time as Fukuyama published his essay, Linda Hutcheon coined the phrase 'historiographic metafiction', a phrase that is still equated with the bulk of postmodernist fiction, clearly conveying that a concern with history is part and parcel of postmodernism. So, after the end of history, history appeared to be coming back – with a vengeance. What is true of fiction is true of film and architecture also: the ghost of the past is questioned, made visible and even foregrounded so as to gothically suggest that the bygone is never bygone and that the whole point of postmodernist art is to problematise the pastness of the past and the deadness of the dead. The reconsideration of ontological categories that are deemed incompatible is very much a common preoccupation of Gothic and postmodernism.

The uneasy inscription of history in neo-Victorian Gothic is at the heart of several chapters in this volume. For Kym Brindle, neo-Victorian (meta)fiction's recurrent use of sensational documents of uncertain ontological nature is meant to reflect the unsettling ambivalence of historical evidence, "impel[ling] readers to assess 'evidence' in the context of a Gothic excess of competing accounts" (this volume: 295). Questioning authority and conveying the instability of epistemology, Brindle argues, is what links neo-Victorian Gothic to the historical novel. According to Max Duperray, the numerous rewritings of the Jack the Ripper mystery similarly highlight the lure of the past and the impossibility of an accurate or conclusive historical reconstitution. The games of substitution and confusion between facts and fiction in these instances end up demonstrating the textuality – if not the mythicality – of history as a patchwork Frankensteinean monster. That the past cannot be trusted is also evinced in Andrew Smith's chapter, which presents the vampiric return of/to the Eastern European and Communist pasts as a new form of strategic political as well as cultural uncanniness, intent on "obscure[ing] the highly ideological constructions of the past [...] via the ethos of a global capitalism that argues that we live in a post-ideological, if not post-political, era" (this volume: 71). Neo-Victorian fiction's repetitive use of unreliable narrators and its appraisal of history through ballads, myths and folktales as much as doubtful 'official' records, reveal a tendency to bear false witness typical of postmodernism's principles of mis- and dis-remembering and (sometimes deliberate) forgetting.

The affinity between the Gothic and postmodernist outlooks is such that Maria Beville recently formulated the hypothesis that the two movements have merged to form a new genre which she calls "Gothic-postmodernism". According to Beville, "the Gothic and the postmodernist have come to be intertwined into a controversial mode of writing that could be referred to as a literary monster", the main characteristics of this new genre being a "fascination with terror, the negative and the irrational, and its hostility toward accepted codes of reality" (Beville 2009: 16). Admittedly, our postmodern civilisation, as Baudrillard has claimed, can be determined by its "spirit of terror" and "culture of death" (Baudrillard 1993: 127), which likens it to a certain Gothic *Zeitgeist*. Similarly, for Jean-François Lyotard, postmodernism's task lies in "presenting the existence of something unpresentable. Showing that there is something we can conceive of that we can neither see nor show"; this evocation of "the unpresentable in presentation itself" represents the postmodernist sublime (Lyotard 1992: 11, 15), manifestly akin to the Gothic unknown and uncanny. But when Beville asserts that in Gothic-postmodernism "all concepts of reality are tinged by the darkness and horror of transgression" or that it represents "a new kind of terror literature; a new language of terror" (Beville 2009: 60, 202), this may be relevant for post 9/11 literature but certainly not for postmodernism in general or neo-Victorianism in particular. For, as Christian Gutleben explains in this volume's final chapter, another major characteristic of postmodernist and neo-Victorian Gothic is its use of humour, adopting an ironic stance towards the literature of terror and the tropes of the uncanny. Fear, and indeed terror, are part and parcel of the thematic concerns of neo-Victorian Gothic, but they are always considered with a distance that encourages reflexion rather than affliction, creating a new type of Gothic where metatextual humour is mixed with metaphysical horror.

So, what also unites postmodernism and the Gothic – and what defines the neo-Victorian Gothic – is a tendency towards playfulness or self-derision. The Gothic is marked out by its "stylized theatricality [...] which is always teetering on the edge of self parody" (Horner and Zlosnik 2005: 12). It is "fundamentally stagey and theatrical in its nature" (Spooner 2004: 1), accounting for recurrent tropes of Victorian theatre/music hall (*Dan Leno and the Limehouse Golem*), stage magic (in the 2006 films *The Prestige* and *The Illusionist*) or staged spiritualist shows (*Affinity* and Maggie Power's *Porphyria's Lover* [1995]) in neo-Victorian Gothic. The postmodernist similarly plays with its own metatextual staging; it is an "overtly ludic (and lusory) form of literature [and art]" (O'Neil 1990: 114). As shown by the frequent use of artificial documents, forged letters/wills or spurious manuscripts, the Gothic revels in unsettling the notions of origins, authenticity and fakery, and these notions are in turn playfully harnessed by postmodernism and its logic of reprise and recycling. Since Gothic "possesses no original", instead taking "the form of a series of revivals, each based on a fantasized idea of the previous one" (Spooner 2006: 32), the neo-Gothic, according to Jerrold Hogle, is "haunted by the ghost of that already spectral past and hence by its refaking of what is already fake and already an emblem of the nearly empty and dead" (Hogle qtd. Spooner 2006: 33). Clearly then, the contemporary attitude towards the Gothic – and this includes both the postmodern and neo-Victorian attitudes – revolves around a playful self-awareness of the artificiality of generic codes, a metatextual understanding of the mode's hyperreality, and Baudrillard's designation of signs, texts or cultural artefacts as referring not to any empirical reality, but merely to other signs, texts or cultural artefacts.

There are (at least) two ways of analysing contemporary Gothic's connection with this hyperreality which is often considered as the main feature of postmodernity. The first interpretation, shared by most critics (Hogle 2000, A.L. Smith 2004, Spooner 2006, Botting 2008a), insists on the standardisation of these games of simulacra, which produce what Fred Botting has called "Disneygothic", "providing an image of dead simulations living on vampirically, freezing all culture and history in their immortal bite" (Botting 2008a: 3). The repetitive, ubiquitous and globalised display of Gothic signs and spectacles "exposes the void at the heart of an advanced consumer society" (Spooner 2006: 155). As Allan Lloyd Smith pithily puts it: "The Gothic heritage becomes *Heritage Gothic*, a use of now conventional tropes that is legitimated simply through previous practice" (A.L. Smith 2004: 126, original emphasis). This reading sees the Gothic as a symptom of postmodernity and its superficial games of self-reflexivity, combined with a mercantile exploitation of sensationalism. And when one considers the practices in advertising, marketing, show business, fashion, television and even, partly, cinema, the commoditisation and spectacularisation of the Gothic are undeniable phenomena affecting neo-Victorian Gothic culture.

Nevertheless, there is another way of interpreting contemporary Gothic's hyperreality if one concentrates on neo-Victorian fiction in particular. Neo-Victorian Gothic does indeed flaunt its reliance on and recycling of other texts, thus signalling "the hyper-reflexivity of post-postmodernism" (Botting 2008b: 107). Yet arguably one can also read this insistence on Gothic's (meta)textual origins as an acknowledgement of the necessity to establish a dialogue with and interrogate neo-Victorianism's sources in cultural 'texts' of all kinds, particularly literary ones, as evident in Holland's *Supping with Panthers* and its self-conscious employment of the trope of the hyperreal. In a sense, the neo-Victorian is *by definition* hyperreal, since it has no direct access to the Victorian real, instead relying entirely on Victorian texts and documents, that is, on *signs* of the past. By foregrounding its hyperreality, then, neo-Victorian Gothic does little else but shift its focus from a referential or axiological priority (such as Enlightenment values, for example) to a literary or cultural dimension. The spectral past is thus presented, interrogated and studied in its sheer (inter/supra)textuality. And there is just no reason to suppose that a greater emphasis put on the literariness of neo-Gothic literature should preclude an exploration or an investigation of the key Gothic concepts such as the other, the marginal, the unknown or the fearful. The postmodernist games with hyperreality therefore modify the manner in which the Gothic is treated and exhibited, but arguably not its purpose.

The foregrounding of sexuality constitutes another neo-Victorian priority where the Gothic meets postmodernism and which substantiates the ambivalence regarding today's handling of the Gothic. The deviant, the perverse, the corrupt, the unnatural have of course always been key ingredients of Gothic, but currently, under the lead of feminists and queer theorists, a disproportionate amount of authorial and critical attention is paid to "non-heteronormative sexualities" (Spooner 2006: 24-25). As Patricia Pulham convincingly argues in her chapter on Colm Tóibín's *The Master* (2004), the transgressive desires revealed in queer Gothic lay bare what we would prefer to ignore about ourselves and aim at de-codifying sexuality, or rather sexualities, even as they may paradoxically re-obscure them: "James's desire, like James himself, becomes a spectral presence that appears and disappears even as we see it" (this volume: 155). The importance attached to queer sexualities – queer being defined as anything that represents "those very alternatives to monolithic orthodoxy" (Hughes and Smith 2009: 2) – can again be construed in two different ways. Because by nature, the Gothic is "always already excessive, grotesque, overspilling its own boundaries and limits" (Wolfreys 2002: 8), the non-orthodox forms and manifestations of sexuality are displaced from the margins, becoming not only central but even invasive and pervasive. Such an exhibitionist tendency might indeed be considered as pandering to "the contemporary lust for spectacle and sensation" (Spooner 2006: 156), for instance in neo-Victorian Gothic's depictions of Rippersesque sex crimes, or *Fingersmith*'s and *The Journal of Dora Damage*'s shameless situation of lesbian and interracial relationships respectively within the context of the pornography business, or in the graphic sex video collection in Will Self's "bonkbuster" (Heawood 2002: 15), *Dorian: An Imitation* (2002). Yet, the degree of staged queerness and 'other' sexual pursuits and pleasures does not alter their primary function: to problematise "the relationship between the marginal and the mainstream, between reciprocal states of queerness and non-queerness", to suggest the possibility of difference and "alternative[s] to all that is non-queer", so as to make "the assigning of Absolutes, in fiction as much as in criticism, a futile act" (Hughes and Smith 2009: 4, 5). Hence Gothic's questioning and valorising of otherness as potentially *both* 'natural' *and* transgressive is not incompatible with a form of brazen exhibitionism. Thought-provoking and fickle, highly ethical and shamelessly commercial, neo-Victorian Gothic is full of paradoxes which it deliberately puts on display.

6.   The Ethical Persistence, After All

Not just neo-Victorian Postmodern Gothic, but neo-Victorian Gothic in all its (mis)shapes comes under the influence of postmodernism's equivocations. Heilmann and Llewellyn have asserted that neo-Victorianism "must in some respect be *self-consciously engaged with the act of (re)interpretation, (re)discovery and (re)vision concerning the Victorians*", yet such self-consciousness can take many forms, not all of which need be characterised by "the self-analytical drive" they claim "accompanies 'neo-Victorianism'" (Heilmann and Llewellyn 2010: 4-5, original emphasis). Indeed, it could be argued that neo-Victorian Gothic's inevitable resort to and reiteration of well-established generic, even clichéd motifs and themes is *inherently* self-conscious – that is, *it cannot be anything else*, if it tried – regardless of whether these elements are employed imitatively or parodically, conservatively or subversively, for stylistic effect or deconstructive critique. The neo-Victorian Gothic, both in what it reprises and how it does so, re-enacts the interstitial balancing act between innovation and imitation, liberation and influence, self and other. Just as Gothic informs the neo-Victorian, so the neo-Victorian infuses twentieth/twenty-first-century Gothic, exploiting as well as contributing to the Gothic's contradictory tendencies that encompass realism and romance, anachronism and nostalgic reiteration, thrilling spectacle and postmodern self-abjection, ethical didacticism and sheer *fun*.

Inevitably, the composite neo-Victorian's use of the heterogeneous concept of the Gothic becomes characterised by a still greater degree of hybridity. Playing sophisticated (but sometimes also quite crude) metafictional and metatextual games with Gothic's tropes and canonical works, exposing the sexy secrets of the society of the spectacle, handling a self-reflexive form of irony about its hyperreal status, exhibiting a paradoxical ethics through fashionable goriness, neo-Victorian Gothic appears as a mixed set of practices, proving as fundamentally ambiguous as the contemporary Gothic to which it contributes:

> It can be progressive or conservative, nostalgic or modern, comic or tragic, political or apolitical, feminine or masculine, erudite or trashy, transcendentally spiritual or doggedly material, sinister or silly. (Spooner 2006: 156)

In spite of neo-Victorian Gothic's constant compromising hybridisation with other genres, modes and codes, particularly those of nineteenth-century Gothic, it is our contention that the Gothic's radical spirit and purpose are never wholly lost. However excessive, however outrageous or mercantile, neo-Victorian Gothic's interest remains its ethical determination to question norms, to value otherness, to nuance identity politics, to interrogate limits and boundaries, and to deconstruct Manichean distinctions – between good and evil, right and wrong, orthodoxy and heterodoxy, light and darkness, life and death and, perhaps most importantly, past and present. An ideal illustration of this paradoxical and hybrid nature of neo-Victorianism's adoption/adaptation of all things Gothic can be found in Alasdair Gray's *Poor Things* (1992). Gray's parodic remodelling of the Frankenstein myth of demiurgic creation is ostentatiously "sham Gothic and sham Victorian" (Davison 2009: 206). It provocatively plays with its (meta)textual (re)creations and hyperreal (fake) origins, shamelessly staging sexual excesses, but it also raises the eminently Gothic question of the legitimacy of creating or destroying life and teaches the eminently Gothic lesson that "no person or nation possesses a monopoly on, or immunity from, monstrosity" (Davison 2009: 211). Like Gray's heroine (and possibly his novel), an oxymoronic "gorgeous monster" (Gray 1993: 91), neo-Victorian Gothic appears full of contradictions, but it keeps challenging established codes, a salutary ethical priority.

The protean neo-Victorian Gothic, then, assumes myriad 'gorgeous monstrous' shapes, building and carrying on, as well as innovating, Victorian Gothic and neo-Gothic traditions, not least by 'mashing' any number of Gothic sub-genres. Infusing and inhabiting our postmodern culture and our cultural unconscious, the othering Victorians whom we simultaneously define ourselves against and in terms of – not least via the Gothic tropes of self-alienation, trauma, obsession and paranoia that underpin postmodern subjectivity – may to some extent be unwanted but, strictly speaking, they are hardly *uninvited* guests. Again and again, twentieth/twenty-first-century arts and media invite them over the threshold and into our homes to abide with us: our resident dream and nightmare, a cherished neurosis of which we do not really wish to be cured. Whether we ever perceive the Victorians in their 'true' shapes (whatever those may be) remains uncertain, since our gothicised vision of them seems inherently and capriciously *dysmorphic*, determined by the very same distorting, hyperreal Gothic tropes through which we attempt to understand and reappraise them. And as we gothically transfigure and resurrect them, so are we ourselves subjected to the transformative othering power with which we invest them.

Bibliography

Arata. Stephen D. 1990. 'The Occidental Tourist: *Dracula* and the Anxiety of Reverse Colonization', *Victorian Studies* 33(4) (Summer): 621-645.
Arias, Rosario. 2010. 'Haunted Places, Haunted Spaces: The Spectral Return of Victorian London in Neo-Victorian Fiction'. In Arias and Pulham (2010a): 133-156.
Arias, Rosario, and Patricia Pulham (eds.). 2010a. *Haunting and Spectrality in Neo-Victorian Fiction: Possessing the Past*. Houndmills, Basingstoke & New York: Palgrave Macmillan.
––––. 2010b. 'Introduction'. In Arias and Pulham (2010a): xi-xxvi.
Armitt, Lucie. 2011. *History of the Gothic: Twentieth-Century Gothic* (Gothic Literary Studies, vol. 3). Cardiff: University of Wales Press.
Baudrillard, Jean. 1993. *Symbolic Exchange and Death* (trans. Ian Hamilton Grant). New York: Sage.
Berthin, Christine. 2010. *Gothic Hauntings: Melancholy Crypts and Textual Ghosts*. Houndmills, Basingstoke & New York: Palgrave Macmillan.
Beville, Maria. 2009. *Gothic-postmodernism: Voicing the Terrors of Postmodernity*. Amsterdam & New York: Rodopi.
Birch, Carol. 2011. *Jamrach's Menagerie*. Edinburgh: Canongate.
Botting, Fred (ed.). 2001a. *The Gothic*. Cambridge: D.S. Brewer.
––––. 2001b. 'Candygothic'. In Botting (2001): 133-151.
––––. 2002. 'Aftergothic: consumption, machines, and black holes'. In Hogle (2002): 277-300.
––––. 2007. 'Gothic Culture'. In Spooner and McEvoy (2007): 199-213.
––––. 2008a. *Limits of Horror: Technology, Bodies, Gothic*. Manchester: Manchester University Press.
––––. 2008b. *Gothic Romanced: Consumption, Gender and Technology in Contemporary Fictions*. London & New York: Routledge.
Bowser, Rachel A., and Brian Croxall (eds.). 2010. 'Introduction: Industrial Evolution', *Neo-Victorian Studies* 3(1), Special Issue: *Steampunk, Science, and (Neo)Victorian Technologies*: 1-45.
Bruhm, Steven. 'The contemporary Gothic: Why we need it'. In Hogle (2002): 259-276.
Byatt, A.S. 2009. *The Children's Book*. London: Chatto & Windus.
Cavale, Jude. 2010. '24 Cool Steampunk Weapons from Another Era' (2 Feb.). On-line at: http://walyou.com/steampunk-weapons/ (consulted 02.4.2012).
Collela, Silvana. 2010. 'Olfactory Ghosts: Michel Faber's *The Crimson Petal and the White*'. In Arias and Pulham (2010a): 85-110.
Davison, Carol Margaret. 2009. 'Monstrous Regiments of Women and Brides of Frankenstein: Gendered Body Politics in Scottish Female Gothic Fiction', in Wallace, Diana, and Andrew Smith (eds.), *The Female Gothic: New Directions*. Houndmills, Basingstoke & New York: Palgrave: 196-214.
D'Haen, Theo. 1995. 'Postmodern Gothic' in Tinkler-Villani, Valeria, Peter Davidson and Jane Stevenson (eds.), *Exhibited by Candlelight: Sources and Developments in the Gothic Tradition*. Amsterdam & Atlanta, Georgia: Rodopi: 283-294.

Edmundson, Mark. 1999. *Nightmare on Main Street: Angels, Sadomasochism, and the Culture of the Gothic* [1997]. Harvard: Harvard University Press. [GOOGLE Books]
Ellis, Markman. 2000. *The History of Gothic Fiction*. Edinburgh: Edinburgh University Press.
Foster, Hal. 1985. *Recodings: Art, Spectacle, Cultural Politics*. Port Townsend, Washington: Bay Press.
Gilbert, Sandra M. and Susan Gubar. 1979. 'Chapter 10: A Dialogue of Self and Soul: Plain Jane's Progress', in *The Madwoman in the Attic: The Woman Writer and the Nineteenth-Century Literary Imagination*. New Haven & London: Yale University Press: 336-371.
Gray, Alasdair. 1993. *Poor Things* [1992]. Harmondsworth: Penguin.
Heawood, Jonathan. 2002. 'The sincerest form' [Review of Will Self's *Dorian: An Imitation*], *The Observer*, Observer Review section (29 September): 15.
Heilmann, Ann, and Mark Llewellyn. 2010. *Neo-Victorianism: The Victorians in the Twenty-First Century, 1999-2009*. Houndmills, Basingstoke & New York: Palgrave Macmillan.
Hogle, Jerrold. 2000. 'The Gothic Ghost of the Counterfeit and the Progress of Abjection'. In Punter (2000): 293-304.
—. (ed.) 2002. *The Cambridge Companion to Gothic Fiction*. Cambridge & New York: Cambridge University Press.
Holland, Tom. *Supping with Panthers*. 1996. London: Little, Brown and Company.
—. 2001. *The Bone Hunter*. London: Little, Brown and Company.
Horner, Avril, and Sue Zlosnik. 2005. *Gothic and the Comic Turn*. Houndmills, Basingstoke & New York: Palgrave Macmillan.
Howard, Jacqueline. 1994. *Reading Gothic Fiction: A Bakhtinian Approach*. Oxford: Clarendon Press.
Hughes, William, and Andrew Smith. 2009. 'Introduction: Queering the Gothic', in Hughes, William, and Andrew Smith (eds.) *Queering the Gothic*. Manchester: Manchester University Press: 1-10.
Hurley, Kelly. 1996. *The Gothic Body: Sexuality, materialism, and degeneration at the* fin de siècle. Cambridge & New York: Cambridge University Press.
—. 2002. 'British Gothic fiction, 1885-1930'. In Hogle (2002): 189-207.
Kaplan, Cora. 2007. *Victoriana – Histories, Fictions, Criticism*. Edinburgh: Edinburgh University Press.
Khair, Tabish. 2009. *The Gothic, Postcolonialism and Otherness: Ghosts from Elsewhere*. Houndmills, Basingstoke & New York: Palgrave Macmillan.
Kincaid, James R. 2000. 'Designing Gourmet Children or, KIDS FOR DINNER!'. In Robbins and Wolfreys (2000): 1-11.
Kneale, Matthew. 2001. *English Passengers* [2000]. London: Penguin.
Kohlke, Marie-Luise, and Christian Gutleben (eds.). 2010a. *Neo-Victorian Tropes of Trauma: The Politics of Bearing After-Witness to Nineteenth-Century Suffering*. Amsterdam & New York: Rodopi.
—, and Christian Gutleben. 2010b. 'Introduction: Bearing After-Witness to the Nineteenth Century'. In Kohlke and Gutleben (2010a): 1-34.
Luckhurst, Roger. 2000. 'Trance-Gothic, 1882-97'. In Robbins and Wolfreys (2000): 148-167.

Lyotard, Jean-François. 1992. *The Postmodern Explained* (trans. Don Barry, Bernadette Maher, Julian Pefanis, Virginia Spate and Morgan Thomas). Minneapolis: University of Minnesota Press.
Mann, George. 2008. *The Affinity Bridge: A Newbury & Hobbes Investigation.* London: Snowbooks.
Mitchell, Kate. 2010. *History and Cultural Memory in Neo-Victorian Fiction: Victorian Afterimages.* Houndmills, Basingstoke & New York: Palgrave Macmillan.
Moretti, Franco. 2000. *The Way of the World: The* Bildungsroman *in European Culture* [1987] (trans. Albert Sbragia), New Edition. London & New York: Verso.
O'Neil, Patrick. 1990. *The Comedy of Entropy: Humour / Narrative / Reading.* Toronto: University of Toronto Press.
Onion, Rebecca. 2008. 'Reclaiming the Machine: An Introductory Look at Steampunk in Everyday Practice', *Neo-Victorian Studies* 1(1) (Autumn): 138-163.
Punter, David (ed.). 2000. *A Companion to the Gothic.* Oxford: Blackwell Publishing.
Rankin. Robert. 2010. *The Japanese Devil Fish Girl and Other Unnatural Attractions: A Novel.* London: Gollanz.
Robbins, Ruth, and Julian Wolfreys (eds.). 2000. *Victorian Gothic: Literary and Cultural Manifestations in the Nineteenth-Century.* Houndmills, Basingstoke & New York: Palgrave.
Rushdie, Salman. 1991. *Imaginary Homelands. Essays and Criticism 1981-1991.* London: Granta Books.
Sadoff, Dianne F. 2010. 'The Neo-Victorian Nation at Home and Abroad: Charles Dickens and Traumatic Rewriting'. In Kohlke and Gutleben (2010a): 163-190.
Sage, Victor, and Allan Lloyd Smith (eds.). 1996a. *Modern Gothic: A Reader.* Manchester & New York: Manchester University Press, 1996.
——. 1996b. 'Introduction'. In Sage and Smith (1996a): 1-5.
Smith, Allan Lloyd. 1996. 'Postmodernism/Gothicism'. In Sage and Smith (1996a): 6-19.
——. 2004. *American Gothic Fiction: An Introduction.* London & New York: Continuum.
Smith, Andrew. 2007a. *Gothic Literature.* Edinburgh: Edinburgh University Press.
——. 2007b. 'Hauntings'. In Spooner and McEvoy (2007): 147-154.
Spooner, Catherine. 2004. *Fashioning Gothic Bodies.* Manchester: Manchester University Press.
——. 2006. *Contemporary Gothic.* London: Reaktion Books.
——. 2007. 'Gothic in the Twentieth Century'. In Spooner and McEvoy (2007): 38-47.
Spooner, Catherine, and Emma McEvoy (eds.). 2007. *The Routledge Companion to Gothic.* London & New York: Routledge.
Warwick, Alexandra. 2007. 'Victorian Gothic'. In Spooner and McEvoy (2007): 29-37.
Williams, Kate. 2012. *The Pleasures of Men.* London: Michael Joseph/Penguin.
Wolfreys, Julian. 2000a. 'Preface: "I could a tale unfold" or, the Promise of Gothic'. In Robbins and Wolfreys (2000): xi-xx.

—. 2000b. '"I wants to make your flesh creep": Notes toward a Reading of the Comic-Gothic in Dickens'. In Robbins and Wolfreys (2000): 31-59.
—. 2002. *Victorian Hauntings: Spectrality, Gothic, the Uncanny and Literature*. Houndmills, Basingstoke: Palgrave Macmillan.
Womack, Kenneth. 2000. '"Withered, Wrinkled, and Loathsome of Visage': Reading the Ethics of the Soul and the Late-Victorian Gothic in *The Picture of Dorian Gray*'. In Robbins and Wolfreys (2000): 168-181.
Zylinska, Joanna. 2001 *On spiders, cyborgs and being scared: The feminine and the sublime*. Manchester & New York: Manchester University Press.

Part I

Imperial Impostures and Improprieties

The Limits of Neo-Victorian History: Elizabeth Kostova's *The Historian* and *The Swan Thieves*

Andrew Smith

Abstract:
This chapter examines how Elizabeth Kostova's *The Historian* (2005) and *The Swan Thieves* (2010) employ the Gothic in their reconstructions of nineteenth-century European history. The explicit use of the Gothic in *The Historian* demonises European history which is variously associated with religious intolerance, fascism and communism – forces which are subject to a possible vampiric return. Whilst *The Historian* can be read as a post 9/11 narrative concerning latent terrorist influences, *The Swan Thieves* attempts to recover the lost history of a French female Impressionist painter. The novels are linked by a shared emphasis on masculine mystique which contrasts the political (Count Dracula in *The Historian*) with the private (Robert Oliver in *The Swan Thieves*). Kostova's use of the Gothic is key to understanding these neo-Victorian engagements and how they relate to politics, Art and gender.

Keywords: *Dracula*, European history, Gender, Gothic, Impressionism, Elizabeth Kostova, Memory Studies.

*****

Critical discussion of neo-Victorian texts has in part focused on the politics involved in such acts of appropriation. Questions raised have addressed whether these texts represent a conservative nostalgia or a radical engagement with how we perceive the Victorians.[1] Whilst it would be problematic to attempt to run these two models together,

---

[1] Christian Gutleben's 2001 study *Nostalgic Postmodernism: The Victorian Tradition and the Contemporary British Novel* provides a detailed analysis of the different political leanings of the neo-Victorian. Also see Andrea Kirchknopf for an overview of critical discussion on the neo-Victorian (Kirchknopf 2008: 53-80).

they are nevertheless both predicated on the possibility of reclaiming the past, which suggests that the Victorians constitute unfinished business. How to conceptualise this connection – either as conservative or radical – suggests that a coherent model of Victorian history is available for such reconstructions.[2] The role of the Gothic in these interventions complicates the picture. In its more radical formations the Gothic provides a way of looking at identity that helps draw out the covert symbolism that inhabits Victorian texts. Sarah Waters's *Affinity* (1999) is exemplary in that regard as it engages with the illicit sexual politics and class complexities which so often characterised the sensation novel. However, in its less challenging modes it can be used to exploit and titillate as witnessed by, to give just one recent example, Dacre Stoker's *Dracula the Un-Dead* (2009). The range of intellectual work which takes place in the Gothic is thus varied and politically complex, and how these issues might relate to the neo-Victorian Gothic will be explored in the work of a writer that arguably falls somewhere between that of Waters and Stoker: Elizabeth Kostova. Kostova's *The Historian* (2005) and *The Swan Thieves* (2010) take up positions on the nineteenth century which helpfully illuminate how the politics of reclaiming the past are closely linked to their engagements with the Gothic.

It should be noted that whilst scholarship on the neo-Victorian has acknowledged that the form trades in images of the Gothic, there has yet to emerge a fully developed examination of what the neo-Victorian does to our understanding of the Gothic. At one level the neo-Victorian could be regarded as a specific modulation of the postmodern in which the use of intertextuality both forges textual connections (as it does in both *The Historian* and *The Swan Thieves*) and poses problems around issues of truth and certainty, which have conventionally been key features of the Gothic text. There is also a related issue which is how to read Gothically. Catherine Spooner, for example, has acknowledged the neo-Victorian view that Sarah Water's *Affinity* uses images of the séance as a conceit for a link to the past, but she moves beyond this by arguing that the more significant Gothic aspect of the novel centres on how "a representative code of

---

[2] The issue of the supposedly conservative political status of nostalgia has been challenged by critics, most recently by Kate Mitchell in her 2010 study *History and Cultural Memory in Neo-Victorian Fiction*.

gender, sexuality and class" is internalised via the image of Bentham's prison Panopticon which positions the Victorians "as the repressed material of modernity" (Spooner 2007: 44). The ideological is what is repressed, and reading the neo-Victorian Gothic for its discrete ideological content is the ambition of this chapter as it attempts to provide both a way of reading the neo-Victorian text and of identifying how such texts broaden our understanding of the Gothic. The Gothic has always been interested in the past and its possible continuing presence, but Kostova's ideologically motivated reconstructions of the past associate Gothic secrets with hidden political realities (*The Historian*) or else use past emotional conflicts as a way of understanding the present (*The Swan Thieves*). The return of the past, as a neo-Victorian uncanniness, is what unites these texts.

Neither *The Historian* nor *The Swan Thieves* are neo-Victorian novels as conventionally understood, because in the main (the exception being some passages in *The Swan Thieves*), they are not set in the nineteenth century. However, *The Historian* engages with a reconstituted idea of the Victorian in its reworking of Bram Stoker's *Dracula* (1897), and Kostova's engagement with late Victorian literature is clearly a self-conscious one given her acknowledgement that *The Swan Thieves* is in part a homage to Conrad's *Lord Jim* (1900). Criticism on the neo-Victorian has also acknowledged that in order to understand our culture's engagement with the past it is necessary to rethink any narrowly defined view of the neo-Victorian that simply depends on the model of a contemporary novel set in the nineteenth century – although this requires a different way of looking at the neo-Victorian which is, as we shall see, illustrated in interesting ways by *The Historian*.[3]

The Historian is set in the present day but moves back to the 1970s, 1950s and 1930s and focuses on how a series of academic historians receive (usually whilst themselves still promising graduate students) a mysterious book, which has as its centrepiece the figure of a dragon. This narrative of textual inheritance is also a personal one as it focuses on the memoir of an unnamed female Oxford historian who

---

[3] Ann Heilmann and Mark Llewellyn outline how our understanding of the neo-Victorian needs to move beyond any easy engagement with texts set in the Victorian period in order to widen discussion of how the nineteenth century itself becomes a complex topic for exploration in other texts and non-text media (see Heilmann and Llewellyn 2010: 1-32).

receives such a book and who recounts her first sighting of a similar volume amongst her father's papers in the 1970s. Her father, Paul, relates much of the story surrounding the book and the links to his PhD supervisor, Professor Rossi, who also received such a volume in the 1930s whilst a graduate student at Oxford. The story that unfolds centres on identifying who the mysterious agent is that has sent out these volumes and what is required of the recipients. The plot reveals that Count Dracula, or more precisely Vlad Tepes, is responsible for distributing these volumes and that the illustration of the dragon is really a map which identifies Dracula's location. The ultimate revelation is that Dracula is looking for a skilled historian to catalogue his vast collection of books, which cover a range of geopolitical issues that, in the main, reflect on his European power base from the fifteenth century. Along the way a family romance is developed in which Paul marries Rossi's daughter, Helen, and they, after many adventures are finally able to defeat Dracula when he is killed by a silver bullet fired by Helen. However, it is also a narrative tinged with tragedy as both Helen and Paul die comparatively young and leave the narrator orphaned. Also, the apparent death of Dracula is inconclusive given that the narrator, some years after the shooting, receives in 2008 a further copy of the volume containing the dragon.[4]

The novel also addresses a number of themes centring on religious conflict between Christian and Islamic beliefs and provides an outline of post World War II European politics, as the novel moves between America, Turkey, Britain, and mainland Europe highlighting religious controversy and a history of political tension – especially in the communist Eastern Europe of the 1950s and 1970s. It is by working through these ideological complexities that the continuing presence of Vlad Tepes is discovered, and he is held to be variously responsible for religious intolerance, fascism and the rise of communism. Indeed he is used as a vehicle through which to demonise European history and to suggest that communism could well be the subject of a possible vampiric return as, like the vampire, it is a dead/undead presence which could be available for political resurrection, were it not for the American focused intervention of

---

[4] 2008 sets Kostova's novel three years into the future of its publication, which seems to be intended as an ominous warning about the near future and the continuing presence of the type of politics that I discuss here.

people like Paul, who manages a peace organisation committed to settling European political conflicts. In some respects this echoes, if in reactionary terms, Derrida's assertion in *Specters of Marx* that the ghost of communism creates an "anticipation" that "is at once impatient, anxious, and fascinated" as the spirit of communism "will end up coming" (Derrida 1994: 4). In *The Historian* the past and place become conflated, meaning that contemporary Europe, as seen through American eyes, such as Paul's and his daughter's (who despite her European connections identifies closely with him), is linked to a particular version of history. The narrator notes of her father's European peace association journeys: "When my father returned from some name on the European map that hung on the wall of our dining room, he smelled like other times and places" (Kostova 2005: 4). How to decode this history requires a process that is imaginative in its engagement with where history is to be found – in folk ballads, myths, literary tales, and above all in *Dracula* – and with how these sources are to be read, rather like how the vampire hunters in *Dracula* approach texts, for their symbolic truths. As Paul tells the narrator, "All the literary stories I read led me into some kind of – exploration – of history" (Kostova 2005: 11), and the setting for much of this relates to an explicit engagement with the Cold War in which communism is figured, at least in the novel's engagement with the 1950s and 1970s, as an ongoing tyranny.

The novel's engagement with a Europe of the 1930s, 1950s and 1970s via Stoker's *Dracula* might seem unusual, especially given that the repeated anxiety about the return of European communism would, from the vantage point of 2005, seem unlikely. However, the references to periods when Stalin consolidated his power (the 1930s) to the 1950s Soviet political buffering of the geographical gains of the 1940s, and the Cold War dramas of the 1970s (and the American led fight against communism in Vietnam during that period), suggest moments of repeated crisis for the West that have not been laid to rest. The novel suggests that these histories never quite die and, as noted in a different context by Derrida, are subject to possible spectral returns which could specifically threaten a model of democracy that is closely associated with America and the global capitalism that helps disseminate it.

Much of the action set in the 1950s centres on Helen's experiences of being raised in the Soviet Bloc and concerns life under the communist regimes in Hungary, Bulgaria, and Romania – with Vlad's supposed burial site in the latter caustically referred to by Rossi as being "now in the possession of our friend socialist Romania" (Kostova 2005: 20). Later Helen also affirms this implied link between communism and Vlad when she tells Paul, "We have been enjoying some freedom in Hungary these days, although everyone wonders how long the Soviets will tolerate that. Speaking of Impalers" (Kostova 2005: 140). For Paul "The Cold War was real to me now, in the person of Helen" (Kostova 2005: 225). The events in Turkey which dwell on Islamic and Christian conflict also become linked to the communist presence via Paul's account of Budapest, which for him is characterised by a strange architectural blending of East and West that symbolises a connection between different forms of religious and political tyranny – all of which coalesce in Rossi's account of Vlad's archive. The archive contains, amongst many others, documents relating to the Ottoman Empire combined with work by Machiavelli, a well-thumbed first edition of *Mein Kampf* and a memo from Stalin to someone in the military consisting of a long list of names of people presumably identified for execution. Rossi also notes that Dracula "*brought his great hand to rest on an early edition of Bram Stoker's novel and smiled*" (Kostova 2005: 643, original emphasis). For Dracula the archived material supports his view that "*History has taught us that the nature of man is evil, sublimely so. Good is not perfectible but evil is*" (Kostova 2005: 644, original emphasis). It is a version of evil that the reluctant vampire hunters contest, and their apparent, if possibly temporary, defeat of Dracula represents a triumph of American western democracy over older European forms of tyranny. The question which one might ask at this point concerns how the politics of Kostova's novel constitute a neo-Victorian engagement with the Gothic and in order to develop this it is necessary to consider what type of European politics were advanced in Stoker's novel and whether Kostova is either appropriating, or moving beyond his political vision.

Matthew Gibson has argued that *Dracula* should be seen within the context of British views on the Balkans from the late 1870s and that the novel represents a conservative and complex view of Balkan politics, in which Dracula is "a valiant fighter on the part of a Christian Europe, and yet the cross has forsaken him and he must be kept out of the West at all costs" (Gibson 2006: 85). However there is a paradox here because, during Harker's journey East to Transylvania, Stoker

> avoids condemning the real Eastern influence, namely Turkey, in keeping with his somewhat self-contradictory desire to suggest that the Turks are the rightful policemen of the Balkans, while the East itself is shambolic and primitive. (Gibson 2006: 83-4)

Stoker thus treads a fine line between seeing the Turks as a restraining influence on an uncontrollable Balkans, whilst wanting to assert the claims of a potentially unified Christian Europe. In other words Stoker wanted to endorse the contemporary British government's view about the need for political stability in the Balkans, whilst being sceptical about how best to police this state of affairs. Kostova's reworking of *Dracula* focuses on a similar terrain but for quite different political ends, as it seems to function as a post 9/11 narrative, in which Islamic culture has been shaped by models of corruption that have their roots within a European history that might come back to life as an enemy of American democracy. Kostova's novel is also variously set in America, Amsterdam, and Britain, and this coalition of the willing reworks the American, Dutch and British vampire hunters from Stoker's novel. However, it redirects a central, if arguably implicit, concern in *Dracula* that relates to American colonial ambitions, which according to Franco Moretti explains the presence and subsequent death of Quincey Morris who symbolically poses a threat to Britain's imperial aspirations (see Moretti 1983: 90-107). *The Historian* thus re-writes anxieties about the imperialist danger posed by a revitalised communist Europe and this process of re-writing raises questions about the relationship between the neo-Victorian and the Gothic.

The issue of rewriting is tied to the idea of the unreliable narrator that so often characterises the Gothic, a genre in which both Stoker and Kostova can be cast as somewhat partial historians in their dramatic reconstructions of the past. However, there are also representations of public and private loss in *The Historian* which can be associated with the neo-Victorian. As Ann Heilmann and Mark Llewellyn note, "[l]oss, mourning, and regeneration are prototypical preoccupations of the neo-Victorian novel which often revolves around the re(dis)covery of a personal and/or collective history" that frequently evokes "repressed memories" (Heilmann and Llewellyn 2010: 34). An engagement with issues about authenticity, repression, and identity (both personal and political) characterises the neo-Victorian Gothic. It is the growing discipline of memory studies which helps us think about the form, even whilst it allows for a reconsideration of the Gothic figure of the unreliable narrator. Indeed Marie-Luise Kohlke has argued that the neo-Victorian text engages with a type of "memory work", which "is actively involved in consciousness-raising and witness-bearing" (Kohlke 2008: 1, 9), and that this illustrates the radicalism of the form as it recovers lost histories – an issue that is certainly relevant to *The Swan Thieves*, but one which is open to challenge in the more explicitly Gothic *The Historian*.

Memory studies have tended to address a tension between what is recorded by historians and what subsists within a culture's collective memory. For Maurice Halbwachs historical accounts represent an intervention which effectively 'stops' history in order to discuss it, whereas "[c]ollective memory" constitutes "continuous thought" (Halbwachs 2008: 140). For Pierre Nora memory "remains in permanent evolution, open to the dialectic of remembering and forgetting", whereas "[h]istory is perpetually suspicious of memory, and its true mission is to suppress and destroy it" (Nora 2008: 146). History, considered in Nora's terms is thus opposed to "reality" (Nora 2008: 146). Michael Rossington's appraisal of Halbwachs and Nora argues the case that it is in literature, or in the "literary-cultural" (Rossington 2008: 137), that the collective memory is stored. However, whilst one key aspect of memory studies is the notion of bearing witness, in the Gothic there is an emphasis on bearing *false* witness, with its unreliable narrators and, in this instance, historians. At one level memory exists in Kostova's novel as accounts of attempts to locate Dracula's lair, but also the past persists through Dracula's memorialisation in a number of largely literary narratives and cultural references, which form part of a folk memory. In structural terms, however, we might say that *The Historian* recalls Stoker's novel through an act of mis-remembering.

Kate Mitchell has explored in depth how neo-Victorian fictions implicate theories of memory as they work to reconstruct politically reorientated versions of the past. She argues that "a re-membering of the past is [...] partial, fragmentary and always open to further re-membering" because "[t]he past only exists in our re-creations of it. Its meaning is produced in and by our very accounts of it" (Mitchell 2010: 37). Memory in *The Historian* also participates in a process of forgetting which is relevant to understanding its specific constructions of European history.

Anne Whitehead notes that Pierre Nora's discussion of memory moves from an account of tradition and embodied cultural gestures to a more modern version of memory associated with the collection of written testimony (Whitehead 2009: 142). Memory thus acquires a form of validation in which its presence becomes archivable, but because a postmodern culture, with its economy of easily consumed and disposed commodities, is no longer able to discriminate between what to keep and what to discard, the archive displaces the conscious act of remembering.[5] Ironically, this means that the archive becomes the receptacle of all that a culture has chosen to forget, as the archive contains what culture cannot be bothered to consciously remember. This takes us back to the central image of Kostova's novel which is the Count's archive that he wishes to make sense of by employing an historian as its cataloguer. Conceived of in terms of memory studies, the novel works to remember the type of histories of tyranny that are found in the archive in order to address them as present rather than as historical concerns with the vampire functioning as a conceit for a history that is not yet dead. As Paul tells Helen's aunt, "It's my belief that the study of history should be our preparation for understanding the present, rather than an escape from it" (Kostova 2005: 335). History and its archive thus function as a precautionary warning about future tyranny unless an intervention is made in the present. Therefore the novel as a whole, with its various accounts of different narrative engagements with Dracula, is about testimony and bearing witness – two chief aspects of memory studies – even whilst it develops a reactionary, because partial and politically slanted, version of latent European political forces that need to be challenged.

---

[5] See also Kohlke's discussion of Simon Joyce's account of memory in his *The Victorians in the Rearview Mirror*, where she refers to the "different kinds of conceptual archives" generated by neo-Victorian texts (Kohlke 2008: 13), which introject twentieth- and twenty-first-century concerns into their adaptations of the Victorian.

At one level Kostova's novel is a reworking and redirecting of Stoker's Balkan politics for a modern age, and this marks out its status as a neo-Victorian Gothic text, which suggests that political instability is also inherited by later generations. For Richard Wasson, "Count Dracula [...] represents those forces in Eastern Europe which seek to overthrow, through violence and subversion, the more progressive democratic civilization of the West" (Wasson 1966: 24). In addition, the reception of Vlad Tepes makes it clear that what is truly unstable is not the politics of the region, but the issue of representation. As Clive Leatherdale has noted, images of Vlad were already contradictory in the Renaissance where he was variously recalled as "one of the great demented psychopaths of history" or an "heroic Christian crusader" (Leatherdale 2001: 95). More recent reconstructions are tinged with Cold War imagery, and in the 1940s Vlad was reworked by the newly formed Romanian Socialist Republic as "the equivalent of England's Robin Hood, someone who took from the rich in order to give to the poor; a freedom fighter who curbed foreign privileges" (Leatherdale 2001: 96). It is this version of Vlad that Kostova's novel seems to take issue with. Representations of Count Dracula also followed certain trends and the example of America is illuminating in that regard, as Leatherdale has noted:

> With the passing of the years the immortal Count has confirmed his adaptability. After 1945 he proved [...] adept at symbolising the Soviet menace in the Cold War. In the McCarthy era, Dracula switched from representing Nazis to representing Reds. He was no longer the exemplar of capitalism: he was now its staunchest enemy. These turnarounds were assisted by the redrawing of Europe's frontiers. Transylvania was again part of Romania, and conveniently lay behind that Iron Curtain. Dracula was a communist, the bogey-man from the East. (Leatherdale 2001: 236)

Or as Helen's mother puts it in *The Historian*, "the vampire can change his shape. He can come to you in many forms" (Kostova 2005: 405). The quintessentially late nineteenth century figure of Count *Dracula* is thus reworked for different ages in order to address later concerns that inform his post-Stoker adaptations.

One might question how self-aware the novel is about these issues of memory, history, and politics. At one level the engagement with Stoker's novel and references to other Victorian texts, such as *Great Expectations* (1860-61) and *Tess of the D'Urbervilles* (1891), is clearly knowing, and there is an explicit argument about history and who gets to write it (the communist bloc or other Western historiographies). However, the politics of the text nervously identify mainland Europe as a possible danger to Western style democracy, even whilst the novel demonstrates a level of self-consciousness about that, with Helen telling Paul "in the East Bloc, we do not like other people stealing our heritage and commenting on it; they usually misunderstand it" (Kostova 2005: 142). Whilst the history of the East Bloc is written as a history of tyranny, the novel is also conscious about what is omitted, and that takes us back to the idea of the archive. Dracula's archive has been constructed on the basis of its confirmation of the prevalence of evil, which supports both his view of the world and the vampire hunters' view of him. What is excluded from the archive and the history of Europe, with which it is associated, therefore constitutes a deliberate act of selection that touches on another key aspect of memory studies that relates to forgetting. Anne Whitehead sees the investigation of forgetting as an enquiry into the various forms of cultural amnesia, which are the absent presences that ghost any history, as the next big area for discussion within memory studies (Whitehead 2009: 153-157). It can also be related to a conceptualisation of the neo-Victorian Gothic as a form which, as in Kostova's novel, deliberately misremembers Stoker's novel by forgetting *Dracula*'s partial vision of Balkan politics in order to redirect that history as underpinning a Cold War communist tyranny. The idea of the archive also becomes significant in the closing pages of the novel.

The narrator, whilst attending a conference in Philadelphia visits the Rosenbach Museum & Library to consult Stoker's working notes on *Dracula*. When she leaves the museum a librarian pursues her as she left her notebook behind. She is also given another book that the librarian assumes belongs to her, which includes the dragon illustration, and so the narrator is enlisted into the tradition of historians recruited to make sense of Dracula's archive. In other words the narrator goes from a real archive of sources for *Dracula* to a fictional archive that belongs to Dracula – a postmodern slip very much in keeping with the neo-Victorian.

Indeed Kostova's novel is about a certain type of bookishness which indicates a self-consciousness in its literary engagements, especially with Stoker, that mark it out as a neo-Victorian text, although one which, in its points of contact with archives, memories, and politics, uses these engagements in order to critique, rather than nostalgically celebrate, European history.[6] As Stoker's novel seems to represent the triumph of British colonialism, so *The Historian* charts the ongoing struggle of a contemporary Anglo-American political class that sees itself as having to address potential global terrorist threats. The final lines of the novel make reference to Dracula's supposed terrorist-like authority, an authority which should feel itself as powerfully circumscribed by the forces which oppose it and yet:

> He looks not at all like a man in constant peril – a leader whose death could occur at any hour, who should be pondering every moment the question of his salvation. He looks instead [...] as if all the world is before him. (Kostova 2005: 704)

And so the novel closes on an image of a persisting terrorist danger.[7]

Whilst *The Historian* reworks a model of European history for ideological purposes, Kostova's *The Swan Thieves* (2010) engages with Europe through aesthetic considerations, which are explicitly related to French Impressionism. This might seem like a radical departure from the type of political imagery, complex plotting and Gothic elements of *The Historian*, but in fact there is a covert relationship between them, which is in part shaped by a reworking of nineteenth-century literary and artistic forms, and in part by an explicit narrative about gender largely elided in *The Historian*.

---

[6] Arguably this technique is more commonly associated with neo-Victorian postcolonial treatments of the iniquities of the British Empire, although *The Historian* redirects this so as to demonise European politics. See Mariadele Boccardi's *The Contemporary British Historical Novel: Representation, Nation, Empire* (2009) for an account of neo-Victorian representation of empire.

[7] Christine L. Krueger argues that post 9/11 images of Victorian empire-building resonated with contemporary fears about America's empire as under threat (Krueger 2002: xi).

The Swan Thieves is set in North America (although like *The Historian*, it also incorporates forays into Europe) and centres on Robert Oliver, a talented modern artist, who is committed to a private medical facility after apparently attacking a nineteenth-century painting titled *Leda* (attributed to the fictional Gilbert Thomas) in the National Gallery in Washington D.C. Robert suffers from elective mutism and his physician, Dr. Andrew Marlow, pieces together Robert's past in order to help solve the mystery of the attack and so restore Robert's health. The key to the mystery lies in a packet of correspondence from the 1870s between a married young French artist, Béatrice de Clerval, and an older painter, Olivier Vignot, who initially acts as her mentor and later becomes her lover. It transpires that Robert had become obsessed both with the work of Béatrice and with the love story between her and Olivier, which he discovered by reading a batch of their letters. His obsession is reflected in his own artwork, which often reproduces images of Béatrice and the Impressionist style of her work; it is an obsession which led to the breakdown of his marriage to Kate and a subsequent relationship with Mary. Both Kate and Mary provide frequent testimony on Robert and their lives with him, which Marlow analytically investigates for evidence concerning Robert's earlier mental condition. The lives of the present day protagonists become inter-related as Marlow begins a relationship with Mary (whom he subsequently marries) and whose own interest in painting forges a point of contact with Robert, in which the supposed links between creativity and temperament focus much of Marlow's psychological investigation. The links to Conrad's *Lord Jim* are revealing as they shape the novel's concern not only about Robert's mental condition, but also Marlow's often problematic attempts to decode that condition. The plotting of the novel relies on the slow revelation of secrets, accounts of mental states and emotional turmoil that are shaped by a Gothic suspense narrative underpinned by images of sexuality, betrayal and mystery.

The novel centres on a debate about contemporary engagements and adaptations of Impressionism that also provides focus to the love story between Béatrice and Olivier, which is brought to life through their letters. For Marlow the initial difficulty is finding a language of empathetic engagement with the Impressionists: "It had been years since I'd looked really deeply into an Impressionist painting; those endless retrospectives, with their accompanying tote bags, mugs, and notepaper, had put me off Impressionism" (Kostova 2010: 47). He further notes that "[w]e postmoderns take them for granted, or disdain them, or love them too easily" (Kostova 2010: 47). How to animate this cultural history is key to the neo-Victorian reconstructions of Robert's art which had originally, before he had become ill, been characterised by a postmodern play with nineteenth-century aesthetics. Marlow visits an art college that Robert taught at, where a former colleague says of Robert's art that one series consisted of:

> still lifes, brilliant, if you like still lifes – fruit, flowers, goblets, kind of like Manet but always with something odd in them like an electrical outlet or a bottle of aspirin – I don't know what. Anomalies. Very nicely done. (Kostova 2010: 230)

Mary recalls other paintings in an Impressionist style but with modern characters, noting that she "liked the contrast between the nineteenth-century brushwork and the contemporary figures" (Kostova 2010: 308). This comment, which indicates a very clear neo-Victorian engagement in which the past is aesthetically transposed into the contemporary moment, also indicates a self-consciousness on Robert's part about his introjected role in such creative acts, as Mary notes of another portrait of a woman that includes a mirror in which Robert is reflected "with his easel, in his rumpled modern clothes, painting himself painting her" (Kostova 2010: 309). Robert's attempt to situate himself within history is also an attempt to resituate the past into the present. Robert's increasingly empathetic engagement with Impressionism contrasts with Marlow's repeated, irritated sense of the cultural consumption of Impressionism, noted earlier in his references to exhibition merchandising ("tote bags, mugs, and notepaper") and later on a visit to New York's Metropolitan Museum of Modern Art, where he quickly becomes "weary from the jostling of the crowd, all these people out gathering impressions of impressions of Impressionists, collecting firsthand images they already knew thirdhand" (Kostova 2010: 366). This observation is in keeping with Marlow's adherence to a discourse of rationality, which he is self-aware enough to realise has culminated in a somewhat emotionally stunted life. Marlow has to learn from Robert (and indeed Mary) about the positive transformation of powerful emotion which is, paradoxically, channelled through the doomed relationship between Béatrice and Olivier that in turn generates the two, linked, mysteries of the novel – why Béatrice stopped painting at a comparatively early age and why Robert has developed elective mutism.

The Historian bears witness to the notion of a dormant communist presence within European political history which could, under certain circumstances, be brought back to life. The novel thus addresses a perceived hidden aspect within that history. *The Swan Thieves* relates the idea of secrecy to what has not been hidden so much as lost – namely, Béatrice's place within Impressionist art history, in which she is symbolically imaged as a lost female voice as the direct, if occulted, consequence of attempted male appropriations of her work that have depended on the exploitation of her secret affair with Olivier.

The central revelation is that Béatrice has been blackmailed by a jealous artist, Gilbert Thomas, and seemingly his art gallery owning brother, who have discovered the affair and agree to secrecy only if Béatrice's subsequent paintings are passed off as the work of Thomas. It is a situation captured in Béatrice's painting *The Swan Thieves*, which is held in a private collection in Paris and has been seen by Robert and later by Marlow. Marlow notes:

> *The Swan Thieves* is not easily put into words. I had expected the beauty in it: I had not expected the evil. It was a largish canvas, about four feet by three, rendered in the bright palette of the Impressionists. It showed two men in rough clothes, brown-haired, one with strangely red lips. They were moving, stealthily toward the viewer, and toward a swan that rose in alarm out of the reeds. (Kostova 2010: 566)

Marlow, whose researches have made him familiar with Thomas's work, understands that the two men are Thomas and his brother and that the painting represents a symbolic assault on Béatrice (whose painting of another swan in *Leda* has been appropriated by Thomas). Marlow reflects that he "had seldom seen such skill in a painting, nor such desperation" (Kostova 2010: 566). The painting "was full of threat and entrapment – and perhaps revenge as well" (Kostova 2010:

567), and it provides him with an insight into why Robert had in fact intended to stab Thomas's self-portrait (in which he is counting coins) and not *Leda*, a work by Béatrice that had been signed by Thomas. It also enables Marlow to reconnect with art as an emotional rather than an academic form – a moment of epiphany in which he admits, "I knew I would never see *The Swan Thieves* again. I had spent five minutes with it, and it had changed the look of the world" (Kostova 2010: 567). Marlow is able to show Robert a final letter by Béatrice that Robert had not previously seen, which confirmed the blackmail that Robert had suspected, and so Robert refinds his voice by reconnecting to a past which, whilst not belonging to him, does nevertheless contain a powerful drama that is for him emotionally and psychologically true as well as personally relevant. He feels this narrative in a deep, visceral, way which had led him to ask Mary, "Have you ever had this feeling that the lives people lived in the past are still real?" (Kostova 2010: 437). History is thus brought to life again, as it is in *The Historian*, although not through folk memory and the partial narrators of the earlier novel. Indeed *The Swan Thieves* suggests that the reclamation of the past is dependent upon witnessing its dramas which will ultimately lead to Marlow's enlightened self-knowledge.

It is clear that *The Historian* and *The Swan Thieves* develop different approaches to the nineteenth century, which in turn shape their formation of the neo-Victorian Gothic. In *The Historian* the past represents the insistent presence of tyranny and a projected terrorism that requires an active and politicised engagement with it so as to neuter its threat. One model of history (the Count's) needs to be challenged by other possible histories (the history of Western democracies), so that a world is built that reflects the triumphant values of freedom and democracy, even whilst the end of the novel suggests that such a battle has yet to be won. In *The Swan Thieves* a lost history of female art is resurrected, and the human drama behind that loss is reworked as a continuing emotional drama, which connects people in the present who were not otherwise associated with it. In the first novel history asserts itself, in the later novel history is recovered. However, at the centre of both novels are figures who represent powerful and enigmatic representations of masculinity: Dracula and Robert Oliver, and this helps clarify the Gothic engagements of both novels.

In *The Historian* Dracula's history is evoked as a model of corruption, in which he is associated with a psychotic abuse of power and with a view of history that he wishes, via his archive, to arrange as both a justification and an explanation of his authority. His shooting by Helen is used in the novel to symbolically represent the triumph of those oppressed by the Soviet Bloc over their rulers, but it also suggests the triumph of a female historian over a male history maker, which challenges his notion of political mastery. This implied gender battle is evoked at the end of the novel, when Helen's daughter inherits the mantle of the new 'historian', who has to seek out Dracula and begin the battle anew. This addresses a gendered narrative relating to who gets to write history and what that history should concern, a process that is not without peril. As the narrator notes, "it is not only reaching back that endangers us; sometimes history itself reaches inexorably forward for us with its shadowy claw" (Kostova 2005: vii). What lies at the heart of that history is an image of political mystique, which is both demonised and associated with the masculine presence of Dracula – who in turn functions as a synecdoche for the male dominated communist party that the narrators (Paul, Helen and Rossi) encounter in 1950s Hungary. A certain type of masculinity is therefore associated with an abuse of power, which is seemingly defeated when Helen shoots him. The challenge posed at the end of the novel is to Helen's daughter as she becomes enlisted as a third generation vampire hunter, which suggests that such abuses of power are ongoing and explicitly gendered through Kostova's closing reference to this new, female, vampire hunter (one who perhaps can, unlike Mina Harker in *Dracula*, play an active, rather than supporting, role in the destruction of the vampire).

The implicit gendering of these political dramas is returned to in the more complex, if self-aware, engagements of *The Swan Thieves*, which also centres on an image of masculine mystique in the figure of Robert Oliver. Marlow initially entertains the idea that Robert's many portraits of Béatrice represent an attempt to emotionally bond with her. He notes of one such image:

> I conjectured that the image might be an expression of his silent rage, and I also speculated about some possible confusion of gender identity within the

patient, although I couldn't get him to respond even
nonverbally to this topic. (Kostova 2010: 28-9)

Later his former wife, Kate, recalls her reaction to one of Robert's portraits of Béatrice: "Perhaps Robert somehow wished he *was* this woman – perhaps this was a portrait of himself as the woman he wanted to be" (Kostova 2010: 158, original emphasis). Although she quickly dismisses such an idea, because he "had always been so hugely male" (Kostova 2010: 158), the idea does implicitly return throughout the novel. Robert's engagement with the romantic narrative of Béatrice and Olivier at one level positions him as a reader of romantic fiction, in which his elective mutism functions as an empathetic reworking of Béatrice's artistic silence. (She ceases to paint after *Leda*, so that Thomas is unable to appropriate more of her work.) Crucially, it is painting rather than literature which functions as the bridge between the real and the unreal, and as in the instance of Robert's postmodern Impressionist paintings, it becomes the site around which much of the neo-Victorian content is elaborated (especially within a debate about artistic 'authenticity' in which Béatrice's place as an artist is restored even whilst, paradoxically, Robert's neo-Victorian paintings seem to challenge the representational scope of such work). In addition Kostova's reworking of *Lord Jim* underpins many of the dramas confronted by Robert and Marlow.

The relationship between Marlow and Robert in *The Swan Thieves* clearly echoes that between Marlow and Jim in *Lord Jim*. Robert, like Jim, is associated with a spirit of adventure in which his immersion in the past projects him into a narrative of romantic, artistic, and political intrigue (including reference to the communards and Olivier's wife, who is killed when innocently caught up in the fighting). Similarly, Marlow's description of a Jim whose "thought would be full of valorous deeds" becomes echoed in Robert's desire for romantic adventure. However, Kostova's Marlow is also foreshadowed by Conrad's Marlow, whose unreliability as a narrator is reflected in Andrew Marlow's difficulty in analysing a mute Robert Oliver. As Conrad's Marlow is dogged by misunderstandings and false impressions so Kostova's Marlow initially cannot decode the seemingly enigmatic behaviour of his patient. Conrad's Marlow's view of Jim could easily stand for Kostova's Marlow's view of Robert:

> The views he let me have of himself were like those glimpses through the shifting rents in a thick fog – bits of vivid and vanishing detail, giving no connected idea of the general aspect of a country. They fed one's curiosity without satisfying it; they were no good for the purposes of orientation. Upon the whole he was misleading. (Conrad 2007: 60)

This problem is compounded because "[h]e was not – if I may say so – clear to me. He was not clear. And there is a suspicion he was not clear to himself either" (Conrad 2007: 135). *The Swan Thieves* explores these entangled relationships by not only having Robert emotionally engage with the lives of Béatrice and Olivier, but also by having Marlow emotionally participate in Robert's life, by which he develops a brief (and seemingly one-sided) attachment to Kate before developing a relationship with Mary. Marlow also increasingly comes to the view that it is psychiatry which enabled him to protect himself by developing emotional distance, but only at the expense of an emotionally fulfilled life – and this generates a relationship with Robert in which, by returning him to health, Marlow is able to re-awaken his own emotions. Towards the end of the novel, Marlow tells the now cured Robert, "You've been here a long time", to which Robert replies with a smile, "So have you" (Kostova 2010: 603). Robert's final words to Marlow are "Thank you for your trouble", and Marlow thinks "*Thank you for your life*, I wanted to tell him, but I didn't. I meant, *Thank you for mine*" (Kostova 2010: 604, original emphasis). These complex relationships are ones which are explicitly worked through in the novel's neo-Victorian engagements with Impressionism. Implicitly these points of contact also suggest the presence of a Gothic uncanny in which characters such as Marlow and Robert come to mirror each other (by inhabiting each other's lives), even whilst they evoke (or uncannily bring to life) characters from Conrad which implicates a truly neo-Victorian model of uncanniness in Kostova's resurrection of the past.

The Swan Thieves indicates a more subtle engagement with the Gothic than *The Historian*. However, as noted, Robert can be read as a modification of the mystique applied to Dracula in *The Historian*. Also, the novel's focus on romantic intrigue, sexual secrets, 'madness', and abuses of power root the novel within a Gothic tradition which has close associations with Melodrama. Marlow notes of Robert's rendering of the shooting of Olivier's wife that it was "terribly alive and yet overdramatic, stilted like a Victorian stage piece" (Kostova 2010: 235). One variant includes the figure of Béatrice bent over the dead body, in which "she had buried her sobs in the dead woman's neck as if drinking her blood or mixing it with her tears – melodramatic, yes, but also wrenchingly moving" (Kostova 2010: 241). Robert's attempts to revivify Victorian art contrast with the explicit experimentalism of the Impressionists, in which Béatrice's *Leda* is coveted by Thomas for its "*perfect combination of old and new, classical and natural painting*" (Kostova 2010: 596, original emphasis). Indeed Robert employs a range of nineteenth-century styles of painting from Victorian melodrama to postmodern takes on Impressionism, which all contribute to the endeavour to bring the past back to life.[8] Victorian art is either associated with various aesthetic experiments or, in its more hackneyed manifestations, such as in the melodramatic rendering of the shooting of Olivier's wife, it becomes "wrenchingly moving": a moment which symbolically, and indeed melodramatically, goes some way to restoring Marlow's emotional life.

The role of art and emotion in *The Swan Thieves* represent less explicitly political themes than those explored in *The Historian*. However, both novels share an interest in nineteenth-century European history, and both rely on earlier Victorian sources for their inspiration. How those sources are reworked indicates either a desire to move beyond the politics of Stoker's *Dracula*, by redirecting it for a modern readership, or to bring a more personal history to life in order to transformationally introject it into the lives of the present day protagonists. The nineteenth century thus still speaks to the contemporary as the modern world (and the battle with the past, as in *Dracula*), resonates with a model of the twenty-first century that is dogged by earlier political struggles and artistic ambitions. The Gothic

---

[8] This suggestion that an emotionally fulfilling engagement with the past is also a feature of neo-Victorian fiction, A. S. Byatt's *Possession: A Romance* (1990) being exemplary in that regard.

aspects are used to either demonise the past or suggest how it shapes discourses of romantic intrigue. The sense that the past is colonised in *The Historian* is clear in its appropriations of European history, which also represent a postmodern engagement with *Dracula*'s reworking of late nineteenth-century colonial dramas. *The Swan Thieves*' evocation of *Lord Jim*, with its representations of colonial power, also implies a reworking of acts of appropriation, in which Béatrice's painting is assumed by Thomas, Robert engages with a nineteenth-century romance that does not properly concern him, and Marlow enters Robert's life so completely that he ends up marrying one of Robert's former partners. Both novels also possess a level of self-consciousness about these colonisations, even if they are represented as political and emotional necessities. Ultimately both rely on a key Gothic conceptual term: ambivalence. The past cannot be escaped because its politically complex and emotionally fraught dramas retain a seemingly disabling grasp on the present. However, the past also, paradoxically, appears to re-energise the present and transforms political views and private lives.

A question which would be appropriate to entertain at this juncture concerns how widely these ideas might be said to characterise the neo-Victorian Gothic. Neither of these novels attempt to aesthetically reconstruct Victorian texts, although they do attempt to reconstruct versions of the Victorian. In that sense they are different in kind to the Gothic reconstructions of Waters or Dacre Stoker. Kostova's brand of neo-Victorian Gothic thus challenges any narrowly considered model of the neo-Victorian Gothic as its metafictional engagements uncannily resurrect the past rather than journey back to it. The past thus needs to be considered differently in her texts. It speaks to us still and seemingly directly, but such overtures are attempts to obscure the highly ideological constructions of the past (especially in *The Historian*) via the ethos of a global capitalism that argues that we live in a post-ideological, if not post-political, era. In other words this new type of Gothic gives itself away even as it attempts to conceal its politics affiliations. In part this is, ironically, because of its very links to the past. However, the central demand placed upon the critic is to draw out the hidden ideologies of such texts and this requires us to read Gothically. In Kostova her instance of the neo-Victorian Gothic appears as a form which captures a highly ambivalent cultural reaction to the nineteenth century, in which the postmodern (seemingly post-ideological world) is unable to go forwards without looking back. How to decode this new expression of a Gothic political unconscious is the challenge posed.

Derrida is in many respects a key radical counterpoint to this model of history. His reading of the Victorian *The German Ideology* (1846) attempts to put back the radical spectral ideological forces that a postmodern, post-ideological world, would conceal from us. He notes that Marx and Engels's text is populated with ghosts:

> it is crawling with them, a crowd of *revenants* are waiting for us there: shrouds, errant souls, clanking chains in the night, groaning, chilling bursts of laughter, and all those heads, so many invisible heads that look at us, the greatest concentration of all specters in the history of humanity. (Derrida 1994: 107, original emphasis)

The radical potential of the Gothic is indicated here, but it is a language that is explicitly used to demonise in *The Historian*. *The Swan Thieves* represents a more subtle exorcism of the past, but they share a powerful message: the past (or more precisely a highly disturbing version of it) cannot be trusted and needs to be laid to rest.

Bibliography

Boccardi, Mariadele. 2009. *The Contemporary British Historical Novel: Representation, Nation, Empire*. Houndmills, Basingstoke: Palgrave Macmillan.

Conrad, Joseph. 2007. *Lord Jim* [1900] (ed. and intro. Allan H. Simmons). Harmondsworth: Penguin.

Derrida, Jacques. 1994. *Specters of Marx*. (trans. Peggy Kamuf; intro. Bernd Magnis and Stephen Cullenberg). London & New York: Routledge.

Gibson, Matthew. 2006. *Dracula and the Eastern Question: British and French Vampire Narratives of the Nineteenth-Century Near East*. Houndmills, Basingstoke: Palgrave Macmillan.

Gutleben, Christian. 2001. *Nostalgic Postmodernism: The Victorian Tradition and the Contemporary British Novel*. Amsterdam & New York: Rodopi.

Halbwachs, Maurice. 2008. '[Extract from] *The Collective Memory* (1950)'. In Rossington and Whitehead (2008): 139-143.

Heilmann, Ann, and Mark Llewellyn. 2010. *Neo-Victorianism: The Victorians in the Twenty-First Century, 1999-2009*. Houndmills, Basingstoke: Palgrave Macmillan.

Joyce, Simon. 2007. *The Victorians in the Rearview Mirror*. Athens, Ohio: Ohio University Press.
Kirchknopf, Andrea. 2008. '(Re)workings of Nineteenth-Century Fiction: Definitions, Terminology, Contexts', *Neo-Victorian Studies* 1:1 (August): 53-80.
Kohlke, Marie-Luise. 2008. 'Introduction: Speculations in and on the Neo-Victorian Encounter', *Neo-Victorian Studies* 1:1 (August): 1-18.
Kostova, Elizabeth. 2005. *The Historian: A Novel*. London: Time Warner.
——. 2010. *The Swan Thieves: A Novel*. London: Sphere.
Krueger, Christine L. 2002. 'Introduction', in Krueger, Christine L. (ed.), *Functions of Victorian Culture at the Present Time*. Athens. Ohio: Ohio University Press: xi-xx.
Leatherdale, Clive. 2001. *Dracula: The Novel and the Legend*. Westcliff-on-Sea: Desert Island Books.
Mitchell, Kate. 2010. *History and Cultural Memory in Neo-Victorian Fiction: Victorian Afterimages*. Houndmills, Basingstoke: Palgrave Macmillan.
Moretti, Franco.1983. *Signs Taken for Wonders: Essays in the Sociology of Literary Forms*. London: Verso.
Nora, Pierre. 2008. 'Between Memory and History: Les Lieux de Memoire (1989)'. In Rossington and Whitehead (2008): 143-149.
Rossington, Michael. 2008. 'Introduction: Collective Memory'. In Rossington and Whitehead (2008): 34-37.
Rossington, Michael, and Anne Whitehead (eds.). 2008. *Theories of Memory: A Reader*. Edinburgh: Edinburgh University Press.
Spooner, Catherine. 2007. 'Gothic in the twentieth century', in Spooner, Catherine and Emma McEvoy (eds.), *The Routledge Companion to Gothic*. London & New York: Routledge: 38-47.
Stoker, Bram. 1996. *Dracula* [1897] (ed. and intro. Maud Ellmann). Oxford: Oxford University Press.
Stoker, Dacre. 2009. *Dracula the Un-Dead*. London: HarperCollins.
Wasson, Richard. 1966. 'The Politics of Dracula', *English Literature in Transition* 9(1): 24-27.
Waters, Sarah. 1999. *Affinity*. London: Virago.
Whitehead, Anne. 2009. *Memory*. London & New York: Routledge.

Reclaiming Plots: Albert Wendt's 'Prospecting' and Victoria Nalani Kneubuhl's *Ola Nā Iwi* as Postcolonial Neo-Victorian Gothic

Cheryl D. Edelson

Abstract:
This essay addresses two neo-Victorian Gothic texts that illuminate the horrors of empire building. In 'Prospecting' (1983), Albert Wendt returns to 1893 for a Polynesian Gothic tale that refuses the narrow options available under western literary genres to conclude with a Samoan funeral that integrates Christianity with indigenous protocols. Victoria Nalani Kneubuhl pursues similar themes in her drama *Ola Nā Iwi* (1994), a ghost story about the repatriation of native Hawaiian remains. Touring Germany with a theatrical company, the Hawaiian actress Kawehi steals the body of deceased kanaka maoli Nanea from a museum in order to repatriate 'living bones'. Inflected with dialogues between Victorian anthropologists who rationalise scientific grave-robbing, *Ola Nā Iwi* dramatises the struggle of native Polynesians to reclaim spaces and selves co-opted under western colonialism. Wendt and Kneubuhl exemplify the postcolonial writer's simultaneous preservation of indigenous culture and exploitation of metropolitan forms and epistemologies.

Keywords: Michel de Certeau, ghost story, Gothic, Hawai'i, Victoria Nalani Kneubuhl, neo-Victorian, Oceania, postcolonial, Samoa, Albert Wendt.

*****

> [Y]ou'd never go and dig up Benjamin Franklin and put him in an exhibit case. (Kneubuhl 2002: xxvi)

For Daniel Candel Bormann, neo-Victorian fiction "provides an ideally stabilising and comforting force" aimed at countering postmodernity's "epistemological challenges, thereby providing a kind of reassuring buffer which allows epistemological questioning to spread its wings without threatening to alienate the reader" (Bormann 2002: 70). But these comforts may also lure us into the disturbing visions of Gothic texts that revisit the Victorian era. With recourse to Gothic pre-texts in Polynesia, as well as theories about physical space, I address two Oceanic artists who adopt the neo-Victorian Gothic to illuminate the horrors of empire building.[1] In 'Prospecting' (1983), Albert Wendt returns to 1893 – a year in which Germany, Great Britain, and the USA vied for control of Samoa. The story begins as a Polynesian Gothic tale that promises little insight into Pacific lifeways: two treasure hunters, the Englishman Barker and his 'sidekick' Mautu, unearth a horrifying Samoan mass grave. But Wendt refuses the narrow options available under western literary genres (the closure of adventure or the exoticist horror of Polynesian Gothic), as he concludes with a Samoan funeral that combines Christianity with indigenous protocols. Victoria Nalani Kneubuhl pursues similar neo-Victorian themes in her drama *Ola Nā Iwi* (*The Bones Live*) (1994), a ghost story about the repatriation of native Hawaiian remains. In this play, the Hawaiian protagonist Kawehi, touring with a theatrical company in Germany, steals the body of deceased kanaka maoli Nanea from a museum. Aided by Nanea's ghost, Kawehi returns to Hawai'i in order to properly bury these 'living bones'. Beginning in the 1800s, the narrative is interspersed with dialogues between nineteenth-century anthropologists who rationalise scientific grave-robbing. Wendt and Kneubuhl, respectively, integrate neo-Victorian motifs into the postcolonial Gothic, realising David Punter and Glennis Byron's observation that

> Gothic tropes of the ghost, the phantom, the revenant, gain curious new life from the need to assert continuity where the lessons of conventional history and geography would claim that all continuity has been broken by the imperial trauma. (Punter and Byron 2004: 58)

---

[1] Jeanne Ellis's analysis of the artist Leora Farber in this collection builds upon the scholarship of Dana Shiller, Mark Llewellyn, and other critics to suggest that the neo-Victorian tends toward subversion, especially when integrated with the postcolonial Gothic, not least as a critique of imperialism. Sebastian Domsch similarly points to the ways in which neo-Victorian texts such as Alan Moore and Kevin O'Neill's *The League of Extraordinary Gentlemen* (1999-2003) move beyond pastiche to investigate "the dominant political, social and sexual ideologies of that time and their afterlife in our own" (this volume: 98), likewise often linked to imperial ideologies and practices.

For Punter and Byron, postcolonial ghost stories resuscitate a literary form that has long been poisoned by imperial/colonial ideologies; this is nowhere more true than in literatures of the Pacific. Perhaps the most well known practitioner of the Polynesian Gothic is Paul Gauguin, who searched Tahiti and the Marquesas Islands for images of Edenic sexuality and fecundity. One of his most controversial images, the 1892 painting *Manao tupapau (The Spirit of the Dead Keeps Watch)*, exemplifies the way in which Gauguin apposes erotic, even pornographic, subject matter with allusions to Oceanic culture and spirituality. A reprise of Edouard Manet's yet more controversial 1863 painting *Olympia* (see Schwarz 1997: 92), the picture sees not a French courtesan but rather a nude Maohi woman lying abed on her stomach, looking invitingly at the viewer. In the opposite but analogous position of Manet's black servant girl, Gauguin installs the strange profile of a black-clad homunculus who treats us to a sidelong glance. Presumably the titular ghost, this figure is likewise Polynesian – the ghost of a departed Maohi who "[k]eeps watch" over the young woman. Gauguin himself suggested that the spirit haunts the girl and that its presence somehow offsets or defamiliarises the 'indecency' of his scene:

> In this rather daring position, quite naked on a bed, what might a young Kanaka girl be doing? Preparing for love? This is indeed in her character, but it is indecent and I do not want that. Sleeping, after the act of love? But that is still indecent. The only possible thing is fear. What kind of fear? ... The tupapau [spirit of the dead] is just the thing... According to Tahitian beliefs, the title Manao Tupapau has a double meaning ... either she thinks of the ghost or the ghost thinks of her. To recapitulate: Musical part – undulating horizontal lines – harmonies in orange and blue linked by yellows and violets, from which they derive. The light and the greenish sparks. Literary part – the spirit of a living girl linked with the spirit of Death. Night and day. (qtd. Bolton 2002: 34, original ellipses)

Later dismissing his own remarks, Gauguin does suggest his aim to assimilate Maohi bodies and meanings into his erotic, aesthetic, and archetypal tableau. More to the point, however, is the way in which Gauguin deploys the motif of haunting within the context of the western/Oceanic colonial encounter. On the one hand, it is only the viewer who looks at the 'Manao'; Gauguin is therefore one of the first to intrigue the implicitly western audience with the vision of an Oceanic spectre. On the other, Gauguin's title may be appropriated as an avenue into another dimension of haunting in Oceanic literature – one in which the "spirit keeps watch" over the indigenous protagonist.

Like Gauguin, many twentieth-century writers turn to the Gothic motif of haunting as a means of representing explorer/settler experience in the Pacific. In tales such as Joseph Conrad's 'The Secret Sharer' (1910), however, the phantom in question is what Frank O'Brien terms a "white shadow" who represents both the freedom and restrictions of life in the island 'haunts' of the colonial periphery. As Jean-Paul Riquelme observes, "the ship becomes a haunted space when it is invaded by a ghost-like character who is eventually exorcised" (Riquelme 2000: 588). But Conrad's novella exercises a light touch, tempering the ghost story with minimalist realism. After taking command of a trading vessel in the Gulf of Siam, the unnamed narrator discovers a luminous nude swimmer hovering around the ship's ladder in an ocean he later describes as "shadowy and silent like a phantom sea" (Conrad 2008: 36). The swimmer is Leggett, an officer from another ship charged with the murder of one of the crewmen. As he harbours Leggett, the narrator clothes the fugitive in a "ghostly gray" sleeping suit and comes to imagine himself party to "a scene of weird witchcraft" in which he enjoys "a quiet confabulation by the wheel with his own gray ghost" (Conrad 2008: 11). The narrator finally puts Leggett ashore, banishing this shade to "the gateway of Erebus", a dark underworld where he may "take his punishment: a free man, a proud swimmer striking out for a new destiny" (Conrad 2008: 44). With this well-known conclusion, Conrad paints Leggett as a modernist hero capable of escaping the constraints of society to follow his own path. By virtue of his phantasmatic, spectral characterisation, however, he is also an absent figure whose very existence (as more than a projected double of the narrator's psyche) remains in doubt.

Other Pacific writers more frankly use haunting as a trope for the failed colonial explorer or settler. The skeptical narrator of Robert Dean Frisbie's 'The Ghost of Alexander Perks, A.B.' (1931) relates yet another spectral remnant of colonial exploration. Marooned on Vostock Island (in Kiribati), Perks perishes and then haunts the atoll as a lonely ghost. He gets a bit of relief with the arrival of the trading schooner *Pirara*, whose "kanaka second mate" Seaside joins him in a game of checkers. Perks is so taken with Seaside that he stows away on the *Pirara*, only to later desert the ship before it sinks. After the *Pirara* goes down, the crew find themselves "in a reef boat [...] pulling the hundred and twenty miles back to Vostock Island" (Frisbie 1964: 161). It is unclear whether Perks's departure has caused or merely foretold the disaster; but he is at the story's end joined by a new band of (albeit living) castaways. Although he indulges in a sentimentalism at odds with modernism, Frisbie, like Conrad, finds in haunting an appropriate conceit for the anomie of the sailors and settlers stranded between metropolis and colony. As David A. Chappell reminds us, however, the true ghost of such a story would be the Polynesian Seaside; Oceanic sailors on European and Euro-American vessels are "double ghosts", he observes, because they are not only deceased physically, but they "survive textually mainly through the biased, selective recollections of their white shipmates. Even the custom of giving *kanaka* crewmen nicknames [...] confuses their identities" (Chappell 1997: xiv). In his dismissive treatment of Seaside, whom the narrator deems a "senile [...] old fool" (Frisbie 1964: 152), Frisbie inadvertently summons the spirit of Pacific Islanders who were likewise displaced by imperial/colonial ventures. Like Gauguin, Seaside may be appropriated as a herald of Oceanic fictions that make very different uses of ghosts and haunting.

As we see in 'The Ghost of Alexander Perks, A.B.', stories of haunting reflect the human impulse to attach oneself to the environment. In *The Practice of Everyday Life*, de Certeau writes that "[t]here is no place that is not haunted by many different spirits hidden there in silence, spirits one can 'evoke' or not. Haunted Places are the only ones people can live in" (de Certeau 1984: 108). He goes on to describe the ways in which haunted sites and many other locales exemplify the "power of place"; these include the pedestrian who transforms the street via walking, the renter who transforms the rented apartment, the factory worker who siphons company time and the reader who peruses and appropriates another's text (de Certeau 1984: xxi-xxii). De Certeau likens space in general to a site haunted by memories, stories, and the presences of those who live there. This experience of physical location "inverts the schema of the Panopticon", because it operates via individual "grassroots" use of space as opposed to top-down surveillance and configuration of human subjects (de Certeau 1984: 108). De Certeau's remarks on the theories of spatial appropriation can be empowering for discussions of the literary Gothic as well as postcolonial resistance cultures. None of de Certeau's examples of spatial counter-culture, for example, is more powerful than that of the native Californians living in the Franciscan missions of the eighteenth and nineteenth centuries:

> Thus the spectacular victory of Spanish colonization over the indigenous Indian cultures was diverted from its intended aims by the use made of it: even when they were subjected, indeed even when they accepted their subjection, the Indians often used the laws, practices, and representations that were imposed on them by force or by fascination to ends other than those of them from within – not by rejecting them or by transforming them (though that occurred as well), but by many different ways of using them in the service of rules, customs or convictions foreign to the colonization which they could not escape. (de Certeau 1984: 32)

Whereas many postcolonial theorists emphasise the coloniser's panoptic control of indigenous peoples, de Certeau reminds us of the ways in which native peoples have appropriated the coloniser's places and practices for the purpose of anti-colonial resistance.

Returning to the world of Victorian empire-building, Albert Wendt and Victoria Nalani Kneubuhl offer Oceanic ghost-stories that reveal the subversive and resistant power of place. In his study *Albert Wendt and Pacific Literature: Circling the Void*, Paul Sharrad argues that Wendt's novel *Black Rainbow* (1992) realises de Certeau's appraisal of quotidian tactics. 'Prospecting' may also be described as a "tactical mix of fantasy, allegory, topical allusion and parody" (Sharrad 2003: 223), as this earlier text enacts and applauds indigenous refashionings of metropolitan culture. Written from the perspective of a young Samoan girl named Peleiupu, this tale relates a quest for gold that alchemically transmutes into a story of cultural redemption and solidarity. I recognise three distinct narrative phases in 'Prospecting', each of which carries a different conception of geographical setting. Beginning with the imperial/colonial adventure's assumption of territorial space, "Prospecting" is interrupted by the 'Polynesian Gothic' and its chaotic, anarchical vision of place. By the conclusion of the story, however, Wendt integrates the idea of place into the fa'a Samoa – the traditional 'Samoan way' – that has survived within and in spite of western colonisation.

As Graham Dawson argues in *Soldier Heroes: British Adventure, Empire, and the Imagining of Masculinities*, literary adventure takes on "a plurality of forms" (Dawson 1994: 57). Evolving from the soldier-of-fortune tales of the sixteenth-century, adventure became associated from the early 1600s onwards with capitalism and imperialism:

> The historical importance to British national development of the acquisition of an empire can be seen here to have become deeply embedded in the English language, giving the cultural significance of 'adventure' in Britain explicitly militarist, capitalist, and colonialist connotations that run right through to the present. (Dawson 1994: 58)

Citing Daniel Defoe's *Robinson Crusoe* (1719) as a prime example, Dawson goes on to suggest that "adventures happen in other peoples' backyards, the other people in question usually being those linked historically with Britain by its adventures overseas" (Dawson 1994: 58). In 'Prospecting', Wendt lures the reader into the assumption that he is paying homage to this metropolitan form. The Englishman Barker is initially described as "[t]he great adventurer that Mautu had told them about", conspicuous in his "black, hobnailed boots", "cartridge belt", and "sun helmet perched precariously on his huge mount of hair" (Wendt 1986 : 74). Rounding out Barker's armament are "his sleek rifle" and "his canvas satchel in which, Peleiupu knew, he carried his pens, pencils and paper" (Wendt 1986: 74). Via this exaggerated figure Wendt invokes the stereotypical western adventure hero who combats harsh terrain, hostile natives, and/or villainous competitors for "god, gold, and glory".

Peleiupu quickly ascertains that Barker and his "loyal native lieutenant Mautu" (Wendt 1986: 75) are after gold; but she tells her family that the duo, being "scientific", might be "mapping the course of the Satoa River", "working out the type of sand, rocks, mud and pebbles found in the valley", or "excavating for the sites of ancient villages, hoping to find priceless artefacts" (Wendt 1986: 79). These speculations reflect Wendt's exposure of the ideology of adventure. Returning to de Certeau, we see that Barker conscripts Mautu into a project of spatial mastery. Enterprises economic, scientific, and military share a drive to distinguish a conquered, subdued place from the unsettled exterior environment (de Certeau 1984: 35-36). In keeping with this will to representational power, Peleiupu notes that Barker's pens and pencils are far more important than his "sleek rifle":

> When the hand clutching the pencil moved, it was like a quick spider drawing with all its legs. Soon black lines, a whole network of them, covered the paper. Peleiupu recognized it as a map of the river valley and the area around it. She had once seen a sketch map in one of Mautu's books. (Wendt 1986: 76)

As we see in the second phase of the story, the ideology of adventure represented by Barker is driven by the economic impulse to liquidate indigenous bodies and natural resources and the scientific or academic impulse to remove natural and cultural objects ("priceless artefacts") from their original context and re-place them in heterotopic institutions such as museums. As Foucault argues, such sites are dedicated, to "the will to enclose in one place all times, all epochs, all forms, all tastes … in an immobile place" (Foucault 1998: 242). Wendt tellingly images Barker's cartographic notations as a spider's web that will ensnare and prey upon native spaces.

While the Victorians often isolated Polynesian indigenes as curiosities, Wendt deploys the neo-Victorian impulse in order to exoticise or gothicise the Victorians. Even early in the story, Wendt drops many clues to his Gothic reinterpretation of the late 1800s colonial adventure genre. If we have not been alerted by the sheer exaggeration of Barker's characterisation, then we might take a hint from Peleiupu's antipathy for the romantic adventurer's dirty, ill-mannered children. These warning signals get louder when Mautu becomes obsessed with the hunt for gold; he neglects his family for Barker's quest, provoking Peleiupu's dream of her father with evident Gothic overtones: "digging his hands into the centre of his chest, he prized open his rib-cage and out of the cavern of his chest gushed a river of liquid gold in which she splashed and laughed and laughed" (Wendt 1986: 78). This dream may constitute a macabre omen of the story's next development or a promise of its redemptive end. Wendt then sends the adventure tale in a different and disturbing direction as Barker and Mautu find not gold, but a "scatter of shallow graves":

> In them, lying in grotesque postures, were the glittering skeletons. Many of them were badly broken, shattered, scattered; many skulls and bones were missing; some of the graves were occupied by more than one skeleton. (Wendt 1986: 87-88)

With this unexpected turn, Wendt stages a Gothic eruption of dark and mysterious forces into the otherwise light-hearted adventure. Three alternatives present themselves as the story proceeds. One of these is the continuation of the Barker's colonial conquest. "Graveyards and dead villages produce wonderful surprises," Barker exclaims, and sets to unearthing the skeletons (Wendt 1986: 84). His treasure-hunt has turned academic: "pulsating with inquisitive blood," Barker intones, "But the mystery, don't you sense the mystery?" (Wendt 1986: 84). However, as we see below, this kind of grave-robbing is itself a form of colonial plunder. As in texts ranging from Bram Stoker's *Jewel of the Seven Stars* (1903) to A.S. Byatt's *Possession* (1990), violation of graves and tombs represents the intersection of the rational drive for knowledge and control with capitalism's impulse to accumulate and liquidate. A different narrative possibility emerges with Mautu's response to the graves; he is haunted by the dead: "'They are here all around me,' he murmured. 'They filled my sleep with their cries, their disquiet, their awful dying!'" (Wendt 1986: 86). This paranormal visitation takes its toll on Mautu, who begins to turn gray and move about "like a creature caught in a self-destructive dream" (Wendt 1986: 87). In light of Barker's curiosity and Mautu's "superstition", the apparition of murder victims and the potential for "aitu and other fearful phantoms" conjures the Polynesian Gothic (Wendt 1986: 84) – native history and culture served up for touristic consumption, as in texts such as A. Grove Day and Becil F. Kirtley's *Horror in Paradise: Grim and Uncanny Tales from Hawaii and the South Seas* (1986). For Day and Kirtley, the "islands of the Pacific have been a favoured region for legend and romance", including "tales of the kahuna cult of Hawaii and the witch doctors of New Guinea, ghosts on high isles and reef-decked atolls, diabolism and fatal tabus" (Day and Kirtley 1986: 1). The conclusion of 'Prospecting', however, broaches a further, more redemptive possibility.

Rod Edmond suggests that 'Prospecting' appears to focus upon the enlightenment of Barker; but Wendt deflects even this comparatively moderate version of the colonial adventure in order to reveal Peleiupu's own understanding of her culture and its traditions. And this revelation constitutes the third and final narrative movement opened by the discovery of the graves. Mautu decides to bring his children to the graves before removing the bodies to Satoa for proper burial. Peleiupu recalls Barker's quest as she views the remains:

> Gold, Peleiupu heard Barker repeat in her head. Gold. Gold. Gold. She gazed down and the heap of bones in the grave in front of her looked golden in the sunlight. All around a golden luminosity was bursting up from the mouths of the graves, and inside her the bones transformed themselves into huge Pua blossoms, and she was floating through a garden of white magic flowers. (Wendt 1986: 88)

These poetic images, which suggest an appropriation and transformation of Barker's 'expedition', also foreshadow the nature of the funeral rites that conclude 'Prospecting'. The Samoan women anoint the bones with cocoanut oil and wrap them in tapa, "as was the custom"; likewise, their "customary funeral wailing" introduces Mautu's Christian sermon (Wendt 1986: 91-92). Wendt leaves us with an almost sentimental ending in which Barker and his family lead the village in "building up the graves with sleek, black stones and pebbles that the young people brought in baskets from the river" (Wendt 1986:

79). Barker himself, the prospector who had crassly poked his fingers into a skull's eye-sockets, voices a – or perhaps *the* – central theme of the story: "I suppose being human like us they needed to be buried decently" (Wendt 1986: 94).

The newly decorated graves of "the people" provide a fitting image for the story's conclusion (Wendt 1986: 87). The burial represents the Satoans' ownership of western funerary practices; decidedly Christian, the burial ceremony also incorporates native elements such as the anointing and 'clothing' of the bones. Moreover, to return to de Certeau's language, the villagers' final touches to the new graves emphasise the notion of the cemetery as space rather than place. In her commentary on this subject, Elizabeth A. Wright points out that the cemetery may be constructed as a heterotopic, even panoptic place that suppresses contestation or as a space filled with "a cacophony of remembrances calling out" and marked with private expressions of commemoration that often bypass the policing of public places (Wright 2005: 60). Wendt emphatically rejects the idea that the Christian burial in Satoa reflects absolute western colonial hegemony. The fact that the villagers manage the graveyard in their own way is consistent with the story's greater emphasis on cultural (re-)appropriation and transformation. Peleiupu has made a gold expedition her own and, in a larger sense, Wendt has reworked the genres of colonial adventure and Polynesian Gothic.

Wendt takes us back to the climax of western colonial power, an age in which metropolitan self-critique was at an ebb and in which Enlightenment culture endorsed rampant despoliation of indigenous peoples. In the early movements of 'Prospecting', the character of Barker hints at the figure of the grave-robber who represents a paradoxical conflation of Enlightenment and Gothic practices. As suggested above, the grave-robbery motif informs neo-Victorian fictions such as Byatt's *Possession*; but the contradictions of this highly charged practice are exposed in the early nineteenth-century by Thomas Hood, whose short poem 'Mary's Ghost' (1826) describes a macabre scene in which the shade of a recently departed girl complains that her "everlasting peace/Is broken into pieces":

> The body-snatchers they have come,
> And made a snatch at me;

> It's very hard them kind of men
> Won't let a body be! (Hood 2004: 174)

The unfortunate Mary goes on to lament that her corpse has been dismembered and parcelled out in the name of medical research. Her arm has gone to Dr. Vyse, while her legs "have gone to walk/The hospital at Guy's" (Hood 2004: 174). Pickled in "spirits and a phial" and wondering about the whereabouts of her head, Mary pleads with her fiancé: "Don't go to weep upon my grave, /And think that there I be;/They haven't left an atom there/Of my anatomie" (Hood 2004: 175) As many scholars point out, 'Mary's Ghost' is usually read for its insight into the contemporary practice of the ironically named 'resurrection men', who would unearth bodies for high paying anatomists; Mary then mournfully reflects that her "trunk" is destined for a lecture hall, to be dissected in front of "Pickford's van" (Hood 2004: l). Roy Porter suggests that poets such as Hood and Robert Southey, along with satiric cartoonists, seized upon this grisly traffic as a sensational and ironic complicity between respectable doctors and criminal, sometimes even murderous body-snatchers (as in the Burke and Hare case, for instance) (Porter 2001: 221).

Grave-robbery associated with medical research was curtailed in Britain in 1832, when the Act for regulating Schools of Anatomy made cadavers legally available. However, body-snatching continued as archaeologists and anthropologists continued to rifle the graves of indigenous peoples encountered in the course of the colonial enterprise. The archaeological grave-robber has attained heroic stature within the colonial imagination (as with the popular representations of Egyptology), but for many native peoples and critics, looting and scholarship come to the same thing. As J. Riding In forcefully argues, while one species of grave-robber is labelled "criminals, Satan worshippers, or imbalanced", others enjoy laudatory "public opinion and loopholes [that] have until recently enabled white society to loot and pillage with impunity American Indian cemeteries" (Riding In 1992: 12). For Riding In, archaeology emerged from and preserves this exploitation of the dead. Haunani-Kay Trask similarly denounces the violation of graves in Hawai'i, calling for "a moratorium on studying, unearthing, slicing, crushing, and analyzing us":

> For many Hawaiians, including myself, archaeologists who dig up our ancestors for money or glory are *maha'oi haole*, that is, rude and invasive white people who go where they do not belong. It is simply wrong, culturally, for non-Natives to dig up our ancestors, to break their bones, to remove them for highways and hotels, and to publish about them. Unlike white people, our culture is not obsessed with "scientific" study of human skeletons. (Trask 1999: 131-132)

Both Riding In and Trask bring home the notion that disinterment of indigenous remains persists, quite literally, as a primary 'site' of contention between indigenous and settler cultures in the United States. Indigenous rights organisations such as the American Indian Movement have successfully lobbied for legislation protecting Native American burial sites. In Hawai'i, Hui Malama I Na Kupuna O Hawaii Nei take even more direct actions as they secure and rebury kanaka maoli remains and moepu (objects), often coming into conflict with other Native Hawaiian groups, developers, the Bishop Museum, and the legal system itself. As Hui Malama P'o Kunani Nihipali argues,

> Some believe that an end (education) justifies the means (removal and desecration). This view is inconsistent with our duties to our kupuna. A major component of our cultural identity is the exercise of our duties as living descendents to protect the sanctity of the graves of our ancestors who gave us the breath of life. (Nihipali 2003)

As Trask and Nihipali imply, this kind of legitimised drive to disinter also reflects a strange moment of deconstructive confluence: on one hand between western discourses of civilisation and savagery, and on the other between Enlightenment rationalism and Gothic excess. The same worldview responsible for what Michel Foucault describes as the modern 'heterotopic' cemetery also inspires the idea of "unearthing, slicing, crushing" the human body; in other words, Enlightenment culture may be seen to produce its monstrous Other.

The cultural theorist Dwight Macdonald already broached such concerns in the late 1950s, when he suggested that horror films reveal modern anxieties about the destructive potential of Enlightenment technological advances: "[S]cience gives man mastery over his environment and is therefore beneficent. But science itself is not understood, therefore not mastered, therefore terrifying because of its very power" (Macdonald 1998: 32). He further suggests that "deep popular intuitions" figure the mysterious and alienating character of the scientist as a monstrous Other,

> to the point, indeed, that if one sees a laboratory in a movie, one shudders, and the white coat of the scientist is as blood-chilling a sight as Count Dracula's black cloak [...] the scientist's laboratory has acquired in Mass Culture a ghastly atmosphere. (Macdonald 1998: 32)

We usually expect to see Enlightenment heroes set in opposition to an irrational and/or savage menace, as in 'The Murders in the Rue Morgue' or *Dracula*; in texts such as Stevenson's *The Strange Case of Dr. Jekyll and Mr. Hyde* (1886), the seemingly polar figures are shown to be one and the same. Macdonald's reading of Gothic horror reworks these conventional associations; he asserts that the protagonists and villains of this genre might not be who we thought they were. As in Hood's poem 'Mary's Ghost', the physician may turn out to be a ghoul and the haunting spectre a victim crying for redress.

These motifs of grave-robbing, colonialism, indigenous resistance, and insurrectionary haunting come together in Victoria Nalani Kneubuhl's drama *Ola Nā Iwi (The Bones Live)*. Kneubuhl presents a postcolonial ghost story about the repatriation of native Hawaiian remains. While touring in Germany, the Hawaiian actress Kawehi steals the body of a long dead kanaka maoli from a museum. Aided by the ghost of the deceased, Kawehi returns to Hawai'i in order to properly bury these 'living bones' – a mission complicated by the Hawaiian activist Pua, on one hand, and the museum operative Gustav, on the other. Like Wendt, Kneubuhl deflects the Polynesian Gothic from its conventional exoticism toward an illumination of the postcolonial quest for repatriation. Living and dead walk the same stage, as Kneubuhl brings to life the indigenous struggle to retain tradition and continuity in the aftermath of colonialism. Kneubuhl makes use of many literary traditions, among them Gothic conventions such as the defamiliarisation of science, the notion of haunting as resistance, and the frustration of the detective story's drive for rational certainty.

As Macdonald suggests, there is a strain of Gothic fiction and film that reinterprets and defamiliarises the scientific and clinical practices of Enlightenment culture. Our understanding of Kneubuhl's participation in this aspect of Gothic literature may be illuminated by Foucault's interpretation of the heterotopic cemeteries and by the larger Gothic preoccupation with violated graveyards. Although Enlightenment culture produced (or at least refined) the heterotopic cemetery, it also inspired its violation in the form of 'academic' grave-robbing. It might not be too much to argue that Gothic literature and Enlightenment clinical discourse jockey for interpretation of this methodology; while researchers and clinicians argue the necessity of disinterment, and dismiss objections as facile sentiment and superstition, Gothic fictions such as Hood's poem, Stevenson's short-story 'The Body Snatcher' (1884), and H.P. Lovecraft's 'Herbert West – Reanimator' (1923), re-present these procurers as ghoulish fiends. Although the indigenous burials staged in Kneubuhl's *Ola Nā Iwi* may not conform to western heterotopic procedures, the play does participate in this representation of grave-robbery as a monstrous form of colonial plunder.

"You'd never go and dig up Benjamin Franklin and put him in an exhibit case", declares Kneubuhl, in an interview with Craig Howes (qtd. Howes 2002: xxvi) – an ironic remark indeed given Franklin's own fascination with heterotopic archives and museums. She began to envision *Ola Nā Iwi* while working as an Education Specialist at the Judiciary History Center in Honolulu. Kneubuhl became familiar with the U.S. Senate hearings on the Native American Graves Protection and Repatriation Act (NAGPRA) and was struck by the idea of "competitions for who could scoop up more human remains and shove them in their collection" (qtd. Howes 2002: xxv-xxvi). In *Ola Nā Iwi: The Bones Live*, Kneubuhl dramatises her sense of horror at such acts through both character and setting. At many points in the drama, Kneubuhl interjects flashback scenes that reveal the depredations of the Victorian body snatchers. These figures fall into two groups: nameless characters known only by allegorical labels and more realistic characters. Consisting of "Graverobber", two "19th Century Professors", and "19th Century Phrenologist", the former series of personae are satiric in nature and represent a mockery of Enlightenment positivism, the ideology that created a market for the remains of indigenous peoples. In his soliloquy in Act I, Graverobber boasts to the audience of his nocturnal forays after Indian skulls:

> I wait until the dead of night, when not even the dogs are stirring. After securing a skull, I have to pass the Indian sentry at the stockade gate, so I never enter with more than one at a time underneath my coat [....] Believing probably at the time that I would never steal his head before he was cold in his grave, they did not keep watch the first night, and thus myself and my two hospital attendants easily secured this fine specimen for you. Perhaps you might decide sometime to honor me as a collector and display it. (Kneubuhl 1994: 177-178)

This soliloquy seems to be addressed to one of the 'legitimate' academics in the play; but in that the actor directs his comments to the 'fourth wall', the audience becomes implicated in the morbid economy between Graverobber and his supposed betters. As represented in *Ola Nā Iwi*, the traffic in human remains spans the obviously Gothic milieu of Graverobber and the sanctified academic world of the nineteenth-Century Professors and historical anthropologists Warren K. Moorehead, George Dorsey, and Franz Boas. In Kneubuhl's mise-en-scène, the latter characters contend for fame and exchange gibes over their respective 'collections'. To Dorsey's boast, "I have recently collected myself, in the field, two skeletons of the Kootenay tribe, which you could never get because they watch their cemeteries very carefully now", Boas responds: "I had already collected and sold many remains to Washington, to Berlin, to important museums throughout Europe before you could even say 'anthropological dig'" (Kneubuhl 1994: 207). Although they are distanced from the outcast Graverobber, these luminaries reveal the prevalence of body-snatching within the academy in general, and museum collections more specifically.

Like the irreverent anatomists in Hood's poem, Graverobber and his colleagues abscond with indigenous bodies in order to 'shove them into collections'. This practice was part of what Foucault describes as a shift between the idiosyncratic collection of the seventeenth-century and the heterotopic museums and libraries dedicated to enclosing elements from various times and places. Arguing that museums cannot be confined to one epoch or ideology, Beth Lord sums up this interpretation of the museum as

> an Enlightenment institution whose power to collect and display objects is a function of capitalism and imperialism, and whose power to form individuals is exercised through the careful ordered deployment of knowledge within an institutionally controlled and publicly monitored space. (Lord 2006: 2)

If the museum belongs to the alienating world of science, then it is also susceptible to popular representation as a site of horror. To repeat Macdonald's previously cited point, "the scientist's laboratory has acquired in Mass Culture a ghastly atmosphere" (Macdonald 1998: 18). As Lord notes, the same may be said of the museum, which has been widely criticised – by Theodor Adorno as a "mausoleum" (Adorno 1981: 175) and by Maurice Merleau-Ponty as a "meditative necropolis" characterised by "mournful light" (Merleau-Ponty 1993: 93). Merleau-Ponty's grotesque imagery is even more suggestive when we consider the relationship between the cemetery and the natural history museum. Heterotopic graves could be opened, but only by overriding this kind of place with another containment facility such as the laboratory, the lecture hall, or museum. While the sterilised environment of the museum becomes a surrogate cemetery, the abjection of the opened grave makes its way into this new repository of human remains.

Kneubuhl recognises the horrific potential of the museum in Act II of *Ola Nā Iwi*:

> Kawehi: Yes, I'm all alone and I'm thinking how dark and cold it is all of a sudden. I look around me at the rows and rows of gray steel storage shelves. Aisle after aisle of bones and bones and the words rushing

> out of nowhere: kupuna kāne, kupuna wahine, nā hulu mamo, *nā lei hiwahiwa (grandfather, grandmother, esteemed elders, precious ones)*, and I feel so lonely, and sad, so isolated in all this chill and gray with the sharp smell of metal and cold, shiny concrete floors. And I'm thinking, how can this be? How can this be real? I look over at one shelf all by itself, with one and only one box on it, and there you are standing next to it, with your arms opened out to me, weeping. (Kneubuhl 1994: 198-199)

Tapping Gothic literary conventions, Kneubuhl defamiliarises the museum; she presents this sanitised environment, with its "rows and rows of gray steel storage shelves", its "sharp smell of metal and cold, shiny concrete floors", as a nightmare world haunted by imprisoned ghosts: "Aisle after aisle of bones and bones and the words rushing out of nowhere." Even as the scientist's lab-coat eclipses Dracula's cape, the orderly regime of the museum takes the place of the haunted house or castle. As I elaborate below, this rendition of haunting is itself part of a distinct Gothic tradition.

In a different sense, museums have frequently appeared in Gothic fiction and film as a stage for terrifying ruptures of normality. H.P. Lovecraft's 'The Horror in the Museum' (1933) is an early example of this sensibility; the tradition continues in films such as *The Mummy* (Karl Freund, 1932), *It!* (Herbert J. Leder, 1966), *Damien: The Omen II* (Don Taylor, 1978), and *The Relic* (Peter Hyams, 1997). There is something more going on here than the contrast between clinical order and abject horror. Within Enlightenment ideology the eruption of a monstrous or polymorphic Other presents a direct affront to and attack upon the museum's heterotopic regime. Like Mautu in Wendt's 'Prospecting', Kawehi is moved by the spirit of the departed Nanea/Liliha; she dupes the anthropologist Dr. Heinrich, removes the bones, and returns with them to Hawai'i, where she hopes to rebury them in a culturally appropriate fashion. In a reversal of imperial/colonial grave-robbing, Kneubuhl allies Kawehi's theft with the motif of haunting and thus clarifies this movement as a form of postcolonial resistance. As de Certeau has suggested, the notion of haunting is related in a fundamental way to the subversive power of lived space. Like Wendt, Kneubuhl presents an indigenous ghost who calls out to her descendent for repatriation. Once she is rescued by Kawehi from the museum, Nanea/Liliha becomes embodied and takes an active role among the living until she is properly laid to rest. Between rescue and burial, however, Nanea has a profound influence upon Kawehi, as well as the German detective Gustav. With the pronouncement "it was you who bound us together" (Kneubuhl 1994: 180), Nanea helps Kawehi to construct a ka'ai, a Hawaiian ossuary; it becomes a symbol of their mutual quest and their connection across time. At the same time, Nanea finds employment as a "living history" tour guide, a position that allows her to offer a counter-narrative to American imperial historiography. She manages to persuade the German detective Gustav of the mana inherent in the bones and the impropriety of his quest to return her remains to Germany. At the conclusion of *Ola Nā Iwi*, Nanea/Liliha assures us that she has found a resting place "in the breathing, beating heart of my beloved aina" and with "the endless, winding procession of torches [...] the faces of every loved one gone before me" (Kneubuhl 1994: 227).

Like Wendt, Kneubuhl revises Polynesian Gothic exoticism toward celebration of the postcolonial struggle for repatriation. Staging Nanea's journey from heterotopic museum to private grave, Kneubuhl dramatises the struggle of native Polynesians to reclaim spaces and selves co-opted under western colonialism. In 'Prospecting' and *Ola Nā Iwi*, respectively, these writers find resources for this project in the neo-Victorian Gothic, which revisits and challenges the Enlightenment ideologies often complicit with imperial domination. Wendt and Kneubuhl write of distinctive and unique Polynesian cultures and histories; but Samoa and Hawai'i do share an experience of what Punter and Byron describe as "imperial trauma", a fracture that has not quite broken all continuity between past and present (Punter and Byron 2004: 57-58). In each text, the ghost of those displaced by the highly suggestive figure of the colonial grave-robber ideally symbolises the spirit of peoples who maintain continuity between generations as well as their attachment to ancestral spaces. Both 'Prospecting' and *Ola Nā Iwi* reflect the postcolonial writers' simultaneous preservation of indigenous culture and exploitation of metropolitan forms and epistemologies. As Wendt suggests in an interview with Vilsoni Hereniko:

the work [of art] is rooted in the culture the artist is from, but in a very individualistic manner. Some are quite political, not necessarily overt. They are redefining who we are, also showing where the art of our countries may be going. (qtd. Hereniko 2006: 61)

Bibliography

Adorno, Theodor. 1981. 'Valéry Proust Museum' (trans. Samuel and Shirley Webber), in *Prisms* [1953]. Cambridge, Massachusetts: MIT: 173-186.

Bolton, Linda, and Paul Gauguin. 2003. *Gauguin*. Edison: Chartwell Books.

Bormann, Daniel Candel. 2002. *The Articulation of Science in the Neo-Victorian Novel: A Poetics (and Two Case Studies)*. Bern & New York: Lang.

Chappell, David A. 1997. *Double Ghosts: Oceanian Voyagers on Euroamerican Ships*. Armonk, New York.: M.E. Sharpe.

Conrad, Joseph. 2008. *The Secret Sharer* [1910]. Teddington, Middlesex: Echo Library.

Dawson, Graham. 1994. *Soldier Heroes: British Adventure, Empire, and the Imagining of Masculinity*. London: Routledge.

Day, A. Grove, and Becil F. Kirtley. 1986. 'Foreward', in Day, A. Grove, and Becil F. Kirtley (eds.), *Horror in Paradise: Grim and Uncanny Tales from Hawaii and the South Seas*. Australia: Mutual Publishing.

de Certeau, Michel. 1984. *The Practice of Everyday Life* (trans. Steven Kendall). Berkeley & Los Angeles: University of California Press.

Edmond, Rod. 1990. 'South Pacific Literature: Post-Colonialism and Post-Modernism', *Wasafiri* 6(12): 20-21.

Foucault, Michel. 1998. 'Of Other Spaces', in Mirzoeff, Nicholas (ed.), *The Visual Culture Reader*. New York: Routledge: 238-244.

Frisbie, Robert Dean. 1964. 'The Ghost of Alexander Perks, A.B.' [1931], in Day, A. Grove, and Carl Stroven (eds.), *Best South Sea Stories*. Honolulu, Hawaii: Mutual Publishing: 150-161.

Hereniko, Vilsoni. 2006. 'Interview with Albert Wendt: Art, Writing, and the Creative Process', *The Contemporary Pacific* 18(1): 59-69.

Hood, Thomas. 2004. 'Mary's Ghost – A Pathetic Ballad', in *The Works of Thomas Hood: Comic and Serious in Prose and Verse with All the Original Illustration Part Four*. London: E. Moxon, Son & Co.: 173-175.

Howes, Craig. 2002. 'Introduction', in Kneubuhl, Victoria Nalani, *Hawai'i Nei: Island Plays*. Honolulu: University of Hawaii Press, ix-xxviii.

Kneubuhl, Victoria Nalani. 2002. *Ola Nā Iwi* [1994], in *Hawai'i Nei: Island Plays*. Honolulu: University of Hawaii Press: 143-227.

Lord, Beth. 2006. 'Foucault's Museum: Difference, Representation, and Genealogy', *Museum and Society* 4(1): 1-14.

Macdonald, Dwight. 1998. 'A Theory of Mass Culture' [1957], in Story, John (ed.), *Cultural Theory and Popular Culture: A Reader*. Athens: University of Georgia Press, 22-36.

Merleau-Ponty, M. 1993. 'Indirect Language and the Voices of Silence' [1952] (trans. R.C. McCleary), in Johnson, G.A. (ed.), *The Merleau-Ponty Aesthetics Reader*. Evanston: Northwestern University Press, 76-120.

Nihipali, Kunani. 2003. 'Seeking the Rightful Homes for Bones, Burial Items', *Honolulu Advertiser* (25 May).

Porter, Roy. 2001. *Bodies Politic: Disease, Death, and Doctors in Britain, 1650-1900*. Ithaca, New York: Cornell University Press.

Punter, David, and Glennis Byron. 2004. *The Gothic*. Oxford: Blackwell.

Riding In, James. 1992. 'Without Ethics and Morality: A Historical Overview of Imperial Archaeology and American Indians', *Arizona State Law Journal* 24(1): 11-34.

Riquelme, John Paul. 2000. 'Introduction: Toward a History of Gothic and Modernism: Dark Modernity from Bram Stoker to Samuel Beckett', *Modern Fiction Studies* 46(3) (Fall):585-605.

Schwarz, Daniel R. 1997. *Reconfiguring Modernism: Explorations in the Relationship between Modern Art and Modern Literature*. New York: St. Martin's Press.

Sharrad, Paul. 2003 *Albert Wendt and Pacific Literature: Circling the Void*. Manchester: Manchester University Press.

Trask, Haunani-Kay. 1999. *From a Native Daughter: Colonialism and Sovereignty in Hawai'i*. Honolulu: University of Hawaii.

Wendt, Albert. 1986. 'Prospecting' [1983], in *The Birth and Death of the Miracle Man and Other Stories*. Auckland: Viking.

Wright, Elizabeth A. 2005. 'Rhetorical Spaces in Memorial Places: The Cemetery as a Rhetorical Memory Place/Space', *Rhetoric Society Quarterly* 35(4) (Fall): 51-82.

Monsters against Empire:
The Politics and Poetics of Neo-Victorian Metafiction in *The League of Extraordinary Gentlemen*

Sebastian Domsch

Abstract:
This chapter analyses the specific way in which Alan Moore and Kevin O'Neill in their graphic novel series *The League of Extraordinary Gentlemen* appropriate Victorian Gothic fiction into a highly elaborate metafictional crossover. Special focus is put on the role of hybridity and otherness, both in the Victorian source material and in the neo-Victorian re-writing, and on the critique of discourses of power.

Keywords: comics, crossover, graphic novel, hybridity, *League of Extraordinary Gentlemen*, metafiction, Alan Moore, Kevin O'Neill, otherness, steampunk.

*****

> The British Empire has always encountered difficulty in distinguishing between its heroes and its monsters. Campion Bond from *Memoirs of an English Intelligencer*. (Moore and O'Neill 2000: Vol. I, 6)

Alan Moore and Kevin O'Neill's graphic novels constituting *The League of Extraordinary Gentlemen* (1999-2009) series are among the most fascinating recent examples of the artistic and political potential of the neo-Victorian Gothic, as they combine a visual and verbal steampunk re-imagination of the more monstrous side of the Victorian era with an almost excessive metafictional playfulness and thorough ideological critique.[1] Moore's fictional world is a world of fictions, a

---

[1] There is not yet that much critical work on the *League* series, even though Alan Moore is one of the few comics authors who has entered the focus of literary scholars. The most substantial and helpful texts are the annotation books by Jess Nevins. Also of note is Ferguson 2009. For texts that concentrate on the movie adaptations are

seemingly inexhaustible pastiche of the Victorian literary tradition, fusing characters, settings, and plot elements from a vast range of the period's literary texts. It is an encyclopaedia of Victorian fantastic fiction at the same time that it is an investigation into the dominant political, social and sexual ideologies of that time and their afterlife in our own. Moore lets us perceive the late Victorian period filtered through the collective prism of its literary imagination, while highlighting the necessary constructedness of such a vision, and thereby providing a genuine neo-Victorian perspective, through his 'illicit' crossing of fictional worlds. His postmodern re-interpretation of so many well-known fictional characters emphasises their embeddedness in discourses of power and gender relations, especially in their interactions with each other and with the institutions of power that are the motors of the stories, most prominently the British Empire. As is already apparent from the title, one of the leitmotifs of the series, a motif that is also at the heart of the Victorian Gothic, and arguably of neo-Victorian Gothic also, is otherness: All the central protagonists of the stories are extraordinary and therefore marginalised figures, social outsiders like Jules Verne's Captain Nemo or Gothic monsters like Mr. Hyde, and their alliance with the imperial powers is always uneasy, ambiguous and more often than not the cause of further conflict and the basis for a larger critique of power. Multi-faceted and highly acclaimed, *The League of Extraordinary Gentlemen* is integral to an understanding of neo-Victorian Gothic.

The narrative of *The League of Extraordinary Gentlemen* consists of a series of graphic novels written by Alan Moore and illustrated by Kevin O'Neill. The first two instalments, simply called *Volume I* and *Volume II*, were published in serialised form from March 1999 to September 2000 and from September 2002 to November 2003 respectively, both having six issues. They were later collected into single bound trade paperbacks. In 2007, a single volume was released under the title *The League of Extraordinary Gentlemen: Black Dossier*, which was rather a source book providing background

---

Duda 2008 and Frenk and Krug 2009. Sometimes, the *League* series is merely referred to briefly, as in Seshagiri 2006: 188 or Perschon 2010: 149. Brewer also briefly mentions the *League* as an example of appropriative use of storytelling (see Brewer 2005: 203-206), but he hardly does justice to the complexity of Moore's and O'Neill's adaptation.

information and a history of the league than a direct continuation of the series. 2009 saw the beginning of a third volume, entitled *Century*, to be published in three instalments of 72 pages, of which only the first two have appeared so far.

The series' storyline generally moves forward in time, with the first two volumes set at the end of the Victorian period in 1898. The *Black Dossier* has a central storyline that takes place in 1958, but the material included reaches back almost all the way through human history. *Volume III* starts in 1910 and is supposed to span the whole of the twentieth century. The central artistic conceit of the series is closely tied to this timeline: all of the characters and places and many of the events in the series are taken directly from other fictional works with the premise that, unless otherwise stated, these events take place at the time of those works' original publication. Thus, for example, the Martian invasion that the second volume deals with is happening in 1898, the year in which H.G. Wells's novel *The War of the Worlds* was published. This time frame is the only limitation to the inclusion of source texts into the fictional world of the *League*, which means that the first two volumes are mainly woven from appropriations of Victorian fiction, mostly of the Gothic mode. In fact, the eponymous league of extraordinary gentlemen can be understood as an anachronistic transposition of the common twentieth-century motif of team-ups of prominent heroic or villainous characters in superhero comics into the Victorian period. This motif provides the answer to the hypothetical question how such a team of superheroes would look, when collected from the Victorian literary imagination and (partially) viewed through Victorian eyes.

Consequently, the league consists of some of the most memorable characters that were created by the Victorian Gothic. Gathered together by a precursor to the British secret service under the control of a figure simply called 'M', the league is led by Mina Harker, the (now divorced) wife of Jonathan Harker from Bram Stoker's *Dracula* (1897), and contains H. Rider Haggard's colonial explorer Allan Quatermain, Jules Verne's Captain Nemo, Robert Louis Stevenson's Dr. Jekyll, and H.G. Wells's invisible man Griffin. The dangers and enemies that they encounter range from Arthur Conan Doyle's Professor Moriarty and Sax Rohmer's Dr. Fu Manchu to Wells's Martian invasion and Dr. Moreau, now turned into a manufacturer of biological weapons. But these are only the most obvious and easily detectable appropriations, while woven into the background is an immensely rich tapestry of allusions to a vast range of Victorian texts, reaching from the classic to the arcane. The depth of this intertextual – and, as Heilmann and Llewellyn have shown, also metafictional (Heilmann and Llewellyn 2010: 174-178) – game very soon had readers rather obsessively hunting for allusions, quotations and references, a hunt that was first organised through websites on the internet, and finally led to the publication of exhaustive companion books to all of the volumes, all edited by Jess Nevins. These books of annotation by far surpass the original publications in the number of pages and nicely illuminate the intricate workings of Moore's and O'Neill's metafictional machine.

The *League* is not Moore's first neo-Victorian fiction. Between 1991 and 1996, together with the artist Eddie Campbell, he published the graphic novel *From Hell*, a fictional account of the Jack the Ripper murders that closely follows Stephen Knight's 1976 theory about the case, expounded in *Jack the Ripper: The Final Solution*. But whereas *From Hell* is as much an engagement with twentieth-century attempts at understanding the case, the so-called Ripperology (as can be most clearly seen in its epilogue, 'The Dance of the gull catchers'),[2] the *League* series takes as its prime source material Victorian literary imagination itself. And yet, the latter series is far more than merely a collection or combination of quotes from the period's texts or fictional ideas. It uses these texts and ideas to highlight some of the period's central concerns and anxieties and provides a critical commentary thereon through the structure of the work: through double-coding, on the one hand, and fictional, generic, and medial hybridisation on the other. It is this combination that makes the first two *League* volumes prime examples of the complexities and capabilities of neo-Victorian Gothic.

1. Fictional Miscegenation

The question of hybridity and otherness is a core element of the Victorian Gothic, and it is one of the elements that neo-Victorian rewritings tend to emphasise. The world of Victorian Gothic fiction is

---

[2] For more on *From Hell* as a metafictional engagement with Victorian culture and its multiple adaptations, see Pietrzak-Franger 2009/2010. Ripperology and neo-Victorian reiterations of the Ripper myth are discussed in Max Duperray's and Sarah E. Maier's contributions to this volume.

one in which the fear of miscegenation looms large. In numerous examples of the most successful stories of the period, in what Patrick Brantlinger has termed 'imperial Gothic' (see Brantlinger 2009: 45-52),[3] national, social, racial, and sexual identities are threatened by contact with the other. Bram Stoker's *Dracula* is perhaps the most elaborate fantasy of a contamination with foreign otherness among the works that Moore draws upon. Its imagery of pure and contaminated blood, of contagion and unholy disease, opposed as they are against Englishness and Christianity, are unmistakeable in their symbolic significance. Similarly, Victorian adventure fiction drew much of its appeal and fascination from an encounter with the other, and some of the most memorable creations of the period's Gothic imagination are images of otherness – strange places, strange creatures, and also strange or different human beings. In the case of adventure stories such as those involving Quatermain, fascinating otherness was located at the edges of the colonial reach, where exoticism bordered on fantasy. But there was a distinct limit to this fascination, a certain distance that the observer needed to uphold, and a breach of this distance bore potential horrors. In more fantastic fiction, this could take on the shape of the horribly disfigured hybrid creatures of Dr. Moreau or of an innocent English girl slowly turned into a vampire after being bitten, but it also figured as the more prosaic racist fear of miscegenation.[4]

---

[3] See also Malchow 1996: 4 and Schmitt 1997: 19.

[4] In H. Rider Haggard's novel *King Solomon's Mines* (1885), three Englishmen travel to an unexplored region in Africa and get mixed up in the politics of an unknown (and fictional) African tribe. At one point, they rescue a black girl called Foulata from being sacrificed. As a consequence, she falls in love with one of the men, Captain Good, nursing him when he is sick and following him into the dangerous mines, and Good seems equally attracted to her. Readers could be titillated with the exotic beauty of the African girl and the possibility of a romantic relationship in this way, though it could not be realised. Instead, the character is conveniently killed off before the threat of miscegenation can be fulfilled, and Quatermain as narrator even seems to recommend the author for this: "I consider her removal was a fortunate occurrence, since, otherwise, complications would have been sure to ensue. [... N]o amount of beauty or refinement could have made an entanglement between Good and herself a desirable occurrence – for, as she herself put it, 'Can the sun mate with the moon, or the white with the black?'" (Haggard 2009: 212) The official Victorian answer to this rhetorical question was unshakeably no, and yet, the idea of a breach of boundaries could not be killed off as easily as the specific embodiments of that idea. For actual high profile cases of miscegenation, see e.g. the epilogue in Howard Malchow's *Gothic Images of Race in Nineteenth-Century Britain*, 'Race, Gender and Moral

It is not the least part of the significance of the Victorian Gothic imagination – and a foundation for neo-Victorian rewritings – that its creations produced an amount of unrest and unease that no attempt at narrative closure could contain. In the Victorian Gothic, literary creation itself becomes "Golem-like [and] uncontainable" (Pulham 2010: 169), undead and haunting. Gothic characters repeatedly transgressed the texts in which they were created (and often enough also killed), or, as Iain Sinclair writes in his neo-Victorian novel *White Chappell, Scarlet Tracings* (1987): "They got out into the stream of time, the ether; they escaped into the labyrinth. They achieved independent existence" (Sinclair 2004: 117). This spectral independence makes them especially interesting for the metafictional game of neo-Victorianism, and turns them into a source of neo-Victorian Gothic.

Most of the monsters taken up in the *League* series, and even many of the heroes, died in the original source texts, but have since then lead a tumultuous afterlife in the form of endless adaptations, (unofficial) continuations, parodies and rewritings. Figures like Jekyll and Hyde or Dracula have become part of our cultural mythology, notwithstanding the fact that in their original stories they ended up dead or destroyed. A fictional death, it seems, is much less stable than a real death – a lesson that the Victorians already learned from the period's most famous rescinded death, that of Sherlock Holmes in 'The Adventure of the Empty House' (1903). Ten years earlier, Conan Doyle had killed his most successful character in 'The Final Problem', in order to be able to write other stories that he deemed more worthy of his attention. But the general demand for Holmes pressed the author into 'resurrecting' Holmes by a re-interpretation of the events that had led to his death.

Moore's metafictional appropriation pays homage to this fact by direct allusion to 'The Final Problem' and through his type of rewritings. Though he is meticulous in the way that all existents are drawn faithfully from Victorian sources, almost all of his central characters owe their continued existence in the fictional crossover-world of the *League* to a rewriting of the ends that their original creators invented for them. In Moore's version, for example, Allan

---

Panic: Miss Jewel's Marriage Revisited' (Malchow 1996: 239-260). See also Young 1995: 142-158.

Quatermain does not die of a lung injury as in Haggard's 1887 novel, but orchestrates his own death in a manner similar to Holmes; Dr. Jekyll does not die through suicide (no explanation is given why he now lives in Paris); instead of being restored to purity and happily bearing a child, Mina Harker divorces her husband, who apparently could not cope with her having once been tainted. And not only do these characters in the *League* live on in a way that denies them the narrative closure that their source texts had deemed important to contain the anxieties that they or their stories provoked, they are also freely and playfully combined into an artwork that incorporates hybridity on three levels: those of genre, of media, and of fiction.

The generic hybridity of the *League* series is itself an inheritance from the source material. Many of the works of Victorian fantasy that Moore uses are themselves literary hybrids, a strangely alluring combination of different genres and literary traditions, drawing on Gothic irrationalism and bringing it into conflict with the scientific empiricism of criminal detection, combining monsters that seem to spring from the deepest recesses of the subconscious with the no less mysterious promises of the most advanced science. Tales of exploration turn into fantastic encounters, as in H. Rider Haggard's *She* (1887), and seemingly fantastic occurrences are explained by ratiocination, as in Edgar Allan Poe's 'The Murders in the Rue Morgue', all referenced in the *League*. This inherent generic hybridity is highlighted and considerably enhanced in the *League* series through the combination of innumerable source texts and consequently source genres. The series can be classified as fantastic fiction, since it contains fantastic elements, but it is at the same time comic, horrific, and tragic, and it mixes the available genres so thoroughly that all clear-cut generic distinctions are effectively dissolved. By genre standards, it is monstrous and unnatural, not only from a Victorian perspective, but also from that of the contemporary comics reader, for whom the intrusion of 'literature' (something that is often regarded as alien to comics) is disturbing because of the lack of boundaries.

The *League* series is also a hybrid in respect to its medium, the comic book. The comparatively new medium of comics combines verbal and visual narrative into something entirely original. The basic characteristics of a comic as medium are sequentiality and the interdependent combination of word and image. Both of these make comics a hybrid of existing media. As the most prominent exclusive writer for the comics medium (as opposed to other writers who sometimes also illustrate, such as Frank Miller), Moore has continuously showcased the hybrid nature of comics by destabilising the medial boundaries, most importantly through the inclusion of long text-only or merely sparsely illustrated text portions. Already in *Watchmen* (1986), each chapter closed with longer texts that were all part of the storyworld, such as characters' autobiographic writings or police records. This structure was also applied to the *League* comics. The first volume contains a story entitled 'Allan and the Sundered Veil', a pastiche of fin-de-siècle boys' magazine fiction starring Allan Quatermain and the Time Traveller among others. In the second volume an even more elaborate 'New Traveller's Almanac' redraws geography according to Victorian and other fiction.[5] Finally, in *The Black Dossier*, the text-only, the predominantly image-based, and the proper comic narratives are balanced in such a way as to make any clear medial ascriptions impossible. This book makes recognition of its hybrid nature inevitable, since it is ultimately undecidable whether it is primarily a comic that quotes extensively from a series of textual pastiches, or whether said series is surrounded by a more or less paratextual graphic narrative. Mediality is further highlighted by the use of different types of paper, printing techniques, and the inclusion of 3D-glasses.

Finally, hybridity is structurally performed in the series through the method of fictional crossovers. Fictional crossovers are hardly an invention by Moore and O'Neill, having long been a feature of literature, but the way that they are used in the *League* series arguably constitutes a direct reflection of their more recent history, a history that is closely connected with medial developments in general, and the medium of comics specifically. There are two main ways to conceptualise fictional worlds, ways that either regard them as self-contained or as additive.[6]

---

[5] 'The New Traveller's Almanac' is a 46-page description of the different regions of the world and the cities, rivers, mountains and other features contained therein, but most of the places described only exist in fiction, such as Jonathan Swift's Laputa, or Margaret Cavendish's *Blazing World* (1666). Most of the fiction used for the almanac is Victorian, though.

[6] These are less theoretical postulations in the sense of "storyworlds *are*...", but different ways in which actual authors and readers understand what a storyworld is

The idea of self-contained fictional worlds is that each narrative creates its own distinct and complete storyworld. Different narrative texts might use the same proper names for existents in their storyworld, but they are not identical, according to this view, as they exist in different and self-contained worlds. Thus, Bram Stoker's Dracula is not the same as the character embodied by Bela Lugosi or Christopher Lee, though they share the same name and many properties. This idea is for example apparent in the acceptance that two stories about the 'same' character will contain an event that can, logically speaking, only happen once, such as the character's death. One major problem of this approach, however, is that it presupposes that one can easily establish the beginning and end of each narrative, especially in distinction to bordering narratives. But does each Sherlock Holmes story written by Conan Doyle really constitute a separate fictional world, something that seems highly counterintuitive, though it would solve the problem of inconsistencies between stories?

The idea of additive storyworlds, on the other hand, is that multiple texts can add to the creation of a single storyworld. This conception could be further subdivided into a canonical and an appropriative form. The canonical form privileges original authorship and clearly distinguishes between authors and readers, with only authors being allowed to legitimately add to the storyworld. In its most restricted form, there is only one author, who is usually the original creator of the storyworld (e.g. Conan Doyle as author of the 'canonical' Holmes stories). In the era of story-franchises, the right of authorship can also be conferred on (multiple) authors by a copyright holder such as a publishing company. Such an idea is apparent in attempts of copyright holders to restrict the use of existents from 'their' storyworlds.[7] The appropriative form, what Brewer has called 'imaginative expansion' (Brewer 2005: 2) and Stern an 'economy of abundance' (Stern 1997: 435), on the other hand, takes the position that a fictional world is principally open to additions from every

---

and how it relates to others. They can be deduced from the way that readers and authors think about characters and other existents across different narratives.

[7] The broader term existents is used here, because storyworlds contain more features that can be appropriated than merely characters, such as places (countries, cities, specific buildings), objects (special weapons or technical devices, fictional books like the *Necronomicon*), or even abstract concepts like 'the force'.

reader, who has the right to become an author at any time, a position taken, for example, by writers of fan fiction.[8]

Throughout the history of narrative, these concepts have been in competing use, and their dominance or negligence has been closely tied to the dominant media. Oral storytelling traditions necessarily rely on an additive-appropriative concept of fictional worlds. Oral narratives are constantly being re-told, with inevitable variations that still leave the story's identity and integrity untouched in the minds of the listeners. No matter how often listeners are being told the story of Ulysses, a story whose textual form will vary each time, for example, they will always assume the identity of the character mentioned to be the same. Oral communication is also the mode most conducive to the synthetic and integrative powers of the discourse of myth, where different stories and different versions of stories are constantly being combined into a larger narrative structure. The pantheon of myth is nothing but a monumental collective crossover fiction. This appropriative mode of storytelling is also conducive to Gothic narrative modes in general (where stories like myths and fables often invade the basic storyworld, and where different narrative traditions are recombined, often to produce some monstrous growth) and to neo-Victorian narratives in particular.

With writing, as texts become fixed, the idea of the integrity of fictional worlds gains strength. Individual versions of a story gain authoritative status, becoming canonical. Ulysses starts to look more and more like Homer's Ulysses, and no one else's. The difference between canon and apocrypha is born out of the idea that a written text has an individual author and fixes a meaning, and this pertains to religious dogma just as it does to the properties of a fictional world. Print only strengthened this process, creating a further clear-cut differentiation between authoritative text (the printed text) and non-authoritative text (hand-written marginalia, or the manuscript as a more fluid text of revisions and rewritings), Stern's 'economy of scarcity' (Stern 1997: 435). Individual and original authorship became prominent as books acquired title pages. But print also brought with it a new factor, one working *against* the compartmentalisation of the fictional worlds that it reinforced, and that was the commercialisation of the literary market. A successful oral storyteller would be able to

---

[8] On fan fiction see Hellekson and Busse 2006.

tell his story again and again, with each performance varying from the other, with constant revisions and additions. But though a printed text can of course be re-read, its fixed nature leaves a desideratum for novelty within familiarity. Readers wanted more of the same, creating a demand. This is where the sequel comes to prominence, and with it the idea of a fictional world as economic property. The second part of Cervantes's *Don Quijote* (1615) is maybe the most famous example of an author's attempt to reclaim canonical authority over his own fictional creation. The eighteenth and nineteenth centuries then developed far-reaching copyright laws that instituted the idea of fictional worlds as a property and of a canonical-additive concept of texts.

Still, these fictional worlds were mostly created and added to by single authors, who were also the prime copyright holders, such as Conan Doyle and Haggard with their Holmes and Quatermain stories. It was only in the twentieth century, with the development of the comic book industry, that the property in fictional worlds moved massively from individual authors to corporations, and the idea of the fictional franchise was born. Multiple authors could work on and add to such a franchise – the stories involving Superman or Batman for example – with fictional authority conferred on them by the company they were working for. And since one company often held the rights to more than one franchise (in fact almost all of them were divided between two companies, Marvel and DC Comics), they could start combining these at will. This was the start of the canonical crossover, establishing the fact that characters who were so far supposed to inhabit their own self-contained fictional world were actually part of a larger fictional world, and could consequently interact with each other (as long as they belonged to the same company). Superman and Batman shake hands. For several decades, this type of crossover was the dominant fictional mode of comics narrative and established the concept firmly in the minds of comics readers. The comics market was and still is flooded with stories of superhero teams and a consequent tangling of storylines that easily outrivaled even the most convoluted chivalric romance. This is part of the rich legacy that Moore and O'Neill bring to the appropriative mode of neo-Victorian fiction. Because all neo-Victorian writing that in any way incorporates Victorian fictional existents into a neo-Victorian storyworld adopts the appropriative view of storyworlds, though often in a self-reflexive way, by showing an awareness of the significance of the adaptation process.

The *League* as a neo-Victorian engagement with pre-existent discourses, both fictional and real, employs the established comics concept of crossover fiction and takes it to its logical extreme by creating a crossover of unprecedented expanse. Moore himself has called it a "literary connect-the-dots puzzle" (qtd. Khoury 2003: 182). In his storytelling practice, no fictional world is left as self-contained and all boundaries are dissolved. Its basic construction premise, that *all* of its existents are to be taken from different pre-existing storyworlds, creates an infinitely rich but at the same time highly unstable tapestry. The comic companies that created large-scale crossover fictions always took a lot of care to guarantee 'continuity' among the different fictional properties that they were combining. This meant that nothing could happen in one storyworld that would contradict another. If, for example, a character died in one story, he could not be alive at the same time in another, if they were connected. This provided stability to the existents of all the fictional worlds, though at the cost of narrative freedom and consequence. In the *League* narrative, on the other hand, Moore combines fictional worlds that should be highly exclusionary, making continuity impossible but for extensive rewritings. Thus, Moore appropriates different fictional worlds, but breaches their integrity through invasive rewritings, enriching his own creation with the pre-existing fictional background of the characters and places he uses, but leaving open the question as to which parts of the background stories apply and which do not. Characters like Mina Harker are at the same time the property of Bram Stoker and of Alan Moore; their status is ultimately ambiguous and hybrid. Moore's text thus becomes a space of competing narrative authorities, those of the source texts and his own, and the characters are as much in the grip of power struggles between forces within the fiction, as between their different authors. The reader is left with the task of integrating what he knows of the sources with their use in the *League* narrative, participating in the creation of a hybrid, a monstrosity of fiction both playful and Gothic that thrives on ambivalence and incongruence.

2. Steampunk and Incongruous Technology

This incongruity is reinforced for the contemporary reader by Moore's use of a significant trend in neo-Victorian writings, a trend that is fed by the fantastic and Gothic elements of Victorian literature. Around the year 2000, real history surpassed the timeframe within which late nineteenth- and early twentieth-century science-fictions had imagined their projections, with the consequence that now both the projected and the actual image of a specific time existed in parallel to each other. In 2001, for example, readers could compare the projections made for that year in the movie *2001: A Space Odyssey* with the actual reality of that same year. But while speculative scientific concepts like robots or spaceships could be equally imagined at the turn of the two millennial turns, their specific look would differ depending on the time of their being imagined. The idea of a submarine might bring to mind a similar *concept* in the minds of a Victorian and someone from 2011, but the concept would most certainly take on a very different concrete *shape*. Interestingly, the projections of early science fiction were often already highly visual in nature, as emphasised through illustrations, book or magazine covers, movies or early comics. This meant that their visual style was to some extent fixed within the aesthetics of their time period. We know – at least in part – how the Victorians thought their future – our own time – would look, and we can now compare these visions with our present. This visual double-coding gave rise to a new, often specifically neo-Victorian sub-genre of science fiction called steampunk.[9] Steampunk stories are usually set in a time period which still employs steam power but also contains numerous science fiction elements, such as space flight or robots. With precursors in the 1980s, the genre really gained prominence with William Gibson and Bruce Sterling's 1990 novel *The Difference Engine*, while the term 'steampunk' became established through Paul Di Filippo's *The Steampunk Trilogy*, published in 1995 (see Bowser and Croxall 2010: 13.[10]

Steampunk indicates a use of outdated images of a future as seen from the past, coupled with new speculative projections, a narrative mode that thrives on anachronism and incongruity and

---

[9] Jason B. Jones has demonstrated in his discussion of Moore that the comic book is especially apt for telling steampunk stories (see Jones 2010: 99). For a general introduction to steampunk as a neo-Victorian genre, see Bowser and Croxall 2010.
[10] For more discussions of steampunk, also see Leavenworth's chapter in this volume.

creates visual hybrids. It is especially congenial to neo-Victorian writing because it highlights the incongruence already inherent in the Victorian conflation of primeval Gothic and scientific speculation. In Victorian fantastic fiction, modernity and science constantly clash with the primeval, whether on a global scale, as in H. Rider Haggard's colonial explorations and encounters with 'savages' or in the menace from the East that is Dracula, or on a more individual scale, as in the split personality of Stevenson's Dr. Jekyll and Mr. Hyde, the scientist and the (atavistic) monster. The neo-Victorian steampunk perspective derives much of its appeal from showcasing these contradictions and dissonances, creating an ambiguous setting that combines the period's technical, social, and philosophical restrictions with the unlimited possibilities of science fiction, understanding the Victorian period as mainly one of transition.

As an amalgamation of Victorian fantastic and Gothic literature, the *League* graphic novels are instantly recognisable as steampunk fiction. The introduction to the series is already a playful and ironic use of the steampunk mode as well as a reflection on its significance. The first page opens with an indication of the time and place of the setting, 'Dover, May, 1898.' The reader immediately knows that this is a past setting. During the panels on the first page, the viewpoint is strongly restricted, with the figures only seen partially and the setting not visually identifiable. Two characters meet somewhere close to the sea, and the page ends with one of them saying: "Simply remarkable, the view here, isn't it?" (Moore and O'Neill 2000: 7) This refers to the view that the two characters have from their own vantage point, but the next page (for which one needs to turn the page, thus heightening the element of surprise) gives the utterance an additional meaning, revealing the even more remarkable view that the reader gets, a view showing not only what the characters are looking *at*, but also what they are looking *away from*: the gigantic construction site of the 'Channel Causeway', a monumental bridge that will connect England and France. Of course, such a bridge was never built in reality, though proposals had existed since the mid 1850s (see Nevins 2003: 26).

Moore and O'Neill's comic, however, not only uses such steampunk images for their spectacular value. From the beginning, they are integrated into the larger context of the books' engagement with Victorian values, visions, and Gothic anxieties.[11] The splash page that shows the channel causeway is also the opening of the first chapter, suggestively entitled 'Empire Dreams'. The statue of a British lion can also be seen decorating the bridge, with the hardly less suggestive inscription 'Albion Reach'. And for those who look closely at the image, they can detect a plaque, on which the engineers of the causeway regret to inform the public that its construction will take longer than originally planned – an ironic comment both on the utopian dreams of the Victorian Empire and the actual construction of the channel tunnel in the late twentieth century, with a decidedly Gothic visual perspective of sublime grandeur. In addition, Jason Jones has highlighted in his examination of the image that the seagulls that can be seen flying here will return later in the series, in a similar visual configuration, but with decidedly more Gothic overtones: on the last page of *Volume III: Century*, one of them is carrying away a human eyeball, snatched from the carnage below (Moore and O'Neill 2009: 75).[12]

The anachronistic perspective of steampunk also highlights another feature of Victorian speculative fiction, a feature that becomes so much more pronounced in retrospect. For a reader of the twenty-first century, the Gothic visions of scientific progress of late Victorian literature can be read as intimations of the end of the Victorian period – and it is the hindsight of neo-Victorian re-engagements that increases the prophetic nature of Victorian fantastic imaginations. Morgan Robertson's 1898 novella *Futility, or the Wreck of the Titan*, about the catastrophic sinking of an ocean liner called Titan in the North Atlantic after striking an iceberg, with high casualties resulting from a lack of lifeboats, was just a regular speculative story at the time of publication, while it holds an eerie fascination for those comparing it to the fate of the Titanic in 1914. Moore alludes to *Futility* through the inclusion of a newspaper headline reading "Maiden Voyage of the

---

[11] Jones is rather (too) positive in his denial of "Moore's interest in steampunk aris[ing] from a material critique of (neo-)Victorian ideology" (Jones 2010: 101), as it is worth noting how Moore consistently appropriates the Victorian language of racism and misogyny for satirical and critical purposes, or for the devastating 'happy end' of the second volume.

[12] See Jones 2010: 115-116. In an interesting aside, the movie adaptation has made the transience of (British) empire all too obvious by including the character of the American Tom Sawyer, who is explicitly asked by Allan Quatermain to take over the responsibility for the world (see Frenk and Krug 2009).

Titan. Ghastly Business" on one of the panels (Moore and O'Neill 2000: 115). This is one of the major shifts from the Victorian to the neo-Victorian engagement with speculation: while the Victorian imagination is looking into the future and at things yet to come, the neo-Victorian return to these imaginations constantly reads them as Gothic intimations of endings, because the neo-Victorian inevitably includes a knowledge of future happenings and consequences. Moore had already employed this neo-Victorian shift in perspective to great effect and in a very explicit way in *From Hell*. There, he contextualised the time of the Ripper murders within worldwide events that bear potentially global consequences, most obviously in the depiction of what is apparently the conception of Adolf Hitler in August 1888. Moore also gives his character Sir William Gull, who is depicted as the murderer, visions of the twentieth century during his murders that can readily be recognised as accurate by twentieth-century readers. And after the final murder, he has Gull say: "It is beginning, Netley. Only just beginning. For better or worse, the twentieth century. I have delivered it" (Moore and Campbell 2009: Ch. Ten, 33). The accuracy of Gull's visions is highly uncanny and is much more conducive to the comic's Gothic effect than the depiction of the murders. Thus it is a true instance of the neo-Victorian Gothic: from a Victorian perspective, the visions are merely an element of the fantastic, but with the hindsight of the neo-Victorian perspective, they are as unexplainable as they are undeniable.

The *League* series intensifies this neo-Victorian Gothic effect by making the uncanny sense of historical repetition between British imperial atrocities and those of later post-imperial nation states a central structural and thematic point. Just as in *From Hell*, in the *League* series the end of the Victorian era – and by implication the beginning of modernity – is marked by a new quality of violence, a type of violence that is in this case made possible through technological advances. In the first volume this is symbolised among other things by Captain Nemo's automatic gun, employed in the league's final battle against Moriarty and his army. Confronted with a mass of enemies, Nemo calmly draws an automatic harpoon gun, advises everybody to "get down", and starts shooting. The ensuing graphically rendered carnage, as dozens of soldiers are killed almost instantly, provokes Mina to cry: "D-dear gracious God! That inhuman mechanism! I-it's... it's so unsporting!" (Moore and O'Neill 2000:

140), echoing a conventional Victorian attitude towards warfare that was quickly becoming anachronistic in 1898. Nemo's weapon is clearly modelled on the Maxim gun, the first self-powered machine gun that had been invented in 1884 and was repeatedly used by British colonial forces at the end of the nineteenth century, for example during the First Matabele War in Rhodesia (1893-1894). In the same year that the events of *Volume I* and *II* occur, Hilaire Belloq wrote his famous couplet: "Whatever happens, we have got / The Maxim gun, and they have not" (Belloq 1898: 41). This rift between the Victorian conception of a 'fair play' war and the grim reality of modern warfare's monstrosities was largely due to a lack of objective visual information on actual wars. Though they surely knew of the existence and effect of weapons like the Maxim or the Gatling gun,[13] the British public of 1898 was 'spared' the very ugly image that Mina has to watch in the comic, that of people being killed indiscriminately and en masse by superior firepower. It is at this point in the comic that the different visual discourses that are being played off against each other enter into a disruptive conflict by merging under the gaze of the characters. Just like William Gull during his murders, Mina and Quatermain get a glimpse of the future to come as the visual depiction of violence turns to an intensity that only late twentieth-century comics can deliver. What to the neo-Victorian perspective constitutes a simultaneous foreshadowing and retrospective witness-bearing of the inevitable – the historical monster waiting in the form of the twentieth century – is something Mina would prefer to suppress by ignoring it altogether: "I... I don't wish to witness this" (Moore and O'Neill 2000: 141).

3. Shadowboxing: Controlling the Monster

As the use of this gun with its implicit geopolitical meaning shows, the *League* narrative constantly re-contextualises Gothic monstrosity into larger social and political frameworks. Most obviously, the individual protagonists are not left to act independently and unrestrained as in their source texts, but are gathered together in a league that is organised and controlled by a government institution, an alliance that is unstable and ambiguous from the beginning, and that is

---

[13] In *King Solomon's Mines*, one of Quatermain's companions, when faced with an overwhelming multitude of African enemies armed with spears, says: "Oh, for a Gatling! [...] I would clear that plain in twenty minutes" (Haggard 2009: 145).

turned on its head both in *Volume I* and *II*. In direct contrast to the superhero teams that they allude to, all of the league's participants lack the total conviction in the rightfulness of the 'bigger cause' they are fighting for. Instead, we find one of the typical Gothic elements where individuals are being caught up in ungraspable power structures and looming conspiracies. In the same sense, the league members are highly suspicious about their shadowy employers, and their suspicions are proven justified time and again. This complicated interplay between the heroic and the monstrous, between the individual and society, is at the core of the series' neo-Victorian engagement with the Gothic and its involvement with discourses of power. Moore and O'Neill's narrative investigates these interconnections by tapping into a Gothic literary tradition that constantly opposes isolation and community and by embedding the characters from the individual source texts into larger structures of power of Moore's own creation.

The antagonism between individual and society is very much at the core of the Gothic experience. The effect of the monstrous is heightened by isolation. On the one hand, the monster is something that needs to be encountered alone to be truly frightful, but the monstrous is also dependent on the monster's isolation – its exclusion and disconnection from society and humanity. The proper exorcism to the Gothic threat of otherness, on the other hand, is an appeal to community. Two examples from fictions used in the *League* series can serve to show this. Dracula is most threatening when he is able to isolate his victims, such as with Jonathan Harker at the beginning of the novel and Lucy and Mina later on. His major threat is a breach of personal enclosure, an entry into the inner circle of an individual beyond the protection of community, symbolised by his ability to turn into fog and thereby to penetrate through the smallest chinks, and, of course, through his bite, the ultimate invasion of the private self. But the table is decidedly turned as soon as his opponents start to pool their resources and to form a group that symbolises the power of Western civilisation. There is social class and financial power in Lord Godalming, English law and justice in Jonathan Harker, scientific knowledge in Dr. Seward and Professor Van Helsing, and manly courage and pugnacity in the American Quincey Morris, all combined with a faith in the Christian god (see Botting 1996: 152-153 and Malchow 1996: 165-166). After being cut off from his own resources (his money, his resting places, and his helpers, both alive and undead), Dracula, the foreign contagion, is effectively isolated and no match anymore for the community he has tried to infiltrate. His only recourse is to flee the country and to return to his place of origin. At this point, the hunter turns into the hunted.

The same thing happens in *The Invisible Man*, where the titular speculative conceit can be read as a parable of isolation. It is the invisibility that alienates the protagonist completely from his peers, as they can and will not recognise him as a fellow human being anymore. Like Dracula, the invisible man casts no shadow. It takes a while for Griffin to accept this fact,[14] but his consequent attempts to find a 'confederate' only result in betrayal and further isolation. Indeed, it is the disclosure of his nature to his former teacher Dr. Kemp that proves his ultimate downfall, as from that moment he turns from the state of 'unseen/unknown/unmarked, because invisible' to that of 'marked/alienated *as* invisible'. And while no individual is safe from Griffin, he becomes increasingly vulnerable the more people he comes up against.[15] In the end, Griffin is beaten to death by a mob.

Both examples show how community expels Gothic otherness by re-defining the other as non-human, therefore legitimising its own functional inhumanity.[16] This discourse of contamination from without is consistent with contemporary racist, sexist or nationalist stereotypes and prejudices, the idea of the superiority of one's identity that leads, among other things, to justifications of colonialism and

---

[14] "I made a mistake, Kemp, a huge mistake, in carrying this thing through alone. I have wasted strength, time, opportunities. Alone – it is wonderful how little a man can do alone! To rob a little, to hurt a little, and there is the end. [...] What I want, Kemp, is a goal-keeper, a helper, and a hiding-place, an arrangement whereby I can sleep and eat and rest in peace, and unsuspected. I must have a confederate. With a confederate, with food and rest – a thousand things are possible" (Wells 2005: 113).

[15] He is terrifying in the scenes in which he is encountered by a single person, but the scenes in which he has to fight against or flee from a group of people easily turn into a gruesome kind of slapstick comedy at his expense. At the end of the novel, when his true nature is detected, he is suddenly opposed by a community that is changed from single individuals into an organised force with a common goal. Again, the alienated social element turns from hunter to hunted, as the community completely expels him, a dehumanisation (note the objection against) exemplified in an exchange between Dr. Kemp and Adye, the chief of the local police, who objects against the unsporting behaviour suggested by Adye (see Wells 2005: 117-118).

[16] While the crowd is here understood as representing the 'moral majority' of society, of which the reader considers himself a part, the Victorian period is also known for turning the crowd (a crowd constituted by social others) itself into a source of Gothic anxiety. See Sussman 1999: 250-251 on Victorian fears about working class mobs.

imperialism. From this perspective, the monstrous other is something that can and needs to be expelled, subdued, controlled, or eradicated. The monster must be found out – recognised as other – hunted down and killed, until purity is regained. This is echoed repeatedly in the *League* series, where to the higher authorities ends always seem to justify means. But while such a position is repeatedly being shown and voiced in the narrative, it is at the same time questioned through an appeal to a second, deeper, and ultimately unsolvable source of Gothic anxiety, namely of the otherness of the self.

While the conventional conception of the Gothic other maintained a clear distinction between self and other, creating the stereotypical fear of tainted purity, of a contamination from outside through contact with the other, another notion lurked somewhat deeper in the shadows of the Victorian Gothic. This was the suspicion that expelling the other would not prove easy, since it might actually be a part of the self (see Brantlinger 2009: 48 and Punter 1980: 241). In this sense, Dracula does not cast a reflection in the mirror, because he *is* the mirror. The story of Frankenstein and his creation is one of the founding myths in Gothic literature, depicting the creation of the monstrous other as a personal birth, and especially the prominent figure of the over-reaching scientist in Victorian fiction, from Griffin to Jekyll and Moreau, made this notion a common one. Personal identity becomes dual and unstable, prototypically in Jekyll and Hyde, and in *The Island of Dr. Moreau* (1896), the nature of humanity itself is questioned, with a breaching of the boundaries between man and animal resulting in an ambivalence towards all humans that echoes Swift's fourth book of *Gulliver's Travels* (1726).[17] One should not forget the fact that, though Dracula is able physically to enter even a locked house almost unhindered, he can only do so after he has been invited by one of the inmates. The key to opening, and hence the transgression of boundaries, is to be found within.[18] This unease lies at the core of the *League*'s neo-Victorian critique of essentialist conceptions of otherness, both Victorian and contemporary, and is the source of its own Gothic effect. While these conceptions are being

---

[17] In the *League* narrative, Gulliver is the leader of an earlier eighteenth-century league.
[18] Stoker rather downplays this element in his novel, having his villain use different ruses to coax invitations, but it remains as a trace of the prime unease about the Gothic.

cited and even emphasised wherever they are found in the source material, they are integrated into an artwork that celebrates hybridity on so many levels and to such an extent that no clearly delineable self is left. It thus downplays Victorian fears of miscegenation and anxieties about purity, while thoroughly criticising the very idea of purity, or of an unquestionable 'heroic' identity.

An example of this is the way that Wells's novel *The Island of Dr. Moreau* is incorporated into the comic. After the beginning of the Martian invasion, Mina and Quatermain are sent to a forest where Dr. Moreau (like many other characters also not dead as in the original story) has been relocated from his island to continue his experiments in creating hybrids between different animals and humans. The original horror experienced by the novel's narrator Prendick in his encounter with the animal-human creatures becomes comical when echoed by Mina and Quatermain in the graphic novel. For what they encounter are recognisable visual depictions of anthropomorphised animals from the period's children's literature, such as Rupert Bear, Beatrix Potter's Peter Rabbit, or Mr. Toad from *The Wind in the Willows* (1908). The real horror lies instead in something the protagonists are not even aware of, namely the hybrid disease hidden away in a box that they are carrying back to London to be used indiscriminately against Martians and humans alike.[19]

The *League* series deals with a number of Victorian heroes and Victorian monsters, and as the epigraph from the first volume indicates, the two are frequently confused. Like much else in the comic, this confusion is doubled between the Victorian and the neo-Victorian perspective. What is clearly seen as monstrous and repulsive through Victorian eyes gets re-evaluated through Moore's narrative and O'Neill's depiction, while some of the heroic norms of Victorian society emerge as truly monstrous. What both hero and monster have in common is that their definition is related to power: the hero is power controlled by the norms of those who confer the ascription of

---

[19] Though not directly referenced by Moore, the use of biological warfare against an 'alien' invading army is an uncanny echo of Matthew Phipps Shiel's 1898 novel *The Yellow Danger*, in which a Japanese-Chinese army is overcome by infecting prisoners of war with cholera and then sending them back, causing some 150 million deaths. Moore was definitively aware of Shiel, since he references his novel *The Purple Cloud* (1901) in the second volume (see Moore and O'Neill 2003: 206 and Nevins 2004: 204).

hero and monster, while the monster is power uncontrolled. In the *League* series, it is the Empire – personified by Campion Bond (an ancestor of 007 of Moore's invention[20]) – that is obsessed with gaining and controlling power, the more monstrous the better, always trying to turn monsters into heroes in its service. Again, Mina's Victorian attitude of propriety (where the monstrous is something that needs to be sanitised away) jars with the power hunger that drives the Empire into modernity. After they have captured the truly monstrous Mr. Hyde, she comments: "Jekyll's being taken from us for some tests. It's hoped that sedatives might ease his strange condition..."; to which Nemo, always more cynical and prescient, answers: "...or control it. Mr. Bond is no philanthropist, I fear. / I fear he collects monsters" (Moore and O'Neill 2000: 41). As he says this last sentence, Nemo is standing in front of a very large tapestry depicting the Hindu goddess of destruction, Kali.

4. Conclusion

The true monster in the *League* stories is Empire, the mistaken dream of endlessly accumulating and successfully controlling power, only seemingly built on Victorian values of decency, propriety and sportsmanship and, most importantly, on the assurance of an untainted and justified identity, but in reality marred by numerous exclusionary discourses that mark an other to be outcast as inferior or monstrous – racial, social, sexual – while suppressing the Gothic knowledge that the other is always already contained in the self. This is the specific shift from one type of Victorian to neo-Victorian anxieties,[21] from the source material used by Moore and O'Neill to their own narrative: where the Victorian anxieties are mostly concerned with a *loss* of power, with a shift of power from oneself (an identity grounded in sex, race, class, or nationality) to the other, the neo-Victorian perspective highlights the deeper Gothic knowledge that there *is* no distinction between self and monstrous other, and that it is the

---

[20] Moore's negative take on James Bond is intensified in *Black Dossier*, where Bond appears rather as a rapist than the stereotypical womanizer (see Moore and O'Neill 2007: 17-18).

[21] Of course, one should not take Moore to intend a criticism of Victorianism in its entirety. Especially through the selection of his source material, he is concentrating on the anxieties described here, which leaves the question of dissenting voices from within the Victorian period open.

possession of power itself that ultimately renders its possessor monstrous. It is power that taints and corrupts and that brings into existence its monstrous other. Here Moore incorporates one of the central but commonly suppressed lessons of the superhero narrative: it is the superhero's own power that creates the demand for a counterforce, and therefore the super-villain. In the same sense, every Empire needs a demonic other to secure the integrity of its identity and to hide its own inherent monstrosity. This is as true for the British empire of Victorian times as it is for the sole remaining superpower at the end of the twentieth century, when Moore starts to write the *League* books.[22] In the first volume, this is made obvious by the revelation that the mysterious 'M', the head of British security who instigated the gathering of the league, is not Sherlock Holmes's brother Mycroft, but his nemesis, Professor Moriarty. A flashback reveals that Moriarty did not die at the Reichenbach falls, either, but was rescued by Campion Bond, both already part of the secret service. Wounded, Moriarty reflects on Holmes's Victorian inability to understand the identity of the self and its monstrous other: "Strange. He thought me... an enemy... of the state... never reasoning... that it might suit the state... to create... its own enemy." / "Shadowboxing, Bond. We're all just... shadowboxing" (Moore and O'Neill 2000: 109).

While Hyde's monstrous ferocity and Nemo's deadly weapons are the most pronounced instances of ambivalently controlled monstrosity in the first volume, the second still goes a step further, in having Dr. Moreau develop a hybrid disease made of anthrax and streptococcus to be used as a biological weapon. In another subtle rewriting, the Martians do not die of the common cold, as in Wells's novel, but of this manufactured bacterium, together with countless humans who will later be propagandistically declared victims of the Martians. To the terror of the remaining members of the league, a final threshold has been crossed; the terrible wars of the twentieth century are at hand. Throughout the volume, there is a subtle shift in the uniforms that the British troops are wearing, from those typical of the Victorian era to ones more reminiscent of World War I, gradually leading the reader from Victorian to neo-Victorian Gothic.

---

[22] It is hardly a coincidence that the questioning of the superhero myth of purely good against an ever-present (and external) evil other, begun in the late eighties, notably by Moore himself, finds its peak in the nineties.

Bibliography

Belloq, Hilaire. 1898. *The Modern Traveller*. London: Edward Arnold.
Botting, Fred. 1996. *Gothic*. London: Routledge.
Bowser, Rachel A., and Brian Croxall. 2010. 'Introduction: Industrial Evolution', *Neo-Victorian Studies* 3(1), Special Issue: *Steampunk, Science, and (Neo)Victorian Technologies*: 1-45.
Brantlinger, Patrick. 2009. *Victorian Literature and Postcolonial Studies*. Edinburgh: Edinburgh University Press.
Brewer, David A. 2005. *The Afterlife of Character, 1726-1825*. Philadelphia: University of Pennsylvania Press.
Duda, Heather L. 2008. *The Monster Hunter in Modern Popular Culture*. Jefferson: McFarland.
Ferguson, Christine. 2009. 'Steam Punk and the Visualization of the Victorian: Teaching Alan Moore's *The League of Extraordinary Gentlemen* and *From Hell*', in Tabachnick, Stephen Ely (ed.) *Teaching the Graphic Novel*. New York: The Modern Language Association of America: 200-207.
Frenk, Joachim and Christian Krug. 2009. 'Handovers of Empire: Transatlantic Transmissions in Popular Culture', in Säckel, Sarah, Walter Göbel and Noha Hamdy (eds.), *Semiotic Encounters: Text, Image and Trans-Nation*. Amsterdam: Rodopi: 191-208.
Haggard, H. Rider. 2009. *King Solomon's Mines & Allan Quatermain* [1885, 1887]. Ware: Wordsworth.
Heilmann, Ann and Mark Llewellyn. 2010. *Neo-Victorianism. The Victorians in the Twenty-First Century, 1999-2009*. Houndmills, Basingstoke: Palgrave Macmillan.
Hellekson, Karen, and Kristina Busse. 2006. *Fan Fiction and Fan Communities in the Age of the Internet: New Essays*. Jefferson: McFarland.
Jones, Jason B. 2010. 'Betrayed by Time: Steampunk and the Neo-Victorian in Alan Moore's *Lost Girls* and *The League of Extraordinary Gentlemen*', *Neo-Victorian Studies* 3(1), Special Issue: *Steampunk, Science, and (Neo)Victorian Technologies*: 99-126.
Khoury, George (ed.). 2003. *The Extraordinary Works of Alan Moore*. Raleigh: Tomorrows.
Knight, Stephen. 1976. *Jack the Ripper: The Final Solution*. London: George G. Harrap & Co.
Malchow, Howard. 1996. *Gothic Images of Race in Nineteenth-Century Britain*. Stanford: Stanford University Press.
Moore, Alan, and Eddie Campbell. 2009. *From Hell: Being a Melodrama in Sixteen Parts* [1999, serialised 1991-1996 in *Taboo*]. Marietta, Georgia: Top Shelf.
Moore, Alan, and Kevin O'Neill. 2000. *The League of Extraordinary Gentlemen: Volume I*. La Jolla, California: America's Best Comics.
—, and Kevin O'Neill. 2003. *The League of Extraordinary Gentlemen: Volume II*. La Jolla, California: America's Best Comics.
—, and Kevin O'Neill. 2007. *The League of Extraordinary Gentlemen: Black Dossier*. La Jolla, California: America's Best Comics.
—, and Kevin O'Neill. 2009. *The League of Extraordinary Gentlemen, Volume III: Century*. Marietta, Georgia: Top Shelf.

Nevins, Jess. 2003. *Heroes and Monsters: The Unofficial Companion to* The League of Extraordinary Gentlemen. Austin: Monkeybrain.
—, 2004. *A Blazing World. The Unofficial Companion to* The League of Extraordinary Gentlemen, *Volume Two*. Austin: Monkeybrain.
—, 2008. *Impossible Territories. The Unofficial Companion to* The League of Extraordinary Gentlemen: The Black Dossier. Austin: Monkeybrain.
Perschon, Mike. 2010. 'Steam Wars', *Neo-Victorian Studies* 3(1), Special Issue: *Steampunk, Science, and (Neo)Victorian Technologies*: 127-166.
Pietrzak-Franger, Monika. 2009/2010. 'Envisioning the Ripper's Visions: Adapting Myth in Alan Moore and Eddie Campbell's *From Hell*', *Neo-Victorian Studies* 2(2) (Winter), Special Issue: *Adapting the Nineteenth Century: Revisiting, Revising and Rewriting the Past*: 157-185.
Pulham, Patricia. 2010. 'Mapping Histories: The Golem and the Serial Killer in *White Chappell, Scarlet Tracings* and *Don Leno and the Limehouse Golem*', in Arias, Rosario, and Patricia Pulham (eds.), *Haunting and Spectrality in Neo-Victorian Fiction: Possessing the Past*. Basingstoke: Palgrave Macmillan: 157-179.
Punter, David. 1980. *The Literature of Terror: A History of Gothic Fictions from 1765 to the Present Day*. London: Longman.
Schmitt, Cannon. 1997. *Alien Nation: Nineteenth-Century Gothic Fictions and English Nationality*. Philadelphia: University of Pennsylvania Press.
Seshagiri, Urmila. 2006. 'Modernity's (Yellow) Perils: Dr. Fu-Manchu and English Race Paranoia', *Cultural Critique* 62 (Winter): 162-194.
Sinclair, Iain. 2004. *White Chappell, Scarlet Tracings*. London: Vintage.
Stern, Simon. 1997. '*Tom Jones* and the Economies of Copyright', *Eighteenth-Century Fiction* 9: 429-444.
Sussman, Herbert. 1999. 'Industrial', in Tucker, Herbert F. (ed.), *A Companion to Victorian Literature and Culture*. Oxford: Blackwell: 244-257.
Wells, H. G. 2005. *The Invisible Man* [1897]. New York: Bantam Dell.
Young, Robert. 1995. *Colonial Desire. Hybridity in Theory, Culture, and Race*. London: Routledge.

A Bodily Metaphorics of Unsettlement: Leora Farber's *Dis-Location / Re- Location* as Neo-Victorian Gothic

Jeanne Ellis

Abstract:
In *Dis-Location / Re-Location*, the South African artist Leora Farber stages the (re)fashioning of a post-apartheid white, female subjectivity rooted in colonial settlement and Jewish diaspora as a gothic horror story of painful metamorphosis through self-inflicted wounding, implantation and hybridisation. At the centre of this performance of a bodily metaphorics of unsettlement is the doubled self of artist and Victorian settler foremother merged into the neo-Victorian composite protagonist Leora-Bertha. In a series of visual narratives, this uncanny figure embodies the sense of (un)belonging and in-betweenness that troubles post-apartheid settler subjectivities that continue to be haunted by the (post)colonial past.

Keywords: *Dis-Location / Re-Location*, Leora Farber, Bertha Marks, metaphorics of unsettlement, Neo-Victorian Gothic, Postcolonial Gothic, colonialism, South Africa, the uncanny.

*****

In the post-1994 period of transition to democracy, South African identities and histories were re-constructed and re-invented under the rubric of the utopian metaphor of the 'rainbow nation' inscribed by Archbishop Desmond Tutu in his Foreword to the Truth and Reconciliation Commission's Final Report. Forming part of the ameliorative discourses of reconciliation and 'nation building', the metaphor invoked a new state of racial harmony which relied on "black and white together [...] to close the chapter on our past".[1] The

---

[1] The Truth and Reconciliation Commission's Final Report (1998) can be found on-line at: http://www.polity.org.za/govdocs/commissions/1998/trc/index.htm. My quotations are from section 1.1 par. 93.

imperative to move forward together as one nation was at that point indisputably urgent, but it also had embedded within it the temptation to forget or repress the horrors and complicities of "our past" – an entanglement of the histories of apartheid with those of colonial settlement (Dutch and English), interspersed with the histories of various diasporas, slavery and indentured labour. Here, with the necessary call for 'closure' on the past, the uncanny obtrudes at the threshold to the new nation to trouble its guiding metaphor, which implicitly references the biblical covenant after the flood, because, as Nicholas Royle reminds us, "the beginning is already haunted" (Royle 2003: 1). For South Africans with a settler colonial genealogy, this haunting continues to accrue to questions of home(land) and (un)belonging, raising the restless spectres of that other originary moment of arrival and settlement, and its consequent displacements and erasures. In Leora Farber's 2007-2008 national travelling exhibition *Dis-Location / Re-Location* (an installation comprising photographic and video work and sculpture), these anxieties and desires are performed in a bodily metaphorics of unsettlement that appropriates and reconfigures the metaphorics of transcendence and rebirth that underpins the legend of the 'rainbow nation'.

By staging "the coming into being" of a post-apartheid white female subjectivity as a process of bodily transformation through "the horror of self-violation", Farber's performance activates the Gothic at the point where postcolonial and neo-Victorian concerns intersect in the trope of hybridity (Farber 2005: 321, 320).[2] Her preoccupation with hybrid identity within the work – enacted as the grafting of plant material into the already uncannily merged body of artist and Victorian settler foremother – is thus mirrored by the hybrid nature of the work itself. This "generic and intertextual hybridity" both appropriates and exceeds what U.C. Knoepflmacher describes as the "blended forms and discursive mixtures" that "incarnated" Victorian writers' interest in hybridity as a subject, and in the Darwinian science that informed it (Knoepflmacher 2010: 3). In its simultaneous invocation of Victorian anxieties about racial purity, miscegenation

---

[2] Distinguishing her work from that of Australian artist Stelarc, Farber explains that "[i]n the series, the graft and its resulting hybrid formations are simulacra – illusionistic re-creations of a metaphorical process created through artistic make-up techniques and materials. Similarly, physical/psychical pain is visually evoked not experienced" (Farber 2005: 325).

and Englishness triggered by the colonial project as coincident with post-apartheid white anxieties about being South African, *Dis-Location / Re-Location* exemplifies Christian Gutleben's definition of neo-Victorianism, in his chapter in this volume and elsewhere, as "an example of postmodernism which systematically hybridises the traditions, genres or works of the past with the contemporary aesthetic and ideological perspective" (this volume: 322; Gutleben 2011: 1).

In the series of photographic stills and video footage of Farber's performances of the three central narratives of *Dis-Location / Re-Location* ('A Room of Her Own', 'The Ties that Bind Her' and 'Aloerosa'), the artist's body, like the Gothic haunted house or body possessed, plays host to or reincarnates its Victorian spectral ancestor in the composite persona of the protagonist, Leora-Bertha. Farber employs this figure in which past and present are irrevocably intertwined to embody the post-apartheid intensification of settler anxieties about the legitimacy of inheritance and ownership, and hence genealogy, and the debts consequent on historical crimes – fears that inform the Gothic's concern with transgenerational haunting (see Castricano 2001: 16; Edwards 2005: xxix). Here, the question of what can be legitimately owned and safely disowned, and what then consequently owed and to whom in expiation or affiliation, shadows Farber's attempts as "a white, middle-class Jewish female of British descent [...] to 'renegotiate' a sense of South African identity" (Farber 2005: 320). Simultaneously, this requires her "to negotiate a sense of being 'African' within a postcolonial environment", given her "feelings of 'displacement' in relation to Johannesburg" and her "identification with [...] South African British colonial history and its current personal and public residues of identity construction" (Farber 2005: 322, 318).

By "[u]sing [her] body as a metonym for [herself] and Bertha Guttman" (Farber 2006: 5), wife of nineteenth-century South African mining magnate and entrepreneur Sammy Marks, Farber initiates a proliferation of allusions and doubles, couplings and becomings, transformations and decompositions played out by and on the body of the protagonist. In its complex hybridity, this Gothic neo-Victorian figure instantiates the "slippage between the central character and the text, between a physical body and the textual corpus" that Ann Heilmann and Mark Llewellyn see in neo-Victorianism's exploration of "the inscription and textuality of the desire to repossess the

Victorian" (Heilmann and Llewellyn 2010: 108). The ambivalent to-and-fro between present and past, here and there, which constitutes the in-between (*dis-* / *re-*)location of the postcolonial settler subject's sense of place and identity is configured by Farber in the fantasy of hybridity enacted by Leora-Bertha as an enfleshment of the metaphor of rootedness. A commonplace in expressions of belonging, this metaphor is still more insidiously present in settler-colonial and nationalist discourses, and also, more recently, in claims to settler indigeneity. Unlike the certitudes that such claims to belonging imply – since to *lay claim* has embedded within it always the risk of clamouring (from the root *clamare*) for the acknowledgement of rights and ownership, and the staking out of territory, the assertion of entitlement – Farber's Postcolonial Neo-Victorian Gothic performs a bodily metaphorics of *un*settlement that invokes the uncanny shifts in meaning of the word *heimlich* circulating in and among the composites 'homeland', 'motherland' and 'homesick'. Her recovery of an unsettled settler foremother, through whom to make sense of her own post-1994 unsettledness, is a gesture similar to the "recovery of a lost or hidden maternal origin" that Jerrold E. Hogle identifies as a Gothic motif in which "a patriarchal lineage and house turns out to be explicitly dependent on and rooted in the unpredictable possibilities of a forgotten, but finally uncovered, womanhood" (Hogle 2002b: 10).

Translated to the South African settler postcolonial context that Leora-Bertha inhabits, however, the metaphor of rootedness implicit in Hogle's description becomes explicitly implicated in what Germaine Greer, writing about her troubled relationship with Australia, her country of origin, describes as "the pain of unbelonging" (Greer qtd. Collingwood-Whittick 2007b: xiv). Greer defines it as "the kind of unremitting and inadmissible psychic pain" felt by white Australians of European descent, which must always be "lesser" and "salutary" when set against the "unbearable anguish" suffered by the Aboriginal peoples who had been "driven out of [their] spiritual landscape" (Greer qtd. Collingwood-Whittick 2007b: xi). Whereas in Australia, Canada and Aotearoa/New Zealand an "independent" and "triumphant" white settler society must negotiate postcolonial identities in relation to and with both marginalised indigenous populations and diverse immigrant populations (Ahluwalia 2001: 65), in post-apartheid South Africa a white minority of largely British and Dutch descent has lost political power but largely retained immense economic power through business and land ownership. As beneficiaries of apartheid, those who have stayed in the country share with other postcolonial white settler subjects what Pal Ahluwalia identifies as the "dual burden" of recovering "their own narratives" and simultaneously acknowledging "that they have blocked the narratives of the indigenous populations which they have rendered invisible" (Ahluwalia 2001: 69).

Writing on the Canadian Postcolonial Gothic, Cynthia Sugars and Gerry Turcotte point out that the pairing of the "tools of the Gothic [...] with the language of the postcolonial in order to articulate and interrogate national identity constructs [...] is unsurprising", because the Gothic "negotiates both internal and external disquiet" and "both enacts and thematizes ambivalence" (Sugars and Turcotte 2009b: xv), a word that recurs in Farber's writing and interviews on the exhibition. Neither does it surprise that it is the spectre of Victorian colonial expansionism that haunts many postcolonial texts, either in a revisionary drive to 'write back' to the literary and historical canon and to give voice to the silenced colonised, or, as is the case with Farber's visual narratives, in an attempt to negotiate the entanglement with colonial settler histories that persists as both identification and disavowal. The latter, often in the guise of the neo-Victorian novel, frequently resembles the first in recuperating marginal figures and revealing hidden histories. In *Jack Maggs* (1997), his revision of Charles Dickens's *Great Expectations* (1860-61), for example, Peter Carey recuperates Magwich, a criminal transported to the Australian penal colony, not only as a fictional character whose story deserves to be told, but as a settler ancestor. The personalised nature of this reinvention of the Victorian fictional character is apparent from an interview in which Carey challenges Dickens's portrayal of Magwich as follows: "Dickens encourages us to think of him as the 'other,' but this was my ancestor, he was not 'other.' I wanted to reinvent him, to possess him, to act as his advocate" (Carey n.d.: 2). The double work of what Dana Shiller describes as neo-Victorian fiction's "essentially revisionist impulse" is evident in Carey's aim "to reconstruct the past by questioning the certitudes of our historical knowledge", which also, by "emphasiz[ing] events that are usually left out of histories [...] manage[s] to preserve and celebrate the Victorian past" (Shiller 1997: 541).

Farber's similar recovery of a settler ancestor, Bertha Marks, is perhaps more burdened with the weight of ambivalence accruing to an historical, as opposed to Carey's fictional, character. In sharp contrast to the disreputable though essentially well-intentioned rogue in both Dickens's and Carey's fictions, the historical Bertha Marks was a middle-class Anglo-Jewish woman brought to South Africa in 1885 as the young wife of Sammy Marks. Marks, a Lithuanian Jew who had come to South Africa via England in 1868, worked his way up from peddling to build an extraordinary business empire which benefited from his alliance with the Boer President Paul Kruger. For most of her married life, Bertha lived at Zwartkoppies, the Highveld property her husband had developed from an old run-down farmhouse to the equivalent of an English country estate. However, her frequent trips to their holiday home at Muizenberg on the Cape coast and sojourns abroad were often a bone of contention between husband and wife, as their correspondence shows, because of Bertha's tendency to extend these visits indefinitely. One is tempted to read Bertha's excursions as an expression of resistance to the landlocked existence at Zwartkoppies, where the domestic demands of raising eight children and hosting Sammy's Sunday lunches for up to forty guests at a time must have been exhausting, in spite of the army of servants they employed, another cause for Sammy's grumbling.[3]

In choosing Bertha Marks as settler foremother, Farber traces a female genealogy based on Anglo-Jewish affiliation, which allows her to return to a point of colonial origin configured as a site of complexity and hybridity. This act of feminist recovery that is often also prevalent in neo-Victorian revisionism follows through on Virginia Woolf's claim that women should "think back" through their foremothers in *A Room of One's Own* (Woolf 1998: 99), a text Farber appropriates for the once-off performance artwork 'A Room of Her Own' with which she launched the exhibition in 2006.[4] In an

---

[3] I rely throughout on Richard Mendelsohn's fascinating account of Bertha Marks and her marriage to Samuel Marks in 'The Gilded Cage: Bertha Marks at Zwartkoppies' (Mendelsohn 2008: 27-39).
[4] Farber launched the travelling exhibition of works produced during a three-year collaborative project with the fashion-design team Strangelove (Carlo Gibson and Siemek Pater) at The Premises Gallery, Johannesburg. The exhibition travelled to six South African national galleries, "chosen for their neocolonial associations" (Farber 2005: 326), and it had a clear didactic purpose in the educational programme and

interview with Sandra Klopper, Farber speaks about "a deep empathy with" Bertha, whom she describes as "an historically marginalised figure" whose "story, one of colonial dis-location and re-location, loneliness, alienation and attempts to transcend these delimitations struck a chord in [her]" (Farber qtd. Klopper 2008: 16, 15). Farber furthermore notes the "paucity of information on Bertha", considering her husband's "well-documented" life, which, she explains, triggered her curiosity and turned Bertha into "an enigmatic figure" for her (Farber qtd. Klopper 2008: 16). Farber's identification of Bertha as "historically marginalised" is implicitly based on the gender politics of the time that relegated her to the silenced realm of the domestic in contrast to the recorded public life of her husband. As Mark Llewellyn points out, neo-Victorian texts "illustrate conflict and difference through their very act of undermining the stability of a presumed hegemonic historical narrative" (Llewellyn 2008: 165), and here, as in other feminist inflected neo-Victorian revisions of colonial history, it is the archive of the domestic, often in the form of letters and journals, that provides a counter narrative. Margaret Atwood, for example, similarly turns to the archive of journals and letters written by Canadian settler pioneer Susanna Moodie, in the first instance to engage in a critical revision of this historical figure in a collection of poetry, *The Journals of Susanna Moodie* (1970), and, in the second, to recover the subaltern voice of Irish servant Grace Marks in the neo-Victorian novel *Alias Grace* (1996).[5] Farber's retrieval of a female genealogy from a strand of South African colonial history often relegated to the margins of official histories, namely the Jewish diaspora, uncovers a woman trapped not only "within the patriarchal social constructs that dictated the day-to-day life of a Victorian wife, mother and woman", but also, significantly, within a state of perpetual "homesickness for England" (Farber qtd. Klopper 2008: 16).

The entrapment and dis-ease of the Victorian woman suggested here recall Sandra Gilbert and Susan Gubar's study of nineteenth-century women's writing that centres on the figure of another Bertha, namely Bertha Mason Rochester in *Jane Eyre* (1847), as eponymously, "*The Madwoman in the Attic*" of female literary

---

supplement, written by Willem van Rensburg (2007), directed at primary, secondary and tertiary students that accompanied it.

[5] See Kym Brindle's chapter in this collection on the role of actual and fictional documents in *Alias Grace*.

imagination. Arguably, however, in its exploration of (post)colonial settler unbelonging, Farber's reincarnation of Bertha Marks as Leora-Bertha more specifically resembles Jean Rhys's recuperation of Bertha Mason as the West Indian Creole Antoinette Cosway in *Wide Sargasso Sea* – one of the first rewrites of a nineteenth-century canonical text in which the Neo-Victorian Gothic intersects with the Postcolonial Gothic to recover a silenced history and "challenge dominant literary, political, and social narratives" (Sugars and Turcotte 2009b: xviii). In both cases, the recovered history is that of a marginalised woman, but one complicit in and contaminated by the colonial world she inhabits. However, in Rhys's novel, that history also reveals the horror of dislocation and relocation suffered by Antoinette/Bertha in England, forcibly taken from the West Indies and incarcerated as the "disgusting secret" of the Rochesters (Brontë 1987: 295). The evident problematic of Creole identity played out in *Jane Eyre*, where, as Jenny Sharpe suggests, "the narrative function of the Creole stereotype is also to disassociate a pure English race from its corrupt West Indian line" (Sharpe 1993: 46), is simultaneously one of English identity. If Englishness in the nineteenth century "was created for the diaspora – an ethnic identity designed for those who were precisely not English, but rather of English descent" (Young 2008: 1), then those returning 'home' to England from the colonies, especially those who had been born abroad, must always confront the possibility of exclusion and alienation, theirs always being an Englishness from elsewhere, not quite homely (*heimlich*), because not native (*heimisch*). As Rhys's novel makes clear, Antoinette, whose Englishness is both diluted by her mother's French blood and stained by her father's association with slavery and miscegenation, is maddened not only by her English husband's treatment of her but by homesickness (*Heimweh*), understood in the eighteenth and nineteenth centuries as "a disease of transplantation" (Dames 2001: 31). Failing to acclimatise to England, the landscape and weather of which are utterly alien to her, Antoinette sickens because of her yearning to return to the West Indies, and it is this, Rhys's novel suggests, that Brontë's novel portrays as excess, pathology and aberration in its refusal of Englishness.

In contrast, Bertha Marks's "homesickness for England" is representative of what was considered a more appropriate and socially sanctioned manifestation of nostalgia (Farber qtd. Klopper 2008: 16), which confirmed the primacy of England in the loyalties of colonial settler subjects abroad whose "identification with the mother country would produce neo-English mimicry" (Veracini 2008: 365). The settler's colonial imperative to put down roots in the new colony – to settle in it and to settle it by taming the wild through cultivation – implicit in the metaphor of transplantation is made overt by Farber's coupling of Bertha's homesickness with "her desire to 'recreate' an English botanical and architectural environment on the Highveld" (Farber qtd. Klopper 2008: 16). Farber's imaginative working through of her own sense of dislocation and alienation in post-1994 South Africa seemingly inverts the process of colonial settlement through transplantation by literalising the metaphor of rootedness in the performative 'grafting' of an aloe plant into the skin of the English rose Leora-Bertha.

The inaugural scene for the staging of Leora-Bertha's transformations in *Dis-Location / Re-Location* is Virginia Woolf's *A Room of One's Own*, relocated to the (recreated) main bedroom of the Sammy Marks Museum in Pretoria, once the home of the Marks family. Although Farber reads this room as "a liberatory space" and "a physical and psychic space of transformation" (Farber qtd. Klopper 2008: 21), in the edited video and photographic stills of the inaugural performance artwork, 'A Room of Her Own', the encroachment of a menacing wild into the rosy domestic interior, doubled by a similar invasion of the protagonist's body, evokes instead a sense of claustrophobia. Here, the museum space becomes "a site of horror", where, as Cheryl D. Edelson in her chapter on Postcolonial Neo-Victorian Gothic points out, "terrifying ruptures of normality" are staged (this volume: 92). In Farber's retelling, a female figure with close-cropped hair, wearing a long white petticoat with corset details worked in leather (a recurrent element in the exhibition), is seemingly engaged in the archetypically feminine activity of embroidery in a room markedly Victorian. Behind her, a glass door leading to a formal rose garden ruptures papered walls covered in an excess of full-blown pink roses, interior decoration magnifying exterior cultivation. What at first seems to be a pretty chocolate-box fantasy, trite and kitsch, tilts into incongruity at the sight of lanceolate aloe leaves among the embroidery tools and thread in the needlework basket on the table next to her. Then, the image shifts into the horror of nightmare: the woman, through the neatly seamed hole worked into the skirt of her petticoat, intricately detailed, is calmly stitching into place six of the aloe leaves that had been inserted into cuts in the skin around a *petit point* rose embroidered into her thigh. In the video sequence, wax roses bloodily melt and drop from the wallpaper in a slow, haunting decomposition. In their place, like uncanny doubles, asserting rightful ownership, as if breaking though the wall itself to take over the house that colonialism had built, uprooting but not quite displacing the interloper English roses, a proliferation of aloes stage a botanical return of the repressed. Simultaneously, the woman's body is undergoing a similar transformation: the aloe leaves implanted into her thigh have withered and the *petit point* rose has metamorphosed into "a new succulent hybrid plant" (Farber qtd. Klopper 2008: 19). No longer seated decorously on her chair – which, in the installation, is shown to have erupted into a proliferation of succulent hybrids – the woman first sits and then falls back onto the carpet in what could be a swoon of ecstasy or death, trails of red embroidery thread unspooling like bloody roots from the protruding veins in her bare leg, her shoe discarded, the white stocking hanging torn from her foot. Fallen into decomposition like the fleshy wax roses that surround her, Leora-Bertha's body becomes ground to the hybrid plant that steadily invades it, and is thus supplanted.

The flesh-and-blood story enacted in 'A Room of Her Own' suggestively hints that Woolf's room too is a bloody chamber, in it the murdered body of the Victorian Angel in the House. In her 1931 lecture 'Professions for Women', Woolf described the act of liberation into writing as "[k]illing the Angel in the House" with a well-aimed inkpot (Woolf 1995: 5), but this humorous account of the woman writer trying to rid herself of the tormenting and inhibiting Victorian foremother also contains an act of much greater, more intimate violence when the writer describes how, driven to desperation, she "caught her by the throat" to finally silence her (Woolf 1995: 4). But the Victorian Angel returns, of course, because what Woolf's humour veils is a Gothic story of ghosts and transgenerational haunting, of "need[ing] to do battle with a certain phantom" again and again because "[i]t is far harder to kill a phantom than a reality" (Woolf 1995: 3, 5). In Farber's appropriation, the phantom of the Victorian Angel in the House is fleshed out in the artist's recovery of and merging with her colonial foremother in the figure of Leora-Bertha, her body the site upon which the "creation of new subjectivities is achieved through traumatically violent interventions" (Farber qtd. Klopper 2008: 17). Relocated to post-1994 South Africa, the room becomes a stage set, a room in a museum, a display case, a cabinet of curiosities, simultaneously a chamber of horrors and a *Wunderkammer*, unsettling and unhomely in its display of self-inflicted wounding and bodily collapse.

In the interview with Klopper, Farber identifies this last image of 'A Room of Her Own', significantly titled 'Redemption', as the final image of the exhibition because, she says, "Bertha/Leora has finally attained this rapturous transformation" (Farber qtd. Klopper 2008: 19). Although the word 'redemption' implies a triumphant resolution, a movement out of the in-between of purgatory that precedes the achievement of atonement, a threshold crossed into the 'New South African Rainbow Nation', Farber paradoxically also describes the "exhibition as inconclusively suspended on this endnote of deep ambivalence" (Farber qtd. Klopper 2008: 19). 'Aloerosa' ends on a similar note of ambivalence, but here the narrative of 'grafting' that mirrors the one in 'A Room of Her Own' is performed outside, firstly in the formal rose garden originally designed by Bertha Marks in the grounds of the Sammy Marks Museum, then in a grove of large aloes, and finally in the African *veld*.[6] In the first image of the sequence, 'Induction', Leora-Bertha with intense concentration 'grafts' the aloe seedling into her forearm, an act of self-mutilation made uncannily domestic by setting it as a typical English colonial afternoon tea in a rose garden. The dissolving of the photograph's lower edges in a blurry mistiness resembles both the clichéd soft-focus prettiness of nostalgic Victoriana and the nebulous images of ghosts in Victorian spirit photographs, but it also anticipates the eventual decomposition of the woman's body implied in the final image of the sequence. The woman at the centre of this first image, however, is encased in a rigid carapace, a corset beautifully crafted from cowhide that covers her breasts and abdomen. In contrast, the rosy flesh into

---

[6] In a note to her article in *Cultural Politics*, Farber defines *veld* as a "South African colloquial term for the bush; Afrikaans in origin. The term could describe many varieties of South African landscape – in this instance, effort was made to locate the shoot in a site that epitomized a dry, uninhabited yellow grass scape, common to the Gauteng province in which Johannesburg and Pretoria are located. This contrasts with the rose garden, which represents a colonial formalizing and cultivation of nature" (Farber 2005: 326).

which she inserts the plant appears shockingly vulnerable, the incision weeping a small tear of blood. In the images that follow, the implanted seedling roots into the veins of her arm, feeding there and, in a vigorous flourishing, in the images titled 'Maturation I' and 'Maturation II', takes over her depleted body, sprawled in a state of abandonment on the ground. Except in the first image in the rose garden, the figure is consistently placed against a dark grey, almost black ground of either aloes, barren rock or menacing expanse of sky, starkly out of place and isolated in a landscape that appears at best neutral, at worst hostile. The transformation Leora-Bertha's body undergoes coincides with the loosening of the corset, its laces pulled open to expose the vulnerable human skin of her stomach between the hard edges of the animal skin, until, in the final image, aptly titled 'Supplantation', all that is left of her is the neatly re-laced corset abandoned in the *veld*, surrounded by young aloe plants.

Like the final image in 'A Room of Her Own', which, troublingly, resembles a glossy photograph of a murder scene – the averted face of the victim's violated body allowing, or inviting, the viewer's complicitous and lingering gaze – the images of the woman's body in 'Maturation I' and 'Maturation II' insinuate the "conflat[ion] of the pin-up with the corpse" that Amelia Jones identifies in the work of Cindy Sherman and Hannah Wilke (Jones 2002: 960). Here, however, it is exaggerated because the woman looking out at the viewer is smiling faintly, almost invitingly, enigmatically. How does one read this look when it is so unnervingly difficult to tell whether she is alive or dead or dying? Considering Farber's assertion of Leora-Bertha's "rapturous transformation" (Farber qtd. Klopper 2008: 19) in 'Redemption', and given her simultaneous acknowledgement of the ambivalence of this image, it is Sylvia Plath's description of the dead woman in 'Edge' (1965) that comes to mind: "The woman is perfected. / Her dead // Body wears the smile of accomplishment" (Plath 1983: 85). However, what is finally accomplished is the erasure of the woman's body from the frame of the closing image of the series: she has been taken out of the picture; she has gone to/turned to ground.

Farber's own description of the implied violence and pain of the transformation in this series relies consistently on references to the Gothic and the uncanny:

> In the "Aloerosa" series, my skin is the site of grotesque disfiguration – the violence of the plant's implied growth is the product of a self-initiated violent action of cutting and insertion, arising from a desire to integrate or "belong," yet it ultimately becomes a metaphor for cultural contamination and contestation. As foreign to the body, the aloe plant signifies insertion of an alien culture, which takes root and disfigures the body through its forceful growth under the skin, turning I / Bertha into something akin to a "monstrous misfit." Such bodily violation implies not only physical but also psychical trauma inherent in the acculturation and contamination processes. (Farber 2005: 323)

Quite unlike the language of ecstatic transcendence she uses when speaking about 'Redemption', here there is an "emphasis on violent transformation" (Trotter 2002: 18), which is reminiscent of what Frederick Jackson Turner in his lecture on 'The Significance of the Frontier in American History' (1893) considered foundational to the forging of a "new product that is American" (Turner qtd. Trotter 2002: 9). Like "[t]he coloniser [who] becomes a coloniser by re-barbarising himself, by immersing himself in an alien culture" (Trotter 2002: 9), the postcolonial settler subject imagined in 'Aloerosa' must undergo a violent assimilation by taking the "alien culture" quite literally into her body (Farber 2005: 323). In Farber's imagined inversion of the project of colonial settlement through transplantation, Leora-Bertha, like the "colonist must want to obliterate [her]self, to turn into [her] opposite" and welcome "the violence with which an old identity is stripped away and a new one forged" (Trotter 2002: 9). Whereas Turner's idea of 'going native' is premised on the colonist first becoming "an Indian in order to become an American" (Trotter 2002: 9) – "he shouts the war cry and takes the scalp in orthodox Indian fashion" (Turner qtd. Trotter 2009: 9) – Farber's turns on the practice of horticultural 'grafting,' the Anglo-Jewish 'rose' body becoming the stock onto which the African aloe is grafted. Here, Farber's project diverges emphatically from the one Turner proposes, because it lacks the conviction of a triumphant regeneration into 'a new product that is South African', to adapt Turner's phrase. Instead, references to the grotesque and the monstrous suggest an ultimately failed experiment, akin to Frankenstein's new creation. Although in both cases Terry Goldie's observation that "[t]he settler 'goes native' in order to 'become of the land' at the very moment that the Native himself conveniently disappears" seems apposite (Goldie qtd. Johnson 2009: 26), in Farber's 'Aloerosa' the solitary white woman who inhabits the landscape – in what could be seen as a reification of the colonial fantasy of *terra nullius* – undergoes a process of transformation that ends in the degeneration and displacement of the coloniser's rather than the indigene's body. As Farber notes, Leora-Bertha's "bodily fluids and tissue serve both as nutrients and host to emergent hybrid specimens" and her "flesh replaces soil" (Farber qtd. Klopper 2008: 18). In the final image of the open *veld* with the discarded skin corset, emptied of her body yet still retaining its ghostly shape, complete transformation of flesh into soil has seemingly been achieved: she becomes part of the land itself as her body is displaced into place.

The violent and intrusive self-fashioning of postcolonial settler identity thus suggested is integral to the enfleshment of the metaphor of rootedness that Farber stages with and on the reincarnated body of Bertha Marks as foremother and 'motherland' into which the new hybrid South African identity is rooted. By insinuating these slippages between foremother, motherland and homeland, she literalises the implied terms of the comparison – that the human body, like a plant, grows from the soil of the country of its birth from which it gains sustenance. In doing so, she uncovers an even older bodily metaphorics that circulates in the primordial metaphor of 'mother earth', revealing there what Luce Irigaray calls the "the body-matter of women" covered over by the abstractions of metaphor (Irigaray 1985: 85), making apparent the "repressed connection between the body and the word" (Best 1995: 190). This evidently also speaks to Freud's claim in 'The Uncanny' that "[w]henever man dreams of a place or a country and says to himself, while he is dreaming: 'this place is familiar to me. I've been here before,' one may interpret the place as being his mother's body" (Freud 1976: 637). In Freud's account of this "beautiful confirmation of the uncanny", the "neurotic" man makes of "the entrance to the former *Heim* [home] of all human beings, to the place where each one of us lived once upon a time and in the beginning" an "*unheimlich* place", thus turning the once homely familiar space of the mother's body into its opposite, the *unheimlich*, where "the prefix '*un*' ['un-'] is the token of repression" (Freud 1976: 637). Hélène Cixous's reading of this section of the 'The Uncanny' is especially evocative in this context. She writes:

> Liebe ist *Heimweh*: Love is a yearning for a country, according to popular wisdom. *Heimweh*: a yearning for a country, is a formulation which is always interrupted by the interpretation which reads: regret and desire for "yearning." But this yearning is also the yearning which renders the country for you a point of destiny. Which country? The one from which we come, "the place where everyone dwelt once upon a time and in the beginning." The country from which we come is always the one to which we are returning. You are on the return road which passes through the country of children in the maternal body. You have already passed through here: you recognize the landscape. You have always been on the return road. Why it is that the maternal landscape, the *heimisch*, and the familiar become so disquieting? The answer is less buried than we might suspect. (Cixous 1976: 544)

The "whole array of intersignifications" evoked when the 'mother earth' metaphor is posited as the primordial substratum for the metaphor of 'rootedness' (the one metaphor in effect rooted in the other) calls to mind Paul Ricoeur's conception of "root metaphors", which are engendered when "[o]ne metaphor, in effect, calls for another and each one stays alive by conserving its power to evoke the whole network" of intersignifications (Ricoeur 1976: 64). The pervasiveness of the metaphor of rootedness in everyday discourse furthermore suggests that Ricoeur's idea of "insistent metaphors – those metaphors that are closest to the symbolic depths of our existence"– also applies (Ricoeur 1976: 68). The implications of this definition is in turn more fully articulated by Hans Blumenberg's proposition of

> absolute metaphors [which] 'answer' those supposedly naïve, principally unanswerable questions whose relevance lies quite simply in the fact that they

> cannot be eliminated because we don't *ask* them, but rather find them *asked* in the foundation of existence [*Daseingrund*]. (Blumenberg qtd. Adams 1991: 156)

Deriving from those spectral questions of origin and belonging that haunt familial and national affiliations – which is also where the postcolonial and the neo-Victorian intersect with the Gothic – the metaphor of rootedness operates as an "absolute metaphor", because it forms "the substructure of thought, [...] the underground, the nutrient of systematic crystallizations" (Blumenberg qtd. Adams 1991: 156).

Yet it is by "giv[ing] the metaphor literal significance", as Catherine Belsey suggests in a different context, and thus "to defamiliarize it, to isolate it for contemplation" (Belsey 1988: 100), that 'rootedness' reveals a fundamental principle of settler societies, namely their aspiration to *settledness*. In his article on settler colonialism and the disavowal of "founding violence", Lorenzo Veracini describes how settler societies draw on entrenched Western political ideologies that view "the 'family settled upon the soil' [Condorcet] as the building unit of the state", so as to consolidate the project of settlement, conceived of "as both an ideal society and as truer and uncorrupted version of the original social body" (Veracini 2008: 366, 365). This ideal is explicitly premised on the fantasy of a depopulated country inviting settlement, a place where "[c]olonial gardens were planted with flowers and vegetables from the old country and the grander settler mansions were surrounded by the reassuringly English décor of rolling lawns and trim green hedges" (Collingwood-Whittick 2007b: xvi). This fantasy sometimes surfaces in neo-Victorian texts as a nostalgic celebration of an 'Out of Africa' or 'White Mischief' colonial chic, thus defaulting on Ann Heilmann and Mark Llewellyn's imperative that neo-Victorian texts "must in some respect be *self-consciously engaged with the act of (re)interpretation, (re)discovery and (re)vision concerning the Victorians*" (Heilmann and Llewellyn 2010: 4, original emphasis). Farber's images to some extent play with this fantasy, only to undermine it with their unsettling Gothic content. Thus, her enfleshment of the metaphor of rootedness, which is central to the colonial "fantasy of indigenization" (Collingwood-Whittick 2007b: xxiii), is made strange and suspect in the South African postcolonial settler context, where it often remains uncritically embedded in discourses of white entitlement to 'indigenous' status that hark back to the settler colonial discourses of nineteenth-century imperialist expansionism. Pursuing a trajectory of recovery and identification that culminates in scenes of apparent bodily decomposition and supplantation, Farber's reincarnation of Bertha Marks performs a fleshy ventriloquism that speaks what Margaret Atwood has termed the "violent duality" of settler (post)colonial identity (Atwood qtd. Staines 1997: x).

Atwood first diagnosed this "violent duality" typical of Gothic configurations of subjectivity in the nineteenth-century English settler Susanna Moodie on whose journals she based her collection of poetry *The Journals of Susanna Moodie*. In the poems, the pervasive unsettledness of settler subjectivity coincides with Moodie's sense of the bewildering encroachment of the bush and its animal and human inhabitants, which makes *being at home* impossible. Reading Farber's work alongside Atwood's poetic ventriloquisms reveals their mutual reliance on the Gothic trope of intergenerational haunting in the uncanny return of a settler foremother, which, whether as spectre or reincarnated body, is always a return to questions of origin, homeland and motherland. In the final poem of the collection, 'A Bus Along St Clair: December', Atwood's Moodie haunts the streets and buses of Toronto as a menacing old woman, "who reveals the city as an unexplored threatening wilderness" (Atwood qtd. Staines 1997: xii): "I am the old woman/ sitting across from you on the bus, / her shoulders drawn up like a shawl; / out of her eyes come secret / hatpins, destroying / the walls, the ceiling" ('A Bus Along St Clair: December' lines 22-27). The wilderness that had once threatened to inhabit her when she "was not ready / altogether to be moved into" ('Departure from the Bush' lines 17-18) has been "bulldoze[d]" into a concrete jungle, a "wilderness of wires" ('A Bus Along St Clair: December' lines 11, 5). Finally absorbed into the landscape, Moodie returns after death as "the spirit of the land she once hated" (Atwood qtd. Staines 1970: 10), but her claim that "this is my kingdom still" rings hollow considering the last lines – both warning and threat – with which the poem and the collection end: "there is no city; / this is the centre of a forest // your place is empty" ('A Bus Along St Clair: December' lines 2, 29-31). This insistence on the return of a repressed wilderness and the emptied out place of settler identity anticipates the perhaps more ambivalent *denouement* of Farber's 'Aloerosa'. Leora-

Bertha's going to ground at the point of narrative closure suggests an achievement of belonging through erasure similar to Moodie's merging with the land through dying and burial. Atwood first introduced this trope in 'Death of a Young Son by Drowning', in which the description of Moodie's young son's burial – "I planted him in this country / like a flag" (lines 28-29) – asserts settlement much more confidently than does her description of the futile attempts of her husband and two male neighbours to cultivate the wilderness in 'The Planters'.

Then as now, Atwood suggests, displacement and alienation are at the heart of settler identity. If Moodie was "divided down the middle", contemporary Canadians fare no better, because they will always be "immigrants […] even if [they] were born [there]: the country is too big for anyone to inhabit completely, and in parts unknown to [them they] move in fear, exiles and invaders" (Atwood qtd. Staines 1997: xi, x). Atwood's description of the landscape as a vast and alienating backdrop against which the settler figure moves, simultaneously "exile and invader", echoes Germaine Greer's description of white Australians as "tourists in their own birthplace, dashing from funny-shaped rock to funny-shaped rock, with only the vaguest idea of what might lie between" (Greer 2007: ix). Similarly, Farber's visual constructions of figure and landscape in 'Aloerosa' are symptomatic of what J.M. Coetzee identifies as an "historical insecurity regarding the place of the artist of European heritage in the African landscape […] an insecurity not without cause" (Coetzee 1989: 62). That there is something there to be known, which yet remains essentially unknowable in the landscape, causes a pervasive sense of anxiety, because, as Justin D. Edwards argues with reference to the Canadian context, "the externalized *unheimlich* space that cannot be settled becomes internalized as part of the geography of the self" (Edwards 2005: xx).

In *Dis-Location / Re-Location*, this uncanny interior landscape of estrangement is shown to be inhabited by the ghosts of settler colonial ancestors. Yet this ghost story is also a flesh-and-blood story, and Farber's embodiment of the haunting entanglement of present and past in the hybrid neo-Victorian figure of Leora-Bertha performs the "formation of self-identity as lodged within the body, bodily borders and the instability of its margins, ambiguity and liminality or a state of 'in-between-ness'" (Farber qtd. Klopper 2008: 14). The metaphorics of transcendent rebirth that underpins the construct of the 'rainbow nation' is here reconfigured as the violent metamorphosis of Leora-Bertha's body: fleshy ground for violent implantations generating "new hybrids" (Farber 2005: 325). As a site and performance of radical unsettlement, then, *Dis-Location / Re-Location*, in attempting to come to terms with a genealogy of settler colonialism, cannot cede easy consolations, and seems to confirm Angela Carter's approving claim that "alienated is the only way to be, after all" (Carter 1997: 12). However, in its ambivalence, the *denouement* of Farber's neo-Victorian Gothic fantasy of hybridity remains haunted by the desire for settler indigenisation through a transformative process imagined as atonement – an 'at-one-ment' with the mother/home/land which must also always be an act of expiation.

Acknowledgement
I would like to thank Marie-Luise Kohlke, Christian Gutleben, the anonymous readers at Rodopi, Meg Samuelson and Dawid de Villiers for their helpful comments and suggestions on earlier drafts of this chapter. I am also grateful to Meg Samuelson for securing the funding from the National Research Foundation of South Africa, under the project 'Southern African Subjectivities', which supported my work on this chapter.

Bibliography
Adams, David. 1991. 'Metaphors for Mankind: The Development of Hans Blumenberg's Anthropological Metaphorology', *Journal of the History of Ideas* 52(1): 152-166.
Ahluwalia, Pal. 2001. 'When Does a Settler Become a Native? Citizenship and Identity in a Settler Society', *Pretexts: Literary and Cultural Studies* 10(1): 63-73.
Atwood, Margaret. 1970. *The Journals of Susanna Moodie*. Oxford: Oxford University Press.
Belsey, Catherine. 1988. *Critical Practice*. London: Routledge.
Best, Sue. 1995. 'Sexualizing Space', in Grosz, Elizabeth, and Elspeth Probyn (eds.), *Sexy Bodies: The Strange Carnalities of Feminism*. London: Routledge, 181-194.
Brontë, Charlotte. 1987. *Jane Eyre* [1847]. Oxford: Oxford University Press.
Carey, Peter. 1997. *Jack Maggs*. London: Faber and Faber.
Carey, Peter. n.d. 'Randomhouse Interview with Peter Carey'. On-line at: http://www.randomhouse.com/boldtype/o399/carey/interview.html (consulted 12.11.2007).
Carter, Angela. 1997. *Shaking a Leg: Collected Journalism and Writings*. London: Chatto & Windus.

Castricano, Jodey. 2001. *Cryptomimesis: The Gothic and Jacques Derrida's Ghost Writing*. Montreal & Kingston: McGill-Queens University Press.

Cixous, Hélène. 1976. 'Fiction and Its Phantoms: A Reading of Freud's *Das Unheimliche* (The "Uncanny")' (trans. Robert Denommé), *New Literary History* 7(3) (Spring): 525-548.

Coetzee, J.M. 1989. *White Writing: The Culture of Letters in South Africa*. Massachusetts: Yale University Press.

Collingwood-Whittick, Sheila (ed.). 2007a. *The Pain of Unbelonging: Alienation and Identity in Australian Literature*. Amsterdam & New York: Rodopi.

——. 2007b. 'Introduction'. In Collingwood-Whittick (2007a): xii-xliii.

Dames, Nicholas. 2001. *Amnesiac Selves: Nostalgia, Forgetting, and British Fiction, 1810-1870*. Oxford: Oxford University Press.

Edwards, Justin D. 2005. *Gothic Canada: Reading the Spectre of a National Literature*. Alberta: University of Alberta Press.

Farber, Leora. 2005. 'Dis-Location/Re-Location: "Aloerosa"', *Cultural Politics* 1(3) : 317-328.

——. 2006. 'Making Room for a Post-colonial Identity', *FADA Research Newsletter* 7: 5.

——. 2007-2008. *Dis-location/Re-location* (Produced in collaboration with Strangelove). Various Sites: National Travelling Exhibition.

Freud, Sigmund. 1976. 'The Uncanny' [1919] (trans. James Strachey), *New Literary History* 7(3) (Spring): 619-645.

Gilbert, Sandra. M., and Susan Gubar. 1984. *The Madwoman in the Attic: The Woman Writer and the Nineteenth-Century Imagination*. New Haven: Yale University Press.

Greer, Germaine. 2007. 'Preface'. In Collingwood-Whittick (2007a): ix-xi.

Gutleben, Christian. 2011. 'Hybridity as oxymoron : An interpretation of the dual nature of neo-Victorian fiction', in Guigney, Vanessa, Catherine Pesso-Miquel and François Specq (eds.), *Hybridity: Forms and Figures in Literature and the Visual Arts*. Newcastle-upon-Tyne: Cambridge Scholars Publishing: 59-70.

Heilmann, Ann, and Mark Llewellyn. 2010. *Neo-Victorianism: The Victorians in the Twenty-First Century, 1999-2009*. Houndmills, Basingstoke: Palgrave Macmillan.

Hogle, Jerrold E. (ed.). 2002a. *The Cambridge Companion to Gothic Fiction*. Cambridge: Cambridge University Press.

——. 2002b. 'Introduction: The Gothic in Western Culture'. In Hogle (2002a): 1-20.

Irigaray, Luce. 1985. *This Sex Which Is Not One* (trans. C. Porter). New York: Cornell University Press.

Johnson, Brian. 2009. 'Viking Graves Revisited: Pre-Colonial Primitivism in Farley Mowat's Northern Gothic'. In Sugars and Turcote (2009a): 23-50.

Jones, Amelia. 2002. 'The "Eternal Return": Self-Portrait Photography as a Technology of Embodiment', *Signs* 27(4): 947-978.

Klopper, Sandra. 2008. 'Bertha Marks Reborn: Leora Farber in Conversation with Sandra Klopper'. In Law-Viljoen (2008): 11-25.

Knoepflmacher, U.C. 2010. 'Introduction: Hybrid Forms and Cultural Anxiety'. In Knoepflmacher and Browning (2010): 1-10.

Knoepflmacher, U.C., and Logan D. Browning. (eds.) 2010. *Victorian Hybridities: Cultural Anxiety and Formal Innovation*. Baltimore: Johns Hopkins University Press.

Law-Viljoen, Bronwyn (ed.). 2008. *Dis-location/Re-location: Exploring Alienation and Identity in South Africa*. Johannesburg: David Krut and The University of Johannesburg Research Centre.

Llewellyn, Mark. 2008. 'What is Neo-Victorian Studies?', *Neo-Victorian Studies* 1(1): 164-185.

Mendelsohn, Richard. 2008. 'The Gilded Cage: Bertha Marks at Zwartkoppies'. In Law-Viljoen (2008): 27-39.

Plath, Sylvia. 1983. *Ariel* [1965]. London: Faber and Faber.

Rhys, Jean. 1997. *Wide Sargasso Sea* [1966]. London: Penguin.

Ricoeur, Paul. 1976. *Interpretation Theory: Discourse and the Surplus of Meaning* (trans. Ted Klein). Fort Worth: Texas Christian University Press.

Royle, Nicholas. 2003. *The Uncanny*. Manchester & New York: Manchester University Press.

Sharpe, Jenny. 1993. *Allegories of Empire: The Female Figure of Woman in the Colonial Text*. Minneapolis: University of Minnesota Press.

Shiller, Dana. 1997. 'The Redemptive Past in the Neo-Victorian Novel', *Studies in the Novel* 29(4): 538-560.

Staines, David. 1997. 'Foreword', in Atwood, Margaret, and Charles Patcher (illus.), *The Journals of Susanna Moodie*. Boston & New York: Houghton Mifflin: ix-xv.

Sugars, Cynthia, and Turcotte, Gerry (eds.). 2009a. *Unsettled Remains: Canadian Literature and the Postcolonial Gothic*. Waterloo, Ontario: Wilfred Laurier University Press.

——. 2009b 'Introduction: Canadian Literature and the Postcolonial Gothic'. In Sugars and Turcotte (2009a): vii-xxvi.

Trotter, David. 2002. 'Colonial Subjects', *Critical Quarterly* 32(3): 3-20.

Veracini, Lorenzo. 2008. 'Settler Collective, Founding Violence and Disavowal: The Settler Colonial Situation', *Journal of Intercultural Studies* 29(4): 363-379.

Woolf, Virginia. 1998. *A Room of One's Own and Three Guineas* [1929]. Oxford: Oxford World Classics.

——. 1995. *Killing the Angel in the House: Seven Essays* [1931]. London: Penguin.

Young, Robert J.C. 2008. *The Idea of English Ethnicity*. Malden, Massachusetts: Blackwell.

Part II

The Horrid and the Sexy

Neo-Victorian Gothic and Spectral Sexuality in Colm Tóibín's *The Master*

Patricia Pulham

Abstract:
Neo-Victorian fiction often displays features of the Freudian uncanny: it 'doubles' the Victorian novel; it reanimates Victorian genres and authors; and functions as a form of revenant that infiltrates our present. In *Victoriana: Histories, Fictions, Criticisms* (2007), Cora Kaplan notes that 'Biofiction', a genre that merges fact and fiction, has achieved increasing popularity in recent years. Colm Tóibín's *The Master* constitutes an example of neo-Victorian biofiction which revives a Victorian author for contemporary consumption. This chapter argues that Tóibín deploys both the Freudian uncanny and James's own uncanny Gothicism in *The Turn of the Screw*, to produce a 'spectral' James, who is himself haunted by his own memories and homoerotic desires.

Keywords: biofiction, Gothic, homosexuality, Henry James, spectrality, Colm Tóibín, the uncanny.

*****

On the 27 April 1890, following his receipt and reading of *Hauntings: Fantastic Stories* (1890), a collection of supernatural tales kindly sent to him by the author, Vernon Lee, Henry James penned a letter of thanks in which he wrote: "The supernatural story, the subject wrought in fantasy, is not the class of fiction I myself most cherish [...]. But that only makes my enjoyment of your artistry more of a subjection" (Edel 1980: 277). Despite this apparent resistance to fantasy Henry James, a realist writer who increasingly specialised in what became termed the 'psychological novel', clearly had in the past succumbed to the supernatural: his ghost story, 'The Romance of Certain Old Clothes' appeared in the *Atlantic Monthly* in February 1868, and he continued, sporadically, to write such fiction throughout his career. For a writer who declared that the supernatural story was "not the class of fiction" he most cherished, it seems ironic that his 1898 novella, *The Turn of the Screw* should be among his best-known works and, indeed, has acquired a cultural afterlife that exceeds the text in numerous television adaptations, film versions, continuing productions of Benjamin Britten's opera of the same name, and in intertextual resonances in the neo-Victorian novel.[1] As Patricia Merivale has observed, *The Turn of the Screw* "draw[s] upon numerous conventions of Gothic fiction – ghosts, doubles, haunted houses", and she argues that Gothic itself

> in its two-hundred year history from *The Castle of Otranto* to the present day is founded in psychological necessity, in the lure of what is at or beyond the edge of the possible [...] in the urge to know what we least wish to know about ourselves. (Merivale 1978: 992)

In James's novella, this urge is explored via the governess's ambiguous narrative, which has been the subject of continuing critical debate. Do the ghosts of her charges' former servant Quint and former governess Miss Jessel, which she sees and suspects of violating the children's innocence, really exist, or are they only figments of her imagination? Can Miles and Florence see the dead, or is the governess incorrectly interpreting their denials as lies? Have they really been corrupted, or is there something in the governess herself which is corrupt or desires corruption, leading to her visions of the infamous servants and, ultimately, to Florence's exile from her home and Miles's death? As critics and readers have found over the years, it is impossible to decide. However, read as a text that informs Colm Tóibín's biofictional novel, *The Master* (2004), the sexual implications of *The Turn of the Screw*, the ghostly sightings, and the battle for possession foster new, if still necessarily ambiguous, readings.

In her article on *The Turn of the Screw*, Merivale identifies "two valid narratives told in the same words for different audiences: a 'surface' plot and a 'shadow' plot" (Merrivale 1978: 998). The same

---

[1] Recent examples include John Harwood's *The Ghost Writer* (2004); Sarah Waters's *Affinity* (2000) and *The Little Stranger* (2009); and A.N. Wilson's, *A Jealous Ghost* (2005).

duality might be said to exist in Tóibín's novel which, on the surface, is a fictional biography of Henry James, shadowed by covert and haunting expressions of homoerotic desire. 2004, the year in which Tóibín's *The Master* was first published became, as David Lodge has termed it, "The Year of Henry James". In the opening pages of the book that bears this same title (published by Harvill Secker in 2006), Lodge quotes from a review of his own James novel, *Author, Author* (2004), that appeared in the *Sunday Times*, 29 August 2004. Peter Kemp wrote: "[i]f anyone deserves to win this year's Man Booker prize, it's Henry James. During 2004, he has been the originator of no fewer than three outstanding novels" (qtd. Lodge 2006: 3). The other works to which Kemp refers are Tóibín's *The Master* and Alan Hollinghurst's *The Line of Beauty*, published respectively in March and April of that year, both of which were shortlisted for the prize which Hollinghurst won. Moreover, as Lodge points out, these novels and his own were not the only James-inspired fictions to appear that year; 2004 also saw Emma Tennant's *Felony* reissued in paperback, while the manuscript of *The Typewriter's Tale* by the South-African writer Michael Heyns (eventually published in 2005) was also with publishers (Lodge 2006: 4).[2]

The plethora of early twenty-first century novels that consider and play with James's "afterlife" and Kemp's reference to him as the "originator", rather than the subject of these texts, suggest a form of spectral visitation. While we may read the word "afterlife" simply in relation to the legacy of James's life and fictions, it also connotes the supernatural and invokes a ghostliness or spectrality. In a sense, as Julian Wolfreys has argued, to engage with the literary text is to always already be "haunted". He writes:

> We announce in various ways the power of texts to survive, as though they could, in fact, live on, without our involvement as readers, researchers, archivists, librarians or bibliographers [...]. So, in some kind of legerdemain, we keep up the plot, the archival burial ground, saying all the while that the life or afterlife of

---

[2] Tennant's novel draws on Henry James's *The Aspern Papers* (1888) and also dramatises the relationship between James and Constance Fenimore Woolson, while Heyns's novel centres on James's secretary, Theodora Bosanquet, and on the affair between Morton Fullerton and Edith Wharton.

> texts is all their own, and not an effect of the embalming processes in which we engage. In such pursuits, and in the paradoxical dead-and-alive situation by which texts are maintained, we find ourselves forced to confront the fact that what we call texts, what we constitute as the identity of texts is, in the words of Jean-Michel Rabaté, 'systematically "haunted" by voices from the past [...] this shows in an exemplary way the ineluctability of spectral returns'. (Wolfreys 2002: xi-xii)

It is, then, only to be expected that neo-Victorianism, a mode which actively engages with the Victorian past and resurrects Victorian authors and texts, should be particularly "haunted". In her introduction to the inaugural edition of the *Neo-Victorian Studies* e-journal, Marie-Luise Kohlke notes that neo-Victorian writing persistently engages "a recurrent spiritualist trope that acts both as metaphor and analogy for our attempted dialogue with the dead and for the lingering traces of the past within the present" (Kohlke 2008: 9). Such engagements can have a psychological dimension: "[h]aunting itself, [...] can be read as indicative of personal and cultural trauma: processed and integrated into consciousness" (Kohlke 2008: 9). Furthermore, as Rosario Arias and I have noted elsewhere, frequently in "dialogue with the dead", neo-Victorian writing manifests a series of recognisable features which Freud describes as uncanny (Arias and Pulham 2010: xv). Freud's list of psychological triggers for uncanny sensations include the double; repetition; the animation of the seemingly dead or, conversely, the death-like nature of the seemingly animate; ghosts or spirits; and the familiar made strange. Many of these uncanny qualities are evident in *The Master* and perhaps necessarily inform the biographical novel which, as David Lodge explains, is a genre that "takes a real person and their real history as the subject matter for imaginative exploration" and extrapolation, "using the novel's techniques for representing subjectivity rather than the objective, evidence-based discourse of biography" (qtd. Russell Perkin 2010: 118).

The Master is an instance of what has become known as Biofiction, a form described by Cora Kaplan as "a hybrid genre", which "can be interpreted in various ways, as highlighting the tension between biography and fiction, as well as marking the overlap between them" (Kaplan 2007: 65). Interestingly, this 'uncanny' engagement with the past is equally present in James's own biographical writings. Describing the process of recollection in his 1913 memoir, *A Small Boy and Others*, James writes: "To look back at all is to meet the apparitional and to find in its ghostly face the silent stare of an appeal. When I fix it, the hovering shade, whether of person or place, it fixes me back and seems the less lost" (James 2001: 49). In *The Master*, Tóibín seems to assimilate James's own ghostly engagement with the past, and his chosen genre, biofiction, offers a liminal space in which to do so – a fitting location for Tóibín's peculiarly uncanny Henry James. In Tóibín's novel, James functions as a 'double' caught between fact and fiction; he is an animated 'corpse', a dead author brought back to life, and yet retains a deathlike, ghostly quality. As Kaplan observes, "Tóibín's James is almost already 'dead' – he is a spectral figure in his own biography" (Kaplan 2007: 71). Moreover, permitted to access the interiority of a well-known writer, yet kept at arm's length by the unspoken, the hidden, and the secret on the cusp of revelation, we are presented with an uncanny example of the familiar made strange. In recent criticism, the "uncanny" nature of Tóibín's text is often encoded within discussions of James's implied homosexuality. Eibhear Walshe writes of the "vanishing homoerotic" in Tóibín's work; he observes that "James is Tóibín's study of life in the closet, a man in late Victorian society carefully suppressing his attraction to other men", and one in which "the gay male body is being controlled, hidden, and allowed to vanish" (Walshe 2006: 134). Similarly, Daniel Hannah notes how "[w]hile scenes exposing James's intense, unconsummated desire for men punctuate Tóibín's novel, homoeroticism remains shrouded in an ambiguous silence of potentiality" (Hannah 2007: 74), and Cora Kaplan remarks that

> *The Master* explores James's homoerotic feelings throughout; they are allowed to rise in conversation and reverie and in a series of imagined and inconclusive encounters [...]. Tóibín never tries to represents [*sic*] James in the way that provocative recent criticism has done, as the avant garde of modern queer fiction. But *The Master*'s interpretation

of James, so structured around the transmutation of loss into writing, suggests what Lodge's [*Author, Author*] goes to some pains to deny, that touch of queerness, in both the sense that James uses it, as 'strange, out of the ordinary', and also in its modern sexualised sense, each inflection connected to the elusiveness of the subjectivity he lived and portrayed. (Kaplan 2007: 69)

This dual understanding of "queerness" is at the heart of Eve Kosofsky Sedgwick's reading of James's 1903 story 'The Beast in the Jungle' in her seminal essay, 'The Beast in the Closet: James and the Writing of Homosexual Panic' (1986), as indeed are secrets, ambiguities and an unnamed dread. Sedgwick explains that, in James's story, "the possibility of an embodied male-homosexual thematic" has "a precisely liminal presence. It is present as a [...] thematics of absence, and specifically of the absence of speech" (Sedgwick 1990: 201). Referring to the supposed "emptiness" of the James's protagonist's John Marcher's secret, and his "unspeakable doom", Sedgwick contends that these may be read in relation to what she describes as "the centuries-long historical chain of substantive uses of space-clearing negatives to void and at the same time to underline the possibility of male same-sex genitality", narratologically manifesting "'that sin which should be neither named nor committed' [...] 'the love that dare not speak its name'" (Sedgwick 199O: 202-203). She further argues that:

> John Marcher's 'secret', 'his singularity', 'the thing' she [May Bartram] knew, which grew to be at last, with the consecration of the years, never mentioned between them save as 'the real truth' about him, 'the great vagueness', 'the secret of the gods' [...] 'dreadful things I couldn't name': the ways the story refers to Marcher's secret fate have the same quasi-nominative, quasi-obliterative structure. (Sedgwick 1990: 203)

In *The Master*, Tóibín seemingly deploys a similarly "quasi-nominative, quasi-obliterative" structure to address James's alleged homosexuality. Writing of his technique, Tóibín tells us how he was interested in creating a sense of "sexual almostness" (Tóibín 2009a: 233). This is particularly evident in relation to incidents – or non-incidents perhaps – of homoerotic tension, a number of which occur in Tóibín's text. For example, the novel begins with Tóibín's James recalling Paul Joukowsky and relating a key moment in their friendship at a distance of twenty years:[3]

> He [James] stood in the beautiful city on a small street in the dusk, gazing upwards, waiting, watching, for the lighting of a lamp in the window on the third story. As the lamp blazed up he had strained to see Paul Joukowsky's face at the window [...]. As night fell, he knew that he himself on the unlit street could not be seen, and he knew also that he could not move [...] – he held his breath even at the thought – to attempt to gain access to Paul's rooms. [...] He wrote down the story of that night and thought then of the rest of the story which could never be written, no matter how secret the paper or how quickly it would be burned or destroyed. The rest of the story was imaginary, and it was something he would never allow himself to put into words. (Tóibín 2004: 10)

Later in the novel he recalls a visit to his cousins the Temples in New Hampshire, and the time he shared a room and bed with Oliver Wendell Holmes. In this scene, James watches Holmes who, naked, resembles "a statue of a young man, tall and muscular", and in bed, "keeping near the edge, yet still touching Holmes", James wonders "if he would ever again be so intensely alive" (Tóibín 2004: 98). Later, James remembers a day "in the fall of 1860", when he entered an artists' studio to find "his cousin Gus Barker standing naked on a pedestal while the advanced students sketched him"; he describes his cousin's form as "beautiful and manly" and is "surprised by his own need to watch him" (Tóibín 2004: 105). These sexually-charged moments, which draw on the homoerotic value of the sculptural body

---

[3] When I use 'James' in the context of *The Master*, it is the fictional, and not the factual Henry James to whom I refer.

in late-Victorian writing,[4] are also implicit in the closing pages of the novel, where James once again refers to a homoerotic encounter, this time with the sculptor Hendric Andersen, which takes place in the Protestant cemetery in Rome. As they stand by Constance Fenimore Woolson's grave, Andersen intuits James's loss and notes that he is crying. Tóibín writes:

> He [James] turned away and tried to regain control but found that he was being held by the sculptor, his shoulders cupped against Andersen's chest and Andersen's hands reaching around to grasp his hands and hold them as firmly as he could. He was surprised at Andersen's strength, the size of his hands. He immediately checked that there was nobody in view before allowing the embrace to continue, feeling the other man's warm, tough body briefly holding him, wanting desperately to allow himself to be held much longer but knowing that this embrace was all the comfort he would receive. (Tóibín 2004: 286-287)

In all the scenes of this nature that Tóibín describes we are left in a state of uncertainty – trapped unsettlingly (and gothically) between truth and conjecture, revelation and secrecy. Any open allusion to homosexual love is discussed at a remove, as in James's conversations with Edmund Gosse regarding Oscar Wilde and John Addington Symonds. Referring to the existence of a list of homosexuals who had, like Wilde, rented boys for sex, Gosse, who had confessed his own love for men to John Addington Symonds, comments "I wondered if you, if perhaps [...]", to which James replies, "You do not wonder. There is nothing to wonder about" (Tóibín 2004: 77). Later, the narrator refers to James's fascination with Symonds and, obliquely, to *A Problem in Greek Ethics* (1883),

---

[4] The sculptural figure, especially that represented in ancient Greek sculpture functions as a homoerotic code in a number of late Victorian works including Walter Pater, *The Renaissance: Studies in Art and Poetry* (1873), John Addington Symonds, *A Problem in Greek Ethics* (1883), and Oscar Wilde, *The Picture of Dorian Gray* (1890-91). This trope is exploited in a neo-Victorian (and lesbian), though not particularly gothic context by Sarah Waters's use of the figure of Antinous – the Roman emperor Hadrian's lover - in *Tipping the Velvet* (1998).

Symonds's defence of homosexual love, sent "to those in England [including Gosse] whom he thought might initiate a debate" (Tóibín 2004: 79).[5]

James's desire, like James himself, becomes a spectral presence that appears and disappears even as we see it. Explaining his approach, Tóibín states:

> I want[ed James] haunted, uneasy but charming; I want[ed] his sexuality to be concealed, unspoken, with no private sexual moments shared with the reader, the reader must be like the wider world, kept at arm's length. (Tóibín 2009a: 231)

Indeed 'haunting' functions as the predominant semantic field in *The Master*, in which James is 'visited' by memories and the ghostly presences of the dead – both male and female. The opening lines of the novel tell us that "[s]ometimes in the night he dreamed about the dead"; like a revenant, the memory of Paris and Paul Joukowsky comes "to haunt him at unlikely moments"; in the years that follow her demise, his cousin Minny Temple "haunt[s] him"; and in the weeks after her suicide, Constance Fenimore Woolson's "spirit", her "fresh ghost", "brushe[s] through his rooms" and returns to him in a series of uncanny encounters (Tóibín 2004: 1, 299, 112, 256). Woolson's 'ghost' functions within the text as a tacit confidante, "the only person he had ever known who was fully skilled at deciphering the unsaid and the unspoken" – thus replicating the role May Bartram plays for John Marcher in 'The Beast in the Jungle' – and the now famous scene in which James "buries" her dresses in the Venetian lagoon, functions as a visual representation of Freud's return of the repressed, the dresses "floating to the surface again like black balloons" (Tóibín 2004: 256, 270).

Adopting this technique, Tóibín not only constructs James as a form of "apparitional homosexual" – a male counterpart to Terry

---

[5] Only ten copies of Symonds's text were initially printed privately and circulated in 1883, before being reprinted, four years after Symonds's death, as an appendix to the English translation of Havelock Ellis's *Sexual Inversion* (1897), now the third volume of seven in *Studies in the Psychology of Sex*. In 1898, Ellis's book was suppressed due to an obscenity case, and only limited editions of *A Problem in Greek Ethics* were later published in 1901.

Castle's "apparitional lesbian" (Castle 1995) – he also subtly invokes James's own style.[6] As Daniel Hannah notes, in *The Master*Tóibín deploys the structural model of James's writing and its interest in the "small gesture standing for a much larger relationship, something hidden suddenly revealed", which both illuminates his "silent handling of homoerotic desire and obfuscates [his] investment in 'gestures' that either refuse to reveal or that reveal uncontainable excess" (Hannah 2007: 75). In drawing attention to the way in which Tóibín plays with James's own writing, Hannah's comments compel us to explore *The Master* in greater detail, to 'spot' those moments which gesture towards James's works. There are many, as over the five years covered – from January 1895 to October 1899 – Tóibín frequently allows us to 'see' the germ of future masterpieces including *The Wings of the Dove* (1902) and *The Golden Bowl* (1904). However, I suggest that the main work that informs *The Master* is James's *The Turn of the Screw*: a text that centres on haunting, that hinges on the 'small gesture' as revelation, that implies sexual corruption even as it obscures it and relies on the ambiguity surrounding its protagonist.

In his fascinating discussion of queer Gothic, George Haggerty demonstrates how Gothic fiction has always served the expression of transgressive desire and behaviour. As he explains:

> A wide range of writers, dispersed historically and culturally, use 'gothic' to evoke a queer world that attempts to transgress the binaries of sexual decorum [...]. It is no mere coincidence that the cult of gothic fiction reached its apex at the very moment when gender and sexuality were beginning to be codified for modern culture. In fact, gothic fiction offered a testing ground for many unauthorized genders and sexualities, including sodomy. (Haggerty 2006: 2)

Interestingly, for Haggerty, "Henry James's *The Turn of the Screw* [...] is the perfect gothic tale", and as Neill Matheson points out, the

---

[6] Castle argues that "[t]o try to write the literary history of lesbianism is to confront, from the start, something ghostly: an impalpability, a misting over, an evaporation or 'whiting out' of possibility" (Castle 1995: 28). This resonates with the ghostly and impalpable nature of James's homosexuality in Tóibín's representation of the writer in *The Master*.

"highly euphemistic quality" of the language James uses in *The Turn of the Screw* "draws heavily on the tropes of Gothic discourse" (Haggerty 2006: 131; Matheson 1999: 710). In addition, the text's allusions to *The Mysteries of Udolpho* (1794) and *Jane Eyre* (1847) explicitly invoke Gothic literature, "especially its characteristic construction of the private as a monstrous 'secret'" (Matheson 1999: 710).[7] In *The Turn of the Screw*, Matheson argues:

> James's habitually indirect erotic language takes an unusually dark and violent form [...] implicating both author and reader in its guilty pleasures. His appropriation of the Gothic genre helps to establish within the story a particularly virulent opposition between private and public, concealment and exposure. (Matheson 1999: 710)

This tension between "private and public, concealment and exposure" is also at the heart of Tóibín's *The Master*. It is perhaps worth noting that the working title for Tóibín's novel was *The Turn of the Century*; moreover January 1895, the point at which Tóibín chooses to open his narrative, is also the month in which James is told the story that inspires him to write *The Turn of the Screw* some years later.[8] Furthermore, as Tóibín acknowledges in an essay on the novella:

---

[7] James's governess asks rhetorically, "Was there a 'secret' at Bly – a mystery of Udolpho or an insane, an unmentionable relative kept in unsuspected confinement?" (James 2007: 27)

[8] In an article in the *Henry James Review*, Tóibín quotes James who, in January 1895, wrote in his notebook: "Note here the ghost-story told me at Addington (evening of Thursday 10th), by the Archbishop of Canterbury [...] the story of the young children [...] left to the care of servants in an old country-house, through the death, presumably, of parents. The servants, wicked and depraved, corrupt and deprave the children [...]. The servants *die* (the story vague about the way of it) and their apparitions, figures, return to haunt the house *and* children, to whom they seem to beckon [...]. It is all obscure and imperfect, the picture, the story, but there is a suggestion of strangely gruesome effect in it. The story to be told [...] by an outside spectator, observer" (Tóibín 2009b: 237). A version of this is quoted in *The Master* (Tóibín 2004: 50). Two and a half years later, James began to work on the story which became *The Turn of the Screw*.

> It is, on one level, a deeply and perhaps unconsciously autobiographical story. Because of their restless father, the James children had no peer group or set of close friends as they were growing up. [...] If an aspect of Henry James himself and his siblings became both Miles and Flora, then a larger part of him became the governess. Composing the story in London while repairs were being done on his first house [Lamb House], imagining with friends and correspondents what it was going to be like to travel alone to live in a home with a history, [h]e was, like his creation, thrilled and frightened at the prospect. (Tóibín 2009b: 238-239)

It is clear that, in *The Master*, Tóibín had already made use of these readings. Here, we are told that James first thought of setting the story in Newport, Rhode Island; that when he began to imagine Flora, "it was his sister's unquiet ghost which came to him"; and that Miles is based on himself. Tóibín's narrator states:

> He gave his story everything he knew: his own life and that of Alice in the years when they were alone in England; the possibility which haunted his family all their lives that the threatening great black shape [which appeared to their father] would return to the window and make their father shudder and howl with fear; and the years he was now facing in an old house to which he would soon go, like his governess, full of hope, but full also of a foreboding which he could not erase.[9] (Tóibín 2004: 50, 52, 152-153)

As I intend to show, the Gothic "great black shape" at the window returns to haunt James in *The Master*, but what is missing in this passage, is any sense of the children's corruption. Interestingly, in an act of displacement, this element is provided in *The Master* by the twinning of Miles and Flora/Henry and Alice with Oscar Wilde's two

---

[9] In 1844, Henry James Sr. experienced a spiritual crisis that prompted a hallucinatory incident which convinced him that he had been visited by demonic forces.

children, "whose very name [...] was disgraced for ever" and who, following the Wilde trials, were taken to Switzerland by their mother (Tóibín 2004: 77). Musing on the events, Tóibín's James imagines their fate:

> For days he thought about them, watchful, beautiful creatures in a country where they could not understand a word of the language, their very names obliterated, their father responsible for some dark, nameless crime. He thought of them in some turreted Swiss apartment house in high rooms with a view of the lake, their nurse refusing to explain why they had all come this way, why there was so much silence [...]. He thought of how little they would need to say to each other about the demons that were around them [...] their father a ghostly memory, standing smiling at them on the bare half-lit landing as they climbed the staircase, beckoning in the shadows. (Tóibín 2004: 78)

Here, the references to "silence" and the unspoken, recall that "thematics of absence" that Sedgwick identifies with the expression of homosexual desire in 'The Beast in the Jungle' (Sedgwick 1990: 201). In addition, Wilde's children, surrounded by "demons", recall Miles and Flora, while Wilde himself becomes a spectral figure akin to Peter Quint, who is similarly responsible for "some dark, nameless crime" and who haunts the tower and staircase at Bly. According to Matheson, James's responses to the Wilde trials inform *The Turn of the Screw*. He contends that:

> The story's casting of sexuality in the mode of Gothic terror and its thematizing of the fear of going public are responses to the climate of anxiety surrounding the nonnormative sexuality in England in the 1890s, embodied for James (and many others) by the sensational trials of Oscar Wilde for 'indecency' in 1895, three years before the story's publication. (Matheson 1999: 711)

He adds that James followed the Wilde trials with both "dismayed fascination and a sense of their dramatic interest" (Matheson 1999: 711). A letter to Edmund Gosse, dated 8 April 1895, illustrates Matheson's point and shows how James draws on the language of Gothic fiction to express his emotions. He writes:

> [I]t has been, it is, hideously, atrociously dramatic and really interesting – so far as one can say that of a thing of which the interest is qualified by such a sickening horribility. It is the squalid gratuitousness of it all – of the mere exposure – that blurs the spectacle. But the fall – from nearly 20 years of a really unique kind of 'brilliant' conspicuity [...] to that sordid prison cell & this gulf of obscenity over which the ghoulish public hangs and gloats – it is beyond any utterance of irony or any pang of compassion! (qtd. Horne 1999: 279)

The hideous "horribility" of the Wilde trials finds a correlative in Quint, one of the spectral abominations of Bly. In *The Master* James, like the governess, is constructed as full of hope and foreboding as he contemplates his move to Lamb House. However, these sentiments become implicitly sexual, as they inform her "longing to meet someone, for a face at the window, a figure in the distance" (Tóibín 2004: 149). In acknowledging that this longing would come to him, too, "as the garden door creaked, or the branches of the trees beat against the window as he read by lamplight, or lay awake in that old house", James merges implicitly with his creation (Tóibín 2004: 149). Here, Tóibín gestures at the original text; not only do we learn in the frame narrative to *The Turn of the Screw* that the governess was "in love", we also discover that the story will not tell us with whom she was in love, at least "not in any literal, vulgar way" (James 2007: 6).

In the story, it is Quint whom she sees on a tower, in the grounds, twice at the window and once on the stairway; and Jessel whom she sees on the stairs, in the schoolroom and across the pond. The encounters with Quint at the window are fraught with tension. The first occurs as she re-enters a room to recover her gloves. As she does so, she becomes "aware of a person on the other side of the window and looking straight in", a face she has seen before; his face is "close to the glass" and she gradually becomes aware that he is not looking at her, but beyond her, as if searching for "someone else" (James 2007: 31). That "someone else", she decides, is Miles. The last disturbing encounter takes place at the end of story, when the governess is alone with Miles, questioning him about a stolen letter; again, Quint's "white face of damnation" appears "close to the glass" (James 2007: 128). As Miles confesses to the theft of the letter, the governess considers herself engaged in a battle for Miles's soul and presses him to acknowledge the abomination in their presence. Yet for all that she is convinced to the contrary, the child does not seem to see what she sees. Asking "Is she *here*?", he appears to think that it is Miss Jessel who is at the window (James 2007: 132). While the governess is "staggered" by this, she continues to press him until he finally declares, "Peter Quint – you devil!", followed immediately by the question: *"Where?"*, before he collapses in her arms and dies (James 2007: 133).

When the governess in *The Turn of the Screw*, speaking of the children, tells Mrs Grose, "They're not mine – they're not ours. They're his and they're hers!" (James 2007: 73), she points to two same-sex couplings: Flora and Miss Jessel; Miles and Quint. Tóibín's suggestion that James based the children in his story on himself and his sister Alice, points equally to a doubling of same-sex desire: like James, who engaged in Romantic friendships with young men, Alice's most intense relationship was with a young woman, her companion, Katherine Loring. In addition, Tóibín claims that the governess contains something of James at the time of writing, a figure who, in the story, is "in love" and wishes to see the longed-for object: "a face at the window" (Tóibín 2004: 149). While it is commonly thought that the governess is in love with her employer, whom she has met only once, her effusive expressions of love are reserved for the children. Like Quint and Jessel, she wishes to "possess" the children; she wants them to be "hers", not "theirs". Interestingly, there are further implicit instances of doubling between the governess and Jessel: remembering a moment of distress, the governess tells how "[t]ormented", she sank down "at the foot of the staircase – suddenly collapsing there on the lowest step" and "with a revulsion, recalling that it was exactly where more than a month before, in the darkness of night and just so bowed with evil things, [she] had seen the spectre of the most horrible of women" (James 2007: 89). Later, recalling the image of Jessel seated at her desk in the schoolroom, the governess declares "[d]ark as midnight in her black dress, her haggard beauty and her unutterable woe, she had looked at me long enough to appear to say that her right to sit at my table was as good as mine to sit at hers" (James 2007: 89). The way in which the governess is doubled with Quint is far more subtle yet, perhaps more significant, and occurs each time Quint appears at or by the windows of Bly, but it is clearest at the moment he appears to her on the staircase, at the "uncovered window" in the "yielding dusk of earliest morning" (James 2007: 61). She recalls how, at this point, they meet as "equals":

> The apparition had reached the landing halfway up and was therefore on the spot nearest the window, where, at sight of me, it stopped short and fixed me exactly as it had fixed me from the tower and from the garden. He knew me as well as I knew him; and so, in the cold, faint twilight, with a glimmer in the high glass and another on the polish of the oak stair below, we faced each other in our common intensity. He was absolutely, on this occasion, a living, detestable, dangerous presence. But that was not the wonder of wonders; I reserve this distinction for quite another circumstance: the circumstance that dread had unmistakably quitted me and that there was nothing in me there that didn't meet and measure him. (James 2007: 61)

In her recent book *Victorian Glassworlds* (2008), Isobel Armstrong argues that "[g]lass is an antithetical material. It holds contrary states within itself as barrier and medium"; "Transparency", she goes on to suggest, "encourages a simple dualism, or, what is the opposite form of the same thing, the collapse of the seer and the seen into one another" (Armstrong 2008: 11). Looking at Quint through or at the window, the governess sees herself: not only her desire to 'possess', but also perhaps her desire for sexual knowledge and experience. As Karen Halttunen observes, glass and mirrors are significant in *The Turn of the Screw* and "[r]eflecting surfaces play an important part in the ghostly appearances themselves" (Halttunen 1988: 480). She notes that Miss Jessel first appears across a lake whose mirrored surface shimmers in the glare of sunshine, and Peter Quint appears against the window panes of the dining room and the tall staircase window (Halttunen 1988: 480). Anticipating Halttunen's theory, Juliet McMaster notes that

> the question that James deliberately raises is whether that glass is a transparent pane, through which Peter Quint can clearly be seen, or whether it is, as it may become at dusk, opaque like a mirror, simply giving back to the governess a reflection of herself. (McMaster 1968: 379)

Given Tóibín's suggestion of an implicit doubling between Henry James and the governess in *The Turn of the Screw*, it is worth looking once more at the significance of the window in *The Master*. As noted earlier, the novel's opening focuses on James's agonised desire to see Paul Joukowsky's face at the window of his Paris hotel, a scene Tóibín based on an anecdote related by Edmund Gosse. Indeed, Tóibín arguably also draws on Gosse's language and imagery of enigma and haunting to construct James's spectral sexuality, which Tóibín never allows him to fully admit even to himself. According to Gosse,

> in profuse and enigmatic language [... James] spoke of standing on the pavement of a city, in the dusk, and of gazing upwards across the misty street, watching, watching for the lighting of a lamp in a window on the third storey. And the lamp blazed out, and through bursting tears he strained to see what was behind it, the unapproachable face. And for hours he stood there, wet with the rain, brushed by the phantom hurrying figures of the scene, and never from behind the lamp was for one moment visible the face. (qtd. Tóibín 1999a: 230)

For Gosse, this "mysterious and poignant revelation" which prompted "an overpowering emotion" prohibited all comment or question (qtd. Tóibín 2009a: 230). Later in the novel, musing on a story that would become *The Aspern Papers* while walking through the haunted streets of Venice, this episode is further obfuscated by being heterosexualised as 'James' catches sight of a woman with "her back to a lighted window" (Tóibín 2004: 240), who reminds him of his dead friend Constance Fenimore Woolson. We are told that "he hungered to be in that room where the woman was talking, he longed to hear her voice and follow whatever it was she was saying" (Tóibín 2004: 240). In *The Master*, Joukowsky and Woolson are posited as doomed close encounters of the romantic kind: the windows, through which James sees, function as literal and metaphoric barriers that prevent any conclusive discernment of hetero- or, indeed, homo-sexuality, both of which remain in spectral abeyance. In addition, these significant figures of James's affection appear in silhouette – male and female versions of those "great black shapes", forms that materialise those unspoken fears and desires which haunt both *The Master* and *The Turn of the Screw*: the demonic creature that appears to Henry James Snr.; Wilde's figure "beckoning in the shadows"; Woolson's dresses "floating to the surface again like black balloons"; Quint's evil ghost at the windows and on the staircase at Bly; and Miss Jessel "[d]ark as midnight in her black dress" (Tóibín 2004: 153,78, 270; James 2007: 89). In their recent book on neo-Victorianism, Ann Heilmann and Mark Llewellyn extend Isabel Armstrong's comments on the nature of glass to collapse the boundary between the spectral and the textual and argue that:

> The mystical, even magical nature of the glass object is always a deception, just as the mirror is never a true reflection of reality. The textuality and materiality of the window, mirror, or lens is thus a filter through which imagination and difference might meet, as closely as possible, the true and authentic. (Heilmann and Llewellyn 2010: 145)

In *The Master*, Henry James becomes that shadowy shape against the glass, in which "imagination and difference" meet the "true and authentic". Employing Gothic tropes and their associations with secrecy and sexual transgression, Tóibín cunningly subverts them. Lured by Gothic conventions into expectations of sensational revelations and access to manifestations of forbidden desire, we are left instead with a James who observes "the world as a mere watcher from a window" (Tóibín 2004: 47). In Tóibín's novel, we simultaneously look up at that window, straining to see Henry James, and see out of it through his fictional consciousness at the troubled world of his late-Victorian narratives and their hidden expressions of desire and sexuality; complicit in his voyeurism, and similarly frustrated in our desire to know the 'truth'.

Bibliography
Arias, Rosario, and Patricia Pulham. 2010. 'Introduction', in Arias, Rosario, and Patricia Pulham (eds.), *Haunting and Spectrality in Neo-Victorian Fiction: Possessing the Past*. Houndmills, Basingstoke: Palgrave Macmillan: xi-xxvi.
Armstrong, Isobel. 2008. *Victorian Glassworlds: Glass Culture and the Imagination 1830-1880*. Oxford: Oxford University Press.
Castle, Terry. 1995. *The Apparitional Lesbian: Female Homosexuality and Modern Culture*. Cambridge: Cambridge University Press.
Edel, Leon (ed.). 1980. *Henry James Letters* [in 4 vols.], Vol. 3, 1883-1895. London: Macmillan.
Haggerty, George E. 2006. *Queer Gothic*. Champain, Illinois: University of Illinois Press.
Halttunen, Karen. 1988. '"Through the Cracked and Fragmented Self": William James and *The Turn of the Screw*', *American Quarterly*, 40(4): 472-490.
Hannah, Daniel. 2007. 'The Private Life, the Public Stage: Henry James in Recent Fiction', *Journal of Modern Literature*, 30(3): 70-94.
Heilmann, Ann, and Mark Llewellyn. 2010. *Neo-Victorianism: The Victorians in the Twenty-First Century, 1999-2009*. Houndmills, Basingstoke: Palgrave Macmillan.
Horne, Philip (ed.). 1999. *Henry James: A Life in Letters*. London: Penguin.
James, Henry. 2001. *A Small Boy and Others* [1913]. London: Gibson Square.
——. 2007. *The Turn of the Screw* [1898]. London: Vintage.
Kaplan, Cora. 2007. *Victoriana: Histories, Fictions, Criticism*. Edinburgh: Edinburgh University Press.
Kohlke, Marie-Luise. 2008. 'Introduction: Speculations on the Neo-Victorian Encounter', *Neo-Victorian Studies*, 1(1) (Autumn): 1-18.
Lodge, David. 2006. *The Year of Henry James*. London: Harvill Secker.
Matheson, Neill. 1999. 'Talking Horrors: James, Euphemism, and the Specter of Wilde', *American Literature*, 71(4): 709-750.
McMaster, Juliet. 1968. '"The Full Image of a Repetition" in *The Turn of the Screw*', *Studies in Short Fiction*, 6 (Summer): 377-382.
Merivale, Patricia. 1978. 'The Esthetics of Perversion: Gothic Artifice in Henry James and Witold Gombrowicz', *PMLA*, 93: 992-1002.
Russell Perkin, James. 2010. 'Imagining Henry: Henry James as a Fictional Character in Colm Tóibín's *The Master* and David Lodge's *Author, Author*', *Journal of Modern Literature*, 33(2): 114-130.

Sedgwick, Eve Kosofsky. 1990. *Epistemology of the Closet*. Berkeley & Los Angeles: University of California Press.
Tóibín, Colm. 2004. *The Master*. Basingstoke & Oxford: Picador.
——. 2009a. 'A More Elaborate Web: Becoming Henry James', *Henry James Review*, 30(3): 227-236.
——. 2009b. 'Pure Evil: *The Turn of the Screw*', *Henry James Review*, 30(3): 237-240.
Walshe, Eibhear. 2006. 'The Vanishing Homoerotic: Colm Tóibín's Gay Fictions', *New Hibernia Review*, 10(4): 122-136.
Wolfreys, Julian. 2002. *Victorian Hauntings: Spectrality, Gothic, the Uncanny and Literature*. Houndmills, Basingstoke: Palgrave Macmillan.

'Jack the Ripper' as Neo-Victorian Gothic Fiction: Twentieth-Century and Contemporary Sallies into a Late Victorian Case and Myth

Max Duperray

Abstract:
Several generations have contributed their share in rewriting the 'Jack the Ripper' mystery in different keys. It is a case in point of fiction and reality coalescing, which seems to concentrate the essence of the late Victorian and urban Gothic era, repackaging it for the present's own desire for sensationalism. From 'new' Sherlock Holmes stories and modern Victorian 'underworld' epics to sheer pastiches and psychological thrillers borrowing from Stevenson, Dickens, Collins, and Stoker, neo-Victorian productions encounter a number of methodological problems in remoulding the historical events. Mary Belloc Lowndes and her now famous *The Lodger* (1911) or Clanash Farjeon's more recent *Autobiography of Jack the Ripper* (2003) both bank on psychotic reminiscences, while Peter Ackroyd's *Dan Leno and The Limehouse Golem* (1994) and Iain Sinclair's *White Chappell, Scarlet Tracings* (1991) plunge readers into a subterranean past as encrypted in the present. The dismembering of Jack the Ripper paradoxically becomes a means of renewing fictional modes.

Keywords: Peter Ackroyd, detective novel, the fantastic, Clanash Farjeon, Mary Bellock Lowndes, pathology, penny dreadful, Ripper literature, Iain Sinclair, Paul West.

*****

The famous serial killer of Whitechapel in 1888 has provided continuous inspiration for storytellers of every description ever since. They have helped rewrite the notorious case of 'Jack the Ripper', but the overall paradigm has been the lure of the past as a Victorian murder mystery or the close connection of the case with early detective stories or crime fiction. It is worthwhile to consider metafictional attempts to bank on the public 'novel' of the Jack Ripper case with a view to assessing the way in which writers have approached facts as fictional material or vice versa. 'Jack the Ripper' is a case in point where fiction and reality coalesce, not only because truths and untruths were blurred indissolubly from the start, but also because the extraordinary case and its overheated reception seem to concentrate the essence of the late Victorian era and the climax of urban Gothic in the midst of the poverty-stricken purlieus of East London. Repeated failures and misconceptions of police enquiries left a vacant space for imaginative minds to fill, not least because the murders echoed mounting anxieties in the impoverished populace and the concomitant uneasiness of the well-to-do in a declining empire; in particular fear of – and fascination for – violations of public order and femininity, as well as social and sexual transgression in a puritanical world bent on dissimulation and dissembling, made it seem as if the sheer brutality of the act was a necessary evil to jolt the contemporaries into wakefulness. The story available for writers to invest in is an incredible vacuum, a blank page to paint in lurid colours, a launching pad for fictionalisation and a neo-Gothic leftover in itself. The prevailing dichotomy is not so much fact versus fantasy as one fiction alongside another. Introducing his novel about the case, the American Paul West writes: "One Ripper specialist's fact is another's fiction" (West 1991: preface). The murders have been steeped in textualities of all kinds, literally from the very outset, growing into the 'ur text' of thrilling mystery in a downtrodden urban context. Letter writing, early high circulation fables or mere fancies, all congregated to frame the plural identity of a neo-Gothic construct, the original matrix for future ideas.

1. A New Victorian 'Everyman'

Those heinous crimes were indeed immediately enmeshed in a cultural background of more or less legendary criminal lore. Fascination for non-resolution propelled into existence the hoax of a legendary figure nicknamed by the press as a new Victorian 'Everyman', Jack, master of the knife. He duplicated the popular figure of the suburban ghost preying on unprotected females, 'Spring Heeled Jack', from the 1830s. Both alien, predatory and familiar, saucy, rebellious in his violation of decency, flaunting his audacity anonymously through public statements in writing, Jack passed off as a member of the motley crew of the Newgate calendar pantheon. The persona struck roots in early Victorian 'Penny Bloods', packed with cut-throat business and memories of the gruesome Ratcliff Highway massacre of 1812, already glossed over by Thomas De Quincey in his 1827 seminal essay 'On Murder Considered as One of the Fine Arts'. Serialised hauntings like those of Sweeney Todd, the 'Demon Barber', notably in *The People's Periodical* 1846-47, under the title of *The String of Pearls,* among other such narratives, helped shape the fascinating figure. Extensive press coverage and media frenzy may thus constitute an inaugural chapter of spontaneous fictionalisation under the guise of the letters sent to the press. They provided the contents of a sensational "reality show", featuring "a figure who craved 'sensation' and who communicated to a 'mass' public through the newspaper" (Walkowitz 1992: 200). They mostly dramatised the illusory pre-eminence of a presence and belief in tantalising authenticity, exactly as fiction dreamt of doing. Remarkably, the likelihood that they were written by practical jokesters worked both ways. It emphasised a quasi gamesmanship, which is not alien to fictional appeal and essential to the construction of the fearsome but sardonic figure. In particular, it articulated the resumption of the late Gothic villain, both absolutely other and compellingly familiar, a hero flouting social strictures and – appealingly – defeating authority and police forces, a creature from beyond, almost crudely Mephistophelian.

The press moreover channelled the imaginative drive of the public, for instance fancying a renewal of Poe's *Rue Morgue* (1841), in which a great ape escapes into the city. As a fictional unit pretending to reflect reality at close quarters, the body of letters fulfilled the role of an artistic artefact, "containing and framing a chaotic situation" (Remington 2004: 216) – allowing readers to think in terms of decipherment of the elusive slasher as the sexually frustrated avenger. A number of hypotheses, thrown into the hot pan of fictitious fancies, composed a possible Gothic story on the spur of the moment, notably in the way its vocation, if nothing else, was to ventilate the real and dark humour elicited by the laughable surmises of the investigators. In fact, early Ripper fiction, properly speaking, first appeared serialised in magazines, such as Mary Belloc Lowndes's famous novel, *The Lodger* (1911), published in the early post-Victorian period

In the early days of his rampage and after, the Ripper could easily slip into the mould of popular penny literature, one heritage of the previous, more aristocratic Gothic century, with its 'frenetic' label, situated somewhere in between a budding sleuth fiction and the older supernatural mode. A penny dreadful, *The Whitechapel Murders or the Mysteries of the East End* (1888) had introduced a police detective – as in a novel of adventure – one Ryder, hot on the trail of the killer, disguising himself, infiltrating gangs of pimps or investigating a Russian forger, while informing the reader about dreadful murders committed before: 'Fairy Fay', supposedly one of the victims of the killer and probably a coined name too, or Emma Smith, allegedly assaulted by a gang and claiming retribution. From the very outset, at the time of the event, another publication, *The Curse Upon Mitre Square,* 1888, under the name of John Francis Brewer, publicised the story of a curse on the fateful area stretching back several centuries – a shameless booklet of sensationalistic appeal, recounting the haunting of a mad monk who was supposed to stalk passageways around Mitre.

Even before a prevailing panic arose following press coverage, the people of the streets had flocked to macabre puppet shows, which re-imagined the gory facts as a mystery play of sorts. The kinship between the outrages and the fiction of the time may find a picturesque illustration in the predicament of the American actor Richard Mansfield, who was impersonating Jekyll on stage. His life-like interpretation of the brute Mr Hyde, thanks to facial transformation by grease paint, was thought to procure undue incitement to murder. Some years later, the manager of Henry Irving's Lyceum Theatre in London, the Irishman Bram Stoker, wrote his vampire tale, *Dracula* (1897), which infused a concoction of violence and eroticism in a legendary lore. It has been suggested that Stoker had the Whitechapel atrocities in mind when he devised his novel. Carol Margaret Davison for one maintains that *Dracula* reads like a cryptic rendering of the Ripper mystery (see Davison 1997). In both cases, fact and fiction, crime and vampire novel, the East assumes an allegorical status, whether it be Transylvania or Eastern Europe transplanted into the heart of the empire – the Carpathians or the inmates of London lousy tenements. Should *Dracula*, then, be read as an early fiction of Jack the Ripper, or the miscreant's writing as vying with *Dracula* as an embodiment of late Victorian, post-romantic, neo-Gothic literature? Alexandra Warwick, in a study of Victorian Gothic, writes: "Jack the Ripper, Dorian Gray, Jekyll and Hyde, Dracula, the Invisible Man and Sherlock Holmes swirl in the popular imagination, condensed into a definitive Gothic code" (Warwick 2007: 36). Jack comes out as a fictitious figure, which literature has one way or another domesticated through detection or fantasy.

2. Urban Gothic and After

A 'Jack the Ripper literature' cannot be dissociated from the rise of an urban fiction which was the inheritor of the Gothic productions of the previous century and also a form of realistic, if not necessarily socially oriented, enterprise. The Whitechapel background, peopled with the patrons of whorehouses, wandering police officers looking for random witnesses, and news from the pinchpenny press of the day, provides a rich context. The mythologisation of the case indeed rests on the late Victorian gothicised notion of degeneracy and the demise of arrogant masculinity against a backdrop of promiscuous sexuality. Gothicism in its nineteenth-century version was soon pervaded by symptoms of contamination, disease and demonology, as Andrew Smith pointedly showed in his remarkable study of medicine and the Gothic at the fin-de-siècle, *Victorian Demons: Medicine, Masculinity, and the Gothic fin-de-siècle* (2004). In the 1820s, De Quincey had inaugurated the ironic Romanticist stance by inoculating himself with the poisonous concoction, laudanum, drop by drop. Later the nauseating effects of Arthur Machen's personal mythologies, the empowerment of the double illustrated by the Jekyll/Hyde divide, regression to bestiality with H.G. Wells's *The Island of Dr Moreau* (1896), Dorian Gray's aesthetic posture, all contributed to a decadent Gothicism, which furnished the background against which fictional grisly crimes took place.[1] More precisely, the stark divide of West/East in the city of London provided the convenient framework for crude visions of ambivalence relating to class or race – with one part of the population preying upon the other – and also laid the groundwork for Gothic fiction to flourish, namely as narrative torn between fascination and repulsion, much as neo-Victorian fiction itself has sometimes been described. The journalist W. T. Stead's often quoted pamphlet, 'The Maiden Tribute of Modern Babylon' in *the Pall Mall Gazette* (1885), about the alleged sexual exploitation of the lower classes by predatory 'viveurs' of the West End – "a

---

[1] Appropriately, Andrew Smith employs 'Gothic London' and 'Gothic Journalism' as chapter headings in his book.

typology of sexual crime" (Walkowitz 1992: 131) – only adds to the much fantasised sexual dangers afoot in the capital. The two-way exchanges between grim fantasies, street publications and documentary chronicles foregrounds the major paradigm of the issue and serves the purpose of later rewriting, whether history or fantasy dominates as a motive.

The fertile basis of a neo-Gothic literature was thus readily available and waiting for use. Widely imagined as the site of deepest depravity, 'Darkest London' as the philanthropists of the time would name it, affords the given setting for dark fiction following in the wake of the street broadsides or George W. M. Reynolds's *Mysteries of London* (1844). But neo-Victorian productions have had to negotiate a number of methodological problems in revamping the given story as history has it and finding some middle path between sheer pastiches – as is the case for the renewal of Sherlock Holmes stories and psychological thrillers which might borrow ideas from Stevenson, Dickens, Collins, Stoker and the likes – or clear departures from them.[2] The so-called postmodernist ventures, whose vocation was to rewrite nineteenth-century realistic masterpieces with an ironic bias, deliberately blurring various biographical, novelistic, and documentary materials, and even literary criticism – starting with John Fowles's *The French Lieutenant's Woman* (1969) – revitalised the old Gothic generic medley of the sentimental and the historic, of the romantic and the grotesque.

Interestingly enough, investigations into the case and tentative solutions have also been a useful resource for fictitious construction: the famous royal conspiracy hypothesis in Stephen Knight's *Jack the Ripper: The Final Solution* (1976) offered one such fabulous scenario. It became the root of a modern-day epic and sensational lyrical fiction about the Victorian underworld and the fin-de-siècle bohemian artistry: *The Women of Whitechapel* (1991), by the American Paul West, who had previously specialised in pseudo-historical tapestries and historiographic biofiction ranging from Lord Byron's doctor to Von Stauffenberg. West's ponderous epic novel is a palimpsestic work, teeming with learned references that evoke a brilliant

---

[2] Michael Didbin's *The Last Sherlock Holmes Story* (1978) or Carole Nelson Douglas, *Chapel Noir: A Novel of Suspense featuring Sherlock Holmes, Irene Adler, and Jack the Ripper* (2001) are obvious examples.

kaleidoscopic picture of late nineteenth-century decadence. Knight's book also prompted the script of the famous *From Hell*, the graphic novel by Alan Moore and Eddie Campbell, 1991-1996 (see Domsch, this volume: 100). The murders are redolent of Masonic rituals and are ascribed to the Duke of Clarence, blackmailed by the woman Kelly. The Prince has an affair with a destitute girl of the lower districts, Annie Crook; she is a model for the painter Walter Sickert, who in turn becomes himself enmeshed in the lethal plot.[3] The sinister Doctor Gull abducts the girl and lobotomises her and thereafter disposes of her friends of the streets who had knowledge of the problem. The most resonant scene of his tortured tale is that of the 'butcher' Gull, who scours Whitechapel accompanied by his complicit coachman Netley, offering grapes to his victims so as to ensnare them. The book unfolds, profusely replete with hallucinatory insights into a degenerate world, highlighting the villain of medical persuasion who personifies the mad doctor of Gothic ascendancy, in the wake of the mad scientist tradition, an echo of Victor Frankenstein or Dr Moreau as enduring prototypes. Furthermore, the tortured Sickert is centrally involved in the world of art, with Oscar Wilde and the bohemian artists helping to infuse the popular melodrama with a modernist vision. Walter Sickert is fascinated by the French transgression inherent in the generation of the Yellow Book – "*peintre maudit* […]. Let us be as *louche* as we can" (West 1991: 28) – and "dresses up as Napoleon, Degas, Whistler, Byron, Burns" (West 1991: 170). The hallmark of West's Gothic lies in its kinship with the grotesque – mostly melodramatic. He saturates the text with piled up notations, as when he depicts Annie Crooke in Mrs Morgan's tobacconist and sweetshop:

> The realm of gratification, she thought (being its queen), had thrones of rubber, cones of catgut, crown jewels made of aching balls, slaves and syrups from Morocco, whips of best Andalusian leather, and photographs so gross they melted. (West 1991: 191)

Or when he reports the coachman Netley on his murderous rides:

---

[3] Patricia Cornwell, of course, has argued that Sickert himself was the actual Ripper (Cornwell 2002).

> Ideally, he thought, they would do their murdering in Dockland next to uninterrupted expanses of oily unrefreshed water, with rats promenading around them for company, ready to lick up the spill [...] the double murder kept him in a state of constant murderousness like a human elevated to godhead and dangling over the entire human race, his fangs unretracted. (West 1991: 345)

The pith of West's bulky epos is indeed its sophisticated language and elaborate craftsmanship, its circumvolutory practice creating a nauseating effect. Paul West thus reactivated, but also remodelled, the typical urban mysteries that had been so attractive for previous generations, based on given ingredients: a true romance, upper stratum conspiracy, love beyond class distinction in the face of annihilation, the villain passed off as therapist – in the tradition of double dealing figures of the Gothic – and the feckless artist bound to participate in the horror against his will.[4]

Mystery, with its uncanny overtones, had first bloomed in the wake of urban Gothic and in a distinctly poetic direction. The French 'fantastique social' of the 1820s, connected to the underworld and its exoticism, beneath the surface of normality and mingling Eros with indomitable violence, harks back to De Quincey's urban wanderings as a 'walker of the street' alongside the destitute 'street walkers'. That school of writing revamped 'l'école frénétique' of the early nineteenth century in France.[5] 'Jack the Ripper', a magnet for Pierre Mac Orlan's trips to London's harbour, in *Sous la lumière froide* (1927), or in *Villes* (1929), epitomised by the memories of Stevenson's Edward Hyde, had its roots in "the sinister fantasy-fiction of German Romanticism" (Hewitt 1987: 44) – thus a reiteration of the prestige of German lore felt by the Gothicists of the eighteenth century, such as 'Monk' Lewis and later Mary Shelley. Pierre Mac Orlan introduced the ghostly presence in his account of his short sojourn near

---

[4] Indirectly, the mad scientist or painter, the quaintness of the world of art, might relate to a relatively common trope of fantastic fiction of the decadent period, to be found in Aubrey Beardsley, Sheridan Le Fanu ('Shalken the Painter' [1839]), Arthur Machen or Vernon Lee.

[5] An expression first introduced by Charles Nodier in 1821 to refer to 'Le roman noir' (see Glinoer 2009).

Commercial Street as in a district of shadows. His guide is a sixty-year-old man who had been Anne Radcliffe's contemporary – and so rather two centuries old. Nostalgia pervades the writer's visions of the London docklands. More than frightful, Jack becomes congenial as an inhabitant of the place, and remains shy and ironically unobtrusive, seemingly inhibited. In *Sous la lumière froide*, the French poet writes the biography of an adolescent brought up in Poplar, Limehouse and Barking, in the vicinity of the 'fallen women', "girls of the Thames" ("*filles de la Tamise*", MacOrlan 1927: 142). His melancholy description of the young Tess, the blind prostitute, harks back to Anne found and lost in *The Confessions of an English Opium Eater* (1822). Crime on the premises is an inbred instinct, he writes, and the poor women fear the cold wintry wind more than the discrete call of Jack the Ripper: "*Les pauvres filles grelottantes craignent plus le vent du Nord que le petit appel timide de Jack l'Eventreur*" (MacOrlan 1927: 166).

Yet the latter's blood-replete ghost haunts the gin-soaked women. Mac Orlan – and to a lesser extent Robert Desnos, in his journalistic series of 1928, staging the supercilious dandy of aristocratic appeal – have inherited the Quincean spell to write atmospheric fiction providing useful signposts and references for future literary renewals.

Before that, however, the unsolved murder case could provide the ideal playground for detection. Edgar Allan Poe or Wilkie Collins had done much to re-channel the Gothic towards the detective novel. Next to De Quincey, Conan Doyle is perhaps *the* iconic figure in Ripper literature. His *Study in Scarlet*, published in 1887, ten years before *Dracula*, is the inaugural novel for his famous series of Sherlock Holmes and Watson stories, an alluring template to investigate the literary 'afterlife' of the Jack the Ripper case.

Versions of fictional killers self-evidently inspired by Jack have featured among a whole tide of crime fiction of every description in the next decades, as well as in neo-Victorian fiction in subsequent centuries. Following hard upon Conan Doyle's dalliances with the Ripper – even though he never addressed the case directly despite many appeals of the public to do so – experiments in Sherlock Holmes's highly expected contribution to the case have proliferated. The temptation was to mix the historical Whitechapel events and the fictional occurrences of the Conan Doyle canon. Despite the somewhat disappointing outcomes of many experiments in this vein, occasionally more interesting fictions have been produced. Among these, Michael Didbin's *The Last Sherlock Holmes Story* (1978) has made a non-canonical contribution by updating the detective's susceptibility to psychosis to the verge of the absurd, making fun of the Sherlockian tradition. He starts by tinkering with the convention of the found manuscript, making Conan Doyle, 'ACD', the alleged publisher of Watson's relations of Holmes's cases for the sake of a somewhat grotesque inversion, as he exposes Holmes himself as the long sought serial killer. Yet the sadness of Watson's discovery that his longtime friend has gone insane makes the book worthwhile, adding a sentimental flavour to the Gothic resumption of the Doppelgänger. An American writer and actress, Lindsay Faye, recently produced a less caricaturish pastiche, *Dust and Shadow: An Account of the Ripper Killings by John H. Watson* (2009), keeping close to historical facts and inserting the detective of great renown in the maze of the actual events of 1888 Tower hamlets, which he penetrates thanks to Mary Ann Monk, a former inmate of Lambeth workhouse. The writer reactivates a near Dickensian London and kicks off a novel of adventure by throwing the detective headlong into the brutal scuffle, exposing him to lethal dangers from which he will barely escape. The mob itself appears in its blind ferocity and threatens anybody suspected of belonging to the medical profession. Ultimately, the criminal returns to his mother, an old hag in Flower and Dean Street, who spends most of her life by the fire with a tailless cat – a plunge back into the universe of The Brothers Grimm's tales or the Dickensian world of Oliver Twist.

Likewise, Iain Sinclair, another major participant in the Ripper reinterpretation project, had started from Conan Doyle when writing his own neo-Gothic novel. Introducing *A Study in Scarlet* for the Penguin Classics edition, he expressly linked Doyle's fiction to the Whitechapel events; that Conan Doyle should have published his book just a year before the Spitalfields/Whitechapel rampage is far from inconsequential in his eyes. In his *White Chappell, Scarlet Tracings* (1987), he staged Watson returning to London from India and becoming a 'flaneur' in the London cesspool, while his master's inactivity and psychosis seemingly finds an outlet in the horrific crisis of the East End, where he can reactivate his skills. Such speculative scenarios in lieu of mundane facts are a flattering suggestion for metaphysical stances such as Sinclair's along Holmes's urban and mental peregrinations; hence the outflow of Sherlock Holmes rebirths for a continuation of detection and thrilling plots with a Gothic flavour.

3. Neo-Victorian Pastiches

From the start the Ripper's unsolved killing spree and concomitant detective fiction had indeed exhibited a kinship with psychosis and madness whether individual or collective. In accordance with growing public awareness and debate surrounding deviance and madness in the late nineteenth century, the hallmark of new Gothic fostered by the Ripper case seems to have been the "process of pathologisation", as Andrew Smith calls it, foregrounding the paradox that "the killer's extraordinariness emerged from his ordinariness" (Smith 2004: 85).

That relationship between individual secret pathology and indiscernible monstrosity gave birth to another seam in the Ripper literature, perhaps the most disquieting of all, starting early in 1911 with Mary Belloc Lowndes's *The Lodger* and, more recently, producing a few gems, among which the pseudo memoir, *A Handbook For Attendants on the Insane: Jack the Ripper's Autobiography as Revealed to Clanash Farjeon* (2003), by a Canadian writer publishing under the titular pseudonym, constitutes the most achieved example. Studies in psychosis, insights into insanity, in the wake of Wilkie Collins or Guy de Maupassant, also produced, in a lesser key, fragments of the fantastic, as Brian L. Porter's *A Study in Red: The Journal of Jack the Ripper* (2008) exemplifies.

Mary Belloc's early attempt to build a fiction out of the case might have been produced by chance rather than intended as a wilful literary project. Remarkably, in the way the first penny dreadfuls or broadsides appeared, it was first serialised in *The Lure Magazine*, in 1911, and was much later picked up by Hitchcock for one of his early masterpieces. It is the first serious novel on the case, close to an adventure thriller that Wilkie Collins could have produced, were it not for the minimalist style of spellbound narration. At a dinner, Belloc had heard a woman say that she had come near a dubious lodger, who could have been the killer himself. Stories about suspect lodgers were plentiful, notably with one major suspect, an American quack doctor, Dr Francis Tumblety. Reported by the German landlady of a boarding house, who claimed to have seen blood on his shirt cuffs, the man was a bizarre collector of human organs, vocal about his hatred for women. Belloc took up the suggestion to write a story in which an elderly couple, who have to take lodgers in order to survive, are confronted by a most curious, elusive individual. As her husband, lost in his avid newspaper reading, remains mostly unconcerned, the landlady, Mrs Bunting, is left largely to her own resources in managing the relationship with the disturbing newcomer. The book is a feat of suspenseful plotting, as data accumulate to implicate the polite, finicky, religious fanatic, who refuses meat and reads the Bible by himself focusing on misogynistic passages, as the killer who terrorises London – albeit in a wider area than the historic zone of Jack's crimes. But beyond that, Belloc explores distress in the face of an agonising moral conflict. The crux of the matter is the gradual slip of the landlady from sheer terror, counteracted by economic necessity, to intense curiosity and secret compassion, as she apprehensively listens to her lodger's nocturnal outings and stealthy moves, as if mesmerised by the snake-like personality that she harbours in her house: a man who discretely carries on so-called scientific experiments behind closed doors while summoning her by ringing a bell for his scanty meals. Each shocking situation adds up to the intensity of that strange relationship developing via innuendoes and indirections, like that of the apparent red ink oozing from the suitcase he has left in the cupboard of his room. Everything unfolds within the gothically confined space of the house – bedrooms upstairs, kitchen below where the 'avenger', as the press calls him, cooks a bizarre and ill-smelling cuisine on the sly, an allusion to the purloined kidney and cannibalistic consumption publicised in one of the letters sent to the press. Most of the spell cast by the narrative lies in the locked room effect: the inner premises seldom open onto the outer world from which news intrudes only via the papers and the voices of the newspaper boys crying out the headlines. Ironically, into this pent-up and cramped locus, truth oozes like blood, while outside the institutional authorities, sometimes embodied by a young policeman, a friend of the family, blunder and fail to understand anything.

The writer has emphasised that paradoxical set-up by calling the strange newcomer 'Mr Sleuth', a curious inversion suggesting that the suspect is paradoxically the investigator calling for the necessity of analysing and deciphering the intricacies of the human brain. To a great extent Mrs Bunting is as much a problem as he is in her enduring reluctance to come to terms with an obvious reality, with the distinctly Other, who nonetheless seems so gentleman like, the very sort of person the Buntings would have chosen as their ideal lodger – Mr Bunting himself being a retired butler who spent his life in the service of the great. Through the demanding mores of the lodger, both principled and reserved, Mrs Bunting vicariously participates in withdrawing from the strictures of humdrum reality and indirectly identifies with the potential 'sacrifice' of the fallen women who, as her husband says, pollute the town of London anyway. She has accepted from the very beginning the glittering gold sovereigns for the rent. She secretly fears that the lodger should be unmasked, not mainly because she would lose her means of survival, but because she gradually feels a deeper and morbid solidarity towards the criminal who took refuge under her roof. Hence her lies to the nosy detective and the lies to herself to try and address the mixture of guilt and desire, hidden like the stowaway in her home, Mr Sleuth, 'S' like Satan. The landlady ultimately exemplifies a case of possession; she becomes evil possessed and the text draws somewhat nearer the madman's diary, though the omniscient narrator's formula precludes that assimilation. Mr Bunting for one ponders the paradox of the situation: that a such a queer gentleman should have made their life so different! A case of selling one's soul in other words. "Strange, was it not, that that odd, luny-like gentleman should have made all the difference to his and Mrs Bunting's happiness and comfort of life" (Belloc Lowndes 2008: 190). The novel indeed reads like a tale, somewhat reminiscent of 'The Monkey's Paw' (1902) by W. W. Jacobs, in which a talisman enables an old couple to make three wishes, but ironically turns out to be a trap and an evil piece of machinery. In Belloc's novel, the landlady, by taking the gold sovereigns, more than normally required for the rent, symbolically sells her soul and connives in the spilling of innocent blood. She epitomises the feminine predicament so familiar to Gothic tradition, more covertly than overtly.

More recently, an English novelist, Pamela Oldfield, has returned to the theme of the enemy within the house in a chilling novel, *Jack's Shadow: A Jack the Ripper's Mystery* (2007), where a woman marries a seemingly perfect loving and rich man, who turns out to be entirely different from what she believes – thus reorienting the deception of the innocent female, so profuse in fiction from *Jane*

Eyre (1847) to *Rebecca* (1938), towards a Ripper tale. Her situation redoubles in that of her niece Lottie, herself orphaned and vulnerable. The heroine Bella's life-story at the time of the Whitechapel events encapsulates memories of Wilkie Collins's *The Woman in White* (1859) or Sheridan Le Fanu's serialised tale *Uncle Silas* (1864) with the grisly destiny of the young orphan Maud, also the victim of unsavoury ravishers, who herself claims kinship with Adeline, the heroine of Mrs Radcliffe's *The Romance of the Forest* (1791): "I feel so like Adeline, in the 'Romance of the Forest', the book I was reading to you last night" (Le Fanu 1966: 358). Endangered but also desiring femininity is a theme which runs through Gothic across generations; "all gothic is generally female" as Anne Williams has it (Williams 1995: 11).

Neo-Victorian reworkings of the Ripper myth have thus banked on the Gothic trope of double personality and the issue of the evil Other behind elaborate and conventional civility. Moreover they have helped the gendered question of the victimised female resurface in all its ambiguity. In most cases indeed, fear of the monstrous slasher also implies a hidden fascination for a ritualistic transgression. Some writers have been more radical in suggesting a female Ripper as Peter Ackroyd did in *Dan Leno* or the Russian Boris Akunin in *The Decorator* (2007).

4. Pseudo Manuscripts Lost and Found

Clanash Farjeon's recent novel *A Handbook for The Attendants of the Insane: The Autobiography of Jack the Ripper* (2003) chooses another strategic bias, granting the murderer himself a voice. It is a further innovation to existing piecemeal Ripper fiction, in so far as Farjeon writes it as the purported biography of another, namely the contemporary psychiatrist and alienist, Lyttleton S. Forbes Winslow, who came to be a suspect himself at the time, so great was his interest in the case and his personal investigation on the premises. He wrote his memoirs in 1910, maintaining that the criminal was responsible for even more than the spectacular crimes usually attributed to him.

In fact 'Farjeon' is a pseudonym, yet another mask, used by the Canadian actor and director Alan Scarfe. The curious authorial name might read like one borrowed from real life by Farjeon/Winslow, since it was also the name of an actual contemporary writer, Benjamin Farjeon. The 'neo-Victorian' Farjeon supposedly writes another's unpalatable biography, but reveals himself as the gruesome Jack, since most of the hero's life-story not only overlaps Winslow's own but seems vindicated by popular obsessive theorising about the frightful murders in question. Critical coverage on the web almost reads as if the autobiography *is* that of the real-life Winslow whose actual memoir, *Handbook For Attendants On The Insane* (1877) is similarly entitled. The game with time sequences is redolent of the fantastic, though unobtrusively so. The narrator protests the current disinterest for his writings from a century before, but asserts that he died in 1913. Hence his allusion to 'Ripperologists', for instance, is sheer anachronism, while the recent publication of the text itself, of course, further highlights the deliberate confusion where chronology is concerned.

Farjeon makes his persona exploit the unique position of the first person's confession, the paradoxical stance of the artist giving vent to a long hidden passion while purportedly remaining free from an emotional entanglement with it as a reporter of his own experience. The speaker's indirect involvement helps keep a distance necessary for expression. The artist as murderer shares a realistic vision of 'normal' people as distinguished from himself, yet calls upon the audience to participate imaginatively in his transgressive career, and endorse the anxiety of alienation.

The first part of the book never derails from the memories of a psychiatrist implicated in famous and extraordinary crime cases. Very rationally reported facts, however, rely on a collation of inherited documents, which he carefully and selectively employs in his investigations, casting more doubt on the veracity of his report. The redoubling effect of a spectator narrator, both strategic director of the show and 'neutral' observer of its reception, is conducive to a narrative of split personality, all the more so as, in the case of the letters sent to the press, he maintains having received some signs by the maniac, before discounting them as his own forgery. Occasionally, he may compare himself to an opium addict or, much later, impart to the reader the idea of writing a madman's diary, as well as of a narrative which might designate James Maybrick as the ideal criminal. This constitutes another way of propelling the persona or cultural myth into the present-day real: in the early 1990s, the probably fake Maybrick manuscript had raised a controversial debate among Ripper experts as to the authenticity of the reemerging manuscript, reminiscent of Edgar Allan Poe's messages found in a bottle. He will also confess playing with fire and pushing his advantage as far as possible in the successful art of dissembling: when meeting the actor Mansfield, Mr Hyde on stage, he takes him to the very scenes of his own crimes. From a literary standpoint the repeated images of make-believe and acting curiously redouble the ambiguous status of the novel itself and the duality of the confessing persona, both the empowered official and the subversive Other. Typically, like so much neo-Victorian writing and more precisely neo-Victorian metafictions, alternate fictionalised stories run parallel to historic records.

Farjeon's overall neo-Victorian project, however, was to narrate the unholy crusade by adopting the deviant psychology of the protagonist and thus see everything from inside, which entails a disturbingly intimate relationship between speaker and listener. The speaker tries his best to distance himself from the monomaniac religious fanatic of murderous tendencies and to ascertain the difference between patient and therapist – a distance which the text patiently and almost silently erodes, as he is both the familiar participant of the scene and the stranger, a unique persona being contaminated by abjection and responsible for it. Similarly, as a talented writer, he harps on the metaphor of the veil: tearing up the veil to unveil transcendental enigmas. One singular image of mental disturbance is the curious dream of collected objects after a robbery and notably the cigarette-cases by a non-smoker. Another memory is that of a killer on a train who was killing for no reason. Meaning and purpose ebb away within a rational discourse of punctilious precision, detachment and imperturbability.

The madman's diary remarkably fits the diseased brain of a Victorian psychopath at the time when Jean-Martin Charcot appeared as a reference in Stoker's *Dracula*. The lure of the personal diary also surfaces in Brian L. Porter's *A Study in Red: The Secret Journal of Jack the Ripper* (2008), the lost manuscript inherited by Dr Robert Cavendish, a contemporary psychiatrist whose forbears have bequeathed the inherited journal of the long-dead infamous killer of the late nineteenth century. Its reading assumes a growing and compelling effect on him. The Gothic theme of an ancestral sin overshadowing future generations surges up when the protagonist comes to understand that his great-grandfather embarked upon a mystic mission of murderous sacrifices to eradicate vice and mock

Christianity and that the curse of his crimes may live on across centuries.

Porter's book more precisely resorts to recipes of the Fantastic, a rereading of Gothic in a more intellectual or ironic mode, inserting the sceptical reception in its poetics. That trend had found its most famous example in the 1940s with 'Yours Truly, Jack the Ripper' (1943), a short story by Robert Bloch, the author of *Psycho* (1959), which exhumed the Melmoth theme of eternal damnation. Transporting the tale to America 1943, and making seedy Chicago a possible uncanny copy of nineteenth-century foggy London, Bloch had focused on a dialogue between two characters, a local psychiatrist and an English visitor who turns out to be an offspring of one of Jack's victims, on the trail of a murderer still alive and kicking. Bloch writes his story as an extended joke. It is mainly a trick played on the reader's expectation, as when the neutral narrator and would-be investigator drops a mask and exclaims: "Call me Jack", the ultimate punch line, in a style which Bloch continued to assume in another darkly humorous story, 'A Toy for Juliette' (1967), replete with Sadean overtones, for which Harlan Ellison wrote a sequel. But he certainly moves away from a purely neo-Victorian transfer.

5. Historiographic Metafiction

Where resumption of neo-Victorian Gothic is concerned though, contemporary novels choosing to collate Victorian references as 'souvenirs' or inserted subtexts, sometimes predicated upon a psychotic echo, abound. Across the century-long span between the first fictional productions, heavily dependent upon the serial narratives produced for the common people, and the latest attempts at renovating an overexploited theme for sophisticated readers, literary stances have succeeded one another in time, helping Gothic survive and prosper by re-negotiating its status within new artistic modes. Moreover, in a growing give and take with the visual arts, graphic literature and the cinema tend to assume increasing importance.

But more to the point are metafictional reconstructions. Peter Ackroyd's novel ranks among the most characteristic example: a throwback to a London past steeped in the universe of popular entertainment. His *Dan Leno and The Limehouse Golem* (1994), not a direct transcription of the case, but a plunge into a revivified subterranean past, reads like the fountainhead of renewed fictional engagement with the Ripper myth, already embroiled in earlier experiments of the same kind by Ackroyd. He had worked on the figure of Nicholas Hawksmoor before, who designed churches in eighteenth-century London, notably Christ Church near Commercial Street. Hence, Hawksmoor and the infamous monster of Whitechapel shared and contributed to "a protean web of mysticism" as *The Literary Guide to the World* phrases it in its article 'Destination Whitechapel and Spitalfields' (Hynes 2006). William Blake's prophetic poems, as well as fantasies like the Royal and Masonic conspiracy, are revisited by contemporary fictions in oneiric directions. Sinclair's *Lud Heat* (2002), both poem and narrative, together with Ackroyd's *Hawksmoor* (1985), where the architect turns sleuth, are major examples. Interestingly, in the latter, the plot is one of a detective story since murders are being committed in the vicinity of the churches, the locations of which, when linked, form a pagan pentagram. In his peculiar surrealistic and arcane fiction, *White Chappel, Sarlet Tracings,* Sinclair, adding another dreamlike twist to Paul West's picturesque epos, shores up an alternative mythology. The macabre overtone inherent in the brutal murders of 1888 resonates in the dark underground history of the city transported into a timeless limbo. It is no wonder that metafiction, and of a historiographic kind to boot, keen on the mystery of palimpsest and vocationally oriented towards the pastiches of previous literary works, should have invested in the open-ended Ripper case, focusing on the coruscating world of the decadent period. The psychotic thriller *Dan Leno and the Limehouse Golem* in particular pays tribute to the music hall stage as the mesmerising hub, the cynosure of all investigating eyes. Contemporary literature feeds on a town which harks back to Dickens, whose fiction was in itself steeped in Gothic overtones.

Dan Leno and the Limehouse Golem assumes both a central and specific position here, first because it fails to resort to a faithful rewriting of historical facts, but deliberately steps into a non-temporal fictitious blend of history and fantasy, mixing fable, crime and popular shows of the Victorian stage and literary criticism also. The novelist steeps his narrative in the subconscious realm of an era, if not in his own mind prone to construct the mystical entity of London, as he has done throughout his writing career. His detailed knowledge of Victorian London as exemplified in *Hawksmoor* and *Chatterton* (1987), after *The Great Fire of London* (1982) and before his bulky

London: The Biography (2000), seeps through, even if documentary knowledge never intrudes. The new genre thus helps build an occult version of capital execution and crime as part and parcel of a Gothic comedy being performed, with a prestigious cast among whom George Gissing and Karl Marx feature as inveterate readers at the Reading Room in the British Museum, the central location of literary creation and meeting point of all the actors of the drama. They tend to read one another's works, Marx reading Gissing's urban novels, while Gissing peruses De Quincey's essay on murder, as if there were indeed no other reality than scriptural. De Quincey's *Confessions* is read in passing in nearly Gothic terms:

> the city [...] a labyrinth of stone, a wilderness of blank walls and doors [...] and his suffering within it, became – if we may borrow a phrase from that great modern poet Charles Baudelaire – the landscape of his imagination. (Ackroyd 1997: 39)

That tends to update the nightmarish framework of the text which is contaminated by the lurid comedy on stage; for Master of them all is Dan Leno, the famous comedian and music-hall entertainer, a historic figure who enables the lost world of entertainment to re-emerge, like clog dancing, recitations of 'The Dramatic Maniac' and popular songs and ballads, mixing pathos, humour and the grotesque. But Ackroyd also installs the cultural background of mystic lore: an old Jewish scholar is found hacked up, and a Hasidic treatise stands open to an entry on the Golem.

Despite the departure from the common run of fictional enterprises on the question, Ackroyd sets a plot in motion from the vantage point of aesthetics: De Quincey, the forlorn poet and walker of the street, serves as the 'ur text' of the world of crime – hence the superposition of the Ratcliff Highway killings of 1812 and the Jack the Ripper ones, revisited as the Jewish bugbear, the Limehouse Golem, during the year 1880. That paradigmatic reference ushers in the domineering concept of the solitary artist, if not genius, whose destiny is to incarnate the city itself just like De Quincey's London with its nautical metaphors, and dubious voyage homewards: "my attempts to steer homewards, upon nautical principles" (De Quincey 1998: 47).

As a result *Dan Leno* is a remarkable transfer of Victorian fear and amusement against the backdrop of gruesome crime in the city of yesteryear and its murky alleyways. It is a reader's world, namely a "Victorian nightmare" as one American journalist described it (Martin 1995). As the text puts it in a self-reflexive comment:

> Charles Dickens and certain 'problem novelists' had described the horrors of urban poverty before but these accounts were characteristically sentimentalised or sensationalised to take account of the public taste for Gothic effects. (Ackroyd 1997: 268)

Reading characters and authors leave it to the reader to read excerpts from the diary of John Cree, a journalist who died an unnatural death and whose wife, Elizabeth Cree, is being examined in court for the alleged poisoning of her husband. History again looms behind, since one of the major suspects in the Jack the Ripper case, Maybrick, died of poison, his wife being arraigned and first condemned for the crime. Elizabeth is the focus of the text. She stands on the scaffold of Camberwell Prison at the outset, and the story unfolds retrospectively. Hers is the life-story of a Dickensian waif becoming the self-made woman, tearing herself away from the poverty-stricken Limehouse marshes of her childhood to step on to the stage of variety theatres. Remarkably, she marries the journalist Cree, a regular attendant of her performances with literary ambitions. She palliates his incapacity to bring a play to completion by replacing him for the job. Her talent at writing ultimately proves to be an unexpected key to the thriller, giving it a shocking twist as melodrama would have it, and throws a retrospective light on the peculiar mores of the woman. Remarkably, her professional talent for disguise is modelled on that of her master, Dan Leno, not to mention that of her creator, Peter Ackroyd himself. Transvestism on the stage suggests a transsexual dissembling process: with male attires on, Elizabeth Cree loves to walk by night through Limehouse and the fated districts where gory murders take place. So according to the rule of the thriller a false lead has indeed been provided all along for the reader to be led astray in the maze of a plot resembling that of the dark passageways of degenerate London with its smoke-filled pubs and rowdy music-halls. Moreover Victorian melodramas might be close at hand in the suggestion of forged identity or disguise and the use of misleading paths or sensational discoveries.

In a sort of self-reflexive logic, melodramas on the stage encapsulate the drama that Ackroyd writes, albeit more highbrow than its models – notably because of a rhythmic succession in focus from one narration to another, to ensure a mirror to the enterprise of devising yet another neo-Gothic resumption of nineteenth-century fiction. It is Victorian sensational fiction through the medium of a postmodernist narrativity, twisting and fracturing viewpoint through the prism of plurality, juxtaposing an omniscient knowledge, Elizabeth's talks, her trial transcripts and the disturbing purported diary of her dubious husband.

As for Sinclair's *White Chappell, Scarlet Tracings*, it is a case apart, a feat of impressionistic wordcraft closer to William Blake's visionary London or Jerusalem, sounding "the midnight harlot's curse" ('London', 1794), than a direct rewriting of the murder case. Despite his alleged starting point – he supposedly works from Conan Doyle – he hardly exhumes a pseudo Victorian piece of writing as Ackroyd would do, but rather picks up the sensational overtone as a starter for his dreamlike investigation of traces – for a travelogue in the 'psychogeographic' universe of itinerant bibliophiles, similar to arrant knaves and errant knights. But this piece of harsh impressionistic poetry reads like a surrealistic fiction on the verge of obscurity, more than a postmodernist plagiarism of previous novels. All the same, the Victorian world of late serves as a reference with half-mythical resonances, interweaving detective fiction and book dealings and the murders of 1888. Victorian Gothic stands as a mental construct revivified in totally new terms. The uncanny narrator is a posthumous Dr Watson, almost incongruous in a metaphysical pseudo-detective novel rather than in a story of detection. Sinclair himself pops up like Hitchcock as a transient actor of his films. The references to *A Study in Scarlet* tend to update words rather than plot. Indirect homage to the 'poètes maudits', Rimbaud and Verlaine, and their sojourn in London years before the events, helps understand the options of a peculiar resumption of the Whitechapel events in a nightmarish, but also poetic, context, by embedding the act of writing in the murdering process: writing and cutting. Dr Gull, the alleged Ripper, is seen cutting, when a child, a white trace into a slate, and that foreshadows later developments. From this viewpoint, the book is an interesting case of rewriting of Gothic ventures recast through the piecemeal fragmentation of postmodernist, almost Derridean, poetics. What remains of a notorious and extraordinary case rises again phoenix-like or looms as gleaming gems within a half darkness of intertextual networks. Textuality is thematised through the characters of the seamy bibliophiles dealing in books, lost in labyrinthine bookshops and crossing Dr Gull or Merrick, the Elephant Man, while giving the whole text its stylistic flavour as it deconstructs the omniscient narrator convention. The overall rationale of the text is given in Chapter 7 when one of the major characters, the sculptor Joblard, finds Knight's *The Final Solution* and pits it against the prophetic writing theory that Stevenson or Conan Doyle have illustrated. Far from the poetics typical of detective fiction focused on unravelling a given crime, the assumed purpose transpires in esoteric pronouncements:

> we want to assemble all the incomplete movements, like cubists, until the point is reached when the crime can commit itself [...] the Whitechapel deeds cauterised the millennial fears, cancelled the promise of revelation. (Sinclair 2004: 51)

The novel is a case in point for the interplay between esoteric fiction and mundane events, the history of the place and that of the book. The exhumation process reads like a poetic transplant of older Gothic into the impressionistic discourse of a demented poet. Dodgy bibliophiles stalk the seedy town obsessed by memories of Jack the Ripper, since "the city is a museum itself" (Sinclair 2004: 111), keeping archives replete with names like those of the Ripper's victims. The idea is of writers as mediums bound to elicit a truth that History conceals:

> I mean that certain fictions laid out a template that was more powerful than any local documentary account, chiefly Conan Doyle, Stevenson, but many others too, the presences they created or figures became too much or too fast to be contained within the conventional limits of that fiction. (Sinclair 2004: 117)

6. The James Family in History and Fable

A fake historical novel by the American academic Paula Marantz-Cohen, *What Alice Knew: A Most Curious Tale of Henry James and Jack the Ripper* (2010), has recently come out, making room for real life figures, notably from the world of arts. Her professional interest in Henry James and her taste for pastiches – she previously tried her hand at imitating Jane Austen in bringing her to an American regional context – urged her to confront James and his family with the criminal case in London where he was staying at the time. Henry's brother William, the pioneering researcher in psychology and philosophy, is summoned to give advice on the murder case and assist in the investigation.

The brilliant family is shot through by the mounting suspicion that artistry and crime might overlap in the milieu of decadent painters like John Singer Sargent and the inevitable Walter Sickert – hence the prevalence of dramatically and ironically pointed remarks about the beauty of murder in the wake of De Quincey and the Gothic trope of the devious creator. In the seamless blend of fact and fiction, for a detective novel seasoned with Gothic innuendoes, the visit to the mortuary where the butchered corpse of the victim has been stitched together again in the semblance of a proper body is certainly more Gothic than anything lurid imaginations may have conceived. But the overall pattern precisely recalls Stoker's masterpiece: like Mina the vampire-smitten heroine who turns into the leading mind of the 'Crew of Light' and directs them from her refuge, bed-ridden Alice, the handicapped sister of the team, investigates and builds up a relationship with Sickert, the eccentric painter who stands as the major suspect – seriously pointed out as the actual murderer by Patricia Cornwell in her 2002 study *Portrait of a Killer: Jack the Ripper – Case Closed*. As might be expected, Marantz-Cohen cannot follow suit despite the number of clues assembled in the novel, but still picks up the artistic guideline, creating a demented subordinate who might do the trick, if an epilogue did not throw this in doubt and maintain Henry's salutary and enduring scepticism as to the 'solution' of the crimes long after the events, when he remains the only survivor of the enquiring family.

The witty portrayals of the characters involved lend a realistic flavour to the context of Jack the Ripper. This is a successful reconstruction of the chief actors' mental Weltanschauung. They participate in the rationalisation of the horrific reality behind the scene, as clues are dropped along the way for the siblings to pick up. Henry James is a somewhat unconcerned ironic spectator helping in the game of detection. Dismal dramatic irony helps the author displace the historical despatch of the cut off kidney to the leader of the Vigilante committee. The fictionalised Alice receives the wrapped up breast of a victim as if it were a chilling harbinger or reminder of the real Alice's fate – she died of breast cancer. Victorian reconstruction based on detective plots helps feed a novel set in the late nineteenth century where the James family inserts the artistic and philosophical dimension, which was looming on the intellectual horizon at the time. But with such a book we are back to a classical detective thriller in a Victorian setting, playfully devising the insertion of famous figures in the given context, and remembering Conan Doyle or Bram Stoker and the world of the late nineteenth-century culture at large.

7. Jack the Ripper, Neo-Victorian Gothic, and Beyond

The myth of Jack the Ripper becoming part and parcel of British culture has served as playground for narrative modes and experiments, a much scrawled upon palimpsest of literature. The myth's literary recyclings cannot be separated from other media – visual that is – as a telling example of a criminal case surpassing anything the Victorian Gothic novel or melodrama might have staged. In the field of the written text, productions have been moulded by literary practices over more than a century now. Pseudo-realistic thrillers, detective novels or works of fantasy, historical epics or neo-romances, vignettes from 'le fantastique social', or downright metafictions, historiographic or poetic and visionary. The Ripper case has flourished as a Victorian nightmare granted an afterlife of strikingly long duration, reproducing as well as subverting older modes of narratives.

Ripper fiction indeed falls into several categories. Exploiting the case as a Victorian novelist would have done is the major temptation for many writers as a ready-made plot is offered to them to rewrite a Victorian Gothic novel in the wake of Le Fanu, Dickens or Collins. Belloc who had overheard a conversation about a landlady's private story, wrote her own, both as a witness and in the tradition of psychic cases like Jekyll's or those found in many ghostly tales, more precisely centred on feminine neurosis. Farjeon went further by choosing the disquieting confessions of the mentally disturbed doctor, keeping close to the reality of Forbes Winslow's autobiography, but implementing a near madman's diary. Adding new episodes to Sherlock Holmes stories, with the Whitechapel murders in them, has become a stock in trade of that fiction. Following suit Brian Porter's book is more interested in reproducing the fantastic trope of the lost and found manuscript in the hypothesis of an inherited testimony.

Basically, the myth born from the open ended case has served as a remarkable locus for a neo-Victorian experiment following the two major lines of the evolving genre in the nineteenth century as Alexandra Warwick defined them: "a bourgeois domestic setting [...] and an urban milieu" (Warwick 2007: 30). Most fictions will tend to recapture the sensibility of the day either in sheer imitation or with a view to reactivating the much fantasised Victorian world and inserting it in the present day. Writing her Dickensian novel, Pamela Oldfield takes more liberty with the history of the case by concentrating on the character of the predatory smooth-tongued crook. Marantz-Cohen writes a fantasised detective novel by mingling it with a pseudo-historical novel, claiming the participation of the James family. But most writers will invest in psychic derangements predicated on the late century obsession with fractured identities. The Jekyll and Hyde syndrome was present during the events themselves since the novella was being played at the Lyceum and was interrupted because of alleged or possible contamination with reality.

The so-called postmodernist school makes a different choice by writing metafictions, i.e. fictional afterthoughts staging critical approaches to the Victorian novel while rewriting it in a new fashion, the old Victorian Gothic construed as memorabilia or leftovers in renovated ventures. Remarkably, modernist novellas like Patrice Chaplin's *By Flower and Dean Street* (1976) focus on the overlap between present day neurosis in London and the return of the killer by making the heroine hear a strange voice pronouncing well-known phrases from nineteenth-century Whitechapel, reminiscent of a ventriloquist's speech, or arcane quotations from a lost hypotext. The elaborate narration, reminding the reader of Charles Brockden Brown's American Gothic, in his novels *Wieland* (1798) and *Edgar Huntly* (1799), dramatises Victorian melodramas as haunting echoes. In more extreme cases such as Paul West's operatic epos or the psychogeographic novel by Iain Sinclair, the move is towards an overall rebellion against genre definitions and constraints, paving the way to a somewhat diffused Gothic with a poetic overtone. Starting with a Victorian reference, namely Conan Doyle's *A Study in Scarlet*, he makes havoc of the model while retaining innuendoes of the story line, a fiction closer to a combination of disparate elements. At one moment the seedy shopkeepers of his are assaulted by hooligans who destroy the shops and its contents:

> They destroyed sensationalist, surrealist, gothic, hermetic, lyric, and domestic literature, with a fine lack of distinction. They also gave Nicholas Lane a bit of a kicking, staving in a couple of ribs and detaching a kidney. (Sinclair 2004: 91)

The apocalypse of literary genres does not prevent the concrete though unemotional reference to mugging and to the kidney torn from the fourth canonical victim of Jack, Catherine Eddowes. But contrary to a neo-Victorian Gothic enterprise, the book takes a distance from its emotional material in favour of a more intellectual or aesthetic stance.

Ripper fiction has helped move generic frontiers in favour of more generic hybridity. But the hallmark certainly lies in "self-reflexive detection" – as Edgar Allan Poe's 'The Man of the Crowd' was already sometimes described (Gutiérrez 2000: 159). A neo-Gothic endeavour ultimately implements a historical, if not critical outlook, one of self-consciousness and reflexiveness, some museographic impulse perhaps. Between the Victorian age and ours, reappropriation has been strongly dependent upon psychoanalysis which radically altered the position of the writers towards their material: Victorian Gothic as a material to be recalled, analysed, revamped, reconstructed or deconstructed. Even such a novel as Marantz-Cohen's, though classical in its imitative impulse, does spring from the author's academic dedication to Henry James.

While Sherlock Holmes is a fictional figure sometimes misconstrued as a non-fictional one, the famous serial killer whose name was a hoax definitely belongs to the world of fiction, however historic the Whitechapel murders were. This accounts for the particular problem posed by neo-Gothic productions, namely an impulse to invent the novel of Jack the Ripper which never came to light at the time, apart from tabloids and popular romances, because of lack of hindsight perhaps. Again Iain Sinclair has a visionary account of the problem at stake by making one of his characters talk about a template to be revisited and enlarged. Hence the move towards a resumption of a fictional appeal escaping the limits of any given genre.

The popular and sometimes sardonic bogeyman who so much remained in Hitchcock's subconscious – the film maker was brought up in the vicinity of the killer's territory – became part of British culture and thus a reference, a byword for a lifetime of terror. His famous film *Frenzy* (1972) could be a stimulating illustration of the problematic of transcription. Hitchcock does not cast his plot on the model of the historical events but centres it around Covent Garden food market, a sort of inverted pastoral Paradise providing apples to be eaten, and also makes it dependent upon the paradigm of femininity. The Victorian town has become referential, picturesque and touristic. The film viewer is induced to travel back to Victorian Gothicism in retrospect as a tourist in the world of literature would.

Another film maker, Stephen Volk, sums up the appeal of the Jack the Ripper case in popular culture past and present, emphasising its omnipresence even if it tends to lose part of its original nature:

> From Hammer horror to Michael Caine. From *Murder by Decree* to graphic novels. From pub signs to walking tours. From lyrics by Nick Cave (or Morrissey) to Spike Milligan's *Phantom Raspberry Blower of Olde London Town.* (Volk 2008: 5)

From muck raking to in-depth psychology, the history of Ripper fiction oscillates, always dedicated to the seductive idea of revelation, however mock it may be, in a somewhat derisory attempt at putting a stop to Jack's career as an anonymous bugbear. For the answer to the protracted enigma can never be unassailable or triumphant. Rather the very impossibility of an answer was the trademark of a flourishing fiction. The failure of detection made it impossible for the writers to opt for a simple emplotment, and they had to step up their inventiveness. By so doing they have promoted a basically self-reflexive type of fiction, with a contemporary flavour tending to interiorise Gothic as Virginia Woolf had interiorised realism. They have provided the readers with a magic looking-glass reflecting both the vanished past and themselves. One way or another, Jack has offered the best insurance premium for his own survival as a promoter of neo-Gothic yarns of Victorian flavour, for readers eager to be 'visited upon', in Horace Walpole's terms, as if by vengeful sins of their forefathers, for generations on end.

Bibliography

Ackroyd, Peter.1985. *Hawksmoor*. London: Abacus Books, Macdonald and Co.
——. 1997. *Dan Leno and the Limehouse Golem* [1994]. London: Vintage
——. 1997. *The Trial of Elizabeth Cree: A Novel of the Limehouse Murders*. New York: Nan A. Talese.
Belloc Lowndes, Marie. 2008. *The Lodger* [1911]. London: Methuen. Sheffield: PJM Publishing.
Bloch, Robert.1943. 'Yours Truly Jack the Ripper', *Weird Tales* 36 (12) (July).
Brewer, John Francis. 1888. *The Curse on Mitre Square... AD 1520-1888, a Penny dreadful*. London: Simpkin, Marshall & New York: Co. John Lowell Company.
Chaplin, Patrice. 1976. *By Flower and Dean Stre*et. London: Gerald Duckworth and Co LTD.
Cornwell, Patricia. 2002. *Portrait of a Killer: Jack the Ripper – Case Closed*. New York: Berkley Books.
Davison, Carol Margaret. 1997. 'Blood Brothers: Dracula and Jack the Ripper in Bram Stoker's *Dracula*', in Davison, Carol Margaret (ed., with Paul Simpson-Housley), *Bram Stoker's Dracula: Sucking through the Century 1897-1997*. Toronto: Dundurn Press: 147-172.
De Quincey, Thomas. 1998. *Confessions of an English Opium-Eater* [1822]. Oxford: Oxford University Press, Oxford World's Classics.
Desnos, Robert. 2008. *Jack l'Eventreur*, articles de *Paris-Matinal* [1928]. Paris: Ed.Allia.
Dibdin, Michael. 1990. *The Last Sherlock Holmes Story* [1978]. London: Jonathan Cape.
Farjeon, Clanash (pseud.). 2003. *A Handbook for Attendants on the Insane: The Autobiography of Jack the Ripper as Revealed to Clanash Farjeon*. Victoria, Canada: Trafford.
Faye, Lindsay. 2009. *Dust and Shadow: An Account of the Ripper Killings by Dr. John H. Watson*. New York: Simon & Schuster.
Glinoer, Anthony. 2009. *La littérature frénétique*. Paris: PUF.
Gutiérrez, Félix, Martin. 2000. 'Edgar Allan Poe: Misery and Mystery in the Man of the Crowd', *Estudios Ingleses de la Universidad Complutense* 8: 153-174.
Hewit, Nicholas. 1987. 'Pirates, Adventurers and their Limitations: Pierre Mac Orlan and the English Tradition', *The Journal of the British Institute in Paris* 3 (Spring): 41-54.
Hynes James. 2006. 'Destination: Whitechapel and Spitalfields', *The Literary Guide to the World*, 15 June. On-line at: http://www.salon.com/2006/06/15/whitechapel/singleton/ (consulted 23.10.2010).

Knight, Stephen. 1976. *Jack the Ripper: The Final Solution*. George G. Harrap & Co Ltd.
Le Fanu. 1966. *Uncle Silas* [1864]. New York: Dover.
Mac Orlan, Pierre. 1927. *Sous la lumière froide* [1926]. Paris: Editions Emile-Paul Frères.
——. 1966. *Villes : Mémoires*. Paris: Gallimard Nrf.
Marantz-Cohen, Paula. 2010. *What Alice Knew: A Most Curious Tale of Henry James and Jack the Ripper*. Naperville, Illinois: Sourcebooks Landmark.
Martin, Valerie. 1995. 'A Victorian Nightmare: *Dan Leno and The Limehouse Golem*, 1994', *The New York Times*, 16 April.
Moore, Alan, and Eddie Campbell. 1999. *From Hell: Being a Melodrama in Sixteen Parts* [serialised 1991-1996 in *Taboo*]. Marietta, Georgia: Top Shelf; London: Knockabout Comics.
Oldfield, Pamela. 2007. *Jack's Shadow: A Jack the Ripper Mystery*. Sutton, Surrey & New York: Severn House Publishers.
Porter, Brian L. 2008. *A Study in Red: The Secret Journal of Jack the Ripper*. Makham, Ontario: Double Dragon Publishing.
Remington, Ted. 2004. 'Dear Boss : Hoax as popular communal narrative in the case of the Jack the Ripper Letters', *Journal of Criminal Justice and Popular Culture* 10(3): 199-221.
Sinclair, Iain. 2004. *White Chappell, Scarlet Tracings* [1987]. London: Penguin Books.
——. 2001. 'Introduction' in Conan Doyle, Arthur, *A Study in Scarlet*. Harmonsdworth: Penguin Classics.
Smith, Andrew. 2004. *Victorian Demons: Medicine, Masculinity and the Gothic at the Fin-de-Siècle*. Manchester: Manchester University Press.
Spooner, Catherine, and Emma McEvoy (eds.). 2007. *The Routledge Companion to Gothic*. London & New York: Routledge.
Volk, Stephen. 2008. 'Alfred and Jack: Ripping Yarns', *Fortean Times* 241 (October): 1-6. On-line at: http://www.stephenvolk.net/Alfred.pdf (consulted 23.10.2011).
Walkowitz, Judith R. 1992. *City of Dreadful Delight: Narratives of Sexual Danger in Late-Victorian London*. Chicago: University of Chicago Press.
Warwick, Alexandra. 2007. 'Victorian Gothic'. In Spooner and McEvoy (2007): 29-38.
West, Paul. 1991. *The Women of Whitechapel and Jack the Ripper*. New York: Random House.
Williams, Anne. 1995. *Art of Darkness: A Poetics of Gothic*. Chicago: University of Chicago Press.

Chasing the Dragon: Bangtails, Toffs, Jack and Johnny in Neo-Victorian Fiction

Sarah E. Maier

Abstract:
Various neo-Victorian Gothic texts explore the implications of the historical Jack the Ripper's cultural mythologisation, while participating in the same process, providing him with a spectral afterlife in the shape of fictional nineteenth-century serial killers who are tracked by their alienist, detective, and profiler counterparts. In such works as Caleb Carr's *The Alienist* (1994), Michael Dibdin's *The Last Sherlock Holmes Story* (1978), and Alan Moore and Eddie Campbell's *From Hell* (1999), the investigator interprets the performative scenes of crime, trauma and victimisation through both literary and psychological means to interrogate the criminal mind that proves emblematic of past and present anxieties of the *fin(s) de siècle(s)*.

Keywords: alienism, Caleb Carr, crime, Michael Dibdin, 'Jack the Ripper', Alan Moore, murder, performance, profiling, *tableaux*.

*****

> "We're in the most extreme and utter region of the human mind, a dim sub-conscious underworld. A radiant abyss where men meet themselves ... Hell, Netley, we're in Hell." (Moore and Campbell 2004: 9.31)

Although Alan Moore and Eddie Campbell's graphic novel *From Hell* (1989) and the 2001 film of the same name are both fictionalised accounts of one of the many theories of Jack the Ripper – indeed, a combination of theories – their recognition that, for the Victorians, the signs and symbols surrounding his heinous crimes were deemed emblematic of a particular *fin-de-siècle* energy encourages us to re-evaluate the place of those same images at the recent twentieth century's end. Indeed, the incessant need to 'solve' the Ripper crimes through a proliferation of theories speaks to the desire to create a sense of closure to the events of 1888, a closure still not felt even in the new millennium where we seek for neo-Victorian crime narratives to inform our own constructions of criminality (Kohlke 2008/2009: ii). The Ripper is symptomatic; the last several years have seen a proliferation of anxiety made manifest in crime serials on television, serial killers at the cinema and serial investigations with 'agents' looking to impose order or understanding in the desire to theorise and, indeed, narrate, the criminal mind. The alternative, to accept banal randomness in the Ripper or any serial killer, leaves society without context or comfort; in particular, neo-Victorian rewritings seek to return the murderer to reality by narrating motivation – the distance from the historical crime can then be regarded with a sense of detachment and re-investigated "curiously, critically or nostalgically, but never 'known' in any authentic sense" (Gamble 2009: 126).

All narratives of Jack the Ripper rely upon minimal factual reports of forensic evidence but a plethora of *fictional* accounts of the Whitechapel killer – a "phantasmagoric criminal, a figment of the gothic imagination" (Milburn 2008: 125) – to contextualise his unexplained monstrosity. To this day, the Ripper remains an unknown perpetrator or a collective of perpetrators, and "Jack has ceased to be one killer but has become a multiplicity of performing personas for the imagination" (Bloom 1988: 124).[1] From Jack the Ripper to his twentieth-century, fictional *fin-de-siècle* twins such as John Doe (*Se7en*, 1995), Jack of all Trades (*Profiler*, 1996-2000), John Beecham/Japheth Dury (*The Alienist*, 1994) and his re-visioned self (*The Last Sherlock Holmes* Story, 1978), these "spectral/textual traces" (Arias 2010: 133) of the Ripper evoke the need to answer the questions who would commit such malignant acts and why they haunt all such fictional representations in their appropriation of Victorian criminality and fledgling detection, particularly in neo-Victorian adaptation(s). At both the approach to and the very cusp of the *fin de siècle*, the popular imagination turned back the clock to embody – literally and literarily – our own anxieties about the blurring of boundaries between sexuality, degeneration, criminality, art,

---

[1] During the investigation into the Whitechapel murders, the police received in excess of two hundred letters ostensibly from the killer. In each of the novels discussed here, interesting use is made of the more infamous letters such as 'Dear Boss' or, of course, the letter addressed 'From Hell'. These early attempts to 'narrate' the killer and his murders are the precursors to the later neo-Victorian fictions discussed here.

technology, science, medicine, deviance, and fiction, all in the shadowy figure of the Ripper.

1. JACK, *n.*[1]; JOHNNY, *n.*

The Oxford English Dictionary makes it clear that "Jack" may be "Applied to a man, or the figure of one. a. (As proper noun.) A familiar by-form of the name *John*; hence, a generic proper name for any representative of the common people." Indeed, in the case of the Whitechapel killer and his various neo-Victorian incarnations discussed here, the generic and/or everyman "Jack" and "John" proliferate. While historically factual, these Jacks and Johns are represented in fragmented narratives of supposition. Indeed, it seems that the serial killer "Jack" cannot be articulated as anything *but* a literary figure because it is a personal narrative which drives him; it is this narrative he purports to tell through a puzzle of clues and entanglement that makes it possible to serialise him for the reading and/or viewing audience or create alternate literary scenarios for his identity and motives.

This continuous obfuscation of fact and fiction into a kind of De Quinceyan neo-Victorian consideration of murder as a fine art is at the heart of *From Hell*, Caleb Carr's *The Alienist*, and Michael Dibdin's *The Last Sherlock Holmes Story*.[2] These literary cases read as case studies of particular predators and profilers, all of which rely upon the shadowy figure of the Ripper as a touchstone of unknowable historical fact. The 'case' of the Ripper can then be read through forensic literary means, both as one interprets a literary text and via forensic science turning to literature for its language of interpretation. Some of that language is drawn from the literary Gothic, fiction that investigates the collapse of distinctions between subjectivity, space, villains, victims, bodies, minds, characters and criminals (Warwick 2006: 561). The facts of the Ripper case become an amalgamation of what can be known and what is constructed as a possible narrative of events that may lead to the characterisation of a particular, preferably evil, person; these 'facts' are then re-interpreted, in many ways, to create further fictional potential, but unverifiable, representations of the Ripper crime(s), victims and possible person(s) responsible as well

---

[2] See Thomas De Quincey's 'On Murder Considered as one of the Fine Arts' (1827) and his follow-up documents 'Second Paper' (1839) and 'Postscript' (1854).

as to posit the solution or capture of the criminal(s). For the reader, the "crime takes place at one remove, in the past, but has continuing and visceral effects within the present" (Spooner 2010: 245) in these works of ongoing reciprocal interpretation – facts into narrative and narrative into facts – which focus upon the killer who, according to the *Pall Mall Gazette* of 14 September 1888, "did his bloody work with the lust it is true of the savage, but with the skill of the savant" (qtd. Cameron 1987: 127).

In the hunt for the perpetrator of serial crimes, one of the required narrative elements is the villain – just who is it that attacks individuals, and by extension, society with repetitive traumatic force? In the case of Jack the Ripper, the villain constitutes the essential missing piece; in each attempt to create the narrative of the Whitechapel murders, the man in the fog-filled streets remains unknown, yet the need to name him and fix his identity or bring his shifting shapes into singular focus is clear. In *From Hell*, there is a quasi-metafictional undercurrent of storytelling when, on their way home from *The Daily Star* office, Mr. Gibbs and Mr. Best decide they are feeling "Creative [....] Y'see, it's like ol'Renwick Williams. 'The Monster.'[3] We need a VILLAIN, Gibbs. And if we can't find one, well ... we shall just have to conjure one up, shan't we!" (Moore and Campbell 2004: 7.37). They proceed to write the "Dear Boss" letter that begins the Gothic hysteria and the mythologising of 'Jack the Ripper'[4] as the 'trade name' for the killer. The reality of the killer's identity is of less importance than the ability to locate and name evil.

The act of serial murder provokes philosophical questioning; a passive, natural scene allows for transformation via questions of who and why. For example, the *tableaux* of death are the multifaceted aesthetic scenes where victims are seemingly staged by the serial

---

[3] The 'London Monster', so named by the press, was a man who allegedly attacked women, stabbing them in the buttocks, in London between 1788 and 1790. Rhynwick Williams was accused but never convicted.

[4] Although many have commented on this idea of the mythologisation of Jack the Ripper, Drew D. Gray's recent *London's Shadows: The Dark Side of the Victorian City*, sets to debunk the differences between the "real Whitechapel murderer from the cultural construction that is Jack the Ripper" to see how "the creation of a modern mythology [...] has in many ways obscured whatever truth there was in the Ripper killings" (Gray 2010: 18). In contrast, I here investigate merely the fictional representations, or the mythologies, of the Ripper without true forensic inquiry into the 'facts' of the case(s). (See also Pietrzak-Franger 2009/2010 and Ferguson 2009.)

killer.⁵ Not only is it the scene of a violent encounter of exchange between the killer, subject and space, but it is also the moment when the victim loses identity to become 'the victim' in "a Gothic failure of distinction" (Warwick 2006: 564). These scenes of death have an eerie parallel in nineteenth-century *tableaux vivants*,⁶ which, by means of allegory and/or representation, would seek to enlighten their audience through the articulation of a particular theme or moment in history. The killers' scenes are, then, 'read' according to the criteria proposed by the alienist/profiler who, in pursuit of the truth, will write the story of the evidence as if part of a genre of fiction.

Well known modern profilers admit that nineteenth-century detectives such as Sir Arthur Conan Doyle's Sherlock Holmes or Edgar Allan Poe's Auguste Dupin are early examples of criminal investigators who tell the tale of their case(s); they bring an exaggerated sense of objectivity, precision and logic to the reading of scenes of crime.⁷ Without exception in such cases, the alienist, scientist and literary detective are master storytellers who seek to critique and explain the murderous performance;⁸ they must act on behalf of the community to collect information and work it into a coherent explanation of the crime that will, hopefully, allow for closure of an aberrant incident of human behaviour – an act of gothicised monstrosity – in an attempt to reassert/re-establish social norms and conventions of acceptability. In each case, the attempt to

---

⁵ I would argue that, in the lineage of Baudelaire, the *tableaux* of the serial killer are an attempt to aestheticise the ugliness of death as a representative *objet d'art*.
⁶ French, for a person (or persons) posed in the manner of a literary work or work of art to create a picturesque scene.
⁷ In his autobiographical consideration of the creation of the Behavioural Analysis Unit at Quantico, Virginia, *Mindhunter*, John Douglas admits that "[o]ur antecedents [...] go back to crime fiction more than crime fact" with training often drawn from film and fiction (qtd. Seltzer 1998: 16).
⁸ In her much-disputed case study, *Portrait of a Killer: Jack the Ripper Case Closed* (2002), Patricia Cornwell 'identifies' Walter Sickert as the Ripper, claiming that he "slipped out of the wings to make his debut in a series of ghastly performances" in a variety of "disguises" to ultimately sketch and/or paint a series of portraits of his crimes (Cornwell 2002: 6, 26). Cornwell claims that his works, such as *What shall we do for the rent?*, indicate more than a passing interest in the crimes of the Ripper; she suggests that, for instance, in *Two Studies of a Venetian Woman's Head* Sickert's drawings resemble the first Ripper victim, Mary Ann Nichols, and that the painting *Putana a Casa* is comparable to the facially-disfigured fourth victim, Catherine Eddowes (Cornwell 2002: 148, 294).

explore, investigate, speculate upon and answer for the nineteenth-century trauma of the Ripper's destabilisation of both social and criminal norms shows the impossibility of closure. In their introduction to *Neo-Victorian Tropes of Trauma*, Marie-Luise Kohlke and Christian Gutleben affirm the psychological impact of literary investigations of historical trauma; relevant here is their assertion that "the nineteenth century has become a prominent focal point" because the "double temporal consciousness typical of the emergent subgenre of [...] the neo-Victorian novel" is able to

> mimic the double temporality of traumatic consciousness, whereby the subject occupies, at one and the same time, both the interminable present moment of the catastrophe which, continuously re-lived, refuses to be relegated to the past, and the post-traumatic present[.] (Kohlke and Gutleben 2010: 2)

The need to revisit the Ripper and his crimes in neo-Victorian fiction, in an act of "excessive metafictional playfulness and thorough ideological critique" (Domsch, this volume: 97), confirms how such unanswered crime becomes an obsessive point of interest while at the same time voyeuristically maintaining the spectacle of violence for the twentieth-century reader audience.

2. Case Study: *From Hell*

Any such historic, or narrative, attempts to 'explain' Jack the Ripper spend much voyeuristic time upon the actual, historic photographic evidence of the *tableaux* of Mary Ann Nichols, Annie Chapman, Elizabeth Stride, Catherine Eddows, and Mary Kelly. Depersonalised in sepia and white, the women become static dissections of the Ripper's deviant psyche to be studied for clues to his identity, not their individual personae. The serial killer narrative is problematic in that it rarely allows for what we consider to be understandable closure. A psychotic, passionate act of single murder is, in some ways, easier to grasp than the violent, sustained purposes of a sane and logical repeat killer who chooses to murder. Murder without apparent motive is much more complex. Such "motivelessness does a great deal towards lifting the serial killer out of history into myth: his actions are portrayed as inscrutable, beyond the reasoning that otherwise explains the world", until the murderer is "filled by the narrator [alienist/profiler] with a variety of speculative motivation" allowing for "both positions of emptiness and fullness simultaneously" (Warwick 2006: 561). Indeed, the neo-Victorian Gothic seeks to fulfil both positions – empty speculation that cannot be filled to create an authentic historical reality yet the fullness of the attempted experience in the hope to achieve a cathartic moment that will allow for movement away from historical stasis of unknowability.

The *modus operandi* of the killer becomes known, but the question of his psyche remains closed except for the *tableaux* that the killer creates as representations of his subjective self; at best, these manifest revelations give us fragments of intelligibility because they are a locus where several discourses collide, but they can never be the complete narrative. The essential problem is the lack of ability to integrate all of the narratives – a collection of self-portraits – into one subjectivity. Indeed, like contemporary scenarios involving real criminals, many neo-Victorian serial killers' attempts at cohesive self-narration seem to contain only randomness with recurrent motifs and stories either borrowed or unfinished that haunts the detective/alienist/profiler and the reader/audience with the desire for impossible closure. The enacting of violence couched in ritual is the serial killer's attempt to establish himself as a unified subject. Most theories of the Ripper grasp at this idea of ritual – what does the extreme disfigurement, the 'ripping' of his victims 'mean' for the killer? Why prostitutes? How does he appear, commit murder, then disappear without notice? The "repetitiveness of his murders serves only to mirror the reproduction of loose stories, unanchored in the *terra firma* of reality, which float around his disintegrating self" (Gomel 1999: 66). Ritualistic killing demonstrates his extreme self-deconstruction and desperation to reconstruct a coherent life-affirming narrative, a kind of psychiatric *Bildungsroman* for himself at the expense of the victims in a clash between his private fantasy and the public performance of that fantasy (Gomel 1999: 62).

Jack the Ripper was profiled as early as 10 November 1888 by Dr. T. Bond in a letter to the Home Office:

> 10. The murderer must have been a man of physical strength and of great coolness and daring. There is no evidence that he had an accomplice. He must in my

opinion be a man subject to periodical attacks of Homicidal and erotic mania. The character of the mutilations indicate that the man may be in a condition sexually, that may be called satyriasis. It is of course possible that the Homicidal impulse may have developed from a revengeful or brooding condition of the mind, or that Religious Mania may have been the original disease, but I do not think either hypothesis is likely. The murderer in external appearance is quite likely to be a quiet, inoffensive looking man probably middle-aged and neatly and respectably dressed. I think he must be in the habit of wearing a cloak or overcoat or he could hardly have escaped notice in the streets if the blood on his hands or clothes were visible.

11. Assuming the murderer to be such a person as I have just described, he would probably be solitary and eccentric in his habits, also he is most likely to be a man without regular occupation, but with some small income or pension. He is possibly living among respectable persons who have some knowledge of his character and habits and who may have grounds for suspicion that he is not quite right in his mind at times. (qtd. Evans and Skinner 2001: 401-402)

In such a profile, the projection of the alienist/profiler – the 'I' of this narrative – into the 'facts' of the case is clear; however, the only evident physical fact here is that the person must have been strong in order to commit such a crime, because all else in the profile is carefully considered conjecture based on details and patterns found at the first four of the five canonical murder scenes. Given the limited resources of science at that precise historical moment of late-Victorian England, this lack of physical evidence is not surprising, but such an attempt to narrate a scene begins the genre of the profile as parallel to a character sketch in a literary text.

In *From Hell*, the graphic novel attempts to bring the reader into the atmosphere of late-Victorian England. Full of despair, poverty, drunkenness and whoredom, the bangtails eke out a living by tossing off the toffs who come to slum it in the back alleys of

Whitechapel. The deaths are posited as a Queen Victoria approved conspiracy of murder by the royal physician, Sir William Gull, to protect Albert (Eddy), the Duke of Clarence, who has fathered a bastard daughter, Alice, with a young woman by the name of Annie Crook. All of the central players are considered (including 'Leather Apron', Walter Sickert, etc.) by Inspector Fred Abberline who is dragged back into the mire of Whitechapel to solve the case(s) of the dead women with the conformist ideas of a police detective seeking out the truth through standard police procedure. Abberline's starting point is a confusion that he cannot unravel with traditional methods; as he admits:

> 'Smith was raped and tortured. That's Cruelty. I can understand cruelty. Tabram was killed by frenzied and repeated stabbing. That's rage. I understand that too. This one's more ... methodical. Someone near enough did surgery on this woman. I don't understand that at all.' (Moore and Campbell 2004: 6.12)

Non-traditional investigations also fail; the visions of the royal psychic, Mr. R. J. Lees, are debunked by his own admission of falsehood, and Abberline is silenced by a conspiracy of both the Masonic and the police brotherhoods. The delusions of historical context and grandeur of his crimes remain intact only for the Ripper in his rantings on the "Fourth Dimension", William Blake, and Masonic history. It is only in the film adaptation, directed by Albert and Allen Hughes, that our own *fin de siècle* fascinations – Johnny Depp, Absinthe, cynicism, New Age psychic abilities, decadent addictions, exoticism, Orientalism and serial killers – combine into the tortured but driven investigator, not the murderer, who is caught chasing an ephemeral shadow figure. Anxiety, opium addiction, laudanum use and intense grief colour Inspector Abberline's abilities to lead him to visions of the Ripper,[9] and, like *Profiler*'s Sam Waters, he visually and forensically interprets his opponent's actions to create and or 'see' a narrative of the crimes. In the film, in particular in Depp's performance of Abberline's visions, the shapeshifting Ripper is

---

[9] The adaptation collapses Lees and Abberline – two characters – into one for the purposes of the film.

"reaffirmed through performing spectacle" via "fragmentation and dismemberment" (Lonsdale 2002: 102, 105) because for the alienist/profiler – and by extension, the reader/viewer of the neo-Victorian serial killer narrative – "[s]uccess in solving the case is wholly dependent upon the novice's ability to identify fully with the killer, to learn […] to desire what the other desires, to inhabit the place of the other's identifications (Fuss 1995: 93).

The more objective Abberline from the graphic novel is transformed into a subjective reader of the Ripper *tableaux*; in the film adaptation, the Ripper's story of the graphic novel becomes, in an act of transformative acceptability, Abberline's story as he investigates the Ripper. He literally envisions the crimes both as the Ripper might commit them and as though he, himself, had committed them. Haunted by his own combination of being chased by the green fairy and chasing a kind of green dragon, as well as his own lustful pursuit of the final victim, Mary Kelly, Abberline's addictions come to include solving the Ripper crime, a fantasy vision of Hell created not from scientific objectivity but rather from subjective interpretations of the Whitechapel hell.

3.   Case Study: *The Alienist*

To set the atmosphere parallel to the fog-filled streets terrorised by Jack the Ripper, Carr's *The Alienist* makes direct reference to the Ripper killings as "three months in London in 1888, when a bloodthirsty ghoul had taken to accosting random prostitutes in the East End and disembowelling them" (Carr 2006: 59). Furthermore, at crucial moments of discovery, connections are made to the Ripper killings as a touchstone for discussions of sanity/insanity, police procedure, victimology and ritual enactment. The New York killer's preference for prostitutes of the Lower East Side provides a suggestive parallel to the East End murders – in both cases the geography is representative of the killer's inner narrative that moves through time and space (Canter 2003: 98, Warwick 2006: 565). Gothic, and I would argue neo-Victorian Gothic, narratives contain fragmented subjects searching for unity; in each case study here, particularly the New York of *The Alienist*, the city itself in its Gothic strangeness may be viewed in terms of what Agnieszka Kliś sees as "a space which perfectly reflects liminal characters" who function in both the Gothic and the familiar space of the urban landscape (Kliś 2010: 378). The incongruity of the space is emphasised by the corresponding unstable identities of the American killer's victims, who are actually young boys parading as girls (e.g. in the case of Giorgio Santorelli "call[ing] itself Gloria" [Carr 2006: 17]), so as to elicit a unique clientele who participate in transvestite sexual performance in bordellos like Paresis Hall. The murders are then enacted to create a *tableau* or scene, unto which the police arrive, of a morbid debauchery akin to the scenes in Whitechapel:

> On the walkway was the body of a young person. I say 'person' because, though the physical attributes were those of an adolescent boy, the clothes [...] and facial paint were those of a girl [...] of dubious repute [...] wrists were trussed behind the back, and the legs were bent in a kneeling position that pressed the face to the steel of the walkway [....] The face did not seem heavily beaten or bruised – the paint or powder were still intact – but where once there had been eyes there were now only bloody, cavernous sockets. A puzzling piece of flesh protruded from the mouth. A wide gash stretched across the throat, though there was little blood near the opening. Large cuts crisscrossed the abdomen, revealing the mass of the inner organs. The right hand had been chopped neatly off. At the groin there was another gaping wound, one that explained the mouth – the genitals had been cut away and stuffed between the jaws. The buttocks, too, had been shorn off [.]
> (Carr 2006: 16)

The careful strokes of the mutilations are reminiscent of some theories of Jack the Ripper as a medical man. Hoping to change the prevalent state of affairs that murders which "appeared insoluble and [...] occurred among the poor or outcast" were "much less investigated" (Carr 2006: 21), Commissioner Theodore Roosevelt asks for the help of his Harvard classmate and gifted alienist, Lazlo Kreizler.

Aware that many different sets of skills will be required to track the man responsible, Kreizler assembles a team of investigators to help find the killer: John Schuyler Moore is his friend and an investigative journalist; Sara Howard is one of the first women employed by the New York City Police Department as an assistant to Roosevelt; Sergeant Marcus Isaacson and Detective Sergeant Lucius Isaacson are detectives on the cutting edge and with a strong interest in forensic investigation. They are accompanied in their work by a team of supporters – Stevie Taggert as a kind of 'man on the street' helper, Cyrus Montrose as a powerful man who silently guards the group, and Mary Palmer as Kreizler's maid and later love interest – who have come to know, respect and protect Kreizler for the care he offered them when each of them was in trouble in the past. In a parallel move, an equally powerful man, James Pierpont Morgan, assembles his own far more conspiratorial team of prominent men who seek to restore order through complicity in a cover up, citing "some precedent" where "[s]imilar efforts, though far more rudimentary, were made during the Ripper murders in London eight years ago" (Carr 2006: 304). The number of murders that take place during the investigation escalates to four – Santorelli, Ali 'Fatima' ibn-Ghazi, Ernst Lohmann and Joseph – with an unnamed boy saved from death as the intended fifth victim. The team discovers that the New York killer has killed a brother and sister (the Zweig children) and two other boys in the same style several years prior to this novel, bringing the overall number of dead to eight from a total of nine victims.

A further connection to the Whitechapel murders is the mention of Forbes Winslow, "an eminent British alienist and an early influence on Kreizler" who had been well known enough "to be able to inject himself into the [Whitechapel] investigation; indeed, he'd claimed that his participation had caused the murders (still unsolved at the time of this writing) to come to an end" (Carr 2006: 59). Drawing upon historical 'fact', Kreizler is influenced by Winslow's work,[10] having adopted the British proto-profiler's idea of constructing an "imaginary man" to "fit the known traits of the murderer" (Carr 2006: 59). Kreizler plans to chase the New York killer of child male prostitutes in a similar manner, claiming "the only thing that *can* be done – is to paint an imaginary picture of the sort of person that *might* commit such acts", adding "[i]f we had such a picture, the significance

---

[10] Lyttelton Stewart Forbes Winslow, MRCP (1844 1913), British psychiatrist involved in the Ripper case and other prominent cases of the late-Victorian era.

of what little evidence we collected would be dramatically magnified" (Carr 2006: 59, original emphasis). In other words, the picture or impression of the killer – here characterised by the non-personal "that" – is to be constructed *before* a consideration of the evidence in a move to add drama, or narrative, to the evidence itself. Once the evidence could be "[j]udged in context, the actions of such patients could be understood and even predicted", Kreizler contends, because in his view such "psychopathic personalities" are not so much mentally diseased as "produced by extreme childhood environments and experiences" while "unafflicted by any true pathology" (Carr 2006: 50-51), a reversal of the traditional Gothic figuration of the perpetrator as evil incarnate. A child-aged killer, Jesse Pomeroy, is identified as one of the journalist Moore's "favourite characters" (Carr 2006: 229), reminding Kreizler and Moore – as well as Carr's readers –that literary license creates mythic personalities of criminals.

The New York killer acts methodically over a period of time, leaving Roosevelt with the uncomfortable question "what *could* drive a man to such things" and to kill children he "doesn't even know", to which Kreizler can only answer, "It is not *knowing* them that is important to him – it is what they *represent*" (Carr 2006: 55). It is this unknown factor that will lead the team to capture their demon because the "creature you seek was created long ago" and "not necessarily here" (Carr 2006: 55), phrases reminiscent of childhood stories of 'once upon a time, long ago and far away' that seek to provide the safety of distance in the face of a rapacious dragon.

The use of forensic science via the practical experience of the Isaacson brothers is an initial attempt to gain dominance over the situation. Not unusual in depictions of serial murder, but certainly a science still in its infancy in the 1890s, the use of technical resources

> becomes a mark of distinction between killer and detective – one characterized by privacy, the other completely devoid of it; one diabolically clever in creating, maintaining, and defending private space, the other resourceful in penetrating his adversary's preemptive strategies. This double-narrative, in which both sides compete for dominance, inevitable culminates in a climactic moment when private space is being ceremonially penetrated. (Hantke 1998: 184)

This penetration can be seen in the novel's culmination with the violent death of Mary, just as she is about to become the acknowledged partner of Kreizler; although they chase a killer, Mary's neck is broken when she is thrown down the stairs in her defense of her friend Stevie. Kreizler's rationalism does not suffice when the loss is personal. Science is not the simple response to the narrative of death; rather, knowing full well "how a broad definition of insanity might make society as a whole feel better but did nothing for mental science", Kreizler continues to push for a narrative to explain the "desperate performances" (Carr 2006: 33, 29).[11] Kreizler theorises that the performative "display[s]", like the Ripper's killings, take place in the open and, as a result, the team "now ha[s] the beginnings of a pattern, something on which to build a general picture of what qualities inspired violence in our killer" (Carr 2006: 146, 93). The argument is for "evidence in the bodies *not of the murderer's derangement but of his sanity*" (Carr 2006: 126). The focus has changed "from criminal act to character of the actor" (Seltzer 1998: 4). When aroused to violence, the New York killer has "complete control over the scene as he play[s] it out" in an "extremely consistent pattern" or ritual (Carr 2006: 190), the key to the performance.

To do so, a war-room of sorts is created at 808 Broadway with a "large chalkboard, on which [...] we would create our imaginary man: physical and psychological clues would be listed, cross-referenced, revised, and combined until the work was done", but "the use of chalk, [Kreizler] said, was an indication of how many mistakes he expected himself and the rest of us to make along the way" (Carr 2006: 120) – in spite of the team being well armed with biological, literary, and philosophical treatises by David Hume, William James, John Locke, Arthur Schopenhauer, Herbert Spencer, Winslow, et al. The argument explicitly made here is that the team must "try not to see the world through [their] own eyes, nor to judge it by [their] own values, but through and by those of [the] killer", because "no good would come of conceiving of this person as a monster, because he was most assuredly a man"; therefore it "was pointless to talk about evil and barbarity and madness" for "none of these concepts would lead us

---

[11] As with Abberline's addictions, and later Holmes's abuses, that seek to calm the psychological turmoil, there is an accompanying sense of desperation in the alcohol dependency of Carr's perpetrator Beecham/Dury as he devolves from coherent social subject into serial child killer.

any closer to him. But if we could capture the human child in our imaginations – then we could capture the man in fact" (Carr 2006: 129). Imagination and knowledge must, ironically, build a reality that can then be presented for judgement, both within the neo-Victorian text and by the reader.

It is this enlistment of the imagination, to create "the imaginary tale" that leads to the danger for the investigator (Carr 2006: 211): the seduction to become the monster to catch the monster. Indeed, Kreizler's concentration causes him to develop a "predatory gaze" and an "increasingly emotional involvement in the case", eventually leading to "uncharacteristic behavior" (Carr 2006: 72, 222). It also initiates a narcissistic interest when the alienist comes to believe that the page of his own article apparently left for him at the scene "was [the killer's] way of *acknowledging* [him], somehow", to entice him to interpret the performance of evil (Carr 2006: 202, original emphasis). It is, in fact, the other team members who realise that Kreizler's objectivity is now in question; the central "fallacy" in "James's *Principles*" is the "business about a psychologist getting his own point of view mixed up with his subject's. That's what's had him in its grip" (Carr 2006: 246). Realising that the "full implications of the document" about Kreizler's own childhood of abuse would lead to questions of his professional objectivity (Carr 2006: 246), Moore and Howard proceed to incinerate it, but it is this moment of kinship, a kind of collapse into affinity, between Kreizler and the New York killer that creates a crisis in the end. The alienist/profiler senses his own weakness and withdraws, exclaiming significantly: "We've been hunting a killer [...] but the killer isn't the real danger – *I* am!" (Carr 2006: 368, original emphasis), thereafter staying away from the case until the moment of capture.

Moore and Kreizler confront "an enormous figure clad in unremarkable black clothing" who was "slowly removing his garments and placing them neatly to one side of the promenade" to reveal a man "more than six feet" and built of "powerful muscles" as part of a "remarkable physical specimen", but Moore is shocked to find he "wasn't prepared for the banality of those features" in a "common sort of face, one that exhibited no hint of the terrible turmoil that boiled without respite deep within the large head" (Carr 2006: 457). This is certainly not the image of the "Red Indian" once posited as a possible Other, possessing the savagery necessary to kill in such a manner (Carr 2006: 196). The insistence in the Ripper crimes that no Englishman could have possibly committed the crimes is reversed;[12] the butchery of Japheth Dury – now self-(re)created as his one-time abuser, George Beecham – enacts his father's photographic images of the Native American, particularly Sioux, massacres (Carr 2006: 326).[13] What follows is the creation of an outcast caught in a "monstrous becoming" emblematic of a *fin de siècle* Gothic narrative that is "convulsed by nostalgia for the 'fully human' subject [but] whose undoing it accomplishes so resolutely" (Hurley 1996: 4). His transformation occurs because of the ramifications of his father's revelations to him in childhood as well as his obsession with photos like that of

> a dead white man: scalped, eviscerated, and emasculated, with arrows protruding from his arms and legs. His eyes were missing. There were no identifying marks on the picture, but it was obviously one of the Reverend Victor Dury's creations. (Carr 2006: 426)

These photographs obsessively state and restage spectacles of abhumanness and trauma done to the human body (Hurley 1996: 4).[14] Moore and Howard recognise the irony:

> "Of course," Sara [Howard] said. "He became the tormentor!"
> I nodded eagerly. "And why the name John?"

---

[12] *From Hell* asserts this point of the non-Englishness of the murders by twice-removing the Whitechapel killer from English correctness by reminding the reader that, after suspicion fell on Leather Apron, "[s]ome people reckon[ed] a Red Indian must have done it. Is Buffalo Bill in England incidentally?" (Moore 2004: 6.13).

[13] It is interesting to note that a cursory look at the name 'Japheth' makes clear the ironic naming of a serial killer who sees himself as John the Baptist but is named for one of the biblical sons of Noah, perhaps the eldest, and as the presumed founder of the "Japhetite" race who promised that "all of his sons should be white" and that the "descendants of Japheth will become proselytes and will study the Law" (*The Book of Genesis* 5.32, 7.6 and 11.10); also see *The Jewish Encyclopedia* (1906: 72).

[14] For full discussions of the possible interpretations of Gothic tropes of the dismembered/mutilated/abjected body, see Hurley 1996 and Harter 1996.

"The Baptist," Sara answered. "The purifier!"
(Carr 2006: 374)

In his mind, rather than seeking or performing monstrous acts, Dury sees himself as performing spiritual cleansing rituals staged throughout New York at significant sights of water infrastructure to cleanse familial, historical and potentially complicit guilt; perhaps these cleansings are similar in nature to how these neo-Victorian narratives of the Ripper revisit the crimes, or a version thereof, to seek absolution for evil not brought to justice on behalf of unfortunates, either women or boys. Rather than the mythic image of the Whitechapel killer, here the white man creates himself as another mythological being, the 'savage', to be reborn from his violent past. Moore's memoir upon the death of Roosevelt in 1919 – the structure of the novel itself – acknowledges that during the events of 1896, the team had "set out on the trail of a murderous monster and ended up coming face-to-face with a frightened child" (Carr 2006: 5). Kreizler, in contrast, looks for answers to his own questions but receives none.

4. Case Study: *The Last Sherlock Holmes Story*

Michael Dibdin's *The Last Sherlock Holmes Story* provides my final example of the incarnation of the alienist/profiler who chases the monstrous subject. It, too, involves the facts and fictions of Jack the Ripper, as well as the fictional detective par excellence, Sherlock Holmes, with his companion John H. Watson, M.D., and his police contact, Inspector G. Lestrade, originally created by Sir Arthur Conan Doyle in 'A Study in Scarlet' that appeared in *Beeton's Christmas Annual* in 1887, the year prior to the Whitechapel murders. Conan Doyle's Holmes provides a commentary on Watson's first narrative attempt to capture the facts of their case:

> Detection is, or ought to be, an exact science and should be treated in the same cold and unemotional manner. You have attempted to tinge it with romanticism, which produces much the same effect as if you worked a love-story [...]. Some facts should be suppressed, or, at least, a just sense of proportion should be observed in treating them. The only point in the case which deserved mention was the curious

> analytical reasoning from effects to causes, by which I succeeded in unraveling it. (Conan Doyle 2003: 100)

It is this sense of hyper-rationality for which Holmes is known; however, in Dibdin's story, it is the toll taken on an individual – here a detective/profiler – in his never-failing search for justice that is explored. In this final case, a kind of counterfactual 'case closed', the separation between monstrosity and civilisation, killer and alienist/profiler, which Kreizler questions at the close of *The Alienist*, collapses into a singular being and creates the need for a secondary profiler reminiscent of Moore and Howard's recognition of suggestive facts in the earlier case.

According to the fictional editors of this last story, 'The Watson Papers' create a "criminological time-bomb" (Dibdin 1999: xii), which can neither be discounted nor proven given the 'evidence' of Sherlock Holmes's last case: Jack the Ripper. Dibdin's text is in itself a complexity of documents and documentation, pseudo-sources intended to lend weight to the narrative before the reader. The 'Introduction' explains the layering effect as a product of lies: Watson is not the author of the cases of Sherlock Holmes; rather, "A.C.D.", a friend of Watson's, decides to "do something based on one of Holmes's cases. What he had in mind was an entirely new type of story that would combine both fact and fiction" (Dibdin 1999: xv, xviii). Indeed, it is the genre of true crime, and for the modern reader of the neo-Victorian narrative outside of the Holmes's universe, it is fictionalised true crime. Watson seeks Holmes's approval for the scheme, to which Holmes merely inquires, "Does he have the humility to follow in my footsteps, telling each link of the iron chain of cause and effect by which I force the truth to reveal itself?" (Dibdin 1999: xix). The disdain of Holmes for what he perceives as the inability of the common mind to appreciate his genius is, ultimately, what collapses the boundary between the profiler and the predator in this last case. A.C.D.'s need to 'dramatise' causes Holmes to dismiss him, stating with oracular perception, that "[w]hoever belittles my opponents, belittles me" in a disdain for the Dionysian performative over the cerebral Apollonian intellect (Dibdin 1999: xxii). Holmes constructs his identity as a detective/profiler in opposition to or in concert with the villain he seeks, and "unless his interest was engaged, Holmes was a mere shadow of the man whose mental powers could seem almost supernatural when they were fully deployed", because he is a "man very finely balanced between reason and hysteria" who resorts to cocaine for "relief" (Dibdin 1999: 2-3). The relief he finds is in escaping a world Watson posits as one "with denizens [that] seem a pale and fraudulent imitation of [Holmes's] own fantasies" (Dibdin 1999: 3). The detachment of the investigator has experienced a Gothic turn; the literal projection and externalisation of Holmes's intense psychological fracture demonstrates that even the most cerebral of men can degenerate to create horrific acts of crime usually kept at bay by intellect, morality, ethics and social convention but, at these *fins-de-siècles* moments, left to develop to cast out his, and the reader's, *ennui*.

Lestrade seeks the investigative talents of Holmes after the first three Whitechapel murders. Watson is noticeably confused that Holmes would be interested, but Holmes quickly points out that the case is "[s]ordid enough and disgusting enough, in all conscience, but redeemed by some quite extraordinary features of interest" (Dibdin 1999: 5), if only Watson was of a like mind to see the murders as "quite insignificant" but recognise that they nonetheless enact a kind of transcendent moment of monstrosity, for

> when the killer tarries by the lifeless body of his victim, deliberately risking capture in order to inflict the most fiendish mutilations on the insensible flesh, then the affair transcends its sordid content and aspires to the realm of the unique and the inspirational. (Dibdin 1999: 9)

Watson raises the hyperbolic vision of the Ripper as a "monster [who] strikes at random, materialising out of the night to do his horrible work, and then vanishing as if by magic!" (Dibdin 1999: 10). This mythologising is cut down by Holmes as mere theorisation; he makes it clear that forensic study is necessary and begins his profile of Jack the Ripper. He warns that Watson must

> put all conventional notions out of your head. We are dealing with an artist of misdirection with an uncanny knack for manipulating the public mind. He knows that organ as well as any great musician knows his

> instrument, and he can make it play whatever medley
> of popular airs will best enshroud the augmented
> tones of his grim *leitmotif.* (Dibdin 1999: 21)

Holmes confirms that there is no "man in London besides [him]self" sufficiently "capable of cutting through this cunning devil's webs of deception, to reveal the unholy genius at the heart of it all" and praises the Ripper as "truly a formidable opponent", rejoicing in finally having found "an adversary wholly worthy of my powers! To destroy him will set a fitting crown upon my life's work" (Dibdin 1999: 58) – much like an author or artist whose entire *oeuvre* will some day be evaluated by a cultural critic. Because he sees a "distinctly theatrical thread running right through this Whitechapel case" (Dibdin 1999: 58), Holmes enacts a drama *en masquerade*, a neo-Victorian Gothic set piece, that we observe as he hunts his prey in a performance of criminality, one dually witnessed by the characters and the reader of the neo-Victorian "after-life" of the crime and its solution (Kohlke 2008/2009: i). Once at the murder scene, it becomes apparent to all present that "some dark power had risen out of the swamps of history, some atavistic freak come to unleash horrors we had thought to meet only in old books and country tales" (Dibdin 1999: 25).[15] It is this idea of atavism or criminal degeneration, invoking images of Cesare Lombroso's criminal type, combined with the provocative image of the folkloric monster, that leads Watson to reassert reason, reminding himself that "this is not a story" and that "fact is stranger than fiction" (Dibdin 1999: 34); however, it also causes him to evaluate Holmes's mood, which he likens

> to that of an artist who pauses during the creation of
> some vast epic canvas to paint a pair of portraits –

---

[15] The idea of atavism – or even the freak and culturally acceptable freakshow – also makes an appearance in *From Hell* in the form of Joseph (John) Merrick (1862-1890), an English man with severe deformities who was 'exhibited' and known as 'The Elephant Man'. His appearance presents the reader/viewer with an interesting confrontation of sympathies: the fascination with the Ripper's crimes is made more inappropriate by the reader/viewer's own reactive desire to quash revulsion and empathise with the deformed man. The conflation of the two images begs the questions who or what exactly Victorian London society – as well as our own – label as degenerate, and who or what it considers a kind of Darwinian success.

light, straightforward, employing only his superb technical skill – while his spirit rests from its intense labours and prepares for renewed struggle. (Dibdin 1999: 37)

Unwittingly, Watson has just profiled the profiler as he either degenerates into madness or elevates into a fantasy of creative monstrosity.[16]

The moment of collapse between the persona of the profiler and the profiled comes when Holmes reveals that he has seen "the very man who was at that moment uppermost in [his] thoughts" in the window across the street and admits "I had hoped to have the advantage of him – to know, and not be known. No doubt it was a vain hope with such a man" (Dibdin 1999: 45). This self-reflective Gothic doubling – via the literal doubling of the of detective and criminal in the window[17] – is a melding of identities "which often makes the detective dangerously complicit" (Spooner 2010: 251), giving the impression that Holmes battles a predatory Other, or, perhaps, attempts to contain his own dragon calmed by cocaine.[18] In another sleight of hand to objectify the evil that has been a constant thread through the Conan Doyle stories, Holmes then removes himself from consideration to posit Professor James Moriarty as the only one

---

[16] Structuralist critic Tzvetan Todorov's definition of fantasy relies on this precise, unsettling moment when the fantastic erupts into the mundane, or when two incompatible spheres of the predicable or mundane and the non-rational world collide, an articulation that appropriately captures the bifurcation/trifurcation, although not supernatural so to speak, of Holmes's persona(e) at this point, because "the fantastic requires the fulfillment of three conditions. First, the text must oblige the reader to consider the world of the characters as a world of living persons and to hesitate between a natural or supernatural explanation of the events described. Second, this hesitation may also be experienced by a character; thus, the reader's role is so to speak entrusted to a character, and at the same time the hesitation is represented, it becomes one of the themes of the work – in the case of naive reading, the actual reader identifies himself with the character. Third, the reader must adopt a certain attitude with regard to the text: he will reject allegorical as well as 'poetic' interpretations" (Todorov 1975: 33).

[17] For an excellent examination of this trope, see Mark Llewellyn 2010.

[18] This moment is particularly suggestive of Robert Louis Stevenson's *The Strange Case of Dr Jekyll and Mr Hyde* (1886) and the battle waged therein by Dr. Henry Jekyll to contain the beast he has brought to life in his alter ego, the monstrous Mr. Edward Hyde.

who is his "intellectual equal" while admitting that the "horror at his crimes was lost in [his] admiration at [Moriarty's] skill" (Dibdin 1999: 37). The reader is confronted by a sense of complicity: the skill of the criminal – the Ripper – and his ability to elude justice has the potential to evoke admiration rather than disgust.

Reassuming his position as detective/profiler, Holmes concludes that Moriarty kills by trade, "murders and mutilates to stave off *ennui*", testing the mettle of Holmes as "his intended opponent", someone who, in spite of his well-known disdain or disinterest in women, will understand with "what consummate artistry [Moriarty] prompts the *vox populi*! No one knows better than he the emotional value of gore and garters […]. To create chaos. To work evil" (Dibdin 1999: 39, 50-51). Lestrade's contempt for Holmes's methods shows itself in a prescient statement: "To hear you talk, anyone would think the killer was a friend of yours. You seem to know his mind better than he does himself" (Dibdin 1999: 82). In the 'facts' of his narrative, Watson soon recognises, reluctantly and via his own profile of Holmes, that the only possible explanation is that Holmes has crossed over into the black of the chess game, because "there were no longer any opponents worthy of his powers"; accordingly, he

> plunged himself into a world of artificial stimulation. There it was, no doubt, in some dark and dismal cavern of the mind unlocked by the spells of cocaine, that a voice had prompted him to move to the other side of the board. (Dibdin 1999: 116)

Dibdin's novel leaves Holmes "mad" although "it was, as one might have expected, a methodical madness" with "[h]is great mind" reduced to "ruins" (Dibdin 1999: 148), thrice split into the neo-Victorian *dramatis personae* of Sherlock Holmes, Jack the Ripper and Professor Moriarty.

These neo-Victorian narratives – these tales of bangtails, toffs, artificial stimulation and dis/eased minds – give pause to the reader to consider the level of complicity, not just of the various investigators, but of the reader in the blurring of boundaries and projection of historical horrors as well as in the need to chase our various elusive dragons. Ultimately, the fictional profiler has become both the factual *and* popular fictional monster(s) of the dual *fin(s) de siècle(s)*.

Bibliography

Arias, Rosario. 2010. 'Haunted Places, Haunted Spaces: The Spectral Return of Victorian London in Neo-Victorian Fiction'. In Arias and Pulham (2010): 133-156.
Arias, Rosario, and Patricia Pulham (eds.). 2010. *Haunting and Spectrality in Neo-Victorian Fiction: Possessing the Past.* Houndmills, Basingstoke: Palgrave Macmillan.
Bloom, Clive. 1988. 'The House that Jack Built: Jack the Ripper, Legend and the Power of the Unknown', in Bloom, Clive (ed.), *Nineteenth-Century Suspense.* London: MacMillan: 120-137.
Cameron, Deborah, and Elizabeth Frazer. 1987. *The Lust to Kill.* New York: Polity Press.
Canter, David. 2003. *Mapping Murder: The Secrets of Geographical Profiling.* London: Virgin.
Carr, Caleb. 2006. *The Alienist* [1994]. New York: Random House.
Conan Doyle, Sir Arthur. 2003. 'The Sign of Four' [1890], in *The Complete Sherlock Holmes*, Vol I (ed. Kyle Freedman). New York: Barnes & Noble Classics: 97-184.
Cornwell, Patricia. 2002. *Portrait of a Killer: Jack the Ripper – Case Closed.* New York: Berkley Books.
De Quincey, Thomas. 2006. *On Murder* [1827]. Oxford: Oxford University Press.
Dibdin, Michael. 1999. *The Last Sherlock Holmes Story* [1978]. London: Faber and Faber.
Evans, Stewart P., and Keith Skinner (eds.). 2001. *The Ultimate Jack the Ripper Companion: An Illustrated Encyclopedia.* New York: Carroll & Graf Publishers.
Ferguson, Christine. 2009. 'Victoria-Arcana and the Misogynistic Poetics of Resistance in Iain Sinclair's *White Chappell Scarlet Tracings* and Alan Moore's *From Hell*', *Literature Interpretation Theory* 20(1-2): 45-64.
Fuss, Diana. 1995. *Identification Papers.* London: Routledge.
Gamble, Sarah. 2009. '"You cannot impersonate what you are": Questions of authenticity in the Neo-Victorian Novel', *Literature Interpretation Theory* 20(1-2): 126-140.
Gomel, Elana. 1999. 'Written in Blood: Serial Killing and Narratives of Identity', *Post Identity* 2(1) (Winter): 24-70.
Gray, Drew D. 2010. *London's Shadows: The Dark Side of the Victorian City.* London: Continuum International Publishing.
Hantke, Steffen. 1998. '"The Kingdom of the Unimaginable": The Construction of Social Space and the Fantasy of Privacy in Serial Killer Narratives', *Literature/Film Quarterly* 26(3): 178-195.
Harter, Deborah A. 1996. *Bodies in Pieces: Fantastic Narrative and the Poetics of the Fragment.* Palo Alto, California: Stanford University Press.
Hughes, Albert, and Allen Hughes (dirs.). 2001. *From Hell.* Perf. Johnny Depp, Heather Graham and Ian Holm. Twentieth Century Fox.
Hurley, Kelly. 1996. *The Gothic Body: Sexuality, materialism and degeneration at the* fin de siècle. Cambridge: Cambridge University Press.

Kliś, Agnieszka. 2010. 'From the Outside to the Inside and the Other Way Round: The Space of Contemporary Gothic Cities' in Ciuk, Andrej, and Katarzuna Molek-Kozakowska (eds.), *Exploring Space: Spatial Notions in Cultural, Literary and Language Studies*, Space in Language Studies, vol. 2. Newcastle upon Tyne: Cambridge Scholars Publishing: 378-386.

Kohlke, Marie-Luise. 2008/2009. 'Editor's Note', *Neo-Victorian Studies* 2:1 (Winter), Special Issue: *"Swing Your Razor Wide...": Sweeney Todd and Other (Neo)Victorian Criminalities*: i-vii.

Kohlke, Marie-Luise, and Christian Gutleben. 2010. 'Introduction: Bearing After-Witness to the Nineteenth Century', in Kohlke, Marie-Luise, and Christian Gutleben (eds.), *Neo-Victorian Tropes of Trauma: The Politics of Bearing After-Witness to Nineteenth-Century Suffering*. Amsterdam & New York: Rodopi: 1-34.

Llewellyn, Mark. 2010. 'Spectrality, S(p)ecularity and Textuality: Or, Some Reflections in the Glass'. In Arias and Pulham (2010): 39-58.

Lonsdale, Kate. 2002. 'Rounding Up the Usual Suspect: Echoing Jack the Ripper', in Krueger, Christine (ed.), *Functions of Victorian Culture at the Present Time*. Chicago: Ohio University Press: 97-114.

Milburn, Colin. 2008. 'Science from Hell: Jack the Ripper and Victorian Vivisection' in Hüppauf, Bernd, and Peter Weingart (eds.), *Science Images and Popular Images of the Sciences*. New York: Routledge: 125-157.

Moore, Alan, and Eddie Campbell. 2004. *From Hell: Being a Melodrama in Sixteen Parts* [1999, serialised 1991-1996 in *Taboo*]. Marietta, Georgia: Top Shelf.

Pietrzak-Franger, Monika. 2009/2010. 'Envisioning the Ripper's Visions: Adapting Myth in Alan Moore and Eddie Campbell's *From Hell*', *Neo-Victorian Studies* 2(2) (Winter), Special Issue: *Adapting the Nineteenth Century: Revisiting, Revising and Rewriting the Past*: 157-185.

Seltzer, Mark. 1998. *Serial Killers: Death and Life in America's Wound Culture*. London: Routledge.

Spooner, Catherine. 2010. 'Crime and the Gothic,' in Rzepka, Charles J., and Lee Horsley (eds.), *A Companion to Crime Fiction*. Oxford: Wiley-Blackwell: 245-257.

Stevenson, Robert Louis. 1998. *Dr Jekyll and Mr Hyde* [1886] */ Weir of Hermiston* [1896] (ed. Emma Letley). London: Oxford University Press.

The Holy Bible. King James Version.

The Jewish Encyclopedia. 1906. On-line at: http://jewishencyclopedia.com (consulted 08.01.2010).

Todorov, Tzvetan. 1975. *The Fantastic: A Structural Approach to a Literary Genre* (trans. Richard Howard). Cornell: Cornell University Press.

Warwick, Alexandra. 2006. 'The Scene of the Crime: Inventing the Serial Killer', *Social & Legal Studies* 15(4): 552-569.

Neo-Victorian Female Gothic: Fantasies of Self-Abjection

Marie-Luise Kohlke

Abstract:
Repeatedly, women writers' turn to Gothic in formulating critiques of past gender inequalities and injustices reproduces insidious patterns of victimisation, which preclude rather than enable female self-actualisation in neo-Victorian fiction. While such denunciations of Victorian wrongs might be regarded as opportunistic, the frustration of female selfhood is also linked to wider Gothic motifs of doubling, abjection and the traumatised subject's spectrality even to itself. Via texts by Marghanita Laski, Maggie Power, and Kate Williams, which reprise aspects of nineteenth-century Gothic, this chapter explores neo-Victorian renegotiations of gender debates centred around essentialism and performativity, around autonomous agency and what might be termed 'subjectless subjectivity'.

Keywords: abjection, the double, Female Gothic, Marghanita Laski, Maggie Power, self-loss, sexual transgression, victim feminism, victimisation, Kate Williams.

*****

Neo-Victorian women writers adopt a distinctly Gothic approach to the histories of gender, sexuality, and women's one-time presumed biological 'destiny' in terms of corporeality and/or marriage, reproduction, and motherhood. This predilection is hardly surprising, since Gothic naturally lends itself to feminist interrogation and critique. As Claire Knowles remarks, "Gothic fiction has, almost from its inception, been concerned with exploring the sufferings visited upon women by the patriarchal cultures in which they live" (Knowles 2007: 141). Furthermore, Susanne Becker ascribes Gothic's resurgence in the late twentieth century to its close relation "to the two most powerful political and aesthetic movements of the time: feminism and postmodernism" (Becker 1999: 1), which call into question the unitary and universalised, self-knowing humanist subject as an ontological given (implicitly male gendered or else presumed to be un-gendered) – movements equally significant to the cultural ascendance of neo-Victorian literature. Almost inevitably, however, this Gothic turn involves a voyeuristic re-victimisation of female characters that at times seems at odds with neo-Victorianism's ethical and liberationist agenda of bearing after-witness to unrecorded traumas of the socially disempowered and marginalised, including women as society's internally colonised subjects or subalterns. For all too often these novels replicate predictable patterns of female oppression, transgression and punishment, as if doubtful about the real extent of change achieved in women's lives since the nineteenth century, participating in on-going critical debates as to whether "'female Gothic' can be read [or *should* be read] as feminist, counter-feminist or anti-feminist discourse" (Kelly 2002: xiii). Displaying a curious ambivalence towards women's liberation, even overtly feminist neo-Victorian novels are likely to end with desolation for their Gothic victim-heroines – or, more accurately, heroine-*victims*.

This chapter interrogates such problematic tensions in three novels that foreground female experiences of victimisation from three stopping-off points in the evolution of neo-Victorian Female Gothic over nearly six decades:[1] Marghanita Laski's *The Victorian Chaise-longue* (1953), Maggie Power's *Lily* (1994), and Kate Williams's more recent *The Pleasures of Men* (2012). To what extent are the neo-Victorian's and Female Gothic's tendencies – of destabilisation, contestation, and/or deconstruction of gender constraints and ideology – mutually reinforcing or, conversely, antipathetic? Does subversion of traditional norms or retro-sexist containment of 'deviance' predominate and why? In pursuit of answers to these questions, I deliberately take recourse to three as yet critically neglected texts,[2] which nonetheless clearly demonstrate the thematic concerns and

---

[1] As advocated by Gary Kelly, I will be employing 'Female Gothic' more as "an interpretative instrument and proposition" than a distinct sub-genre or mode (Kelly 2002: xiv). For used in the latter senses, Andrew Smith and Diana Wallace have argued, 'Female Gothic' has become "too much an umbrella term, and, possibly, too essentialising", resulting in contemporary critics preferring to resort to alternative designations, such as "'women's Gothic', 'feminine Gothic', 'lesbian Gothic', even 'Gothic feminism'" (Smith and Wallace 2004: 1), or sometimes 'postfeminist Gothic'.
[2] The interest generated by William's novel, however, suggests it likely will receive significant critical attention in future.

narrative strategies dominating neo-Victorian gender politics more generally. In view of Gothic's one-time despised, subaltern status within 'high' literature and culture (despite its perennial popularity), it seems fitting to resist neo-Victorian criticism's own inclinations towards canonising exclusivity – something the diversity of texts discussed in this volume likewise aims to do.

Neo-Victorian women's writing, this chapter proposes, highlights potential contradictions within Female Gothic's (as well as neo-Victorianism's own) transgressive emancipatory and pessimistic reactionary tendencies, with the latter defusing – at times risking to negate altogether – the celebration of modern-day women's comparative (if by no means wholly achieved) liberation and self-realisation. Repeatedly the notion of female selfhood per se is called into question by tropes of fragmented, abjected, and haunted identities that appear unable to ever completely 'possess' or 'own' themselves, let alone attain genuine control over their own lives, resulting in what might be termed 'subjectless subjectivity'. How should we read these disturbing fantasies of self-abjection in neo-Victorian texts?

1. A Feminist Impasse?

Most neo-Victorian Female Gothic novels eschew the restorative justice of the Radcliffean happy ending, which is either relegated to comic-gothic texts like Angela Carter's *Nights at the Circus* (1984) and Elaine di Rollo's *The Peachgrowers' Almanac* (2008), or else disturbingly attenuated by ambiguity, as in Margaret Atwood's *Alias Grace* (1996) and Sarah Waters's *Fingersmith* (2002). In this sense, the latter texts mirror Victorian "classics of late gothic feminism", such as the Brontë sisters' *Wuthering Heights* (1847), *Jane Eyre* (1847), and *Villette* (1853), which Diane Long Hoeveler describes as "indictments of the limitations" of the Gothic, "end[ing] on a compromised note" (Hoeveler 1998: 186). At times, neo-Victorian women writers likewise seem to compromise their agendas of historical recovery and symbolic retrospective liberation by working in the formulaic Gothic vein.

The close of Waters's novel, for instance, parodies Female Gothic's traditional motif of the persecuted heroine's quest for the lost mother, reuniting the lesbian protagonists Maud Lilly and Susan Trinder only at the cost of the renewed loss of the mother figure, the arch manipulator Mrs Sucksby. Moreover, the heroines begin their 'new' life together at the Gothic mansion Briar, primary scene of Maud's traumatic scribal enslavement to her 'uncle' Christopher Lilly's monomania with cataloguing his pornographic collection, much of which she destroys after his death. (The protagonists having been switched at birth, Lilly is in fact Susan's rather than Maud's uncle.) Liberation from both the villainous father figure and the 'bad' mother is further compromised by Maud's resort to writing pornography for a living, spectrally reconstituting her uncle's collection by providing new additions for other collectors' stock and thus condemning herself to re-live her former abjection. On a Gothic reading, the novel's 'happy ending' turns into a feminist dead-end.[3] Similarly, at the close of Atwood's novel, the new husband of the pardoned murderess Grace Marks continuously makes her re-live the day of the killings and her executed accomplice McDermott's sexual aggression as a form of titillating foreplay to their marital relations, traumatically re-playing the implied (actual and/or attempted) sexual abuse Grace was subjected to throughout her life by various male authority figures, including her father. Grace's indeterminate condition, possibly a late middle-age pregnancy or a cancerous tumour, either of which may kill her, likewise functions as the spectre of Gothic retribution. In these examples, though re-imagined from more egalitarian and 'liberated' post-Victorian perspectives, *any* female sexual activity, whether within or outside sanctioned marriage, still seems to invite disastrous, even interminable punishment. Women's victimisation and the cultural 'prison house' of gender prove inescapable.

Hence from one point of view, neo-Victorian Female Gothic evinces strains of so-called "victim feminism" whereby, according to Naomi Wolf, women underhandedly seek "power through an identity of powerlessness" and redress for their culturally disadvantaged state "on the basis of feminine specialness" (Wolf 1994: 147). Put

---

[3] My reading thus diverges significantly from the better known critical views represented by Cora Kaplan, Kathleen A. Miller, Kate Mitchell, and Heta Pyrhönen, who view the female protagonists as subversive agents, empowered by their appropriation of the formerly male-defined space, role, and profession (see Kaplan 2007: 113, Miller 2007, especially para. 3-5 and 25, Mitchell 2010: 140, and Pyrhönen 2010: 192). For a darker reading of the ending's equivocation, focusing on *Fingersmith*'s analogy between women's literacy and poison, see Armitt 2007: 28 and Muller 2009/2010: 122-123.

differently, victim feminism advocates special pleading for women as purportedly hapless victims of male persecution, thus ingeniously disavowing their own capacity for aggression and violence – though that capacity is clearly evident in Waters's Maud and Susan and Atwood's Grace.[4] Other critics, like Rene Denfeld in *The New Victorians*, have gone still further, claiming that second-wave feminists' reiterations of Gothic plots of a patriarchal conspiracy against morally superior femininity sustain an antiquated "victim mythology" of women as "politically powerless – and perpetually martyred", naively reminiscent of nineteenth-century feminist discourse, especially social purity movements (qtd. Meyers 2001: 5; see also 8-9). While Hoeveler does not specifically focus on contemporary or neo-Victorian texts,[5] her coinage "gothic feminism" similarly highlights passive aggression and the performance of masochism as typical subversive strategies by which female characters surreptitiously gain power through the cultivated "appearance of their very powerlessness" (Hoeveler 1998: 7). Hoeveler suggests that early Female Gothic writers "imagined a world where a wily little woman would triumph through her skilful use of femininity as manipulation and guile", teaching "women that pretended weakness was strength, and that the pose, the masquerade of innocent victim, would lead ultimately to possessing the master's goods and property" (Hoeveler 1998: 246). Yet what crucially differentiates neo-Victorian Female Gothic fictions from earlier works of gothic feminism is their much greater scepticism regarding the very possibility of women's self-actualisation and empowerment, be it via self-conscious masquerade of victimhood, equivocal celebrations of female eroticism, madness and visionary imagination, or (backfiring) parodies of Gothic narrative patterns and tropes.

The depictions of victimisation resulting in self-abjection in *The Victorian Chaise-longue*, *Lily*, and *The Pleasures of Men* critique

---

[4] However, neo-Victorian Female Gothic's frequent foregrounding of the female perpetrator or violent avenger is not wholly at odds with victim feminism, since the latter's supporters often advocate on behalf of female criminals convicted of the murder of abusive men or of being accessories to murder (for example, of children) by violent partners, whose actions they were supposedly unable to oppose due to their own victimisation (see Wolf 1994: 211-215, and 222-227).
[5] Bar passing references to Margaret Mitchell's *Gone with the Wind* (1936) and Daphne du Maurier's *Rebecca* (1938) in her brief 'Afterword'.

not just the foundations of patriarchy in violence, but also, implicitly, some of the basic tenants of feminism. For as Anne Williams argues, comparable to Enlightenment notions of all men's equality that informed Gothic's original radicalism, "liberal or bourgeois feminism is founded on the so-called liberal self, the assumption that we are free to act independently according to our will and desires, free of any external determinants", so that ultimately it holds Gothic heroines "responsible for their own fates" (Williams 2007: 88-89). However, Gothic themes of doubling and otherness often short-circuit such liberal/liberational aspirations for female characters (and indeed, as will be seen, for male characters also). Whether read in terms of biological or ideological destiny, these women's fates have as much to do with what can be done *to* women than what women can do for themselves. If as Helene Meyers argues, Gothic's "femicidal plots" provide a particularly useful lens to negotiate feminist controversies about "violence against women", exploring "the sometimes vexed relationship between the literal, fear-inspiring violation of female bodies [and psyches] and the theoretical status and limits of the female subject" (Meyers 2001: 2), neo-Victorian Female Gothic pursues those debates to their logical extremity by imagining different kinds of vanishing points for subjectivity itself.

2. The Victorian Succubus: Draining Women's Vitality

More than a decade before Jean Rhys's seminal *Wide Sargasso Sea* (1966), Marghanita Laski re-worked a similar complex of traditional Gothic tropes – self-destructive desire, sexual transgression, dysfunctional family relations, mental instability, and self-alienation, as well as female physical imprisonment, persecution, and painful death – in her horror story of an inadvertent twentieth-century time-traveller, Melanie Langdon, who falls asleep on the titular antique to be precipitated back in time to 1864. *The Victorian Chaise-longue* depicts femininity as a state of terrifying powerlessness, as the new mother Melanie, recovering from a life-threatening pregnancy that aggravated her tubercular condition, awakens in the dying Victorian body of a consumptive 'fallen' woman. As described by P.D. James, Laski's novel "involves the reader in that most atavistic of human horror, confusion of identity and the realisation that one is inexorably trapped by circumstances which one can neither influence nor understand" (James 2006: v). The confusion of identity relates not only to that between Melanie (or 'Melly' as her husband Guy calls her) and her Victorian alter-ego Milly, but also between character and reader. For the protagonist's time-travel imitates the reader's vicarious immersion in the recreated nineteenth century, eager to encounter the period 'first-hand' in its full sensual immediacy. Yet in this case the fantasy of physically reliving or 'inhabiting' the past turns out to be horrific rather than exotic and exhilarating, as Melanie, acting as the reader's stand-in, becomes literally trapped in Milly's dying body.

The Victorian Chaise-longue 'springs' the trap of abjected female corporeality without egress and hence the interminable cultural reproduction of female 'Nature' as inimical destiny. Initially, Melanie's tortured consciousness vigorously rejects Milly's body as an Hyde-like other to herself, but as the story progresses, difference segues into heterogeneous identity.[6] Very much a *fallen* 'Angel of the House', the unmarried Milly's sexual transgression not only contributes to her own postpartum decline, as she awaits death imprisoned in the domestic sphere she never leaves throughout the story, but also mysteriously occasions the married twentieth-century mother's 'fall' into her double's body. Laski's novel thus distinctly recalls Ellen Moers's influential analysis of Female Gothic, summarised by Andrew Smith and Diana Wallace "as the coded expression of women's fears of entrapment within the domestic and within the female body, most terrifyingly experienced in childbirth" (Smith and Wallace 2004: 1), the birthing process also transforming the one into a multiplicity of beings akin to Melanie's experience. Yet Laski's text stages a generic repetition with variation: the typical patriarchal tyrant or other male Gothic villain is replaced by the far more insidious threat of debilitating ideological legacies perpetuated by and with the collusion of women as they victimise themselves and each other. For above all, it is the venomous Adelaide, Milly's sister, who condemns her sibling for bringing shame on the family name and, having disposed of Milly's illegitimate child, cruelly refuses to

---

[6] One of the most excruciating moments occurs when, needing to urinate, the protagonist realises that Milly's body, long since decomposed in Melanie's own time, can still "make its demands upon her" (Laski 2006: 42), collapsing her mental self-separation from her 'alien' vessel. Later, in a possible echo of Robert Louis Stevenson's classic horror story of split identity, she increasingly fears "Melanie again being overwhelmed by Milly, that the moments when Melanie could be only, surely Melanie would grow shorter and shorter" (Laski 2006: 77).

disclose its fate in spite of her dying sister's agonised pleas to be told what became of the infant. The narrative context of respectable domesticity hiding sexual and family scandals distinctly evokes nineteenth-century sensation fiction, a genre intersecting and overlapping with both Victorian and neo-Victorian Gothic, which are equally obsessed with secrets, transgressive desires, and undisclosed crimes, as well as the disjunction between public and private lives.

Why the "good obedient", pampered, modern Melanie should be so afflicted is never made explicit (Laski 2006: 2), unless even her legitimate enjoyment of the sexual aspects of her marriage renders her liable to Gothic punishment. Indeed, in some ways Melanie is presented as a Gothic femme fatale, albeit more a construct of male fantasy than a self-conscious seducer. Early on, as she undergoes an updated version of the nineteenth-century rest cure, still weakened from pregnancy and disease, "the doctor wondered again how it was that Melanie's smile seemed always to invite delights he was sure she had never known" (Laski 2006: 1). He suspects Guy of seeking his pleasures elsewhere while unable to enjoy them with his ill wife, suggesting that Victorian double standards are still very much alive in the post-Victorian age,[7] and regards Melanie herself as mercurially "cunning" – "the purely feminine creature who makes herself into anything her man wants her to be" (Laski 2006: 5). Implicitly, Melanie is viewed as an amorphous shape-shifter, a Lamia-like seductive monster, yet one who remains conveniently blind to her husband's indiscretions. The doctor's reflections not only collapse the traditional virgin/mother–fallen woman/whore binary, but depict the protagonist as a radically unstable, discontinuous and morphically interchangeable subject. Her continuous state of *un*-becoming, self-fission and re-formation displays a contingent performative identity that facilitates her temporal substitution.

It is worth stressing that Melanie's time-slip into Victorian otherness occurs only once the nuclear family is complete, almost as if, with her new maternal role, she will no longer be able to satisfy her husband's craving for an innocuous child-wife solely concerned with accommodating *his* needs. Julia Kristeva, of course, draws a specific link between the maternal and abjection, proposing that the latter

---

[7] The exact temporal setting of the modern-day part of story remains uncertain, as no dates or identifying historical contexts are provided.

commemorates "the archaism of pre-objectal relationship, in the immemorial violence with which a body becomes separated from another body in order to be", that is, the self's "source in the non-ego" (Kristeva 1982: 10, 15). Arguably, Melanie' amorphous selfhood is connected to her recent experience of giving birth. The protagonist's trans-historical imprisonment within Milly's body may thus be read as an ironic representation of the longed-for death or rather *killing* of the Victorian maternal Angel of the House, famously advocated by Virginia Woolf in *A Room of One's Own* (1929) and 'Professions for Women' (1931), as well as an indictment of the death-like stasis threatened by the long shadow that nineteenth-century idealisations (and demonisations) of femininity continue to cast over women's lives. As Cora Kaplan pertinently notes of neo-Victorian narratives with dual time-frames, "our own moment is seen to suffer as much from the hypocrisy of liberation as the Victorian did from the effects of repression" (Kaplan 2007: 98) – or, perhaps more accurately, our own moment suffers from the false or unachieved promise of true liberation.

Rather than the achievement of a confident feminist consciousness, Laski's novel dramatises women's on-going struggle with and Gothic reversion to disabling gender roles inherited from the Victorians, which vampirically drain the life-force of later generations of women. Through subtle intertextuality with nineteenth-century Gothic classics, her narrative weaves what might otherwise appear to be reactionary tendencies into a resonant feminist critique. It seems no coincidence that Melanie's rest cure calls to mind the treatment the narrator of Charlotte Perkins Gilman's 'The Yellow Wallpaper' (1892) is subjected to by her doctor husband, which eventually drives her mad – although Melanie's husband Guy is actually a lawyer. Melanie's doctor recalls that "for eight months she had obediently lain still in bed, but with the stillness of taut anger and resentment and never the demanded relaxation" (Laski 2006: 7).[8] As if fulfilling the

---

[8] The novel's unsettling pathologisation of feminine reproductive capability, reminiscent of Elaine Showalter's notion of "the female malady" (Showalter 1987), raises the possibility – though never explicitly pursued by Laski – that Melanie's time-travel constitutes a psychotic projection, a traumatic response to her fear of death (and likely motherhood also), with which the novel opens. "Will you give me your word of honour," Melanie asks her doctor, "that I am not going to die?" (Laski 2006: 1). Towards the end of the novel, Melanie's thoughts raise this possibility more

fairytale adage that 'you should be careful what you wish for', Melanie's supine confinement renders literal "her body's need to lie on the Victorian chaise-longue" that overwhelms her on first seeing it in the antique shop, together with a half-formed, seemingly psychometric impression of a sexual act consummated thereon (Laski 2006: 19). Unconsciously, Melanie conspires in the masochistic Victorian fantasy of women's assumed helplessness and passivity, underlined by the later implication that Milly's 'fall' on the chaise-longue may have been a forcible violation rather than voluntary seduction, possibly by the local curate Gilbert Charters.[9] Though covered in a faded rose pattern, the chaise-longue hardly proves a 'bed of roses'. The ominous stain in the pattern, which Melanie dismisses as inconsequential when buying the antique, could be read as indicative of her contamination by (or 'buying into') outmoded gender ideology, which insidiously colonises her psyche analogous to the patch on her lungs that spreads unseen to the point of endangering her vitality.

Implicitly, Laski critiques even modern marriage and motherhood as likely forms of self-loss for women rather than genuine means of fulfilment and self-actualisation. Not coincidentally, when Melanie wakes the second time in the uncanny Victorian setting – having willed herself back asleep hoping to escape what she initially takes to be a bad dream – she recalls a visit with Guy to a junk-shop, which he dismissed as not worth calling into: "she half played the foolish little woman, the man knowing better", pleading with him to let her browse nonetheless, and "gazed up at him, miming the playful but obedient kitten" (Laski 2006: 31). Melanie's defining desire to be indulged and cherished makes her repeatedly guilty of self-diminishment to the point of complete self-abjection. This accounts for her instinctive horror on realising that Milly's body is already "all dead and rotten long ago [...] rotted filthily [...] stinking, rotten dead", with its "flesh crawled away, [...] turned green and liquescent and at last become damp dust with the damp crumbling coffin wood"

---

directly: "I have only to wait and the illusion that clouds my mind must pass" (Laski 2006: 93). In this sense, Laski's novel can also be read as a 'hysterical' text.
[9] When Melanie/Milly begins to 'remember' the seduction scene, suddenly "enormous disgust blotted the picture out" (Laski 2006: 77), though this is ascribed to her horrified realisation that Milly's lover too is already dead and decomposed, evoking the Gothic archetype of the spectral bridegroom.

(Laski 2006: 41-42), in effect a *thing* drained of personhood, all distinguishability lost – a sign of ultimate otherness and abjection. Unknowingly, Melanie *already* existed in a state of quasi living death, at best a simulated or putative *proto*-subject, a liminal not-quite self. Having wasted her life,[10] the protagonist now literally wastes away. Body horror merely reveals the Victorian 'rottenness' already within her, inhabiting her like a psychic succubus.

The extent to which she has internalised retro-sexist gender norms is emphasised when, as yet unaware of her double's transgression, Melanie contemplates the possibility of Milly having changed places with her and enjoying her husband's loving attentions. Immediately Melanie fears Guy "liking her better than me" (Laski 2006: 46), suggesting that for the protagonist the fantasy of the 'good' self-effacing Victorian woman, vacuously doll-like or childish, constitutes the ideal model of femininity. When she fruitlessly tries to convince the visiting vicar of her switched identity, only persuading him further of Milly's mental instability on account of unconfessed sins, her "simulacrum of ecstasy" during his prayer makes the same point: "a total withdrawal into timeless *selflessness*, the transfiguration of the burden of self into its apotheosis, all this, though sincerely sought, had been feigned" (Laski 2006: 69, added emphasis). Melanie's search for transcendence of her imprisoning embodiment takes the form of would-be projection into unbounded otherness, resembling an encounter with uplifting sublimity. Yet instead of re-affirming or exalting the self, this move paradoxically risks suspending it altogether; apotheosis becomes dissolution. Since in the Gothic "the transcendence associated with the sublime might also be described as self-loss," Donna Heiland aptly notes, "one must wonder whether it is a truly desirable experience" (Heiland 2004: 34). Immediately thereafter Melanie remembers her guilty pleasure during pre-marital sex with Guy, comparing it to an earlier religious experience of self-transcendence: "the ecstasy identical, whether from man or from God" (Laski 2006: 70). Her transgression, then, is an uncommon one for Female Gothic – not the wilful assertion of her

---

[10] Nowhere does Melanie express any personal aspirations beyond those of a decorative wife and homemaker, although at one point she bemoans her inadequate education, which prevents her from recalling historical facts about the Victorians that might prove of use: "If I was one of those educated women, she thought angrily, an old resentment, long buried in marriage, rearing its head again" (Laski 2006: 57).

own desires, but rather their absolute negation. In elevating her husband to the role of God and (re-)creating herself in his desired image of her, Melanie has bought into "a useless magic" that ultimately fails her (Laski 2006: 69), akin to what Angela Carter resonantly called the myths by which women "allow themselves to be consoled" for their disempowerment in culture and society, "consolatory nonsenses [sic]" that only serve to "obscur[e] the real conditions of life" (Carter 1993: 5). Fittingly, Melanie concludes that "[i]t is the ecstasy that is to be feared" (Laski 2006: 70) – the consuming ecstasy (or abyss) of women's culturally inculcated desired/desirable self-loss, prescribing a trajectory of symbolic death.

Yet the dawning of this "darker, disastrous knowledge" is insufficient for Melanie's liberation from her ideological entrapment (Laski 2006: 86). Upon the appearance of her apparent seducer, and later again at the arrival of the doctor, Philip Blundell, she promptly falls back into a coy little girl role, posturing and seeking to please. Evidently attracted to her himself and angered by her sexual transgression with an unknown rival, Blundell takes her flirtation amiss, painfully grasping her shoulders and threatening her: "You like to be hurt, don't you? You don't always scream and flutter and protest when a man hurts you" (Laski 2006: 84). His words reiterate the Gothic theme of female masochism while, much as does Adelaide, squarely placing the blame on the woman as inviting, even desiring, any physical or sexual violence committed against her. After the doctor's departure, fearful of wholly merging with Milly, Melanie tries to reaffirm her distinct sense of self through an exploration of 'her' body: "if I know anything in the world I know my body" (Laski 2006: 95). The protagonist unselfconsciously re-enacts the very essentialism Laski's text problematises in its emphasis on the cultural construction and performance of gender, so typical of neo-Victorian fiction.[11] Unexpectedly discovering milk-heavy breasts, Melanie/Milly panics and screams for her baby, resulting in Adelaide rushing in and condemning her as "foul" and "mad" (Laski 2006: 97). Melanie/Milly becomes Gothic's quintessential madwoman. Indeed, the room she is confined to, with its "red-brown plush curtains" and "heavy red

---

[11] This tendency is arguably most apparent in narratives involving cross-dressing and/or cross-gender identities, as in Sarah Waters's *Affinity* (1999) or Wesley Stace's comic-gothic *Misfortune* (2005).

wallpaper, patterned like the ceiling in textures that formed shapes and then shifted as she looked" (Laski 2006: 24, 30), evokes both the terrifying red room in *Jane Eyre*, which pre-figures the madwoman's attic, and the attic room of 'The Yellow Wallpaper' where Gilman's narrator discerns strange shapes and movements behind the wall covering, which she comes to regard as the figure of a woman straining to break free.

In Brontë's text, of course, the mad woman's fiery exorcism facilitates the heroine's eventual accommodation with normative gender expectations and renewed (self-)repression of her 'unfeminine' rebelliousness as the crippled Rochester's helpmeet, while in Gilman's story the protagonist collapses with/into the madwoman. Laski's story opts for a more inconclusive ending. Adelaide offers to allow Milly to see her baby, but only if she discloses its father's name, precipitating the final ignominious revelation of the text, as Milly confesses she cannot, "for I do not know" (Laski 2006: 98). Ironically, from the viewpoint of sexual self-expression, Milly could be regarded as *more* liberated than the twentieth-century protagonist, who at one point recalls Guy describing her as a Jane Eyresque "puritan at heart" (Laski 2006: 70). Laski depicts a reincarnated Victorian sensibility inhabiting the present-day protagonist, who ironically haunts her past alter-ego rather than vice versa.

Maddened to frenzy by Milly's confession, Adelaide violently attacks her both verbally and physically, striking her sister until the invalid vomits blood over the chaise-longue's roses and succumbs to a fatal coughing fit. In an apparent out-of-body experience, Melanie sees both Milly's deathbed and, beyond it, what may be her own twentieth-century deathbed scene. Laski's novel ends on Melanie's "fading vision", followed by "nothing but darkness, and in the darkness the ecstasy, and after the ecstasy, death and life" (Laski 2006: 99). Yet what sort of twentieth-century "life" she may be reborn into, if at all, remains doubtful in view of the implication that Melanie has all the time been living a lie, an invalided/invalidated existence or non-life. Her earlier cited admission that "ecstasy […] is to be feared" updates Gothic's traditional warning about obsessive desire for a fetishised person, object, or state rebounding upon the desiring subject, redefining the end of female desire not as total possession of the other, but rather absolute self-*dispossession*.

The Victorian Chaise-longue, it must be remembered, was written in the vanguard of second-wave feminism and the 1960s sexual revolution. In Gothic form, the novel anticipates women's anxieties and dissatisfactions with their assigned lot highlighted in a seminal work like Betty Friedan's *The Feminine Mystique*, published a decade later in 1963. Laski attacks femininity from within the residual but tenacious cultural norm, deconstructing gender essentialism from the inside out via Melanie's 'performance' as Milly, which the reader at least recognises as merely a *repeat* performance of her modern femininity. Nowadays, Laski's representation of the Victorians as punitively repressed – mirrored in her own text's deliberate sexual obliquity – might strike readers as too simplistic and stereotypical, not to say over-done by later neo-Victorian writers. Yet her figuration of the succubus-like Victorian colonising present-day subjects effectively pre-empts the dual subversive and reactionary tendencies of later "Victoriana" in fictional and other forms, foreshadowing what Kaplan describes as the

> oddly contradictory conjuncture, when the libertarian impulses of the 1960s, so invested on the one hand in driving a final stake through the heart of Victorian values, reanimated them on the other through its prurient curiosity about the period. (Kaplan 2007: 86)

If as some critics assert, the historical settings in Gothic fictions may serve to ameliorate depicted horrors by "tell[ing] a comforting story about how far we have travelled from" the repressive past (Killeen 2009: 5), or "fill[ing] us with relief at our exemption from the dangers they represent" (Heiland 2004: 2), Laski's neo-Victorian Female Gothic refuses such reassurance. Distance and difference collapse into simultaneity and sameness, accounting for the deeply unpleasant frisson of *The Victorian Chaise-longue*. Significantly, the reader is never shown Melanie as a resurrected modern woman, having learnt her overdue feminist lesson, only as a transplanted, reanimated and replicated (neo-)Victorian.

3. The Revenge of Withering Femininity

Maggie Power's *Lily*, published four decades after Laski's novel, likewise redeploys tropes of sexual transgression, disease, madness, and death, albeit with a much more vicious feminist twist and in a still more densely intertextual context. Power's novel reworks and combines aspects from various Gothic classics, again reprising both *Jane Eyre* and 'The Yellow Wallpaper', as well as *Wide Sargasso Sea*, Emily Brontë's *Wuthering Heights* (1847), Wilkie Collins's *The Woman in White* (1859-60), and Edgar Allan Poe's 'The Fall of the House of Usher' (1839). In addition, the male protagonist's name Jonathan Hopgate references Jonathan Harker from Bram Stoker's *Dracula* (1897), with Power describing her novel as "a vampire novel without a vampire" (Power qtd. Kohlke 2011: 88). Written in the context of second-wave cultural and literary feminism, not least Sandra M. Gilbert and Susan Gubar's seminal 1979 study *The Madwoman in the Attic*, which Power cites as a significant influence on her work (Power qtd. Kohlke 2011: 86), *Lily* could be read as a feminist 'Reclaim the Gothic' campaign. While Hopgate's wife Lily reincarnates the theme of female masochism, the novel's main focus actually falls on the husband's progressive self-loss, paradoxically precipitated by his exploitation of unequal gender roles and opportunities. In a dramatic volte-face – and powerful critique of Gothic's gendered politics of the objectifying male gaze – the Byronic hero-villain is condemned to suffer the fate of entrapment in abjected corporeality traditionally reserved for female victims. Such "critical reversals of […] victim status", Fred Botting has aptly noted, "shift the identification of monstrosity from [women's] sexualised otherness to tyrannical patriarchal systems" (Botting 2007: 170). Power opportunistically employs strains of victim feminism as a 'cover story' for a subversive story of an entirely different sort, deliberately playing with and overturning reader expectations of the Female Gothic, not least those derived from her literary intertexts.

Last scion of a dissolute gentry family, the impoverished drawing master Jonathan – in an ironic nod to Walter Hartright in *The Woman in White* – enters a mercenary union with his invalid pupil Lily Flood, heiress of a widowed nouveau riche industrialist, so as to redeem his ancestral home High Withens from his dead father's creditors and restore the decaying moorland estate with her substantial dowry. While Brontë's Rochester binds himself in marriage to a Creole heiress who unbeknownst to him suffers from her mother's inherited insanity, Jonathan – who fittingly has a penchant for Jamaican rum – calculatingly weds the magnate's daughter, having been assured that "[t]he consumption's after her like it galloped off with her mother before her" (Power 1994: 27). Only needing to await Lily's imminent death to fully enjoy his good fortune, he instead becomes infatuated with the local curate's daughter, the angelic motherless Agnes Slane, a perfect counterfoil (à la Jane Eyre, albeit more beautiful) to his dark-skinned sickly wife. Yet when Agnes in turn falls victim to "the fatal spell" of Jonathan's Rochester-like, dark brooding looks (Power 1994: 19), the Byronic hero proves quite prepared to assume a role more akin to that of Sir Percy Glyde or Count Fosco in his eagerness to dispose of his new bride. Although disgusted with Lily's unseemly passion for him, he encourages her, against her doctor's express advice, to consume increased doses of her pills so as to make herself well enough to resume their marital relations, and later even administers the medicine himself. Revealing himself as a Bluebeardesque tyrant, he views their lovemaking as "the foreplay to killing her" (Power 1994: 126).[12]

Yet if, as Anne Williams suggests, the Bluebeard trope exposes "patriarchy's secret, founding 'truth' about the female: women as mortal, expendable matter/*mater*" (Williams 1995: 43), that same matter comes back to haunt Jonathan with a vengeance. His fate is foreshadowed by his relationship with High Withens which, although regarded by Jonathan as his patriarchal "inheritance", can also be read in terms of the abjected maternal body, rendering his obsessive self-identification with the house – "I *am* High Withens" – gothically incestuous and his exclamation upon his first sight of the estate after his wedding – "my destiny!" – uncannily and ironically prophetic (Power 1994: 65-66, 2, original emphasis). Indeed, his prior visit with Lily's father, which sees Jonathan "[r]eturning like an ardent lover to the arms of a long lost mistress; going back to [his] first love that leaves its mark forever" (Power 1994: 29), suggests an unresolved Oedipal conflict, exacerbated by a domineering, women-

---

[12] On their very first morning at the ancestral home, Jonathan thinks, "Let her die, let her die" (Power 1994: 7), echoing Antoinette's words in *Wide Sargasso Sea*: "Say die and I will die" (Rhys 1993: 77). Bluebeard imagery is subtly inverted in the scene of Jonathan and Mr Flood's initial visit to High Withens, when his future father-in-law hands over the "[k]eys to unlock the heart and its illimitable desires" (Power 1994: 33). Later, during Jonathan's forcible seduction of Agnes while Lily's body is barely cold, he overcomes Agnes's resistance by threatening to strangle her "like Porphyria's lover" (Power 1994: 152).

abusing father whom the son comes to mirror. Having taken up permanent residence, Jonathan compares the "little ruinations" in the house's fabric to an enticing and "intriguing history of seductions" that experience has written "on the face of a courtesan", and he spends the first few days after his return in an eroticised re-discovery of High Withens that reads both like a sexual conquest of feminised Gothic space and engulfment therein:

> Days passed in rapt exploration of the most secret inner chambers and labyrinthine passages, distilling his breath on the streaming windows, penetrating every curtained recess, prying open cupboards, forcing doors ajar, until he had inventoried every item of neglect and abandonment. (Power 1994: 12-13)

High Withens thus represents Jonathan's conflicted relation to maternity and femininity, a jealous unconscious desire for non-differentiation or being-other, simultaneously longed for and abhorred. His exploitative treatment of femininity is underlined by his reminiscence of an affair with Christina, a governess whom he playfully re-named Christabel, "a small faery of a woman" (Power 1994: 9) – evoking Rochester's first meeting with Jane Eyre and imagining a darker alternative ending for Brontë's heroine had she succumbed to Rochester's insistent pleas to remain with him unwed. For after seducing Christina and causing her to lose her position, Jonathan briefly kept her as his mistress (albeit making her work as a nude artist's model for her keep), before callously palming her off on an artist friend to be passed round among the latter's associates, now opium-addicted and "no better than a dollymop" (Power 1994: 11).

Christina/Christabel's self-loss reproduces the Gothic trope of women's conspiracy in their own victimisation, replicated in Lily's self-abasing relationship with her husband: "[h]er masochism astonished him" (Power 1994: 52). Yet Lily also functions as a version of the Gothic's monstrous other. For Jonathan experiences distaste, verging on horror, for his wife's embraces; Lily's "slaver[ing]" kisses remind him of "Lamia and Geraldine and all the female monsters, the serpent women the poets wrote of", and he finds her body disgustingly "hot, salamandrous, as it wreathed over him" (Power 1994: 85). Her perceived loathsomeness evokes fears of what

Kelly Hurley terms the "abhuman", characteristic of fin-de-siècle Victorian Gothic, which "in place of the possibility of human transcendence" offers only "the prospect of an existence circumscribed within the realities of gross corporeality" (Hurley 2004: 3) – directly opposed to Jonathan's view of himself as an innate aesthete, offended by all things vulgar and base. He only manages to forget his aversion to Lily while drunk, as when he eventually consummates their marriage in the gazebo in the High Withens gardens, thus sealing his own 'Fall' into consuming and (self-)obliterating materiality.

Lily herself proves the forbidden or, more accurately, poisonous fruit, transformed into an ironic version of Gothic's spectral lover who draws the unwary to a premature grave.[13] As much is implied when an inebriated Jonathan claims his conjugal rights, imagining a sexual union with Agnes instead: "He saw the other woman's mouth and eyes efface Lily's for a brief moment before the vision faded. Then there were black holes where Agnes's eyes had been, a terrible absence instead of her mouth" (Power 1994: 52). Recalling Victor Frankenstein's dream of his beloved Elizabeth transformed into the decaying corpse of his dead mother, Jonathan's nightmarish vision is haunted by the fear of abjected female matter/maternity. Yet Lily further acts as his own Doppelgänger here, as on his pre-marital visit to High Withens a "trick of the light" made it appear to his future father-in-law as if Jonathan's features were suddenly erased, leaving only "an abyss, a chasm like the mouth of hell, where a man's face should have been" (Power 1994: 33). Contrary to Gothic's traditional spectral lover, Lily's sinister power has a very material cause: shortly after her death, Jonathan discovers his wife's true illness to have been syphilis, of which Lily and her father were kept in ignorance by a compassionate doctor,[14] along with

---

[13] In an early dream, Jonathan sings a ballad on this theme – "'Last night I lay sleeping,/ When my dead love came in...'" – and later he thinks Lily "looked already like a cadaver" (Power 1994: 5, 47, original ellipses). After her death he has nightmares in which "Lily wouldn't stay dead. She always came back for her tardy lover" (Power 1994: 170).

[14] Having warned Lily against having marital relations, the doctor had assumed her husband would not inflict himself on a dying woman. Curiously, venereal disease remains a largely neglected topic in neo-Victorian fiction in spite of the prevalent focus on sexuality and/or prostitution in the genre. For instance, it is not explicitly addressed in Carter's *Nights at the Circus*, Waters's (non-Gothic) *Tipping the Velvet*

his own virulent infection, already passed on to the seduced Agnes, his soon-to-be second wife. Despite her virginal name, Lily had been unchaste, having contracted "the Italian plague" from her former dancing master Giovanni (Power 1994: 166).[15] Syphilis proves the unredeemed Byronic hero's true inheritance.[16]

As in Power's first novel *Goblin Fruit* (1987), the man's previous lover demonically haunts his future relationship, though in this case in the shape of transmitted disease which will live on beyond him through Agnes: "Lily was in them both, a rank poison who had got into bed with them" (Power 1994: 169). Hence what Heta Pyrhönen terms "Bluebeard's sacrificial cycle" continues, not even ending with the "scapegoat[ed]" Bluebeard's own death via which the family or community is traditionally cleansed (Pyrhönen 2010: 161). As in Laski's novel, desire consumes the desirer, who inadvertently mistakes the end of desire for total possession of the (m)other rather than self-dispossession in a state of non-differentiation. The decaying High Withens turns into the pre-Oedipal womb, where Lily, Jonathan, and his mother (and, presumably, in due course Agnes also) will merge into sameness, realising what Leona F. Sherman, in a discussion with Norman N. Holland, describes as "the primary motivating fear in gothic", namely "nothingness and nonseparation" (Holland and Sherman 1977: 283). Yet crucially the inflicted self-loss is distributed equally between women *and* men and, in so far as the disease stems from Giovanni, implicates *male* rather than female desire as the source of 'original sin' and transgression.

As might be expected, Lily ends her life largely confined to an attic room, albeit a spacious chamber re-decorated in rose rather than red or yellow. Though she views it as a welcome change from her

---

(1998) or Michel Faber's *The Crimson Petal and the White* (2002). Among the still comparatively rare exceptions, Charles Palliser's *The Quincunx* (1989) briefly mentions it, while D.M. Thomas's *Charlotte* (2000) treats the issue in the twentieth-first-century context of AIDS.

[15] Indeed, observant readers' suspicions will already have been aroused by repeated references to the curvature of Lily's spine, her recurrent bouts of fever, mercury medicines, "running sore[s]", and "the silvery moons of pigmentation that pocked her chest", just as her sexual transgression is pre-figured in the triptych "Daughter of Intemperance" hanging in her father's house (Power 194: 39, 89, 21).

[16] Power's novel thus renders explicit what critics have long suspected of *Jane Eyre* – that Bertha may be suffering from tertiary syphilis and that Rochester's blinding in the Thornfield fire symbolically evokes one of the side-effects of the disease.

damp marital bedroom with its "infernal scratching" behind the wainscoting, the sounds eventually resurface to torment her in her new chamber: "The walls of the old house were gossiping as if the long dead mistresses of High Withens had been buried alive in them" (Power 1994: 105, 133-134). Lily is thus aligned with Brontë's Bertha and Gilman's imprisoned narrator, as well as Bluebeard's brides. Yet what sets Power's neo-Victorian novel apart from these Gothic narratives is how she aggressively, even savagely, modulates the madwoman/victim trope. As foreshadowed by the doubling leitmotif, Lily's vacated place in the attic is eventually taken up by none other than Jonathan himself. I am not suggesting that Power engages in blunt reversal here along the lines of cultural feminism, simply inverting gender hierarchies in a fictional form of men-bashing demonising misandry; indeed the text displays a fascinated sympathy with its predatory male protagonist and never imputes moral superiority to its female characters. Nor does Power chart a way out of the potential impasse of Gothic victim feminism – but she does show this impasse to be a self-destructive ideological dead-end for *both* heteronormative genders. In a fitting and wonderfully ironic re-write of the male protagonist's re-naming of Antoinette to Bertha in *Wide Sargasso Sea*, Lily addresses her husband by her first lover's name shortly before she dies, pre-figuring his subsequent literal self-loss to the ravages of the disease: "'My name is Jonathan,' he said. 'Give me my English name'" (Power 1994: 141).

Jonathan's second marriage is dominated by Agnes's long vacations apart from him in seaside spas, trying to cleanse herself of his "filth" (Power 1994: 196). Increasingly, Agnes leaves him alone at High Withens to be haunted by echoes of his dead wife's Bertha-like "harsh laugh", Lily's sickly mix of perfume, mercury ointment and corruption that seems to infuse the atmosphere, and her spectral footsteps echoing through the house – to the point that "he almost forgot he had another wife" (Power 1994: 225). Rational masculinity is left radically unhinged. In spite of his Victorian credentials, Jonathan can thus be read as a version of contemporary Gothic's "Postfeminist Man", linked to what Benjamin A. Brabon terms the "spectral phallus": "the symbol historically associated with masculinity – the phallus – has become a ghostly form for men", he asserts, representing both "presence and absence – the manifestation of an aggressive masculine identity and a lack thereof", simultaneously "emasculated and whole, impotent and virile" (Brabon 2007: 57-58). Via the trope of venereal disease, centred on the literal male genitalia, Power emasculates the hero-villain-turned-victim and renders him, rather than the monstrous female, as abject. Hence she inverts the male subject's traditional alignment with transcendence compared to femininity's identification with materiality, instead "positing absolute corporeality as the ineluctable condition of both masculinity and femininity alike", yet without the potential *jouissance* of its willing embrace that Hurley locates in late Victorian Gothic's deployment of the trope (Hurley 2004: 147; see also 4). The very basis of symbolic law, threats to which Victorian Gothic so often ends up re-containing, becomes the source of that law's systematic undoing. At the end of the novel, the dominant potent masculine subject is reduced to subject-less subjectivity, the phallus-less object of the gaze. Jonathan ends his days confined to the attic, having lost not only his mind and powers of speech, but his inheritance once more, being without issue and even without name; when the doctor asks him who he is, he answers, "Me, Lily" (Power 1994: 257).

Rather than the House of Hopgate sinking in Poe-esque fashion into a primordial swamp, its master's body, so closely identified with High Withens, begins to literally disintegrate. Tormented by the servant-guard employed to watch over him, Jonathan is subjected to the added indignity – though one he can no longer even register – of being sketched in his progressive physical deterioration. The one-time drawing master made good becomes the scientific object of study for the purpose of illustrating medical texts on syphilis. "The last portrait" of him is a truly horrific itemisation of the noseless, mouthless master of High Withens as a staring "death's head" with its "rictus of diseased flesh", reduced to a mass of "rotting matter" (Power 1994: 259).

4. Festering Femininity and Puppet-Play

Kate Williams's post-millennial *The Pleasures of Men* plays with the trope of the self possessed by another's malevolent subjectivity like a puppet manipulated by external will, rather than focusing on disembodied ideology that haunts the pseudo self or on excessive 'corporealisation' that likewise produces a subjectless subject. Her novel dramatises the female protagonist's quasi merger with and take-over by other entities or consciousnesses. Although this does not involve any genetic manipulation/alteration, which Botting links to his coinage of "chiasmosis", the novel's protagonist Catherine Sorgeiul is, in effect, the object of a pseudo-scientific experiment by her sinister anthropologist uncle Mr Crenabon and his associates as well as a victim of manipulation by the serial killer dubbed the Man of Crows. This results in what might be viewed as a psychological version of chiasmosis – an apparent conflation of 'chiasmus' and 'osmosis' – whereby, "in the crossing and reversal of terms" and "the breach between oppositions", subject and object collapse, infusing and taking up each other's ("empty"/emptied) place (Botting 2007: 171). Precipitating the loss of individuation, the resulting adulterated subjectivity underlines the performative nature of Gothic femininity, but voids the subversive potential of victim feminism, since a puppet does not self-consciously enact the role it is forced to play.

Initially, however, *The Pleasures of Men* tempts its readers and its traumatised, mentally fragile protagonist to think differently, as Catherine projects herself into the role of active would-be criminal investigator, reminiscent of Abberline in the film adaptation of Alan Moore and Eddie Campbell's *From Hell* (1999) discussed in Maier's chapter (this volume: 202-206). Catherine, too, imagines a psychic communion with a serial killer, who terrorises the streets of Spitalfields, London, mutilating women (albeit in the 1840s, long before Jack the Ripper), so as to track him down by imaginatively and physically retracing his steps and writing herself into his mind through her diary. However, as Miriam E. Burstein argues, one of Williams's most interesting moves is what she does with the trope common to "both neo-Victorian fiction and feminist theory more generally: she deconstructs the connection between women's writing and self-empowerment". Burstein describes the protagonist's explicit desire to "throw [her]self into the Man of Crows, be bound up into him and his atrocity and find release" (Williams 2012: 43) as partaking of an "orgasmic" and "perversely Keatsian" quality, which renders it an "act of subjective self-erasure, *becoming* the character" (Burstein 2012: n.p., original emphasis) – or becoming wholly other – paradoxically an evacuation rather than actualisation of subjectivity, akin to Melanie's ecstasy in *The Victorian Chaise-longue*.

The Pleasures of Men is as much a dissection of Catherine's at times near-delirious psyche as that of the killer, with abrupt narrative shifts between their perspectives inviting confusion between their identities, evoking what Andrew Smith calls Gothic's typical "fragile, because permeable, models of subjectivity" (Smith 2007: 95). Indeed the protagonist's self-professed psychic affinity with the killer is predicated on the belief of her own inherent evil: "Others were too much of the world to recognize him, but I was darker and crueller and more wrong than them all so *I would be able to see him*" (Williams 2012: 44, original emphasis). She blames herself for childhood dreams of wishing her sibling and parents dead, which appeared to come true when her younger brother Louis was snatched in London's streets never to be seen again while Catherine, herself still a child, stood by helpless, an event that precipitated her mother's suicide and her father's self-exile from England, leading to his death at sea. Existing in a state of permanent anxiety, Catherine has interiorised self-blame to the point where she feels that she draws evil to herself and others around her, a conviction seemingly confirmed by her maid's unexplained disappearance, the accidental death of a magician's female volunteer at a theatre show she attends, and the murder of a new friend. Catherine's quest for the killer is thus a perverse search for self; her visionary empathy constitutes a communion with her own feared and loathed otherness, hidden beneath the placid exterior of decorous Victorian femininity.

Fittingly, the killer eventually turns out to be Catherine's innocuous and solicitous next-door neighbour, Mr Kent – of all things a painter of the quaint supernatural subject of fairies, for which he employs young female models he picks up from the capital's streets. His name almost seems a deliberate play on 'ken', meaning an intuitive cognisance, discerning perception or recognition, as well as vision or (in its archaic sense) *descrying* – in Catherine's case, this is nothing less than discovering herself in the other / the other within herself. It is this disturbing intimate *proximity* of evil, its apparent sameness to and convergence with ordinary everyday selves that the Victorian Gothic explored in characters like Jekyll/Hyde and Dorian Gray and which the neo-Victorian Gothic revisits, albeit more often in the context of psychoanalytically inflected trauma discourse rather than explorations of scientific or supernatural monstrosity.

Kent, it turns out, has been intruding into the Crenabon home to read Catherine's diary, violating the boundaries between self and other, 'inhabiting' her secret self, so to speak. Analogous to a victim of mesmerism, she has been invaded and manipulated, adopting a 'stray' cat, which Kent actually sent as a gift, and following his spectral instructions left on the pages of her journal, such as "*Write about your maid*" (Williams 2012: 362, original italics), the disappeared Grace. In reciprocal mutuality, Kent now demands that *she* write *his* story, determining his future self via a narrative of the repentant killer no longer wishing to continue with his crimes. Williams's resolution is somewhat clumsy and contrived, with Catherine managing to escape through the convenient intervention of Kent's mother, a spectre-like Miss Havisham figure,[17] as her great expectations of redeeming her own evil by overcoming the killer crumble to nothing. Yet the oblique, trance-like writing of the scene is curiously fitting:

> 'Mother!'
> 'You should let Miss Sorgeiul leave,' she said, her voice as strangely high as his. 'I think she would like to go.'
> And those were my words. [...] (Williams 2012: 364-365)

The "strangely high" voice, reminiscent of a ventriloquist's projection, Mrs Kent's articulation of Catherine's wish to escape, her uttering, as Catherine puts it, "my words" while sounding like her son, and the fact that Catherine has been compelled to write the killer's story – all combine to render indefinite who exactly is the producer of the scene and, indeed, the crimes which precipitated it. Even once she has managed to flee, Catherine admits, "I heard his voice in my mind: *Shall we begin?*" (Williams 2012: 365, original italics). Has Catherine, trance-like, been acting out Kent's desires/instructions or vice versa?[18]

---

[17] As much is indictaed by the following passage: "Mrs Kent stood there in her nightgown, her grey hair hanging loose around her face. I saw the wrinkled skin of her hands as she raised them. Her gown was netted with holes, a giant spider's web. She was like a child's version of a Greek goddess, Hecate, perhaps, with leaves in her hair" (Williams 2012: 364).

[18] Burstein argues that, "[a]lthough it's easy to miss, Catherine is the author of the plot's alternative POV [point of view] narratives: the prologue, for example, features an 'I' who is actually the Man of Crows". While a definite possibility, I would suggest that the narrative remains deliberately vague as to the seguing of their subjectivities and the boundaries between them. Whereas Burstein reads Catherine as "yearn[ing] to occupy both positions simultaneously", perpetrator *and* victim, it also makes sense to

The situation is rendered still more indefinite by the two earlier discovery scenes. The first is set in her uncle's Bluebeardesque secret study, where Catherine find various personal items, which had mysteriously vanished from her room causing her to question her sanity; the second takes place in Catherine's derelict former family home, where it is revealed that Crenabon has manipulated her life and events all along. He too has been encouraging Catherine's diary-writing and reading her journal, as well as deliberately exposing the household servant girls as well as his niece to danger – all so that he and his esoteric associates might determine how the killer selects his victims and, by Catherine's anticipated violent death, prove their belief "that people attract evil to themselves" (Williams 2012: 350). This suggests that even Catherine's deepest held belief may not be her own so much as implanted, that she may be a wholly 'constructed' subject reminiscent of an automaton wound-up and set in motion, first by Crenabon and later by Kent. As she realises early on during her uncle's confession, "*I was a toy for you*" (Williams 2012: 246, original emphasis); any 'agency' on Catherine's part has taken the form of inadvertent complicity in her own and others' victimisation rather than conscious choice. The Gothic dread of the scene is further heightened by its accompanying revelations, which paradoxically validate her paranoia: of her uncle's closest associate, Mr Trelawny – a man Catherine is instinctively terrified of – having been the man who snatched her brother to exploit him for criminal purposes (akin to Oliver Twist); of Louis's subsequent suicide; of Crenabon's incestuous relationship with Catherine's mother and the possibility that he may, in fact, be her biological father, all of which further undermine her precarious sense of self. Like Maud and Susan's victimisation in *Fingersmith*, that of Catherine serves the discovery that, quite literally, she may be someone else entirely.

In a self-consciously postmodern twist, Catherine's subsequent confrontation with Kent also implicates reader (and author) in the confusion of identities. For Kent, like Crenabon, has been our stand-in, following Catherine's inconclusive diary entries in a seductive game of deferred desire. Indeed, he metafictionally

---

read her in terms of Botting's chiasmosis as victim-perpetrator. Indeed, as much is implied by Burstein's later questions: "Who, or what, has been writing all along? [...] Who is the subject and who is the object here?" (Burstein 2012: n.p.).

admonishes Catherine for not fulfilling her responsibilities as a writer towards him (and, implicitly, us):

> ['']I became rather intent on reading the next instalment. I felt such disappointment when I arrived and found you had not progressed.' He wagged a forefinger at me. 'Authoresses are supposed to entertain their public, madam.' (Williams 2012: 363)

Similarly, Kent points out that "you did not explore the need for society to project evil on to such a man" (Williams 2012: 363), turning the readers' gaze back on themselves. Implicitly, Williams invites readers to question their investment in a narrative of graphic violence against women, implying voyeuristic complicity with, even sadistic desire for the crimes to take place, as if, akin to Catherine's obsessive quest – possibly encouraged by her own predilection for horrid novels (see Williams 2012: 123) – the horridness and depravity sought actually constitute self-reflections.

Indeed, some reviewers have seized on this aspect of the novel to question Williams's feminist credentials and intentions as a writer, especially in contrast to her highly respected work as a historian on women's lives and contributions to history. Mark Ravenhill suggests that Williams "seems to relish" the "artistic model" proposed by the nineteenth-century Parisian dramatist Victorien Sardou, who "once advised that the secret of a good plot was to 'torture the heroine'" (Ravenhill 2012: n.p.).[19] Similarly, Bidisha wonders "why Williams participates in the literary fetishisation of men who kill women", but also reports Williams's revealing response to the effect that

> it's the fetishisation itself that interests her: "Why do we invest murderers with this amazing existential greatness [....] rather than us thinking these are

---

[19] His subsequent dismissal of the novel as "a dose of gothic-lite, decaf Dickens", which risks "becoming a theme park ride with notes by Freud and Foucault", seems to rely heavily on what he describes as the overfamiliarity of "[t]he interlocking of male power, madness and violence" (Ravenhill 2010: n.p.), aligning him with postfeminist concerns.

pathetic figures [...]? We don't invest victims with such greatness." (Williams qtd. Bidisha 2012: n. p.)[20]

Hence the novel's ultimately unsatisfying resolution may be deemed a deliberate (feminist) refusal to satisfy/vindicate such dubious desires on the part of Gothic's readers. Somewhat unbelievably, Catherine, who has spent a life of domestic and institutional confinement prior to her night-time excursions in search of the killer, ingeniously manages to flee to Egypt to assume a new identity as a teacher at an expatriate girls schools. Although she escapes the prescribed role of Gothic female victim, she does so only by opting for a form of renewed enclosure, seldom going beyond the confines of the school and her rented room. Crucially, however, Williams does not pursue the strand of possible heterosexual romance with the potential 'hero' figure, Constantine Jannisser, the son of a friend of her uncle, who bashes the vile Crenabon over the head with a candlestick. Nor does she conflate Catherine's powerlessness with virtue or innocence – after all, when forced to decide which of the children the criminals would abduct, she designated her brother, and she never reports Kent to the authorities or brings him (or her uncle) to justice. At the same time, however, this move enables Williams to refocus on the victim rather than perpetrator and divests the latter of his phallic power as another version of Brabon's "Postfeminist Man". The Man of Crows is finally as much a subjectless subject as Catherine, a being constructed, impelled, and empowered by others' projected desires, including the reader's own.

5. Epilogue: Gothic Defeatism?

The triumph of rational sensibility over supernatural explanation at the end of *The Pleasures of Men*, so typical of traditional Female Gothic, provides little comfort. As in the case of Melanie's death/rebirth and Lily's conquest over her husband only once dead, ambiguity once again attenuates the protagonist's liberation. Although neo-Victorian heroine-victims are never completely subjugated to the point of unquestioning and unresistant abjection, they remain unable to mount

---

[20] Compare Leslie A. Fiedler's contention, from *Love and Death in the American Novel*, that Gothic's *proper* focus is the male perpetrator rather than his female victims: "[T]he fully developed Gothic centers not in the heroine (the persecuted principle of salvation) but in the villain (the persecuting principle of damnation)" (Fiedler qtd. Meyers 2001: 18).

effective resistance to patriarchal oppression or postulate – yet alone achieve – an autonomous subjectivity, assuming full responsibility for their actions and fates. None of the female protagonists manages a definitive escape from confining cultural norms; each can only seek a different form of accommodation therewith and negotiation therein, calling into doubt Benjamin A. Brabon and Stéphanie Genz's proposition that, in an age of asserted postfeminism, "we might have crossed a psychological barrier and reached a new critical space beyond the Female Gothic (and its ghosts of essentialism and universalism)" (Brabon and Genz 2007b: 7). Rather, neo-Victorian Gothic fictions' obsessive recourse to just these same ghosts, highlighted by their nineteenth-century normative settings, emphasise the continuing relevance of these concerns in the present time of writing – and the feminist work still to be done in Gothic fiction and criticism, as well as 'Gothic culture'.

As such, neo-Victorianism makes a crucial contribution to a "new generation of feminine writing", much of it in a "neo-gothic" vein, as described by Becker:

> It evokes and reveals established images of femininity, but does not propose new role models [*The Victorian Chaise-longue*]; it evokes and re-writes familiar narrative forms, but undermines their established effects [*Lily*]; it evokes and repeats ideological constructions of established power structures, but defamiliarises their 'natural' existence [*The Pleasures of Men*]. (Becker 1999: 253, 3)

Neo-Victorian Female Gothic contests postfeminism's presumption of the liberal subject credited with unrestricted agency and potential for self-actualisation, which would dismiss 'gender oppression' itself as essentialising rubbish and an outdated delusion of 'old' feminism. *The Victorian Chaise-longue*, *Lily*, and *The Pleasures of Men* do not reify women as victims, so much as self-consciously critique and contest cultural processes of subject formation and representation (including the Gothic itself) as complicit in perpetuating essentialising tendencies, norms, and ideals that continue to reduce fictive and real women to readily victimised and/or disposable irrational matter. Victimisation, these texts propose, is not a pose voluntarily adopted or subversively indulged, but rather a state of abjection forcibly inculcated and imposed, the logical endpoint/vanishing point of which is a chimerical subjectless subjectivity. Neo-Victorian Gothic is finally haunted by desire for a very different object than the maternal body that once underpinned the Female Gothic quest – that has been superseded by the indefinitely deferred, fully liberated daughter's female self, as yet to be written into existence.

Bibliography

Armitt, Lucie. 2007. 'Dark Departures: Contemporary Women's Writing after the Gothic'. In Brabon and Genz (2007a): 16-29.
Becker, Susanne. 1999. *Gothic Forms of Feminine Fictions*. Manchester & New York: Manchester University Press.
Bidisha [ShonarKoli Mamata]. 2012. 'Kate Williams joins the queens of historical fiction', *The Guardian*, 16 January: n. p. On-line at: http://www.guardian.co.uk/lifeandstyle/2012/jan/16/kate-williams-queens-historical-fiction (consulted 23.05.12).
Botting, Fred. 2007. 'Flight of the Heroine'. In Brabon and Genz (2007a): 170-185.
Brabon, Benjamin A. 2007. 'The Spectral Phallus: Re-Membering the Postfeminist Man'. In Brabon and Genz (2007a): 56-67.
Brabon, Benjamin A., and Stéphanie Genz (eds.). 2007a. *Postfeminist Gothic: Critical Interventions in Contemporary Culture*. Houndmills, Basingstoke: Palgrave Macmillan.
––––. 2007b. 'Introduction: Postfeminist Gothic'. In Brabon and Genz (2007a): 1-15.
Burstein, Miriam E. 2012. '*The Pleasures of Men*', The Little Professor [Blog], 15 April: n.p. On-line at: http://littleprofessor.typepad.com/the_little_professor/2012/04/the-pleasures-of-men-.html (consulted 23.05.12).
Carter, Angela. 1993. *The Sadeian Woman* [1979]. London: Virago.
Heiland, Donna. 2004. *Gothic & Gender: An Introduction*. Malden, Massachusetts & Oxford: Blackwell Publishing.
Hoeveler, Diane Long. 1998. *Gothic Feminism: The Professionalization of Gender from Charlotte Smith to the Brontës*. University Park, Pennsylvania: The Pennsylvania State University Press.
Holland, Norman N., and Leona F. Sherman. 1977. 'Gothic Possibilities', *New Literary History* 8: 278-294.
Hurley, Kelly. 2004. *The Gothic Body: Sexuality, materialism, and degeneration at the* fin de siècle [1996]. Cambridge & New York: Cambridge University Press.
James, P.D. 2006. 'Preface' [1999]. In Laski (2006): v-ix.
Kaplan, Cora. 2007. *Victoriana: Histories, Fictions, Criticism*. Edinburgh: Edinburgh University Press.

Kelly, Gary. 2002. 'General Introduction', in Kelly, Gary (ed.), *Varieties of Female Gothic*, Vol. 1: *Enlightenment Gothic and Terror Gothic*. London: Pickering & Chatto: xi-lx.

Killeen, Jarlath. 2009. *History of the Gothic: Gothic Literature 1825-1914*. Gothic Literary Studies. Cardiff: University of Wales Press.

Knowles, Claire. 2007. 'Sensibility Gone Mad: Or, Drusilla, Buffy and the (D)evolution of the Heroine of Sensibility'. In Brabon and Genz (2007a): 140-153.

Kohlke, Marie-Luise. 2011. 'Neo-Victorian Goblin Fruit: Maggie Power on the Gothic Fascinations of Demon Lovers and Re-Imagining the Victorians', *Neo-Victorian Studies* 4(1): 77-92.

Kristeva, Julia. 1982. *Powers of Horror: An Essay on Abjection* (trans. Leon S. Roudiez). New York: Columbia University Press.

Laski, Marghanita. 2006. *The Victorian Chaise-longue* [1953] (preface P.D. James). London: Persephone Books.

Meyers, Helene. 2001. *Femicidal Fears: Narratives of the Female Gothic Experience*. Albany: State University of New York Press.

Miller, Kathleen A. 2007. 'Sarah Waters's *Fingersmith*: Leaving Women's Fingerprints on Victorian Pornography', *Nineteenth-Century Gender Studies*, 4:1, para. 1-30.

Mitchell, Kate. 2010. *History and Cultural Memory in Neo-Victorian Fiction: Victorian Afterimages*. Basingstoke & New York: Palgrave Macmillan.

Muller, Nadine. 2009/2010. 'Not My Mother's Daughter: Matrilinealism: Third-wave Feminism & Neo-Victorian Fiction', *Neo-Victorian Studies* 2:2, Special Issue: *Adapting the Nineteenth Century: Revisiting, Revising and Rewriting the Past*: 109-136.

Power, Maggie. 1994. *Lily*. London: Simon & Schuster.

Pyrhönen, Heta. 2010. *Bluebeard Gothic: Jane Eyre and its Progeny*. Toronto, Buffalo & London: University of Toronto Press.

Ravenhill, Mark. 2012. 'The Pleasures of Men by Kate Williams – review: A gothic novel pastiche fails to convince', *The Guardian*, 27 January: n.p. On-line at: http://www.guardian.co.uk/books/2012/jan/27/pleasures-men-kate-williams-review (consulted 23.05.12).

Rhys, Jean. 1993. *Wide Sargasso Sea* [1966]. London: Penguin.

Showalter, Elaine. 1987. *The Female Malady: Women, Madness, and English Culture, 1830–1980* [1985]. London: Virago.

Smith, Andrew. 2007. *Gothic Literature*. Edinburgh: Edinburgh University Press.

Smith, Andrew, and Diana Wallace. 2004. 'The Female Gothic: Then and Now', *Gothic Studies* 6(1) (May), Special Issue: *Female Gothic*: 1-7.

Williams, Anne. 1995. *Art of Darkness: A Poetics of Gothic*. Chicago & London: University of Chicago Press.

——. 2007. '*The Stepford Wives*: What's a Living Doll to Do in a Postfeminist World?'. In Brabon and Genz (2007a): 85-98.

Williams, Kate. 2012. *The Pleasures of Men*. London: Michael Joseph/ Penguin.

Wolf, Naomi. 1994. *Fire with Fire: The New Female Power and How It Will Change the 21st Century* [1993]. London: Vintage.

Part III

Hybrid Forms

Epistemological Rupture and the Gothic Sublime in *Slouching Towards Bedlam*

Van Leavenworth

Abstract:
This chapter examines how Gothic effects of the sublime are generated by the incomprehensible phenomenon at the centre of an interactively produced steampunk narrative. Set in a re-imagined London in 1855, the interactive fiction *Slouching Towards Bedlam* explores links between Victorian and contemporary anxieties regarding the individually and socially transformative dangers of infection. The work reflects the Victorian zeal for classification both in the player's role and the narrative produced via interaction. However, the classification failures that develop in this narrative point to a subversion of the Victorian epistemological framework and are further shown to constrict the player's agency. These ruptures and constrictions enact the Gothic sublime in a manner that links the fears of the Victorian period to those of today.

Keywords: classification, epistemology, Star C. Foster, Gothic sublime, interactive fiction, Daniel Ravipinto, steampunk, virus.

*****

In the introduction to *Victorian Afterlife*, Dianne F. Sadoff and John Kucich contend that re-envisionings of the nineteenth century are on the rise because contemporary culture "fetishizes notions of cultural emergence, and because the nineteenth century provides multiple eligible sites for theorizing such emergence" (Sadoff and Kucich 2000: xv). This chapter considers the ramifications of this claim as it explores how forging a link to the re-imagined Victorian past creates a "fetishized" Gothic experience for the player of the interactive fiction *Slouching Towards Bedlam* (2003), written by Star C. Foster and

Daniel Ravipinto.[1] I investigate how effects of the Gothic sublime may be generated by an unclassifiable, threatening phenomenon in this steampunk work, a sense of traumatic disturbance intertwined with a particular version of 'the Victorian' and its legacies in the present day.

As an interactive narrative form, *Slouching* provides the player with a neo-Victorian experience that is distinct from reading and yet also readerly. Interactive fiction is often subsumed within what has come to be called 'electronic literature', a term for works that are "created on a computer and (usually) meant to be read on a computer", but which actively partake in literary traditions (Hayles 2008: 3). Although ground-breaking work exploring interactive fiction's formal and aesthetic properties has been carried out by scholars such as Nick Montfort and Jeremy Douglass (see Montfort 2003, 2007; Douglass 2007), interactive fictions remain underrepresented in cultural and literary criticism. This lack of critical attention is particularly noticeable within Gothic criticism, where despite the fact that the genre has "never been a solely literary phenomenon [. . . .] the [contemporary] proliferation of Gothic media still remains a relatively under-researched area" (Spooner 2007: 195). The same concern applies to neo-Victorian scholarship. Foster and Ravipinto's interactive fiction is wholly text-based, which is to say that it contains no sound or images, and proceeds in alternating steps of textual output from the software (describing a setting, an action, a character, etc.) and typed input from the player. Conceptually, the work presents a re-imagined Victorian story world that the player explores through an avatar-like entity called the 'player character'. The simple text commands that the player inputs (such as 'read patient file', 'talk to James', etc.) function as instructions that direct the player character. A typical exchange from *Slouching*, with player commands written in capitals after the prompt (>), looks like this:

> Office
> A massive cedar desk, well-polished and worn, looks
> elegantly out-of-place among the chaos. Papers, files,

---

[1] My arguments in this chapter derive partly from the fourth chapter of my doctoral dissertation, *The Gothic in Contemporary Interactive Fictions* [Umeå University, 2010]. Although I provide a different interpretation of *Slouching* here, the reader will recognise certain ideas and sub-arguments from that chapter.

and books cover nearly every flat surface in the room.

There is a phonograph on the table near the window.

Triage sits near the door to the south.

>EXAMINE DESK
A deep green blotter, dotted with black ink stains, sits in the center of the desk, mostly covered by files and papers. One side of the blotter seems slightly higher than the other.

The corner of a sandalwood box is visible beneath a stack of thick folders.

The desk contains a large central drawer, which is currently closed.

>LOOK UNDER BLOTTER
Beneath the blotter is a small key, easily taken. It carries a small tag labeled '2D'. (Office)[2]

As this exchange indicates, clues to what to examine or interact with are embedded in the passages output from the software, and so play involves a good deal of (re-)reading and thinking on the part of the player before s/he inputs a command.

In fact, the term 'player' is slightly misleading as *Slouching* has a strong narrative emphasis that tends to overshadow the interactive, ludic elements. In the work, the player guides the player character, Bethlehem ('Bedlam') Hospital Superintendent Dr Thomas Xavier, as he re-examines the fate of a strangely afflicted asylum patient who apparently became 'infected' as a result of a mystical-technological communication with an ambiguous, uncertain entity or phenomenon he terms the 'Logos'. As it is eventually revealed to the player that Xavier is also infected, and that the surprisingly contagious

---

[2] Specific information from the interactive fiction will be cited either by reference to a document which the player encounters or by reference to the name of the room where an event occurs, as is the case here. In most interactive fictions, rooms are the primary means of localising the narrative details produced through play.

Logos seems to be an agent of profound social upheaval, the player must interpret the information available in various records and character diaries in order to determine the best way to handle the entity/phenomenon. This plot and the several possible outcomes that the interactive fiction allows are generated through the player's interactive control of Xavier. However, a large portion of the narrative comes from documents discovered during play but describing events prior to the start of *Slouching*. Although the player only gradually pieces together this background story or 'back story', it is important to note that it provides a 'static' narrative prelude to the story produced through interaction. In this manner the interactive fiction literalises a praxis of neo-Victorian fiction, utilising prior knowledge and (mis)conceptions of 'the Victorians' as a back story that the present day player/reader engages with for a contemporary purpose. Xavier may thus be considered both as the main character in the back story that the player reads *and* the player character that the player must control in order to interact with the software and produce further narrative(s). My analysis of the interactive fiction will examine both aspects.

Slouching is a steampunk work in which shared epistemological concerns of the present and the re-imagined past are emphasised through the use of anachronistic technology. Steampunk fiction elides easy definition, but much of it tends to feature a mixture of Victorian historical detail and imaginative technology in order to connect perceived perspectives of the period to aspects of contemporary culture. Popular steampunk works, such as William Gibson and Bruce Sterling's *The Difference Engine* (1990) and Alan Moore and Kevin O'Neill's graphic novel series *The League of Extraordinary Gentleman* (1999-present), achieve this connection by blending history and fiction in order to produce an alternative view of the nineteenth century.[3] Rachel A. Bowser and Brian Croxall assert that steampunk is "a genre that revels in anachronism while exposing history's overlapping layers" and, in so doing, "creates a new paradigm in which technologies, aesthetics, and ideas mark different times simultaneously" (Bowser and Croxall 2010: 1, 3). This temporal simultaneity is central to the player's experience of the interactive

---

[3] Sebastian Domsch discusses this process in Moore and O'Neill's series in specific relation to the 'monstrous' politics of Empire (this volume: 97-121).

fiction. *Slouching*, set in London in 1855, establishes a historical setting via locations such as Newgate Prison, popular ideas such as Urquhart and Bentham's Panopticon Plan, and individuals of historical record such as the alienist Sir John Charles Bucknill. However, the interactive fiction also indicates the fantastic quality of this setting through the use of anachronistic devices, which dually signify plausible machines of the time and the media technologies of today's society. Like many other steampunk fictions, *Slouching* draws overt "parallels between the Industrial Revolution of the nineteenth century and the Information Revolution of the late twentieth century" (Jagoda 2010: 47). These 'IR' apparatuses include a 'magnetophone' that functions like a short-wave radio, a phonograph that both plays and records, a mechanical spider that retrieves files from a vast archive, a 'personal analytical engine' that stores, categorises and analyses data, a panopticon device for watching and listening to asylum inmates unobtrusively, and an executioner automaton. Aside from embodying qualities of the past and present, these devices indicate shared epistemological concerns of the Victorian and contemporary periods. Through their various communicative, recording, archival, surveillance and corrective functions, they suggest the importance attached to knowing the world as a means of being able to control it, and of being in control through knowledge: the intertwined power-knowledge relationship which Michel Foucault suggests has long been endemic to Western societies in *Discipline and Punish* (see Foucault 1991, 27). Information gathering and record keeping were central to Victorian notions of social stability, and *Slouching* emphasises their continued importance with regard to increasingly social networks of information in present-day society.

Representing objects in the world in hierarchical classificatory systems was an explicit endeavour for the Victorians, and this is reflected in *Slouching*. As the boundaries of the empire expanded and as continuing industrial revolution drastically altered the fabric of domestic society, classificatory endeavours, both scientific and popular, blossomed. This development suggests that the Victorian 'classification project', as I will call it, functioned as a means through which to combat the potential destabilisation accompanying these changes. For example, David Spurr contends that empirical methods in natural sciences shored up a hierarchical difference between Western and non-Western ideologies and thence civilisations. By the end of the eighteenth century it was assumed that the inherent traits of an object of study could be deduced from its observable exterior functions and qualities. Spurr argues that such

> a system of understanding – one that orders natural beings according to function and establishes a hierarchy based on internal character – has consequences for the classification of human races in the Western mind. (Spurr 2004: 63)

In other words, classification became a possible means to reinforce social and racial hierarchies by validating their foundational normative values as 'natural'. A similar function of classification existed domestically, where

> [e]xhibitions, museums, and print advertisements organized objects with symbolic or representative (metaphorical) significance in a spatial arrangement where the contiguity of objects to one another as well as to the larger area related to organizing taxonomic schemes such as anatomy, geography, ethnography, evolution, nation, industry or history […]. In cordoning off, setting forth, and protecting, display technologies not only signaled an artifact's value and fragility, but […] enabled its neat resignification within a Victorian Anglocentric worldview, producing their meaning as they organized and situated the trophies of exploration and the innovations of science and industry. (Roof 2000: 103)

Re-signification through classification asserted stability and continuity by emphasising the perceived progress of society and the nation-state. As these examples suggest, on both foreign and domestic fronts the Victorian classification project worked to maintain a variety of meta-narratives in support of the status quo. In *Slouching*, the importance of creating order out of empirical observation is reflected in Xavier's dated journal entries, the panopticon device, the analytical engine that follows Xavier everywhere, Bethlehem's vast archive system, several patient files that the player may retrieve and read, other miscellaneous documents, and some of the appendices that become available after reaching various endings. These aspects allude to the Victorian classification project and also involve the player in it, as s/he must discover information about the Logos and interpret those details in order to 'solve' the dangerous problem it represents. The ramifications of the player's actions in trying to solve the problem are shown to affect all of London and the rest of the world, either maintaining the status quo or disrupting it irreversibly.

As classification functions to assert and maintain social norms and control, profound resistance to classification, implicitly a resistance to systematic re-presentation, carries the potential to be threatening enough to enact the Gothic sublime. Gothic narratives explore anxieties regarding the coherence or stability of the self, and so the genre may be conceived of as investigating the dangers incumbent on all kinds of epistemological and ideological "boundaries and their instabilities" (Horner and Zlosnik 2000: 243). Victorian classification systems define the boundaries of normalcy by including exemplary Victorians within the hierarchy; those people or things not easily subsumed into the system are threatening as contact points beyond a regulated boundary and, more seriously, for their implied critique of the system itself. Great attention is given to these concerns in Victorian fiction, where the large number of encounters with "strange places, strange creatures, and also strange or different human beings" may be explained as part of a collective wish to narratively contain the threateningly inexplicable (Domsch, this volume: 101). Such threats (potentially) undermine a particular way of knowing the world, a systematic epistemological framework, and are embodied in monstrous dangers depicted in Gothic writings from the Enlightenment to today (see Castle 1995: 7-9; Bruhm 2004: 170). In *Slouching*, failures of classification tied to the Logos and its effects produce anxieties reflective of the Victorian period, which anachronistically echo those of contemporary society. These anxieties enable the Gothic sublime, which may be generally described as the awe-inspiring realisation that things which are perceived to be knowable (and hence classifiable) defy representation, a terrifying realisation that calls into question the efficacy of meaning-making systems and, by extension, the human mind's ability to fully comprehend objects in the world (Beville 2009: 8; Mishra 1994: 16).[4] Furthermore, the Logos enacts the Gothic sublime via its uncertain qualification as (super)natural phenomenon or technologically manifested entity. The interactive fiction produces these effects for the player character and configures them, through play, for the player also.

Within the narrative of the back story, Xavier experiences the Gothic sublime when the principles and methods of his specific Victorian classificatory endeavour, the diagnosis of mental illness, not only fail to treat the asylum patient Cleve Anderson, but actually encourage and accelerate the spread of his 'disease'. The ramifications of this failure suggest that the system poses a hazard to itself, and the manner in which this produces destabilising anxieties for Xavier will be analysed in the first section of this chapter. The second section investigates the nature of the anxieties which are configured, with modern-day relevance, in the player's interaction with the interactive fiction. Whereas Cleve's illness is seen to be a significant danger to the rationally ordered view of the world that sustains social hierarchies in the nineteenth-century context, the ambiguous Logos's viral potential to spread itself through communication highlights contemporary fears related to biological and technological infection. As all of these anxieties in *Slouching* are magnified by the potential for revolutionary change inherent to the Logos, the interactive fiction implies that Gothic fears of today culturally emerge from and uncannily replicate fears of the Victorian period.

1. Diagnostic Failure in Bethlehem

Slouching deals with anxieties related to two areas of the nineteenth-century classification project: the medical science concerned with insanity and biological taxonomy. Both of these areas assert a normative vision of the (sane) human being as occupying a dominant

---

[4] The Gothic effects of these classificatory failures derive from *Slouching*'s steampunk traits. Steffen Hantke claims that steampunk plots often force their protagonists to glimpse "Victorian culture's dark double, its seamy underside or secret truth", an act that simultaneously produces "profound disillusionment" for the characters and negates the efficacy of scientific knowledge that "appears as an inadequate, conceited, or mystifying set of dogmas that have little to do with the newly revealed reality" (Hantke 1999: 251). The Gothic takes these ideas further by indicating the ultimate incomprehensibility of this "secret truth" and emphasising the threatening epistemological upheaval that accompanies this revelation.

position in social and biological hierarchies. When (afflicted) individuals resist classification via these systems, they destabilise the coherence of conceptions of the human being *per se* and, when their resistance becomes outright rejection, they potentially provoke the incoherent awe associated with the sublime. In reading *Slouching*'s back story, the player learns that the Gothic sublime develops for Xavier not in spite of, but as a direct result of his attempts to diagnose and treat the enigmatic asylum patient Cleve Anderson.

The insane asylum setting in *Slouching* foregrounds the ideological boundary between classifiable and unclassifiable knowledge. Insanity was implicitly problematic for Victorian knowledge schemata, particularly in so far as sufferers' internal qualities were not easily deduced (however misguidedly) from casual surface representation. The difficulty of this endeavour is reflected in the nineteenth-century development of "increasingly complex symptomatological taxonomies" which were, nonetheless, the subject of much disagreement among medical professionals (Wiesenthal 1997: 5). In parallel to professional attempts at diagnosis, popular beliefs about the origins and identification of insanity reveal similar problems with classification. In *The Invisible Plague: The Rise of Mental Illness from 1750 to the Present*, E. Fuller Torrey and Judy Miller note a wide range of proposed causes of insanity in Victorian England, ranging from physical ailments (e.g. "constipation", "bee stings") to 'inappropriate' behaviour (e.g. stimulating the uterus, tight clothing, studying astrology) to dangerous technology (e.g. "[r]ailway travel, which was thought to injure the brain") (Torrey and Miller 2002: 98). Collectively, these strange catalysts demonstrate both the interest in finding a means for diagnosis of the insane and the empirical difficulty of doing so. As the "[r]ailway travel" cause hints at, the sharp rise in the number of insane persons during the nineteenth century coincided with development of industrialization, a link that led many to believe that 'civilisation' was primarily at fault (see Torrey and Miller 2002: 43-102, 328-329). The diagnosis of madness was thus regarded as significant for the safe development of civilisation. In an article from *The Times* in 1856, for instance, the anonymous author initially lauds medical authorities for achieving undeniable progress for mankind with the implementation of more humane methods of treating the insane. However, the article concludes with a concern regarding the uncertain exterior-interior causality of diagnostic methods.

> We should have felt still more obliged to [mental health expert] Dr. Conolly, had he pointed out the connexion which often subsists between bodily and mental derangement, and the right method of dealing with such cases. We have good grounds for saying that the medical profession, as well as the public, need enlightening on this point, and whoever succeeds in dispelling the clouds of ignorance with which this branch of the subject is at present encompassed will render a great service to mankind. (Anon. 1856: 4)

Establishing the link between "bodily and mental derangement", between external symptom and internal aspect, is here presented in no uncertain terms as beneficial to humanity for its epistemological value of "dispelling [...] ignorance". This uncertain causal link constituted a difficulty for mental health care that had ideological repercussions for larger classification systems based on the same empirical principle, such as the racial hierarchies 'identified' through anthropometric methods in the nascent field of physical anthropology. However, such uncertainty was more acceptable than it may have been in anthropological schemata as long as the insane were segregated from society and controlled, posing a reduced threat to the status quo. In *Slouching*'s Victorian asylum setting, Xavier is seen to tolerate a certain degree of uncertainty while trying to diagnose Cleve's illness and, in so doing, makes the ramifications of his failure all the greater.

Xavier's attempts to diagnose Cleve's condition demonstrate the failure of taxonomical classification and the inapplicability of empirical observation. When he is brought to Bethlehem Hospital and while he remains there, Cleve refuses to speak for fear of spreading an unusual infection. Xavier lists several possible diagnoses in Cleve's patient file, but the basis for these diagnoses is faulty, because Cleve is no longer a human being *per se*. When Xavier repeatedly says Cleve's name in an effort to get him to speak, Cleve angrily responds by writing that he is "NOT WHO", but rather "SOMETHING NEW" as a result of "INFECTION" (Patient File F6A142). Cleve's transformation into a 'thing' has the potential to undermine Xavier's diagnostic systems and, because he is not visually distinct from other humans, the taxonomical system for ordering species based on their external characteristics. However, with the alienist-inmate hierarchy in place to cognitively and physically control Cleve's 'insane' beliefs, Xavier does not appear to believe Cleve or recognise the potential subversion the patient's 'thingness' may pose to his classificatory methodology. Instead, he relies on the principles of observation and control and uses the panopticon device to remotely view Cleve in his room and listen to him through the listening tube (Patient File F6A142). In doing so, he hears Cleve speaking in his sleep and, though he does not realise it, is infected with Cleve's disease. Xavier's mistake is epistemological at heart in that he does not allow for the failure of his classification system or method.

As he gradually realises the extent of this mistake, Xavier questions his own actions and purpose and ultimately rejects an epistemological perspective that asserts that the world may be comprehended in its totality. Xavier initially believes he has simply misdiagnosed Cleve. In the last entry in the case file, he describes the unexpected violent argument he had with the patient, which resulted in Cleve's accidental death. For this death, a result of profoundly misdiagnosing Cleve's propensity toward violence, Xavier admonishes himself, writing that "[e]verything has told me one thing and I have thought another – my own hubris is such as to put whatever Cleve thought he did to shame" (Patient File F6A142). As corrupt authorities have confined Cleve to Bedlam to make him 'disappear' from society, Xavier simply seals the case file and hopes to forget about it. However, he realises the faulty epistemological foundation of his actions several days later. His method is no longer at fault, instead he notes, "I discredit my profession; examining madness as if the world were a fluent thing and sanity as malleable as the warm wax of a candle" (Journal, March 16th). Xavier's comment calls to mind a Gothic dilemma that Eve Kosofsky Sedgwick describes as the tyranny of unintelligibility that only occurs with the conviction that "the elements of the universe are so orderly they are seen as being meant to be interpreted, as being a transparent medium for a 'meaning'" (Sedgwick 1986: 52). In dismissing his profession, Xavier dismisses his former beliefs that the world may be comprehended, that it communicates itself, as well as the concept of humankind being able to control or mould things which are not understood. These rejections call into question the very grounds and purpose of the Victorian classification project.

With his epistemological framework undermined, Xavier experiences a Victorian conception of the Gothic sublime. In Gothic writings of the Romantic era, sublimity occurs in recognitions of the vast and infinite in nature, which may terrifyingly endanger the coherence of the self (Burke 2008: 39, 57-58; Hogle 2004b: 14). In the Victorian period the sublime shifts, along with Gothic fiction, to urban contexts and engages with metropolitan social issues. For instance, the dehumanising potential of working solely for money is featured in Charles Dickens's *A Christmas Carol* (1843), and the seedy, criminal activity which the labyrinthine city enables is foregrounded in the weekly serial started by G. W. M. Reynolds, *The Mysteries of London* (1844-48). Decoupled from infinite vistas, experiences of the sublime – the terrifying recognition of something incomprehensible which drastically undermines the coherence of one's self – refocus themselves in more personal and intimate ways. These proximate experiences of the sublime create a sense of isolation, while simultaneously threatening the orderly foundations of society. In *Slouching*, Xavier comments in his journal that he has "found what I have sought, and I shall now pay the price for it", lamenting that he is probably "going mad" (Journal, March 16th). Xavier's mental destabilisation derives from an affliction he has brought upon himself but which he does not comprehend. His affliction is "a growing mystery" that "lays [sic] heavily on both my mind and heart", and while he expresses a desire to confide what he knows of it to others and wonders how he can "bear it alone", he ultimately concludes: "No. I can trust no one, in the end […]. Perhaps soon … not even myself" (Journal, March 16th, unbracketed ellipses in the original). Encumbered with an unclassifiable and untreatable affliction that it is dangerous even to possess knowledge of, Xavier's terrible sense of isolation negatively indicates the ever-present threat of contamination by infectious diseases in a heavily populated urban centre. In *Slouching*'s re-imagined Victorian context, Xavier's experience of the sublime derives from a rupture of the classificatory system that not only maintains the normative foundations of society but also his (professional) identity.

2. The Ramifications of Infection in Bedlam

The terrible portents of Xavier's March 16th journal entry are the first thing the player reads in *Slouching*, setting up a quasi-detective story impetus for the player to carry out an investigation in order to discover what infects Xavier, so that he may be cured. However, despite being encouraged, in several ways, to proceed by classifying and interpreting information gleaned during play, the player's potential for success is undercut by several classification failures that cumulatively point to a rupture in the epistemological perspective established in the re-imagined Victorian setting. These failures demonstrate that the Logos signifies multiple dangers within the contexts of Victorian and contemporary societies. As these threats are enacted within the story world and also coded into the software in such a way as to blur the boundary between fiction and reality, *Slouching* is likely to simulate effects of the Gothic sublime for the player, analogous to those encountered by Xavier.

The player's unstated goal in playing *Slouching* is to continue the work Xavier began in the back story. This involves using classification methods to discern the nature of Cleve's and Xavier's affliction as the grounds for discovering a cure for Xavier. While player interpretation may be considered standard practice in interactive fiction due to a generic tendency toward puzzle-solving, Foster and Ravipinto's work requires an unusual amount of sifting through details before being able to act with any sense of purpose. For instance, one reviewer of *Slouching* emphasises its narrative rather than ludic qualities and notes that "you are constantly encouraged to explore, read, assimilate, and find a pattern amongst all the information you collect" (Bardinelli 2009). Alongside the many documents (journals, patient files, etc.) to be read, the player's classification project bears similarity to Victorian explorations of the world. Specimen-collecting natural scientists (or lay enthusiasts) were standard personnel on expeditions in the late eighteenth century, and this trend continued well into the nineteenth century (Pratt 2005: 27-28; Spurr 2004: 63). In *Slouching*, as the player guides the player character through re-imagined London spaces, s/he performs a similar information-gathering and ordering process. In effect, the interactive fiction makes the twenty-first century player an 'explorer' of the re-imagined Victorian environment, an environment that is ostensibly familiar due to popular historical (mis)conceptions but which nonetheless needs to be (re)discovered in this work. In this respect, *Slouching* is similar to other neo-Victorian fiction that overtly positions the reader in the spatial historical setting, such as Michel Faber's *The Crimson Petal and the White* (2003) or Sarah Waters's *Affinity* (1999).

In the *interactive* fiction, however, the player's active exploration is central to developing the work, and s/he does this with the help of the Triage, a personal analytical engine that can scan objects and people and then organise information about them into strict hierarchies based on their category, utility and particulars (see *Operator's Manual*).[5] Perhaps the most overtly steampunk device in *Slouching*, the Triage symbolises the cultural emergence of personal computers of today in Charles Babbage's nineteenth-century designs for an analytical engine, a mechanical computational device that could be configured for various operations with the help of punch-card programming. Although Babbage never completed the engine, many steampunk works not only feature it but creatively rectify this technological dead end. For example, Gibson and Sterling's *The Difference Engine* (1990) sees Babbage's completion of the engine as a prelude to sweeping societal change in Victorian England, and Michael Flynn's *In the Country of the Blind* (1990) makes the nineteenth-century engine central to the development of a prophetic mathematical science which eventually allows a shadowy group to control the twentieth-century world. The popularity of the analytical engine in steampunk fiction illustrates the (sub)genre's fascination with "what would have happened if twentieth-century technologies had appeared or been invented in the nineteenth century", or if technology had developed along "a different path during the steam age" (Pike 2010: 264). In this sense, Babbage's engines are ideal narrative buds, because computers have so profoundly transformed present-day society that it is difficult not to imagine that a completed analytical engine would have had similar effects in the Victorian era. However, in contrast to such positive treatment in steampunk fiction faithful to its science fiction roots (see Hantke 1999: 246), the Triage in the more Gothic *Slouching* does not precipitate sweeping social change. Instead, its function as an everyday helpmate (or fantasy

---

[5] The *Operator's Manual* is a document in the storyworld that provides instructions for using the Triage.

Victorian naturalist device), while beneficial for play, ultimately asserts the limits of its classificatory power for the player. One reviewer refers to the Triage as "the ideal thing to have along" in an interactive fiction, because it follows the player around of its own accord, interprets codes and suggests how Xavier should interact with items in the environment (Knoch 2003). These are the kinds of things a player would normally have to do on his or her own, and so the Triage performs a central role in determining the systems of meaning that govern the player character's interactions with elements in the environment.

Since the Triage appears to validate an endeavour to map the world onto ordered schemata, its failure to classify Xavier is likely to destabilise the player's sense of purpose. As the player explores the environment through the player character, there is a certain amount of learning involved in understanding Xavier both as a character and as an interface for existing in the story world. This is not the same as developing a readerly identification with Xavier (though that may occur), but rather a question of learning how Xavier's personal issues, concerns and goals coincide with those designed for the player. The Triage's failure to classify Xavier as a human within its taxonomical system thus impacts the player's ability to knowingly direct the player character. When prompted to analyse other characters in the work, the Triage provides discrete information regarding the subject's physical category, utility (function), and identifying particulars. Xavier's assistant James, for example, is described as a "LIVING.HUMAN / MALE", whose primary function is "COMMUN / ICATION" and whose particular identification is "JAMES.HOULIHAN" (Lobby). However, if the Triage is instructed to scan Xavier, it produces the following response:

CAT:LIVING......
*CATASTROPHIC.ER
RROR.A042.CATEGO
RY.INDEX.OUT.OF.
RANGE.STACK.OVER
FLOW*PART:ID=DR.

THOMAS.XAVIER=CU
RRENT.OPERATOR..[6]

Although Xavier's mortal condition and identification are apparent, the Triage fails to determine his species and utility, which suggests that, like Cleve, he is a thing rather than a human. In fact, Xavier is infected, from the very beginning of *Slouching*, with the same virus that Cleve had. Whether or not the player has realised this, Xavier's thingness asserts the epistemological limits of the player's Triage-enabled classification project. The destabilising ramifications of this failure to subsume Xavier into a taxonomic hierarchy are underscored by the fact that this is the only instance in *Slouching* when an internal error prohibits the Triage from issuing a report. Xavier is not difficult to classify, as some items appear to be in the work; rather, he *cannot be classified*.

Having discovered that the Logos is what afflicted Cleve and infects Xavier, the player's main concern becomes dealing with it; however, since it is unclassifiable, it presents an epistemological dilemma whose significance is all the greater because the entity/phenomenon embodies several Victorian and contemporary anxieties. Some of these anxieties are apparent before the player learns anything specific about the Logos. Prior to reading Cleve's diary and a letter he wrote, the player knows that the problem involves a highly infectious disease and the degeneration of people into things, two prominent sources of anxiety in Gothic works written in the Victorian period. With the majority of the population in mid-century Britain "concentrated in urban areas, and more than a tenth of the whole population in London", highly transmittable diseases were a realistic source of fear, which often took monstrous, particularly vampiric, forms in Gothic fiction (Warwick 2007: 33; Pick 2004: 291).[7] A more literal investigation of the world-changing threat of disease occurs in Mary Shelley's *The Last Man* (1826). In a related vein, threats to the coherence of the human being brought on by, among other things,

---

[6] As a mechanical device, the Triage does not have a screen but rather a grid of symbols that turn and flip to indicate various characters. Reports from the Triage are arranged to represent its 16 x 8 display.

[7] For a comprehensive examination of the viral similarities shared by the Logos and the Victorian era's seminal vampire, Dracula, see chapter four in *The Gothic in Contemporary Interactive Fictions* (Leavenworth 2010: 144-179).

Charles Darwin's organising theory of natural selection, led to a fear of and subsequent Gothic works about what Kelly Hurley calls the *"abhuman* body". Example fiction in this vein includes H. G. Wells's *The Island of Doctor Moreau* (1896) and Richard Marsh's *The Beetle: A Mystery* (1897). Hurley notes that the abhuman "retains vestiges of its human identity, but has already become, or is in the process of becoming, some half-human other", or else "some unimaginable 'thing'" that incorporates, mimics or assumes human form, "thereby constituting another kind of threat to the integrity of human identity" (Hurley 2002: 190). As Hurley suggests, the abhuman is threatening as it implies that being human is not a stable position or fixed location in the normalising classification systems that order the world. Hence, potentially, *anyone* may become other to her/himself, calling into question humanity's status at the apex of the evolutionary hierarchy.

However, when the player reads about the Logos in Cleve's writings, two more anxieties come to light regarding communication technologies and profound social change. First, the Logos seems to embody the threatening potential of 'new' communication technologies in both the nineteenth-century context and contemporary culture. In later Victorian culture and fiction, communication technologies with the ability to reproduce disembodied sounds and images are frequently seen as evidence of mysticism or the supernatural. As Alison Chapman notes, "psychic influence" is associated with uncanny technologies such as "telegraphy, electric light, phonograph, radio, the telephone, and, primarily, photography", and as a result these technologies are "seen to disrupt and confuse the relationship between a whole range of binary terms: subject/other, viewer/viewed, nature/culture, time/space, inside/outside" (Chapman 2000: 109-110). The living/dead and natural/supernatural binaries are also disrupted by uncanny technologies, evident in the Victorian fascination with spiritualism (e.g. via séances and spirit photography) and neo-Victorian fiction's similar interest in the supernatural (see Arias and Pulham 2010).

This technological-mystical link is apparent in Cleve's means of contacting the Logos. In an attempt to ingratiate himself with a secret society that believes in the "development of new technologies to unlock the mysteries of the Universe", Cleve contacts what he thinks of as the "mind of God", using the society's custom-made engines (Cleve's Letter, Cleve's Diary). The experience is transcendent, and Cleve discovers what he terms the Logos, noting "[t]hat is all I can call it – what else can one call language given sentience, an idea that breathes, a thought that thinks itself?" (Cleve's Diary). His contact with the Logos happens when he speaks and hears his words echoed and changed, a communication that mutates rapidly, so that he finds himself forming a symbiosis with the Logos and is "spoken" by it (Cleve's Diary). The engines sustaining this contact fail shortly after this, but in his diary Cleve indicates that the Logos remains with him as a presence that increasingly floods his head with words and compels him to speak in a language he does not understand, making him an unwilling 'spirit' medium. This entity or phenomenon thus mediates the technological-mystical link through disembodied communication technologies of the later nineteenth-century, such as the telegraph or phonograph, as well as the dangers of contemporary technologies that, through the medium of code, receive and transmit potentially malicious information or programs of which the user is unaware. The Logos, whether supernatural entity or technological creation, suggests the dangers of humankind's hubris in both areas.

Second, the Logos's uncertain classification is all the more problematic for the player because, as it spreads like a virus, it has the potential to radically change society. *Slouching Towards Bedlam* takes its name from W. B. Yeats's poem 'The Second Coming', and the Logos, like the beast in the poem that "[s]louches towards Bethlehem", is a motley ambivalent presence that heralds a coming revolutionary change (Yeats 1993: l. 22). Although *Slouching*'s use of this modernist poem suggests a non-Victorian site of cultural emergence, the sublime, apocalyptic theme of the poem repeatedly appears in Gothic fiction from the eighteenth century to the present. Donald E. Hall describes Yeats's poem as presenting "a new era of thinking brutally", which functions as a "diagnosis" or possibly "revelation" of the present age (Hall 2004: 73-74), an ambivalence which suggests that the reader is put in the position of interpreting this second coming and, possibly, attempting to avert it. *Slouching*'s player occupies a similar position. The Logos alludes to multiple interpretations simultaneously without allowing any one to emerge as entirely valid. For instance, the term connotes a revelatory meaning in Christian scripture, 'kai theos en ho logos' (a phrase Cleve uses initially to describe it), Greek for 'and God was the word' from John

1.1 (Cleve's Letter). Similarly, in Jacques Derrida's investigation of language (a classification system) and meaning in *Of Grammatology*, the 'logos' is a site of origin for metaphysical truth and scientific, rational log*ic*, meanings that also surround the term in various ways as it is explored in Western philosophy (Derrida 1997). However, Cleve later questions his initial idea that the Logos is a deity and the player is never given any indication that it represents truth or logic, a classification problem that calls into question the validity of meta-narratives in general. Whatever it may be, the Logos spreads quickly and deteriorates the health of the characters exposed to it (Patient File F6A142). The epidemic danger it represents requires action, but the player's inability to classify the Logos points to the destabilising inefficacy of the epistemological framework of the re-imagined Victorian setting and forces the player to, as Xavier did with Cleve, judge without any firm basis as to how to proceed.

In providing the player with this unclassifiable threat and encouraging her or him to deal with it, *Slouching* configures a situation in which the player's actions are unwittingly damaging. The very process of gathering information, the player's empirical method, allows the Logos to spread. In unravelling the mystery of what happened to Cleve and what is happening to Xavier, the player may meet three characters: Xavier's assistant James, an unnamed hansom cab driver, and Alexandra Du Monde, head of the secret society. Initial conversations that the player character may have with these characters include Logos utterances, which characters seem to recognise as language without understanding them. The cab driver, for instance, notes that it sounds "like something foreign" (Courtyard). The Logos transmits to others via these utterances and, significantly, they happen unexpectedly, without the player's prompting – even if the player has not commanded the player character to initiate a conversation. For example, when Xavier first enters Bethlehem's Lobby, he speaks to James using Logos-speak, excerpted here in the following four lines:

/(reachgrabfeel|possibility|probability)\
/(actionpositiveaffirmative|destroyingfrictionbreaking growth|positiveyes)\
/(livinggrowthfrictionfurtherspreadingoutwardstretchi

ngyestouchingyes)\
/(yesdoneyes)\[8]

This unexpected outburst of Xavier's, written in this unique manner, indicates to the player that something odd happened. When read, with some effort, these lines describe the insistent extension of the Logos to James, though the player will not realise this as a viral transmission because s/he has not had access to Cleve's patient file yet. Instead, s/he is likely to attribute this odd communication to the mental instability Xavier confesses to in his journal. With similar ignorance, the player may, via Xavier, infect the cabbie and, quite possibly, Alexandra in her/his quest for information. If this happens, at the end of the interactive fiction the infection spreads, beginning with these characters, throughout the population of London and then the world.

Slouching further indicates the fallacy of a belief in the comprehensibility of the world by encouraging the player to replay the work in an attempt to contain the Logos, despite the fact that no such result is possible. Replay has its benefits: with each new attempt the player is aided by an increased knowledge of the re-imagined Victorian setting, the infection and how to restrict its spread. As this information may help the player achieve better and better endings, s/he is likely to develop a sense that an ending where the Logos is neutralised or defeated is possible. For example, in the ending most players probably encounter first, Xavier infects the three characters mentioned above and they spread the virus onwards. In another ending, the player directs Xavier to kill these three characters in order to curtail the outbreak but fails to kill Xavier himself, again allowing the virus to proliferate. Alternatively, another ending results from killing the three characters and commanding Xavier to commit suicide (via the steam-driven executioner automaton). Finally, the player may direct Xavier to kill himself very early in the interactive fiction, before he investigates anything or talks to anyone. (The fifth ending is different: if the player interprets the Logos as a divine presence, s/he may broadcast the Logos to the London populace using Xavier's magnetophone. This ending does not provide an explicitly positive resolution, however, and so the Logos's 'true' nature remains occluded.) Of the five possible endings to *Slouching*, the last two

---

[8] All Logos utterances are formatted like this.

'containment' scenarios imply that the spread of the Logos has been stopped with the benefit of the player's applied knowledge. However, the world-changing danger of the Logos is asserted in these endings as well, as indicated by altered lines from 'The Second Coming'. The image of coming revolution presented in the poem is alluded to in each of the endings as they all conclude with the following:

/(and what rough beast)\
/(its hour come round at last)\
/(slouches towards)\
/(bethlehem)\
/(?behtlehem?)\
/(BEDLAM)\
/(to be born?)\

With the last two lines of Yeats's poem formed as Logos utterances and corrupted (the promise of Bethlehem changed to bedlam), the persistence of the Logos and the profound change it heralds is assured in every ending, including the two where it is apparently contained. The player is encouraged to classify and subvert the Logos yet denied any possibility of doing so, comprehensively demonstrating the failure of both the re-imagined Victorian systems for ordering and understanding the world presented in the work and any alternative knowledge system the player might postulate.

The effects of the Gothic sublime that the player may experience derive from a successive undercutting of the efficacy and, ultimately, validity of the player's classification project. The player's unknowing agency in carrying out this project only functions to make him or her culpable in enabling the Logos epidemic. As this fatal dynamic is eventually revealed to the player, though not in a manner that allows him or her to comprehend the Logos or effectively combat it, the player is made to experience a sense of constriction and impotence which may produce the effects of the Gothic sublime. Vijay Mishra describes this experience as "being hostage to the unpresentable", that is, as desiring to pass beyond an "abyss that incapacitates the powers of cognition" but knowing, without understanding why, that there is no way to do so (Mishra 1994: 17). The player is thus placed in a position of fatal realisation similar to that occupied by Xavier.

In addition, this position is reinforced on another level, as *Slouching* worries the boundary between fiction and reality. The organically harmful word-virus of the storyworld also appears to have infected the work itself, so that the player's interaction with the interactive fiction software shows signs of Logos infection. Alongside commands directing the player character, there are meta-level commands that govern the running of the program, such as 'save', 'restore' and 'quit'. The program executes these commands but confirms their execution in Logos-speak, indicating that that the player is communicating with infected software, a source of great anxiety today. In today's digitally-networked societies, computer viruses are threatening for their unavoidable transmission, their parasitic surveillance, their incomprehensible spread, their seeming agency and, of course, for their ability to fundamentally destabilise or destroy (the flow of) information. This contemporary anxiety, though it alludes to the isolating fear of contagion in the Victorian metropolis, suggests a postmodern conception of the sublime, which Joseph Tabbi contends is connected to "technological structures [. . .] beyond the comprehension of any one mind or imagination" (Tabbi 1995: ix). Although the player may or may not respond with fearful awe to *Slouching*'s dual-level configuration of the Gothic sublime, the interactive fiction nonetheless demonstrates a significant reworking of this trope within the context of present-day fears.

3. Conclusion: Being Captive to the Incomprehensible

As a steampunk fiction, *Slouching* refigures the neo-Victorian praxis of creating links to the re-imagined past in a more speculative manner, forging connections to an alternative historical setting through, among other things, anachronistic technologies. This speculative framework does not diminish the contemporary relevance of Victorian sites of cultural emergence, but instead allows for a comprehensive investigation of the anxieties that derive from them, particularly as the player encounters them at multiple levels of story and simulation. The Victorian attempt to organise and master the world for the social 'good' foregrounds on-going attempts to manage and oversee the 'normal' flows of information in the mediated networks that are integral to everyday life in Western societies. *Slouching* demonstrates how failures in these linked endeavours produce both pragmatic dangers and profound fears of the incomprehensible, which are recognisable as the effects of the Gothic sublime. Through fears related to corporeal and technological viruses and the mystic sentience of communication technologies, the interactive fiction plays on worries about the drastic social changes that may ensue should human classification projects and the empirical frameworks that support them fail.

The focal point of this failure is the Logos, an entity/phenomenon whose uncertain essence (if it has one) demonstrates the profound limits of knowledge about the Victorian past and contemporary present. The Logos is understood to usher in revolutionary change in *Slouching*'s story world but every ending concludes at the cusp of this transition, leaving the player with no evidence as to what the Logos represents. What sort of 'rough beast' is it? The knowing player may link the Logos to God, metaphysical truth or even rationality and logic, but under scrutiny it resists identification with any one of these things. In postmodern fashion, it simultaneously suggests and discounts the possibility that it represents a unifying means to create order, subverting the validity of the meta-narratives that seek to make the world knowable. The only thing that is certain is that drastic change happens, and so the recognizable Victorian historical setting, although already fictionally altered, is implied to be transformed into something else entirely, unrecognizable in our history. This signals a playful but extreme perspective on neo-Victorian attempts to re-envision the nineteenth century as a site of cultural emergence for contemporary culture. The question becomes not whether present-day cultural elements emerged from Victorian culture, but *what* it is that has emerged. What viral, revolutionary 'thing' have we inherited from the Victorians?

If the (potential) monster we must face is no longer comprehensible, not even, perhaps, as a monster, how do we combat the threatening paradigm shift it may produce? How, indeed, do we do so when our very basis of knowing the world and our agency within it serve as the conduits for ushering in such a monster? *Slouching Towards Bedlam* suggests that there is no way to combat it, that it is already too late in the present and perhaps was already too late in the Victorian period, and so the more relevant question is what our perspective of this unfolding paradigm shift will be.

Bibliography

Anon. 1856. 'Conolly on Treatment of the Insane', *The Times* (16 October): 4.
Arias, Rosario, and Patricia Pulham (eds.). 2010. *Haunting and Spectrality in Neo-Victorian Fiction: Possessing the Past*. Houndmills, Basingstoke & New York: Palgrave Macmillan.
Bardinelli, John. 2009. Review of Foster and Ravipinto (2003). On-line at: http://jayisgames.com/archives/2009/06/slouching_towards_bedlam.php (consulted 15.11.2011).
Beville, Maria. 2009. *Gothic Postmodernism: Voicing the Terrors of Postmodernity*. Amsterdam & New York: Rodopi.
Botting, Fred, and Dale Townshend (eds.). 2004. *Gothic: Critical Concepts in Literary and Cultural Studies*, Vol. 3. London & New York: Routledge.
Bowser, Rachel A., and Brian Croxall. 2010. 'Introduction: Industrial Evolution', *Neo-Victorian Studies* 3(1), Special Issue: *Steampunk, Science, and (Neo)Victorian Technologies*: 1-45.
Bruhm, Steven. 2004. 'On Stephen King's Phallus; Or The Postmodern Gothic'. In Botting and Townshend (2004): 170-190.
Burke, Edmund. 2008. *A Philosophical Enquiry into the Sublime and Beautiful* [1757] (ed. James T. Boulton). London & New York: Routledge Classics.
Castle, Terry. 1995. *The Female Thermometer: 18th-Century Culture and the Invention of the Uncanny*. New York & Oxford: Oxford University Press.
Chapman, Alison. 2000. 'Mary Elizabeth Coleridge, Literary Influences and Technologies of the Uncanny', in Robbins, Ruth, and Julian Wolfreys, (eds.), *Victorian Gothic: Literary and Cultural Manifestations in the Nineteenth Century*. Basingstoke & New York: Palgrave, 109-128.
Derrida, Jacques. 1997. *Of Grammatology* [1967] (trans. Gayatri. C. Spivak). Baltimore & London: The Johns Hopkins University Press.
Dickens, Charles. 1985. *The Christmas Books, Volume 1* [1843] (ed. M. Slater). New York & London: Penguin.
Douglass, Jeremy. 2007. *Command Lines: Aesthetics and Technique in Interactive Fiction and New Media*. PhD Thesis. University of California, Santa Barbara.
Faber, Michel. 2003. *The Crimson Petal and the White*. Edinburgh: Canongate.
Flynn, Michael. 2001. *In the Country of the Blind* [1990]. New York: Tor.
Foster, Star C., and Daniel Ravipinto. 2003. *Slouching Towards Bedlam*. On-line at: http://www.wurb.com/if/game/2186 (consulted 15.11.2011).
Foucault, Michel. 1991. *Discipline and Punish: The Birth of the Prison* [1975] (trans. A. Sheridan). London: Penguin.
Gibson, William, and Bruce Sterling. 2011. *The Difference Engine: 20th Anniversary Edition* [1990]. New York: Ballantine.
Hall, Donald E. 2004. *Subjectivity*. New York & London: Routledge.
Hantke, Steffen. 1999. 'Difference Engines and Other Infernal Devices: History According to Steampunk', *Extrapolation* 40(3) (Fall): 244-254.
Hayles, N. Katherine. 2008. *Electronic Literature: New Horizons for the Literary*. Notre Dame, Indiana: University of Notre Dame.
Hogle, Jerrold E. (ed.). 2004a. *The Cambridge Companion to Gothic Fiction*. Cambridge: Cambridge University Press.

———. 2004b. 'Introduction: The Gothic in Western Culture'. In Hogle (2004a): 1-20.
Horner, Avril, and Sue Zlosnik. 2000. 'Comic Gothic', in Punter, David (ed.), *A Companion to the Gothic*. Oxford: Blackwell, 242-254.
Hurley, Kelly. 2002. 'British Gothic Fiction, 1885-1930'. In Hogle (2004a): 189-207.
Jagoda, Patrick. 2010. 'Clacking Control Societies: Steampunk, History, and the Difference Engine of Escape', *Neo-Victorian Studies* 3(1), Special Issue: *Steampunk, Science, and (Neo)Victorian Technologies*: 46-71.
Knoch, Jessica. 2003. Review of Foster and Ravipinto (2003), *SPAG: Society for the Promotion of Adventure Games* 35 (Winter). On-line at: http://www.sparkynet.com/spag/s.html#slouching (consulted 15.11.2011).
Kucich, John, and Dianne F. Sadoff (eds.). 2000. *Victorian Afterlife: Postmodern Culture Rewrites the Nineteenth Century*. Minneapolis & London: University of Minnesota Press.
Leavenworth, Van. 2010. *The Gothic in Contemporary Interactive Fictions* (Umeå Studies in Language and Literature 11). PhD Thesis. University of Umeå. Umeå, Sweden.
Marsh, Richard. 2007. *The Beetle: A Mystery* [1897]. Tales of Mystery and the Supernatural. Ware, UK: Wordsworth Editions.
Mishra, Vijay. 1994. *The Gothic Sublime*. Albany, New York: University of New York Press.
Montfort, Nick. 2007. 'Playing to Solve *Saviore-Faire*', in Atkins, Barry, and Tanya Krzywinska (eds.), *Videogame, Player, Text*. Manchester: Manchester University Press, 175-190.
———. 2003. *Twisty Little Passages: An Approach to Interactive Fiction*. Cambridge, Massachusetts: MIT Press.
Moore, Alan, Kevin O'Neill, Ben Dimagmaliw and Bill Oakley. 2000. *The League of Extraordinary Gentlemen* [1999], Ser. l. America's Best Comics.
Pick, Daniel. 2004. '"Terrors of the Night": *Dracula* and "Degeneration" in the Late Nineteenth Century'. In Botting and Townshend (2004): 287-303.
Pike, David L. 2010. 'Afterimages of the Victorian City', *Journal of Victorian Culture* 15(2): 254-267.
Pratt, Marie Louise. 2005. *Imperial Eyes: Travel Writing and Transculturation*. London: Routledge.
Reynolds, G.W.M. 1998. *The Mysteries of London* [1844] (ed. T. Thomas). Edinburgh: Edinburgh University Press.
Roof, Judith. 2000. 'Display Cases'. In Kucich and Sadoff (2000): 101-121.
Sadoff, Dianne F., and John Kucich (eds.). 2000. 'Introduction: Histories of the Present'. In Kucich and Sadoff (2000): ix-xxx.
Sedgwick, Eve Kosofsky. 1986. *The Coherence of Gothic Conventions*. New York: Methuen.
Shelley, Mary. 1985. *The Last Man* [1826]. London: Hogarth Press.
Spooner, Catherine. 2007. 'Gothic Media'. In Spooner and McEvoy (2007): 195-197.
Spooner, Catherine, and Emma McEvoy (eds.). 2007. *The Routledge Companion to Gothic*. London & New York: Routledge.
Spurr, David. 2004. *The Rhetoric of Empire: Colonial Discourse in Journalism, Travel Writing, and Imperial Administration*. London: Duke University Press.

Tabbi, Joseph. 1995. *Postmodern Sublime: Technology and American Writing from Mailer to Cyberpunk*. London & Ithaca, New York: Cornell University Press.

Torrey, E. Fuller, and Judy Miller. 2002. *The Invisible Plague: The Rise of Mental Illness from 1750 to the Present*. New Jersey & London: Rutgers University Press.

Warwick, Alexandra. 2007. 'Victorian Gothic'. In Spooner and McEvoy (2007): 29-37.

Waters, Sarah. 1999. *Affinity*. London: Virago.

Wells, H.G. 1946. *The Island of Doctor Moreau* [1896]. New York & Harmondsworth, UK: Penguin.

Wiesenthal, Chris. 1997. *Figuring Madness in Nineteenth-Century Fiction*. London: Macmillan.

Yeats, W. B. 1993. 'The Second Coming' [1920], in Abrams, M. H. et al. (eds.), *The Norton Anthology of English Literature*. 6th ed., Vol. 2. New York & London: Norton, 1880-1881.

Dead Words and Fatal Secrets: Rediscovering the Sensational Document in Neo-Victorian Gothic

Kym Brindle

Abstract:
The lost and found document convention is a significant framing feature of eighteenth-century Gothic fiction that metamorphoses into a trend for intercalated documents in nineteenth-century sensation novels. This essay considers how neo-Victorian fiction reworks both preceding uses of the convention and considers Margaret Atwood's *Alias Grace* (1996) and Beryl Bainbridge's *Watson's Apology* (1984) as case studies. I examine how prefatorial and postfacing author's notes frame document extracts in novels that revisit the documented history of two infamous nineteenth-century murders. The texts illustrate historiographic metafiction's affiliation with Gothic 'spaces of absence', as readings, misreadings, and evolving interpretations emphasise enduring secrets that sustain Gothic imaginations.

Keywords: Margaret Atwood, Beryl Bainbridge, found document, Gothic, Neo-Victorian, sensation fiction.

*****

In *Victorian Studies in Scarlet*, Richard Altick suggests that for the Victorians "murder was all the more dreadful, in a most agreeable sort of way, when the criminal and his victim wore the everyday dress of the present" (Altick 1970: 69). Revisiting the same crimes that sensationalised the Victorians, neo-Victorian writers now satisfy an appetite for murder wearing nineteenth-century dress stitched with Gothic thread. The stories of infamous nineteenth-century cases like the Road Hill Murder, the Stockwell Tragedy, or that of Canadian murderess, Grace Marks, as well as a host of famous female poisoners including Edith Carew, Adelaide Bartlett, Florence Maybrick, and Madeleine Smith have all been adapted by novelists for contemporary audiences.[1] Sensation and scandal may live on beyond Victorian times but neo-Victorian writers are most preoccupied with emphasising uncertain channels of communication between past and present. Margaret Atwood's 1996 novel *Alias Grace* and Beryl Bainbridge's 1984 work *Watson's Apology* revisit infamous Victorian crimes to orchestrate an unstable narrative mix of citation and invention that exploits inconsistencies, gaps, and secrets in historical documents that claim to evidence the "awful truths of human existence" (Bainbridge 1992a: 124). Readings and misreadings of the past are confronted within historiographic metafictions that imagine scenarios of motivation that resonate with Catherine Spooner's identification of Gothic's fascination with "spaces of absence" (Spooner 2006: 48).

While it is possible to speak of the Gothic as a historical phenomenon originating in its literary sense in the eighteenth century, David Punter and Glennis Byron put forward

> a more radical claim that there are very few actual literary texts that are 'Gothic' and the Gothic is more to do with particular moments, tropes, repeated motifs that can be found scattered, or disseminated, through the modern western literary tradition. (Punter and Byron 2004: xviii)

This chapter considers the evolution of the discovered manuscript trope as one such Gothic motif that is widely disseminated in neo-Victorian fiction. As a significant feature of traditional Gothic, the lost and/or discovered document endures in altered shape from its origins as a framing device in the eighteenth century to a trend for intercalated documents in nineteenth-century sensation fiction.[2] This essay will explore how neo-Victorian's turn to the past employs the convention in both guises for postmodern narratives that conform to what Ann

---

[1] For a detailed study and bibliography of true crime's influence on fiction and drama, see Haste 1997.

[2] Leading Gothic critics habitually cite the discovered manuscript as a "stock Gothic device", used "as the means by which the past haunts and threatens the present" (Mighall 2003: 113). Spooner notes that "postmodern Gothic has seized on the idea of the found manuscript" (Spooner 2007: 45) and Punter further argues that "the increasing complexity of the concept of the discovered manuscript is a significant part of the history of the Gothic novel" (Punter 1996: 49).

Heilmann and Mark Llewellyn identify as "the self-analytical drive" that accompanies texts, which qualify in their critical terms as neo-Victorian (Heilmann and Llewellyn 2010: 5).[3]

1. Gothic Manuscripts Lost and Found

The discovered manuscript convention is originally identified as a framing device of Gothic fiction tradition. Its origins are attributed to Horace Walpole's influential 1764 novel, *The Castle of Otranto: A Gothic Story*, which had an original preface stating that the tale was "found in the library of an ancient catholic family in the north of England" (Walpole 2008: 5). Walpole later revised the text with a second preface that refuted the first's claims to authenticity by confessing that he was author and not editor of the tale.[4] Walpole's counterfeit assertion and subsequent disavowal doubly emphasises writerly authority by creating an aura of authenticity for the narrative before revealing this to be a ruse controlled by the author. Like Walpole, who explained that his motivation was "an attempt to blend the two kinds of romance, the ancient and the modern" (Walpole 2008: 9), neo-Victorianists frame their texts as innovative blends of past and present. In paratextual authorial notes, Atwood and Bainbridge claim literary license to ironically fuse imagination and probability, echoing Walpole's wish to make characters "think, speak and act, as it might be supposed mere men and women would in extraordinary positions" (Walpole 2008: 10).

Exposing contradictions in the story of a "celebrated murderess" (Atwood 2006a: 25), Atwood echoes the Gothic discovered manuscript convention with an author's 'Note' that frames a narrative that is densely organised with intercalated actual document extracts. *Alias Grace* revisits the tale of an infamous double murder that took place in 1843 Toronto when a sixteen-year-old servant girl achieved widespread notoriety for her suspected part in the crime.

---

[3] Heilmann and Llewellyn argue for parameters of the genre defined by texts that "must in some respect be *self-consciously engaged with the act of (re)interpretation, (re)discovery and (re)vision concerning the Victorians*" (Heilmann and Llewellyn 2010: 4, original emphasis).

[4] The reputation of Walpole's eminent Gothic novel lies as much in the history of faked claims to authenticity and authorial confession of trickery as it does in the merits of the story, as discussed by Andrew Smith: "it is important to note that critical discussion of *Otranto* has focused as much on the novel's two prefaces as it has on the novel itself" (Smith 2007: 18).

Grace Marks and her fellow employee, James McDermott, were found guilty of the murder of their employer, Thomas Kinnear, and also suspected of killing his housekeeper, Nancy Montgomery. Grace and McDermott were tried, convicted, and sentenced to death. However, Grace's sentence was commuted to life imprisonment because of her comparative young age of sixteen. She served nearly thirty years in Kingston Penitentiary, Toronto before eventually being pardoned in 1872. She was then accompanied to New York state and thereafter no record of her life exists. In a spirit of Gothic textual excess, Atwood embeds frame within frame in a novel that debates Grace's guilt or innocence.

Bainbridge's little discussed novel similarly explores an infamous nineteenth-century murder when a husband of thirty years brutally bludgeoned his wife to death. The Reverend John Selby Watson became a cause célèbre when, like Grace Marks, his initial sentence to death was commuted to life imprisonment on controversial grounds of temporary insanity that granted him "Royal clemency" (Bainbridge 1992a: 230). There was widespread suspicion that this decision was made to appease public resistance to the idea that such a visceral crime could occur in a respectable middle-class home.[5] With a reputation as a mordant writer and an extensive collection of novels exploring the tensions that characterise failing marriages, Bainbridge, like Atwood, employs a particular form of Gothic that concentrates on what Spooner identifies as "the disintegration of boundaries between inside and outside, body and mind, villain and victim, not to mention a preoccupation with mortality and decay, [that] marks [crime] narratives as peculiarly Gothic" (Spooner 2010: 255). Like Atwood, Bainbridge frames her text with an authorial 'Note' that explains her adaptation of historical documents.

There is a creative consensus that prefatory notes acknowledge factual sources whilst concomitantly promoting imaginative license for fiction. Readers of revisionist fiction may be

---

[5] Bainbridge addresses this subject by intercalating a newspaper article from *The Globe*, dated 26 January 1872, which states that "Watson is the 'Revd Mr Watson', Mr Watson, 'the clergyman', the 'venerable looking prisoner'. Would the same sympathy have been felt if a Mr Mick Connor had knocked his wife's brains out with a pick-axe? There are cases which make one wonder if an unconscious feeling for respectable people has not influenced exertions to save such persons" (Bainbridge, 1992a: 231).

ostensibly removed from anticipation of the 'real' in a postmodern climate of doubt, yet writers continually disrupt readerly understanding by incorporating actual historical documents within fiction. For example, Julian Barnes postfaces his novel, *Arthur and George* (2005), with a 'Note' that points out that quotation from letters, newspapers, government reports, proceedings in Parliaments, and the interpolated writings of Sir Arthur Conan Doyle are all 'authentic' documentary sources. Michèle Roberts, by contrast, prefaces her novel, *In the Red Kitchen* (1991), with a 'Note' that states she has "freely adapted the (disputed) facts" of the life of the nineteenth-century medium Florence Cook for *fiction* (Roberts 1991: n.p., original emphasis).[6]

Neo-Victorian writers paratextually acknowledge inspiration found in historical documents and also frame narrative as an interrogation of the provenance and transmission of documented events. 'Notes' function as metafictional devices to organise what Patricia Waugh describes as the simultaneous "construction of a fictional illusion (as in traditional realism) and the laying bare of that illusion" (Waugh 2002: 6); they reinforce Heilmann's and Llewellyn's argument that "the higher end of neo-Victorianism seeks to illuminate its own trickeries" (Heilmann and Llewellyn 2010: 23). Moreover, they may also indicate that writers are in some sense captured by stories found in documented history, with narrative providing a release from spells cast on the imagination by the past and its elisions. Evoking Andrew Smith's argument in this collection that "[t]he Gothic has always been interested in the past and its possible continuing presence" (this volume: 53), Atwood confesses that early readings of a nineteenth-century writer, Susanna Moodie – who met and recorded her encounters with Grace Marks – "began to haunt her" (Atwood 2006d: 72), and Bainbridge, in addition to replaying her parents' dysfunctional marriage, admits that her fiction is also pervaded by an influence of tragedy and horror gained at an early age from documentary footage of the Belsen concentration camp (see

---

[6] Kate Summerscale alternatively introduces her 2008 documentary book, *The Suspicions of Mr Whicher* by tracing the palimpsestuous history of the 1860 Road Hill Murder. Summerscale acknowledges her use of "some of the devices of detective fiction", but states that in her book "the content, though, aims to be factual" (Summerscale 2008: xiii).

Guppy 2000: n.p.).⁷ Gothic proves the medium for both writers to embrace the obsessive and irrational hold of the past to reanimate haunting tales of neurosis and morbidity.

With a notable ironic tone, Bainbridge's and Atwood's 'Notes' acknowledge frameworks of fact whilst declaring that documents are freely adapted and licensed by fiction as works of imagination. Atwood notes that "*Alias Grace* is a work of fiction although it is based on reality [...] I have not changed any known facts, although the written accounts are so contradictory that few facts emerge as unequivocally 'known'" (Atwood 2006b: 537), and Bainbridge asserts, "this novel is based on a true story. The documents presented have been edited here and there to fit the needs of the narrative, but are otherwise authentic" (Bainbridge 1992b: n.p.). Such exercises in authorial framing and interpretative direction question an authoritative and authentic version of the past – official or mainstream history's account of events; they illustrate Gothic's fractured flow of information, which, as Eve Kosofsky Sedgwick points out, results in a difficulty in getting the tale told, with a fully legible manuscript or uninterrupted narrative notably rare in the genre (see Sedgwick 1986: 13).⁸ Atwood's and Bainbridge's 'Notes' dissolve divisions between story and 'fact' in an essential Gothic and postmodern indeterminacy: Bainbridge's vague suggestion that she has "edited here and there" parallels Atwood's communicated sense of the undecidable and uncertain. Both writers undermine historical accounts whilst simultaneously asserting that a new author[ity] is firmly located in neo-Victorian novels that also incorporate fractured documents in ways that substantiate a legacy from nineteenth-century sensation fiction.

---

⁷ Atwood describes a halting progression of "involvement" with Moodie that begins with her early rejection of Moodie's works found on the family bookshelf and ends with a "vivid dream" of writing about Moodie – a discovery made by her unconscious, that Atwood observes resulted in Moodie "haunting" her (Atwood 2006d: 71-72).
⁸ In her study *Legitimate Histories: Scott, Gothic and the Authorities of Fiction*, Fiona Robertson observes that "frame narratives and other formal paratexts (including editorial introductions and explanatory notes) are exercises of authorial control and tests of competing narratorial and historiographical authorities" (Robertson 1994: 118).

2. A Sensational Legacy

Revisionist writers adapt both strategic and thematic inheritance from Victorian sensation fiction, with buried writing unfolding contemporary rewritings of dark desires and social transgression. Wilkie Collins is perhaps the best example of a nineteenth-century writer who substantially intercalates documents for a sensationalist agenda. Collins's tales of domestic crime, including murder, were narrated with invented documents as part of what one Victorian reviewer deemed a "peculiar new scheme of writing a tale in the words of a dozen different narrators" (Anon. 2005: 99).[9] Reconfiguring a relationship with sensationalist media, Atwood and Bainbridge review ideological debates on domestic crime, as strategies of textual excess underline neo-Victorianism's connectedness to the sensation school of Gothic. *Alias Grace* and *Watson's Apology* are Gothic fictions of the domestic kind; they reinforce Susanne Becker's point that "after all, gothic horror is domestic horror" (Becker 1999: 4) and resonate with Punter's and Byron's explanation of the sensation school:

> Sensation fiction, sometimes called 'domesticated Gothic' because of the way in which it transfers Gothic events to the heart of a supposedly respectable Victorian society, focuses upon secrets, social taboos, the irrational elements of the psyche, and questions of identity. Murder, adultery, bigamy, blackmail, fraud and disguise are common components of the plot. (Punter and Byron 2004: 94)

Found documents play key roles in revealing Collins's sensational secrets as seen in his 1874 work, *The Law and the Lady*. Following *The Moonstone*'s success at the height of the sensational 1860s, with details borrowed from the Road Hill Murder, Collins casts Valeria Woodville as an early type of detective figure attempting to clear her husband of poisoning his first wife. Ultimately, she provides proof of his innocence by supervising the reconstruction of a torn and

---

[9] Demonstrating an incestuous relationship with sensational journalism, Collins's novels like *The Woman in White* (1860), *Armadale* (1866), *The Moonstone* (1868), and *The Legacy of Cain* (1888) illustrate what Altick calls "the perennial Victorian delight in murder" (Altick 1970: 302).

scattered confessional letter, as "precious morsels of paper" are recovered (quite fantastically) from beneath three years of refuse in the "dust-heap" (Collins 1998: 339). Within such sensational plots of suspense and discovery, documented secrets are sooner or later revealed. Drawing on Kathleen Tillotson's definition of these texts as "novels with a secret" (Tillotson 1969: xv), Kelly Marsh notes that "sensation novels, by definition, work on the assumption that present enigmas are the result of secrets hidden in the past, and that these secrets are discoverable" (Marsh 1995: 102). Unearthed and exposed, documents disclose material 'evidence' to avidly awaiting audiences seeking resolution and restoration of social order.

Neo-Victorianism employs fragmented documents quite differently to those in nineteenth-century fiction. For the sensation school, discovered documents provide restorative hermeneutic evidence for fictional worlds under threat from social and sexual transgression. Unlike nineteenth-century narratives of exposed and explained secrets, postmodern fiction tends not to emphasise documents uncovering 'truths', but rather deconstructs how investigatory reading and interpretation take place. Documents read in a postmodern framework of ambiguity, discontinuity, and self-conscious narrations reveal decentred and destructured subjects. Manipulating documentary 'evidence', contemporary writers play with histories, cultural ideas, and critical representations of the Victorians in ways that deconstruct how we see and perceive their lives. Unlike sensation fiction's focus on plot over character, neo-Victorian novels use intercalated diary extracts, ruptured letter exchanges, and lurid newspaper reports to more closely explore the violent psychological recesses of murderous minds. This is indicative of what Robert Mighall identifies as Gothic's new emphasis on the bodies, minds or psyches of criminals (see Mighall 2003: 26), and is particularly evident as novelists play to the idea that "murder is the Gothic act par excellence" (Botting 1995: 88).

3. Fatal Correspondences

With literary reputations affiliated to Gothic themes, Atwood and Bainbridge manipulate real people and events in historiographic metafictional ways. Retracing society's fears, prejudices, and misreadings, Bainbridge frames fragments of writing as part of a *Daily Telegraph* report (undated) and also structures the fourth and final part of her novel with trial documents and public commentary, including court reports, witness testimony, newspaper articles, and a series of letters to *The Times* newspaper. Atwood similarly assembles an assortment of documents within her novel, but these are, in contrast, arranged as collected epigraphs, introducing chapters with quilt pattern titles like 'The Letter X', 'Secret Drawer', and 'Pandora's Box'. Nineteenth-century commentary on Grace Marks's case appears in the form of a ballad, newspapers reports, and prison records, together with extracts from Moodie's work. Historical sources are arranged sequentially with quotations from Victorian prose and verse for a non-hierarchal mix of fact and fiction that Magali Cornier Michael argues "not only destabilizes the authority of official documents but also recuperates previously de-authorized texts and discourses".[10]

Atwood's found documents are many and varied, but they all radiate from her personal discovery of Moodie's work.[11] As a nineteenth-century pioneer and writer, Moodie recorded her impressions of Grace Marks in her work, *Life in the Clearings Versus the Bush* (1853). She first visited Grace in Kingston Penitentiary and later witnessed her short incarceration in the Lunatic Asylum in Toronto. Moodie's sensational accounts (reported from memory) are, however, deemed unreliable, and she is suspected of inflaming sensational interest in Grace; yet for a long time, she was nonetheless regarded as a particularly authoritative commentator on Grace's story. Responding to the materiality and reading of history in ways that organise Gothic's witnessing and responding to ghosts (see Wolfreys 2002: 11), Atwood was provoked by Moodie's discrepancies to write *Alias Grace*. For this research, she returned to the paper trail that documented Grace's story, but found the available information partial and frustratingly contradictory.

In *Alias Grace*, Atwood imaginatively reconstructs Grace's family background: her migratory journey from Ireland, early work experience and relationships before focussing on the events that led to the murders. Bainbridge similarly begins her novel with six actual

---

[10] Magali Cornier Michael. 2001. 'Rethinking History as Patchwork: The Case of Atwood's *Alias Grace*', *Modern Fiction Studies* 47: 2 (Summer), 421-447 (p. 426).
[11] Atwood's long critical relationship with Moodie begins with a 1970 series of poems, entitled *The Journals of Susanna Moodie*, and a later television play based on Moodie's reports of the murder.

courtship letters sent by Watson to Anne Armstrong before imaginatively recreating scenes of an abusive marriage. *Watson's Apology* depicts a long, slow build-up of tensions and verbal warfare that culminates in a macabre scene of murderous violence, as a doctor discovers "a woman under a filthy blanket, jack-knifed in the corner like an old battered doll" (Bainbridge 1992a: 165). The murder is thereafter explicitly represented from various viewpoints in transcribed court and medical evidence and newspaper reports, and just as Atwood describes the crime and crime scene and aftermath of arrest and incarceration from Grace's point of view, Bainbridge imagines Watson's psychological state of mind as he endures a gruelling prison life haunted by memories of his crime.

Bainbridge fills the gap between courtship letters and later documentation of the murder by imagining a union driven by loneliness, distorted memory and Anne's urgent need to escape a Gissing-like 'odd woman' life of poverty and despair.[12] Effectively strangers, Watson's courtly yet significantly opaque letters give Anne "no clear picture of the man behind the words" (Bainbridge 1992a: 22), but we do gain a picture of Anne through the lens of Watson's epistolary expectations. Framing his prospective wife as a woman whose perceived 'staid, quiet and domestic habits' (Bainbridge 1992a: 9) conform to his understanding of proper femininity, Watson is, at first, reassured on meeting Anne that he "has found his ideal" (Bainbridge 1992a: 47). However, relief at materialising the "sparkling" (Bainbridge 1992a: 42) eyes of a ghost from distant youth is displaced as more "theatrical eyes" (Bainbridge 1992a: 149) reveal an emotional excess that is abhorrent to him. From Watson's point of view, Anne's passions and sexuality are animalised from their first conjugal encounter:

> He dreamt he was at the hotel, caressing the ears of the mongrel dog. The coarse hairs on its neck dragged against his wrist. For some reason, though he knew it was a dog squatting there, he thoughts its mouth was a purse and he was curious to know how much money it

---

[12] George Gissing's 1893 novel *The Odd Women* discusses the straitened circumstances of Victorian unmarried women who grow old alone or marry to escape poverty.

contained. He stroked the close muzzle, searching for an opening. The dog squirmed under his touch but he persisted. At last his fingers penetrated the fiery warmth of its jaws, and he looked into its pumpkin-coloured eyes and slid his thumb across the moist and silken lining of its gums. He was sure the brute would never bite him. (Bainbridge 1992a: 56)

For Watson, dream-state sexual exploration becomes a waking nightmare, as Anne's embrace of her sexuality – her "long-drawn-out howl of abandonment" (Bainbridge 1992a: 57) – recasts her as a dangerously sexual Gothic anti-heroine. In the tradition of Bertha Mason – *Jane Eyre*'s original dangerous 'mad woman in the attic' – "some strange wild animal" (Brontë 1999: 258) – Watson sees his "woman of sense", "lady of great excellence" (Bainbridge 1992a: 7-8) "ravaged" by "impure joy" (Bainbridge 1992a: 57): a transformative and monstrous duality. Now defined by emotional excess and violent outbursts, Anne, "no longer modest" (Bainbridge 1992a: 57) is characterised by malice and melodrama evident in frequent outbursts termed by Watson as his wife's "scenes" (Bainbridge 1992a: 143). It is evident, however, that both submit to violent emotions: he "trembling with fury" (Bainbridge 1992a: 115), grinds his teeth and clenches his fists (Bainbridge 1992a: 113); ink spilled on a library book causes him to become "so angry he pounded the table" (Bainbridge 1992a: 112), whilst she, continuing to believe "she doted on him", awaits his presence: "if he didn't unlock the library on the stroke of five o'clock she took a hammer to the door" (Bainbridge 1992a: 135). Anne, first angry and then bitter, finally attaches herself to Watson with an unnatural obsession as, "by some atrocious quirk of fate he had become her whole life. Whatever emotion she had substituted for love, it now consumed her" (Bainbridge 1992a: 115). Ultimately, excessive and distorted emotions lead to a final conflict resulting in Anne's violent death and Watson's consequent failed suicide attempt.

Admitting to an uncanny replaying of her parents' troubled relationship in much of her fiction, Bainbridge imagines the claustrophobia and tortured atmosphere of a disintegrating marriage as reason for Watson's reported 'sudden' loss of control.[13] Motive remains unexplained in the historical record of the case; as Bainbridge explains in her 'Note', "what has defeated historical inquiry has been the motives of the characters, their conversations and their feelings. These it has been the task of the novelist to supply" (Bainbridge 1992b: n.p.). She provides this in conjunction with document extracts presented without narrative commentary, but with a reading response nevertheless prefatorially primed to incite uncertainty and scepticism. Documents are depicted as discovered and used as trial evidence; for example, a series of writings extracted from a *Daily Telegraph* report are introduced under the heading: "excerpts from some writing found in a carpet bag in Horsemonger Lane Gaol, said to have been written by Mr Watson while awaiting trial for his life and entitled: 'Dead: A Contemplation'" (Bainbridge 1992a: 168). In these fragmented writings, Watson abstractedly muses on his wife's life and death with mixed emotions of regret, nostalgia, compassion, and detachment, which communicates an uneasy sense that she lingers un-exorcised.

Adopting second person holy language, he attempts to distance himself as an impassionate observer of her dead body: "she is dead. She lies motionless. That which once animated her, animates her no longer. Thou canst not disturb her" (Bainbridge 1992a: 168). However, he reveals that she haunts him – he cannot escape "her presence", as "sleeping or waking, she is with thee where thou goest. She cannot be excluded" (Bainbridge 1992a: 168). Just as Atwood debates Grace's insanity in troubling dream sequences, Bainbridge presents Watson tormented by memories of the murder scene. He imagines a graphic image of Anne "[wearing] her brains on the top of her head like a squashed flower, like a bunch of crimson ribbon" (Bainbridge 1992a: 251). Such macabre coalescence of femininity and horror reminds of the fate of Gothic's female monsters like, for instance, *Dracula*'s Lucy Westenra, savagely rendered "no longer the foul Thing" and restored as a "holy" memory (Stoker 2000: 179-80) by Stoker's "Crew of Light" (See Craft 1994). Watson may similarly

---

[13] Death predominates in Bainbridge's fiction. Willa Petschek notes: "there is inevitably a death in Bainbridge novels. The death may come by illness, accident or a vicious clout, but the effect is a sharp reminder, she says, that the most innocent are guilty of murderous thoughts, and that sometimes the thought becomes deed. Her next novel is about the murder of the 19th-century clergyman, John Selby Watson. He will, she supposes, be based on her father" (Petschek 1981: n.p.).

believes that in bludgeoning Anne to death, he is "merely rid[ding] her of the bad things" (Bainbridge 1992a: 255), but Anne's dangerous, vampiric sexuality and "fatal imagination" (Bainbridge 1992a: 24) remain an 'unholy' memory despite Watson's attempt to sanctify her in his record.

Watson's writings are immediately followed by a report on the murder from *The Times* newspaper that voices the horrors of finding a "primaeval murder" in "a decent neighbourhood, at a clergyman's hearth, on a Sunday afternoon after a morning's visit to church" (Bainbridge 1992a: 171). Like much reportage on Grace Marks's case, the article adopts a Gothic register to further sensationalise the event, with emphasis of "horrors as fearful spectacles" and "spectres dogging our steps" (Bainbridge 1992a: 170). A rhetorical question: "is our everyday human nature such a mere crust over a seething abyss?" (Bainbridge 1992a: 170) is reminiscent of sensation fiction's focus on crime and disorder disturbing façades of domestic respectability and raises anxieties that continue today.

Bainbridge's strategy of intercalation is contrasted by Atwood's epigraphic positioning of her documentary sources. Epigraphs can function, as suggested by Gérard Genette, as "a mute gesture whose interpretation is left to the reader"; but I propose that Atwood's epigraphs, in fact, adhere more to Genette's second argument for a canonical function that comments "on the *text*, whose meaning it indirectly specifies or emphasizes" (Genette 1997: 156-157, original emphasis). The reason for this is that Atwood problematises the quotations as "mute gesture[s]" for they are always in dialogue with her 'Note's' guidance. Atwood's epigraphs proliferate with official (found) documentary sources and selected creative extracts. This creates a dialogic tension between fact and fiction whereby, for example, a quotation from Alfred Lord Tennyson's epic verse *Maud* (1855), with its ambiguous speaker – potentially madman or commentator – offers critical commentary on a letter by Moodie. Discussing her husband's "ingenious" Spiritoscope, which she believes enables her to contact the dead and produce a form of automatic writing, Moodie concludes an animated account by stating, "now, do not think me mad or possessed by evil spirits" (qtd. Atwood 2006a: 457). Moodie may have Gothicised Grace's state of mind by way of sensationalised descriptions of madness as a "frightful malady", with Grace "lighted up with the fire of insanity" – "hideous and fiend-like", "shrieking away like a phantom", forever "haunted" by memory of a brutal crime (qtd. Atwood 2006a: 51); yet Atwood illustrates that Moodie's own self-confessed "possession" is, by contrast, distinguished by her as "a glorious madness" (qtd. Atwood 2006a: 457) that she wishes all could share.

In an earlier epigraph, Moodie authoritatively diagnoses Grace's insanity. An extract from *Life in the Clearings* appears with a letter from Dr Joseph Workman, Medical Superintendent of the Provincial Lunatic Asylum in Toronto, in which he frankly acknowledges a troubling blindness in science, confessing that "the human psyche cannot be dissected nor the brain's workings put out on the table to display" (qtd. Atwood 2006a: 51). His admission that limitations in scientific knowledge leave him "blindfolded, groping my way" (qtd. Atwood 2006a: 51) works as a careful critique of Moodie who, as a lay commentator, remains nonetheless supremely confident in her diagnostic gaze. Workman and Moodie are then supplemented by a verse of Emily Dickinson's:

> One need not be a Chamber – to be Haunted –
> One need not be a House –
> The Brain has Corridors – surpassing –
> Material Place –
> ...
> Ourself behind ourself, concealed –
> Should startle most –
> Assassin hid in our Apartment
> Be Horror's least. ... (qtd. Atwood 2006a: 52)

Atwood's selected creative commentary transforms the haunted house – a staple of Gothic literature – to symbolise greater horrors hidden in the "corridors" of the mind. Workman's identification of an interior invisible world is consequently emphasised as mysterious and unknowable from the dual perspective of science *and* creative imagination.

Bainbridge similarly debates mysteries of the psyche with an exchange of letters published in *The Times* newspaper under the heading "Mr Watson's Latinity" (Bainbridge 1992a: 196). This correspondence responds to a Latin phrase "found among Mr Watson's papers" (Bainbridge 1992a: 196) and used as evidence against Watson by the Crown Prosecutor, Mr Denman. Various correspondents vie to translate the phrase "s*aepe olim amanti nocuit semper amare*" (Bainbridge 1992a: 196), with no definition agreed upon.[14] Ultimately the editor closes the correspondence with the issue unresolved as scholars pour polite scorn on contending translations of "bad Latin" (Bainbridge 1992a: 198). The final letter further complicates the matter by suggesting that Watson may not have been referring to himself with this phrase, before confusing the issue still further by questioning the legibility of Watson's handwriting "in this time of stress. Did he perhaps write not 'amare' (to love) but 'amari' (to be loved) – not 'amanti' (lover) but 'amenti' (madman)?" (Bainbridge 1992a: 199). Bainbridge thereby emphasises instability in found documents, which prove open to limitless interpretations; in this instance, any potential for illuminating Watson's state of mind is indeed lost in translation.

Contending and revised interpretations are explored by both writers, with Atwood considering the role of retrospect as events recede into the historical past. A newspaper article entitled, 'Recollections of the Kinnear Tragedy', written for the *Newmarket Era* in 1908 appears in dialogue with Christina Rossetti's sonnet 'Remember' (1849). The reporter William Harrison recollects the murder decades after the event and admits imaginative license for his reconstruction of McDermott and Grace; allowing "plenty of room for [...] supposition", he concludes with the somewhat ironic judgement that McDermott's "disregard for truth" was "well-known" (Atwood 2006a: 213). Atwood therefore allows imaginative licence for factual reporting and uses creative support to illustrate that as events inevitably slide into the past they become increasingly open to reinterpretation and Gothic story-telling. As Rossetti's verse indicates, "For if the darkness and corruption leave/A vestige of the thoughts that once I had" (Atwood 2006a: 213), past horrors offer interpretative potential – a trace – for neo-Victorian writers to speculatively explore psychological recesses unilluminated by historical record. This is arguably the raison d'être of neo-Victorian fiction as it freely revisits and rewrites nineteenth-century crimes that have long faded from a

---

[14] The first interpretation is given as "To a person who has loved often in former times, living has never been anything but a trial and an injury" (Bainbridge 1992a: 175).

visceral reality. As historical distance opens the past to creative hypothesising and debate, an inescapable Gothic sensibility comes into play as writers imagine "thoughts [...] once had" with creative liberty that allows what Marie-Luise Kohlke observes is the neo-Victorian "desire [to make] the spectres dance to our tune delimiting what we choose to hear when we make the ghosts speak or speak for them" (Kohlke 2008: 14).

Atwood chooses the patchwork quilt as a controlling frame to speak about and for ghosts. As readers negotiate epigraphic borders of competing texts, the chapters of *Alias Grace* are further framed by the names and designs of quilt patterns. Much is made of the quilting metaphor as a structural and controlling intertext in various critical responses to the novel. Most commentators focus on quilting as women's cultural expression or argue for their function as metafiction.[15] What becomes particularly significant about quilting from a Gothic point of view is not only their function as a framing device, but also the spectral quality of recycled materials that record memory as text[ile] fragment. After many imprisoned years sewing for others, Grace stitches her own quilt when free to do so. Choosing the 'Tree of Paradise' pattern, she once again "changes the pattern a little to suit [her] own ideas" (Atwood 2006a: 533), adapting story by piecing three extra fragments of scrap fabric into her quilt. These are cut from clothing – as tradition demands –with triangles of cloth taken from Grace's prison nightgown, the petticoat that Mary Whitney (her alias) was wearing when she died, and a dress originally belonging to Nancy Montgomery. In this way Grace stitches her private memories together, commenting: "and so we will all be together" (Atwood 2006a: 534).[16]

Grace's quilt provides an oblique representation of her personal history. Three women's intertwined stories become part of the fabric of Grace's textile narrative. Construction of the quilt closes Atwood's novel by opposing sensationalised media retelling of the murder. This was typified by the prison Governor's wife's scrapbook

---

[15] Michael acknowledges that a resurgent interest and radical reassessment of the quilt as art was concomitant with the advent of the women's movement in the 1970s. (See also Ingersoll 2001, Murray 2001, and Wilson 2003.)

[16] Significantly, Nancy's dress was worn by Grace during her aborted attempt to flee after Nancy's murder; it appears with uncanny repetition throughout the dream/hallucination sequences that disturb the text.

– a collection of famous and sensationalised crime reports that Grace was obliged to read. Finding herself part of a collated, pieced and pasted narrative that satisfied the Governor's wife's penchant to shock and "horrify her acquaintances" (Atwood 2006a: 29), Grace notes that the scrapbook is kept on a table covered by a silk shawl illustrated with "branches like vines intertwined, with flowers and red fruit and blue birds, it is really one large tree" (Atwood 2006a: 27). With vines flowers, fruits, *and* disguised snakes, Grace's 'Tree of Paradise' quilt closes Atwood's novel by memorialising the ghosts of Nancy Montgomery and Mary Whitney. Three women's stories are bound firmly together in a narrative that is not destined to be sensationalised or circulated, but will preserve private memory as part of the domestic fabric of Grace's new life. Crucially, this final episode of Grace's life is wholly lost to the historical record. The patchwork fragments represent the enduring secrets of the tale. They gesture towards the visible but essentially unreadable trace and demonstrate a secret that provokes the telling and retelling of a familiar Gothic tale of good, evil, temptation, and retribution.

4. Conclusion: Gothic Traces

Alias Grace and *Watson's Apology* debate historiographic metafiction's familiar idea that history is only found in partial documentary traces. Murder for the Victorians was rigorously debated and documented in newspapers, trial documents, confessions, social commentary, and fictional accounts. There was a symbiotic relationship with veracity as newspapers reported actual crimes and sensation fiction drew on such reports; as Altick observes, "they added verisimilitude to extravagance, and thus made the extravagant credible" (Altick 1970: 79). Now neo-Victorianism imitates the processes of reading documentary traces in order to stress the role of interpretation and impel readers to assess 'evidence' in the context of a Gothic excess of competing accounts; what Becker might term "interrogative texture and generic excess" (Becker 1999: 285). Moving beyond nineteenth-century thematics of resolution and punishment, contemporary writers probe deeper into the motivations and mysteries of minds driven to murder.

Evidencing Cora Kaplan's view of neo-Victorianism as coloniser of genres (See Kaplan 2007: 4), Atwood's and Bainbridge's postmodern narratives rework crime and history and inescapably borrow elements of the Gothic and sensation. Spooner indeed argues that "there are traces of Gothic in most crime narratives, just as there are crimes in most Gothic novels" (Spooner 2010: 246). Criminal psyches are explored in postmodern and Gothic ways, which illustrate Maria Beville's point that

> some of the issues that are explored separately in Gothic and postmodernist fiction, are one and the same, namely: crises of identity, fragmentation of the self, the darkness of the human psyche, and the philosophy of being and knowing. (Beville 2009: 53)

Adapting the nineteenth century in spectral and material ways, Atwood and Bainbridge explore the paradox of postmodernism as complex and indirect representations; they imagine, install, and manipulate 'found' documents remaking Gothic traditions to demonstrate processes that result in "unresolved contradictions" (Hutcheon 1995: 67). Adapting the themes and techniques of sensation fiction, neo-Victorian writers again focus on horrors hidden in domestic settings, exploiting anxieties that continue unabated in the modern world. An atmosphere of doubt dominates both novels as documentary evidence is tested for reliability, with reading, interpretation, and fact-making processes effectively put on trial. As partial material traces continue to tell incomplete stories with an emphasis on secrets and Gothic imaginations. Gothic and postmodernism find coherence in historiographic metafiction, the "ascendancy" of which, Spooner points out, has "laid the past open for Gothic rewriting"; with the Victorian era becoming a particular focus (Spooner 2007: 43-44).[17] As contemporary writers revisit an era which, Alexandra Warwick points out is, in the popular imagination, "in many ways *the* Gothic period" (Warwick 2007: 29, original emphasis), any rewritings of the period are destined to produce uncanny repetitions of Gothic themes, tropes, and structure. Angela Carter's much quoted refrain "we live in Gothic times" (Carter) strikes a new note, as neo-Victorianists re-live Victorian times in cyclical

---

[17] Spooner explains that "although historiographic metafiction is not always written in the Gothic mode, its concern with marginal voices, untold tales, and the difficulties history has in getting told lends itself naturally to Gothic treatment" (Spooner 2007: 43-44).

returns and fragmentary conditions that creatively reanimate spectres of the past for new audiences.

Bibliography

Anon. 2005. 'Unsigned Review, *The Times*, October 1860' [1860]. In Page (2005): 99.
Altick, Richard D. 1970. *Victorian Studies in Scarlet*. New York: W. W. Norton.
Atwood, Margaret. 1997. *The Journals of Susanna Moodie* [1970]. London: Bloomsbury Publishing.
——. 2006a. *Alias Grace* [1996]. London: Vintage.
——. 2006b. 'Author Afterword'. In Atwood (2006a): 537-542.
——. 2006c. *Curious Pursuits: Occasional Writing 1970-2005*. London: Virago.
——. 2006d. 'Introduction to *Roughing It in the Bush*' In Atwood (2006c): 71-94.
——. 'In Search of *Alias Grace*: On Writing Canadian Historical Fiction'. In Atwood (2006c): 209-234.
Bainbridge, Beryl. 1992a. *Watson's Apology* [1984]. London: Penguin.
——. 1992b. 'Author's Note'. In Bainbridge (1992a): n.p.
Barnes, Julian. 2005. *Arthur and George*. London: Jonathan Cape.
Becker, Susanne. 1999. *Gothic Forms of Feminine Fictions*. Manchester: Manchester University Press.
Beville, Maria. 2009. *Gothic-Postmodernism: Voicing the Terrors of Postmodernity*. Amsterdam: Rodopi.
Botting, Fred. 1995. *Gothic*. London: Routledge.
Brontë, Charlotte. 1999. *Jane Eyre* [1847]. Hertfordshire: Wordsworth.
Collins, Wilkie. 2003a. *The Woman in White* [1860]. London: Penguin.
——. 2003b. *The Moonstone* [1868]. London: Penguin.
——. 1998. *The Law and the Lady* [1875]. London: Penguin.
Craft, Christopher. 1994. *Another Kind of Love: Male Homosexual Desire in English Discourse 1850-1920*. Berkley: University of California Press.
Genette, Gérard. 1997. *Paratexts: Thresholds of Interpretation* (trans. Jane E. Lewin). Cambridge: Cambridge University Press.
Gissing, George. 2000. *The Odd Women* [1893]. Oxford: Oxford University Press.
Guppy, Shusha. 2000. 'Beryl Bainbridge: The Art of Fiction', *The Paris Review* 157 (Winter). On-line at: http://www.theparisreview.org/interviews/561/the-art-of-fiction-no-164-beryl-bainbridge (consulted 03.11.2011).
Haste, Steve. 1997. *Criminal Sentences: True Crime in Fiction and Drama*. London: Cygnus Arts.
Heilmann, Ann, and Mark Llelwellyn. 2010. Neo-*Victorianism: The Victorians in the Twenty-First Century, 1999-2009*. Houndmills, Basingstoke: Palgrave Macmillan.
Hutcheon, Linda. 1995. *The Politics of Postmodernism*, 2nd edn. London: Routledge.
Ingersoll, Earl G. 2001. 'Engendering Metafiction: Textuality and Closure in Margaret Atwood's *Alias Grace*', *The American Review of Canadian Studies*, 31(3) (Autumn): 385-401.
Kaplan, Cora. 2007. *Victoriana – Histories, Fictions, Criticism*. Edinburgh: Edinburgh University Press.

Kohlke, Marie-Luise. 2008. 'Introduction: Speculations in and on the Neo-Victorian Encounter', *Neo-Victorian Studies*, 1(1) (Autumn): 1-18.
Marsh, Kelly A. 1995. 'The Neo-Sensation Novel: A Contemporary Genre in the Victorian Tradition', *Philological Quarterly* 74(1) (Winter): 99-123.
Michael, Magali Cornier. 2001. 'Rethinking History as Patchwork: The Case of Atwood's *Alias Grace*', *Modern Fiction Studies* 47(2) (Summer): 421-447.
Mighall, Robert. 2003. *A Geography of Victorian Gothic: Mapping History's Nightmares*. Oxford: Oxford University Press.
Moodie, Susanna. 1989. *Life in the Clearings Versus the Bush* [1853]. Ontario: McClelland and Stewart.
Murray, Jennifer. 2001. 'Historical Figures and Paradoxical Patterns: The Quilting Metaphor in Margaret Atwood's *Alias Grace*', *Studies in Canadian Literature*, 26(1): 65-83.
Petschek, Willa. 1981. 'Beryl Bainbridge and Her Tenth Novel', *New York Times*, 1 March. On-line at: http://www2.nytimes.com/books/98/11/29/specials/bainbridge-tenth.html (consulted 03.11.2011).
Punter, David. 1996. *The Literature of Terror: The Gothic Tradition Volume 1*. London: Longman.
Punter, David, and Glennis Byron. 2004. *The Gothic*. Blackwell Guides to Literature. Oxford: Blackwell.
Roberts, Michèle. 1991. *In the Red Kitchen*. London: Minerva.
Robertson, Fiona. 1994. *Legitimate Histories: Scott, Gothic, and the Authorities of Fiction*. Oxford: Oxford University Press.
Sedgwick, Eve Kosofsky. 1986. *The Coherence of Gothic Conventions*. London: Routledge.
Smith, Andrew. 2007. *Gothic Literature*. Edinburgh: Edinburgh University Press.
Spooner, Catherine. 2006. *Contemporary Gothic*. London: Reaktion Books.
—. 2007. 'Gothic in the Twentieth-Century'. In Spooner and McEvoy (2007): 38-47.
—. 2010. 'Crime and the Gothic', in Rzepka, Charles J., and Lee Horsley (eds.), *A Companion to Crime Fiction*. London: Blackwell: 245-257.
Spooner, Catherine, and Emma McEvoy (eds.). 2007. *The Routledge Companion to Gothic*. London: Routledge
Stoker, Bram. 2000. *Dracula* [1899]. Hertfordshire: Wordsworth.
Summerscale, Kate. 2008. *The Suspicions of Mr Whicher or The Murder at Road Hill House*. London: Bloomsbury.
Tillotson, Kathleen. 1969. 'The Lighter Reading of the Eighteen-sixties' [introduction]. In Collins (2003a): ix-xxvi.
Walpole, Horace. 2008. *The Castle of Otranto* [1764]. Oxford: Oxford University Press.
Warwick, Alexandra. 2007. 'Victorian Gothic'. In Spooner and McEvoy (2007): 29-37.
Waugh, Patricia. 2002. *Metafiction: The Theory and Practice of Self-Conscious Fiction*. London: Routledge.
Wilson, Sharon R. 2003. 'Quilting as Narrative Art: Metafictional Construction in *Alias Grace*', in Wilson, Sharon Rose (ed.), *Margaret Atwood's Textual*

Assassinations: Recent Poetry and Fiction. Ohio: Ohio University Press, 121-34.
Wolfreys, Julian. 2002. *Victorian Hauntings: Spectrality, Gothic, the Uncanny and Literature.* Houndmills, Basingstoke: Palgrave Macmillan.

'Fear is Fun and Fun is Fear':
A Reflexion on Humour in Neo-Victorian Gothic

Christian Gutleben

Abstract:
Starting with the idea that neo-Victorianism's humour privileges an intertextual form of irony typical of postmodernism, this chapter argues that the association of humour and Gothic produces a critical distance towards Gothic texts and tropes a detached perspective which is also an efficient anti-nostalgic device. What a humorous treatment of Victorian Gothic also allows is an ontological reconsideration of the concepts of otherness, the uncanny and the monstrous, precisely because humour encourages a reflexive attitude. The result of the playful hybridisation of humour and Victorian Gothic is a new novelistic species in keeping with the neo-Victorian cult of heterosis. Humour creating hermeneutic ambiguity and Gothic relying on conceptual uncertainty, the association of the two necessarily increases textual indeterminacy, and it is the challenge of this interpretative plurality that explains critics' continued interest in the puzzles of neo-Victorian Gothic.

Keywords: Gothic, humour, hybridisation, irony, monstrosity, neo-Victorian fiction, otherness, parody, the uncanny, *unheimlich*.

*****

Reflecting upon the contemporary association of fear and fun, or of horror and humour, does not mean asserting that this association is new or specific to today's culture. Far be it from me to contest Avril Horner and Sue Zlosnik's hypothesis that the hybridity of Gothic fiction includes a fundamental "incongruity [which] opens up the possibility of a comic turn in the presence of horror or terror". This unexpected phenomenon of the "comic turn in Gothic", the authors claim,

> is not an aberration or a corruption of a 'serious' genre; rather, it is intrinsic to a mode of writing that

> has been hybrid since its very inception. [...] The comic Gothic turn self-consciously uses Gothic's propensity to bare the device in order to allay the reader's response to fear, horror and anxiety when encountering certain plots and tropes. [...] In this sense, the comic Gothic turn is the Gothic's own *doppelgänger* [*sic*]. (Horner and Zlosnik 2005: 3-4)[1]

Hence, I am not proposing a reconsideration of the Gothic tradition here, but rather an analysis, in the context of neo-Victorian Gothic texts, of the specifically contemporary meaning of the generalised presence of humour.[2] As Fred Botting has convincingly demonstrated, Gothic has invaded all cultural areas: not only cinema, literature and entertainment, but also "[c]lothes, puppets, masks, lifestyles, dolls, sweets", in other words, the whole "machine of popular culture" (Botting 2007: 199, 201). Catherine Spooner confirms that "[t]he passion for Gothic shows no sign of abating", adding that our Gothic culture is "intrinsically concerned with the production of pleasurable fear" (Spooner 2006: 22, 31), an enjoyment to which humour arguably contributes. It is on this oxymoronic combination of pleasure and fear that my reflexion will dwell. As the pervasive phenomenon of Gothic film parodies having already been widely studied, notably by Kamilla Elliott (2007), I prefer to concentrate on literature and particularly neo-Victorian literature, because the breakthroughs of neo-Gothic and neo-Victorianism appear strikingly parallel and concurrent. The point of the ensuing discussion is of course to determine the function(s) of humour in the recreation of Gothic episodes in a neo-Victorian context. What does it mean to systematically and ironically reconsider the myths and motifs of Victorian Gothic? What happens to the Gothic questioning of rationality when it is treated playfully or

---

[1] The idea presented here by Horner and Zlosnik had already been voiced by Fred Botting – and in strikingly similar terms: "The play of fear and laughter has been inscribed in Gothic texts since their inception" (Botting 1996: 168).

[2] The notion of humour seems preferable to the comic because the former concerns a vision of life which includes sympathy and the possibility "to *marvel smilingly* at the reach and diversity of human nature" (O'Neil 1990: 41, added emphasis) whereas the latter is directly linked to laughter and "the minimisation of some particular thing to be taken seriously" (Olson 1968: 23), and it is precisely my intention to show that the humour of neo-Victorianism contributes to the serious reconsideration of the Gothic's themes and questions.

parodically? Is the Gothic challenge to the concepts of otherness and familiarity weakened or strengthened by the intrusion of humour? And, from an aesthetic point of view, what is the result of the amalgamation of the neo-Victorian Gothic and humorous modes? To try and answer these questions I will suggest three main analytical possibilities. My first hypothesis consists in stipulating that the recourse to humour in neo-Victorian Gothic constitutes a distancing device meant to assert an anti-nostalgic stance both towards an imaginary original Gothic and the Victorian production of its own Gothic myths. In a second movement, this new perspective on the genres' intersection provokes a reconsideration of key neo-Victorian Gothic concepts such as otherness, the uncanny and monstrosity. Finally, the seemingly unnatural union of fear and fun serves an essential aesthetic function of diversification: hybridising the Gothic and the ludic modes makes room for new generic, modal and stylistic combinations.

1. The Hegemonic Rule of Postmodernist Irony

To characterise postmodernism and its endeavour "to settle scores with the past" – exactly what is at stake in this study of the neo-Victorian version of Gothic – Umberto Eco famously insisted on the role of irony, one of humour's favourite tools:

> The postmodern reply to the modern consists of recognizing that the past, since it cannot really be destroyed, since its destruction leads to silence, must be revisited: but with irony, not innocently. (Eco 1994: 67)

If Eco's definition remarkably applies to postmodernism in general, it seems even more relevant in the case of neo-Victorianism in particular. Neo-Victorian literature takes Eco's injunction to revisit the past with irony to the letter. Implementing a double or multiple narrative and temporal stance, displaying a metafictional awareness, or using deliberate anachronisms (in language, ideology, cultural reference or thematic concerns), the neo-Victorian systematically adopts the distanced and dual perspective typical of irony. For Ann Heilmann and Mark Llewellyn the dominant characteristic of neo-Victorianism is "a series of metatextual and metahistorical conjunctions" which allows the contemporary movement to "be *self-consciously engaged with the act of (re)interpretation, (re)discovery and (re)vision concerning the Victorians*" (Heilmann and Llewellyn 2010: 4, original emphasis). Neo-Victorian self-reflexivity and metatextuality are indeed at the origin of a particular form of irony since they allow – or force – the contemporary reader to simultaneously contemplate a Victorian referent and a postmodernist technique, a world of the past and a device of the present. Metafiction in neo-Victorian texts plays another ironical game since, by "allowing us insight into how the illusion is produced", it challenges us to "embrace a double vision which satisfies our desire for […] a visible myth of origin even as it is engaged in deconstructing it" (Heilmann and Llewellyn 2010: 210). The concomitant creation and subversion of illusion through double-layered metatextuality is singularly at stake in the neo-Victorian version of Gothic insofar as the mysteriousness, gloominess and uncanniness intrinsic to Gothic are self-consciously offset by intertextual or metatextual indications which counterbalance the atmosphere of terror or fear.

One of the most famous representatives of neo-Victorian fiction, A.S. Byatt's *Possession: A Romance* (1990), immediately shows how the Gothic episodes are carefully framed by metafictional devices which encourage critical reflection rather than fictional illusion. The central Gothic scene revolves around a spiritualist session and the (surmised) death of a baby,[3] but the practice of spiritualism is discredited throughout the novel, starting with one of the two opening epigraphs taken from Robert Browning's 'Mr Sludge, "The Medium"' in which the poet notoriously voices his scepticism and exclaims: "How good men have desired to see a ghost" (Browning 1864, l. 143). The episode itself is narrated in an extract from the autobiography of Mrs Lees, herself a medium, but, again, the reliability of this embedded narrative fragment is pre-empted by the

---

[3] The other main Gothic scene concerns the desecration of the Victorian poet's grave, and, strikingly, if Gothic literature "represent[s] excess and exaggeration" (Punter 1980: 5), then this passage is written in a parodic vein as the excess of excess, since it incorporates a redundant accumulation of Gothic signs – a storm, a churchyard, yew trees, the moonlight, a white owl, the howling wind, "small bones", "a *presence*, not of someone, but of some mobile *thing*", "a chorus of groans and creaking sighs", and "a creature from another dimension" (Byatt 1990: 493-494, original emphases) – all of which creates narrative saturation and generic invalidation.

context. Mrs Lees is first presented by Randolph Ash, the (fictional) Victorian poet who, very much like Browning, condemns those who "conduct or orchestrate as it were the vulnerable passions of the bereaved and the desperate" and denounces the "trickery" of Mrs Lees's séance (Byatt 1990: 390-391). She is then introduced and described by the twentieth-century extradiegetic narrator as someone "accustomed to seeing threads and clouds of odylic light run about the heads and shoulders of the Elders" and as someone who pretends "she had provoked winds in closed rooms, and had seen her dead grandmother perched on the end of the bed, singing and smiling" (Byatt 1990: 393). After such implicit but unmistakable incredulity stemming from the framing narrative, the framed narrative and its revelation of a crying baby can only be perceived as a fraud, and hence as a fake Gothic reconstruction.

Inserted in a modern narrative, edited by a twentieth-century narrator and enclosed in a context denouncing mediumistic charlatanism, the Victorian Gothic episode can only be read through the deforming prism of contemporary scepticism. Byatt's ironic inclusion of Gothic in her polyphonic and polymodal novel is not only made apparent through her narrative techniques, but also highlighted by the very structure of the novel. Only the carefully planned 'Postscript 1868', available to the sole reader and to none of the diegetic characters, makes it possible to understand the Gothic episode of spiritualist communication with a lost child. It is only this concluding passage that reveals that the spiritualists, far from being clairvoyant, were in fact utterly blind. This piece of structural irony apparently further subverts the Gothic ambiguity of the limits between life and death, but Byatt's ultimate tour de force consists on the contrary in suggesting, subtly and indirectly, that the aforementioned passage can and must be read as a Gothic passage – although not in its mediumistic context. Indeed, talking about the spirits, the Victorian poet makes this crucial revelation: "They speak to me too, through the medium of language" (Byatt 1990: 395). As the ironic use of the term "medium" clearly signals, the Gothic dimension of the novel does not reside in the dubious proceedings of any spiritualist medium, but in the process of writing itself. It is Randolph Ash's poetry, and of course Byatt's whole text, which prove to be Gothic, giving a voice, a presence, a life to the dead. The deadness of the dead and the pastness of the past are indeed challenged in Byatt's seminal novel which demonstrates, quite brilliantly in my view, that the neo-Victorian enterprise is by its very essence Gothic, bent as it is on exhuming the remains of the past and breathing life into the spectres of Victorianism. As much is suggested by the latest studies of neo-Victorianism when they argue that the neo-Victorian novel "functions as a form of revenant, a ghostly visitor from the past that infiltrates the present" (Arias and Pulham 2010: xv) or when they insist on

> the centrality of the figure of the ghost [...] as a metaphor for both the persistence of the past and our relationship to it today. Reversing the conventional image of the beckoning ghost returning to make a claim upon the present, in these fictions the ghost does not reach out to us, rather we seek it out, conjure it up. (Mitchell 2010: 180)

In 'The Conjugial Angel' (1992), the second novella in *Angels and Insects*', Byatt starts by signposting and displaying the Gothic nature of her narrative through a series of intertextual and self-reflexive commentaries. The quotations integrated by Byatt seem to have been chosen to exemplify the variety of human attempts to try and establish a communication with the deceased. The extracts from Arthur's Hallam's paper 'Ghost' (1829), Poe's 'The Raven' (1845) or Keats's 'Isabella, or the Pot of Basil' (1820) all insist on "the colossal Presences of the Past" stemming from "the inmost gloom" (Byatt 1993: 186). The Gothic idea of a glimmer of light issuing from the shadows of death is also taken up and developed in the numerous extracts from Tennyson's 'In Memoriam' (1850). The weighty presence of Tennyson's masterpiece inevitably introduces "a set of speculations on how the dead might survive and [...] a meditation on types of posthumous returns" (O'Gorman 2010). Indented as they are, the multiple and lengthy quotes end up forming a sort of parallel text, almost independent from the diegetic narrative, illustrating the Gothic trope of spectrality, celebrating the living endurance of the dead, constituting a poetic "ghostology" (O'Gorman 2010) which, Hamlet-like, speculates on the undying life of the spirits and on the poet's mediumistic role of providing a link between vacuity and substance, loss and gain, obliteration and creation.

The irony in Byatt's novella is generated by the juxtaposition of these poetic exercises in transcendence and the prosaic attempts of the actual characters of the narrative. The intertexts' loftiness is opposed to the text's lowliness and the poet's spiritual endeavours contrast with the characters' physical, or even physiological, realities. Mrs Earnshaw would like to establish a contact with the spirit of her deceased children, but the narrative voice insists instead on the fleshy encumbrance of "her big breasts" (Byatt 1993: 200). Mr Hawke preaches the purity of the spiritual world inhabited by the angel-like departed, but the narrative depicts him as "a lascivious man" who literally leaps on one of his fellow spiritualists "so that his hands scrabbled at her bosom, and his breath, heavy with port wine, invaded her lips and nostrils (Byatt 1993: 214, 215). As for Mrs Papagay, her yearning for her lost husband is not at all disincarnate, since she dreams of "male arms around her in the scent of marriage-sheets" (Byatt 1993: 191). What is more, during the séances which give rise to the quotation or transcription of spirit-seeking poetry, Mrs Papagay's "irrepressible imagination" repeatedly ventures into the other participants' "conjugal bedroom[s]", going so far as to picture "the seed rushing in" (Byatt 1993: 199). Let it be added that the séances which structure the narrative are punctuated by the "scraps of flesh" that are being fed to the threatening raven and by the dog's "popping little farts" (Byatt 1993: 183, 286), and it will be clear that Byatt's strategy is a typical strategy of grotesque "decrowning" such as Mikhail Bakhtin described in his work on the carnivalesque function of parodic literature, a "decrowning" which systematically and comically inverts the sacred and the profane, high and low, top and bottom, face and backside (Bakhtin 1973: 123-124).

If Byatt derives much humour from the contrast between the characters' discourse and quotations about spirits, on the one hand, and their pragmatic, material or even sexual thoughts (revealed thanks to an astute system of shifting internal focalisations), on the other, the function of this contrast remains to be seen. Does the repeated emphasis on bodily needs mean that the Gothic suggestion of ghostly existences is debunked? This is indeed not the case for the number and beauty of the quoted texts provide convincing evidence of a communication of a spiritualist kind, and, even in the diegetic context, certain scenes are presented without irony, as in the case of the imagined return of the dead Arthur Hallam who confides: "I walk.

Between. Outside. I cannot tell you. I am part of nothing. Impotent and baffled" (Byatt 1993: 250). The paratactic dislocation of the syntax, the semantic bafflement created by the juxtaposition of "between" and "outside", and the metonymic (and desperate) claim of nothingness, all contribute to conveying the speaking dead's Gothic otherness. Manifestly then, a single text can be, if not simultaneously, at least successively, humorous and Gothic. In other terms, humour and Gothic do not exclude each other but can be complementary.

To prove this complementary relation, another narrative fragment must be evoked. When Alfred Tennyson in his old age becomes the subject of the narrative, the disclosure of his dark thoughts is regularly interrupted by the mention of his pathetic failures to button up his nightshirt and the indication of his vain satisfaction about "the good phrase[s]" and the "wonderful line[s]" he has written (Byatt 1993: 267). In this context of disparagement, what is stressed is the poet's terrible perception of his "decaying" body, the "body of this death", "this nothing" (Byatt 1993: 272). Strikingly, it is the "nothing" which unites the living Tennyson and the dead Hallam, as if Byatt wanted to give expression to an ontological continuity between existence and nonexistence. And since the narrative voice is unashamedly modern in its linguistic outspokenness, it is tempting to see in the narrator's cynical denunciation of corruptible flesh the modern vision of death in life as opposed to the nineteenth-century poets' vision of life in death. But, as the title of Byatt's collection, *Angels and Insects*, clearly indicates, her purpose is not to oppose a spiritualist and a materialist conception of life, but, rather, to combine them. In this combination must be seen the postmodernist, and indeed the neo-Victorian, stance consisting in conflating the spiritualist conception of Gothic inherited from the past and the meaty, if not gory, conception of Gothic typical of the present. By associating the hopeful spiritualism of the Victorians and today's dejected vision of a humanity governed by its flesh, Byatt revisits the past in Eco's ironical fashion, but she also modalises *both* the hopes and the dejection, casting a relativistic glance on *both* the past and the present.

This ironical double discourse, in which the Victorian Gothic is framed by metafictional and sometimes metacritical guidelines, can be found in most neo-Victorian Gothic novels. In *Poor Things* (1992), Alasdair Gray stages the fabrication of his protagonist by an experimental doctor so as to make the link with *Frankenstein* unmistakable. The doctor's name, Godwin Baxter, refers directly to Mary Shelley's father, William Godwin, and the final narrative document produced by the protagonist herself denounces the fact that the main narrative is full of "ghouleries from the works of Mary Shelley and Edgar Allan Poe" (Gray 1993: 272). Gray's novel, then, is necessarily read as a double of Mary Shelley's Gothic creation, but, as a playful, humorous double as is made clear by the caricature reproduced at the thresholds of the main narrative, representing the upper part of a naked woman leaning out of the jaws of a magnified skull (Gray 1993: 1, 248). A sexy, female Frankenstein is what Gray heralds in his fiction, self-reflexively described by the protagonist as "sham-gothic [which] stinks of Victorianism" (Gray 2003: 275).

In Peter Ackroyd's *Dan Leno and the Limehouse Golem* (1994) Thomas De Quincey's 'On Murder Considered As One of the Fine Arts' (1827) constitutes the structuring hypotext. The story's Jack-the-Ripperish murderess finds a constant source of inspiration in De Quincey's essay, and the bulk of the narrative concerns the murderess's grotesquely inappropriate attempts to put De Quincey's satirical theory into literal practice. After each murder she tries to show that she is the equal of the artist described by De Quincey, aspiring to create "a spectacle", for example by placing "the intestinal tract [as] a very pretty decoration beside the womb" of one of her victims or by disposing a further victim's cut-off penis, "another work of God", on an open book (Ackroyd 1998: 62, 86).[4] The irony in Ackroyd's text stems from the discrepancy between the source work written as a satire and the responding text which utterly fails to perceive the mockery of its model. This discrepancy is nowhere more evident than in the literary pretensions of the slaughtering psychopath who appropriates Shakespeare's poetry and butchers it into coarse Gothic prose: "What a work is man, how subtle in faculties and how infinite in entrails!" (Ackroyd 1998: 62).

In A.N. Wilson's *A Jealous Ghost* (2005), the extradiegetic framing narrative is contemporary, and it is the sub-text, intertext or hypotext which is (late-)Victorian, but the principle of metafictional irony remains constant. Wilson's narrative's duplication of the

---

[4] The precise location of the penis is "Hartlib's *Knowledge of Sacred Things* across the entry for 'golem'" (Ackroyd 1998: 92). By thus juxtaposing a penis and a golem, Ackroyd provocatively suggests a visual metaphor illustrating the ever-potent association of the grotesque and the Gothic.

diegetic structure and motifs of Henry James's *The Turn of the Screw* (1898) is explicitly acknowledged, since the protagonist is writing a thesis on James's Gothic novel and repeatedly summarises parts of the plot, quotes from, refers to and comments upon the original text, always in relation to her own parallel situation. Metafiction therefore tends to invade the narrative, and it is crucial to understand that these metafictional remarks, like any metadiscourse, function like an ironical discourse because they have simultaneously two semantic fields of application concerning as they do both the hypotextual model and the narrative itself, both the late-Victorian text and the contemporary text. As such, they illustrate D.C. Muecke's contemporary conception of irony as "a perpetual deferment of signification":

> The old definition of irony – saying one thing and giving to understand the contrary – is superseded; irony is saying something in a way that activates not one but an endless series of subversive interpretations.
> (Muecke 1982: 31)

Metafiction, then, invites the addressee to read the novel as an ironical double-discourse, constituting the texts as a ghost of fiction, as James's novella's spectral double. The spectre works at several levels in Wilson's Gothic rewriting: it not only provides a thematic leitmotif but also a structural device, for Wilson's novel unfolds alongside the ghostly presence of James's text. As a fascinating consequence of this spectral construction, it is precisely when the revenant text and the ghost text cease to coincide that the narrative stands out in its sheer otherness. In other words, Wilson recontextualises James's novel and follows the master's storyline so as to create specific narrative expectations; yet it is by *thwarting* these same expectations and unexpectedly diverging from the master narrative, leaving the ghost behind in the process, that the contemporary text highlights its originality. Just as the ghost of the children's departed mother is finally explained away in Wilson's narrative,[5] just so the ghost of James's text is finally dispelled as Wilson's epilogue proves entirely

---

[5] What the unhinged governess takes for a ghost is in fact the actual mother who had simply been banished from the house and who was not at all dead as surmised.

different from James's ending. Hence, while Wilson acknowledges and integrates the Victorian masterpiece into his contemporary narrative, he manifestly juxtaposes an antiquated and a modern version of the Gothic tale, though not to denigrate the old version so much as underline the fundamental difference and originality of his own ghost-story, which resurrects the ghosts of the past the better to dismiss, if not to exorcise, them.

What all these examples tend to show is that neo-Victorian fiction's treatment of Gothic is typical of postmodernism's ironical *modus operandi* as described by Eco. Just as in metafiction the illusion of fiction is simultaneously recreated and acknowledged as an illusion, just so in neo-Victorianism, the Victorian Gothic is recreated and at the same time, through metatextual or intertextual reminders, ironically acknowledged as mock- or neo-Gothic. The omnipresence of often comic irony is neo-Victorianism's most efficient device to signal its anti-nostalgic stance.[6] What is manifest in the self-conscious humour with which the myths and tropes of Victorian Gothic are reconstituted is the distance and the difference – not the imitation or the repetition – of the contemporary texts in relation to their spectral ancestors. To a certain extent, Gothic itself is thus held at a distance, almost observed and analysed, even while it is being revived, and it is necessary to ponder the purpose of this humoristic and self-conscious examination.

2. Rethinking the Fearful

If Victorian Gothic is preoccupied with the creation of fear, the staging of the irrational and "the destabilization of the domestic scene" (Wolfreys 2002: 5), then a humorous, self-conscious revision of Victorian Gothic necessarily undertakes a reconsideration of these Gothic concepts. The ghost that has just been evoked in the context of

---

[6] This insistence on the anti-nostalgic stance of neo-Victorianism extends, rather than contradicts, my earlier argument in *Nostalgic Postmodernism*, which has sometimes been misinterpreted as "posit[ing] a more simplistic [...] sense of 'nostalgia'" (Arias and Pulham 2010: xiv) or asserting "that a nostalgic text *cannot* be subversive" (Mitchell 2010: 179). The third part of the study contends that neo-Victorianism's relation to nostalgia is fundamentally complex, ambiguous and paradoxical, so that, even though many texts incorporate subversive elements, neo-Victorian fiction as a whole "cannot be deemed *radically* subversive" (Gutleben 2001: 218, added emphasis).

The Turn of the Screw's neo-Victorian rewriting represents a pertinent starting point to highlight one aspect of the difference between the Victorian and neo-Victorian perspectives. In James's novella the apparition of Quint's and Miss Jessel's ghosts creates a zone of undecidability whose ambiguity is never cleared up in the narrative: the absent ghost fully corresponds to the link with the mother that is broken and continued at the same time, the definitive absence that is also a continued presence, "that which is neither alive nor dead", that "[t]hing which is not a thing, [and] comes to defy semantics and ontology" (Derrida 1994: 12, 6). In Wilson's neo-Victorian version, the mother's ghost looms in similar conditions, but it is later proven a delusion, the ghost having been all along the actual *living* mother.[7] This revelation creates an *a posteriori* irony, also instigated and intended by the novel's title, which derides the reader's gullibility and invites a reflexion on the belief in ghosts – rather than on the nature of ghosts. By thus inviting a hermeneutic blunder, Wilson creates the appropriate context to demonstrate that Gothic effects can be achieved by the spectral presence of a text – and not of any 'literal' ghost, spirit or phantom. In other words, Wilson highlights the lure of intertextuality and the self-reflexive nature of neo-Victorian Gothic writing and reading, in which the Gothic mode and mood are produced by Gothic fiction itself – and not by any diegetic reality. By resurrecting James's text, Wilson masterfully evinces the spectral nature and power of Victorian Gothic.

The jealous ghost of Wilson's novel and ghosts in general in neo-Victorian fiction are treated with an ironical distance that dispels their frightening power and their supernatural ontology. To reveal the imposture of ghosts is, of course, in keeping with contemporary culture's emphasis on simulations and simulacra; it is also in keeping with the extraordinary current commoditisation of ghosts which, as Catherine Spooner clearly explains "are mass-produced and altogether fail to terrify", having become fundamentally "domesticated" (Spooner 2006: 27). Ubiquitous in the toy industry, in comics, cartoons and computer games, in fashion, in advertising, entertainment and leisure, the ghosts fully partake of "Disneygothic" and "become ordinary figures for the operations of new technologies

---

[7] In contrast, Patricia Pulham's contribution to this volume discusses how the ghost of James's unacknowledged homosexuality haunts Colm Tóibín's *The Master* (2004).

and their hallucinatory, virtual effects" (Botting 2008: 2, 10). The way contemporary fiction plays at unveiling its diegetic ghosts shows, firstly, that neo-Victorianism fully shares the postmodern *Zeitgeist*, according to which simulations are not only practised as the rule of the day but are also revealed as such, and, secondly, that ghosts can no longer be read or seen literally.[8]

Nevertheless, ghosts, or illusions of ghosts, are incorporated over and over again into neo-Victorian fiction, and this repeated presence must have a meaning – if not literal then necessarily metaphorical. Inviting a critical distance through humour or irony, these neo-Victorian texts also invite a reassessment of the figure, the idea or the myth of the ghost. In this sense, neo-Victorianism follows the tendency of the critics who, in the wake of Derrida's publication of *Specters of Marx*, have reconsidered the concepts of ghosts and spectres in order to move away from interpretations stressing the ambiguous limits of life and death and to define haunting as a principle, a literary and temporal principle. The literary dimension of haunting is not restricted to the intertextual presence-absence of revenant texts; it also concerns the very opacity of language, the enigmas of meaning, or the aporia of interpretation. Accordingly, the fictionalisation of ghosts is also a means of questioning "the jarring elements within language in order to account for the unsaid of an utterance and to reinstate the excommunicated in communication" (Berthin 2010: 39). The temporal dimension bears upon the problematic persistence of the past in the present and "the crucial elements of revenant history" (Spooner 2007: 45), which critics on the Gothic have repeatedly theorised:

> How to represent the past is one of the central concerns and the figure of the ghost is used to raise questions about making visible that which a culture has lost or has been forced to forget. [...] Ghosts are never just ghosts; they provide us with an insight into what haunts our culture. (Smith 2007: 152-153)

---

[8] The presence of actual ghosts in neo-Victorian novels such as Toni Morrison's *Beloved* (1987), Carol Goodman's *The Ghost Orchid* (2007) or Joanne Harris's *Sleep Pale Sister* (2005) does not alter the matter: neo-Victorian ghosts embody distinct cultural metaphors.

The deconstruction of the (mock-)ghosts of the nineteenth century, then, is obliquely, often humorously and quite manifestly, a reminder of "what haunts our culture", that is, of the continuous non-existent existence of Victorianism and the history of Victorian culture in (the supposedly post-historical or a-historical) postmodernity.

If the ghost is necessarily rethought and redefined because derisively revealed as a sham, another Gothic motif, namely that of the monster, is presented in an entirely new light when treated with humour. Admittedly, the monstrous has always been a staple of Gothic fiction, its function consisting in challenging the rational categories and the essentialist conception of man inherited from the Enlightenment. The terrorising creatures of Gothic, the "species of non-species" (Derrida 1978: 293), radically blur the frontiers between the human and the non-human, between the self and the other. The monster inevitably questions the relation of the self to otherness but also the possibility of otherness within the self. What, then, is the specificity of the monster presented in a humorous light? Firstly and quite categorically, the monster does not lose its capacity to stimulate thought simply by becoming 'funny'. Humour does not prevent critical reflection; rather it encourages it by creating a critical distance from its target. The monster, even the humorous monster, then, produces an effect of ontological destabilisation, for the very "idea of the monstrous contains in itself a sense of the contingency of any definition of the human (Gibson 1996: 239). To probe into the further functions of neo-Victorian Gothic humour, which are necessarily additional functions, one has to consider some concrete examples.

What effects do Liz Jensen's promiscuous "Gentleman Monkey" (Jensen 1998: 170), Alasdair Gray's uninhibited woman with a child's brain and Angela Carter's picaresque bird-woman produce? The main impression derived from the monstrosity of humanity is, paradoxically, the humanity of monstrosity. Humour humanises the monster and, instead of insisting on the essentialist crisis provoked by the spectacle of muddled identity, it celebrates the richness and plurality of the various forms of human otherness. Carter, in particular, revels in the cult of monstrosity when, in *Nights at the Circus* (1984), she describes the Gothic "vault or crypt" in Madame Schreck's Museum of Female Monsters, an exhibition of freaks comprising the "Living Skeleton" and "[d]ear old Fanny Four-Eyes; and the Sleeping Beauty; and the Wiltshire Wonder, who was not three foot high; and Albert/Albertina, who was bipartite, that is to say, half and half and neither of either" (Carter 1994: 61, 59). By thus underlining bodily aberrations, Carter's humorous strategy integrates the grotesque, and "the grotesque is never far from Gothic modes of representation" (Wolfreys 2002: 43). As Kelly Hurley further explains, the grotesque in a Gothic context has a Bakhtinian function of "celebrating the idea of a human body without proper boundaries" (Hurley 2007: 140). So what Carter's grotesque Gothic demonstrates is that the boundlessness of human nature might be terrifying but can also be exhilarating and empowering. That Carter's neo-Victorian novel is a text bent on exultation is obvious in the comic similes used to describe the setting of the Gothic exhibition – "a mighty marble staircase that went up with a flourish like, pardon me, a whore's bum" and a "drawing-room [...] snug as a groin" (Carter 1994: 26, 27) – and this exultation makes it clear that Carter wants to highlight the seduction of monstrosity, the pleasure of otherness and "the *gleeful excessiveness* of Gothic horror" (Hurley 2007: 142, original emphasis).

Humour's main function is to illustrate the "joyous relativity" of all things (Olsen 1990: 31), so when applied to Gothic monsters, it logically illustrates the "joyous relativity" of man's nature and definition. The fundamental anxiety related to human ontology is not eliminated in neo-Victorian Gothic, but it is accompanied by a concomitant debunking of anxiety. This omnipresent sense of derision ultimately helps us "face the 'monstrous' within ourselves, [...] making us tremble simultaneously with laughter *and* fear" (Wolfreys 2002: 53, original emphasis). The playful representation of monsters shows, then, that horror and humour can, delightfully and thought-provokingly, coexist (in fiction) and that, as the Shakespearian title of this chapter suggests, fear can be fun and fun can be related to fear.

The presence of the monstrous in neo-Victorian fiction brings about an element of unexpectedness and produces an effect of defamiliarisation typical of the Gothic uncanny. The uncanny in a Gothic context corresponds to Freud's concept of the *unheimlich*, which is always defined in relation to its opposite: the *heimlich*; it derives from the disquieting irruption of the unfamiliar in the familiar and

> it represents a feeling which relates to a dialectic between that which is *known* and that which is *unknown*. If we are afraid, then more often that not it is because we are experiencing fear of the unknown: but if we have a sense of the uncanny, it is because the barriers between the known and the unknown are teetering on the brink of collapse. (Punter 2007: 130, original emphases)

In view of such a definition, it is of course tempting to consider the whole nineteenth century, and perhaps even the general idea of the past, as the privileged site of the uncanny for neo-Victorianism insofar as the Victorian period is at the same time (over-)familiar and always eluding the limits of knowledge. Above all, what fascinates neo-Victorianism is what is unknown in the known Victorian context,[9] and this fascination seems to be of the order of the uncanny.

Relying as it does on the dialectic of the known and the unknown, the uncanny is necessarily redefined in neo-Victorian fiction, since the limits of the known are constantly renegotiated. And since it seems impossible to share the sense of defamiliarisation experienced in another civilisation by people with an utterly different perception of the world, neo-Victorianism introduces the Victorian uncanny through the anamorphic perspective of humour.[10] In both Liz Jensen's *My Dirty Little Book of Stolen Time* (2006) and Miranda Miller's *Nina in Utopia* (2010), the Victorian heroines are, mysteriously or science-fictionally, transported into our contemporary era. A fundamental discrepancy is then established between the protagonists' perspectives, whose familiar world is radically unsettled, and the reader's perspective, whose familiar world is perceived through alien eyes, with this discrepancy invariably engendering

---

[9] Impressively voluminous as the Victorian archives may be, many personal or social secrets remain hidden, many stories of suffering remain untold, and many horrors remain unexplained and unexplored: those dark, unrecognised areas of history, however small in scale, constitute the privileged focus of attention of neo-Victorian Gothic and its fascination with mysteriousness and concealment.

[10] As Jeanne Ellis shows in her chapter on the postcolonial sense of the Gothic, the uncanny can also be introduced through an alien culture or an alien perspective and particularly the perspective of the "monstrous misfit" (Farber qtd. Ellis, this volume: 135).

comic effects. What scares the cross-world heroines is the utterly alien (to us utterly ordinary) commodities such as a "teavea" or "kaas" (Miller 2010: 31, 33), the car being perceived, in a similar alienated vision, as "a foul-tempered hippopotamus" (Jensen 2007: 88) and a "racing behemoth" (Miller 2010: 19). Certain concepts also show how the same referent can be frightening or amusing according to the particular perspective, for example when Jensen's protagonist is horrified by the idea of 'the Third World': "O Lord, [...] there are now three? Spare me, Sir, I pray!" (Jensen 2007: 128). But it is the comic fear occasioned by the black taxi driver which best illustrates neo-Victorian's humorous appropriation of the uncanny: what makes the heroine want to "scream in terror" is "the cannibal driver whose white-teethed fury scared the wits out from me, for I had visions of him tearing us limb from limb & munching on our bones, just as they do in the godless realms of Afric" (Jensen 2007: 88). From the twenty-first-century point of view, the comic inadequacy does not reside in the object or the referent of the stereotype but in the out-of-place subject and speaker.

As these novels (fake to) discover our contemporary world, their encounter with the (pseudo-)unknown includes a critical (re)assessment. If Jensen insists upon the dystopian side of modern council houses – these "multi-storeyed pig farms that stretched to the sky [in which] people are moody & dejected" (Jensen 2007; 95) – Miller, as the title of her novel heralds, focuses on our society's utopian aspects insisting on the – at least for a Victorian woman – incredible improvements in gender relations. And in spite of the naivety of the Victorian heroine's perception of our society as disencumbered of money because of the use the credit cards – which ironically underlines the paramount role of money – strikingly, these evaluations force us to reconsider our modern civilisation just as much as they force us to reconsider our perception of the Victorian civilisation. The humorous relativity of the uncanny is, then, a very efficient means to highlight the dialectics of neo-Victorian fiction, which works according to the principle of refraction, as defined by Susana Onega and myself, which establishes a dialogue between two periods and two sets of texts where each fosters a new understanding of the other and "where each sheds light on the other" (Onega and Gutleben 2004: 9).

3. Fear, Fun and the Evolution of Neo-Victorian Fiction

That fear and fun can coexist in a single work seems widely accepted at least since Shakespeare interspersed his tragedies with comic interludes. These instances of comic relief come after or before the manifestations of horror, though they are never simultaneous. Similarly, Horner and Zlosnik's theory of the intrinsic "possibility of a comic turn in the presence of horror or terror" relies on the idea of the "juxtaposition of incongruous textual effects" (Horner and Zlosnik 2005: 3). The question arising, then, may be formulated as follows: are fear and fun, humour and Gothic, necessarily successive or juxtaposed? Can they ever be concomitant and mingled? It is, of course, this chapter's contention that, in Neo-Victorian Gothic, fear and fun are constantly intertwined so as to redefine their conventional Gothic role.

Let us take two examples to consider the intersection and concurrence of humour and Gothic. The first comes from Dan Simmons's *Drood* (2009), which introduces Wilkie Collins's first-person narrative of Dickens's final years and which concerns Dickens's confrontation with dislocated bodies and a ghoulish creature hovering near the site of the Staplehurst train accident:

> In his five remaining years after Staplehurst, Dickens would only say about what he saw in that riverbed – 'It was unimaginable' – and of what he heard there – 'Unintelligible.' This from the man generally agreed to have the greatest imagination, after Sir Walter Scott, of any English writer. And from a man whose stories were, if nothing else, always eminently intelligible. (Simmons 2009: 13)

The vocabulary used here ("unimaginable", "Unintelligible") and mainly related to the eponymous Drood, a Dracula-like figure who can take any shape and materialise in any substance, is typical of the Gothic's attempts at saying the ineffable and the uncanny, that is, at playing with the limits of representation – just as with any limits. The challenge of presenting the unpresentable is precisely the poetic challenge that urges Gothic fiction to look for and multiply circumlocutionary discursive devices such as similes, metaphors, parallel or embedded narratives. It is the short-circuiting of this poetic quest and the mockery of this failure which are unusual here and which introduce the humorous element of discrepancy. It is also the contrast between the hyperbolic description of Dickens ("the greatest imagination [...] of any English writer") and the minimal expression of his descriptive power that engenders a derisive tonality. The passage's crucial irony that affects the whole novel is that (Simmon's version of) Wilkie Collins playfully launches into a 771-page narrative trying to elaborate on Dickens's two-word account and demonstrate Collins's own superior power of description. Nevertheless, the mysterious nature of the spectral Drood remains unsolved at the end of the long narrative, and the central presence of the uncanny is reinforced, rather than undermined or deconstructed, by the humorous approach of the deliberately Dickensian narrative. Humour does not function as an addition to the Gothic here; it playfully constitutes the Gothic itself, since the dreadful Drood, sometimes presented as Dickens's dark *Doppelgänger*, is considered as an enigma that the perspicacious narrator is bent on cracking. The dark side of Dickens-Drood appears constantly *both* fearful and entertaining, *both* Gothic and humorous.

The second example, taken from Susan Barrett's *Fixing Shadows* (2005), concerns a character specialising in "[p]ost-mortem photography, or mourning memorial", for whom "the modern mechanism by which the living may hold on to the dead became her business" (Barrett 2005: 259):

> Aurora has taught herself how to use hidden props and ties to create a relaxed pose suggestive of life interrupted rather than ended. She grew especially skilled at finding ways to mimic the painless slip from waking to post-prandial snoozing despite the conundrum of how stiffened feet might be fitted back into shoes, or a casual newspaper slotted into hands clenched like claws by the death spasm. (Barrett 2005: 260)

Here again humour and Gothic are not separate or successive, they feed off and accentuate each other. Quite remarkably, this passage seems to illustrate almost literally Henri Bergson's definition of the comic as "a certain mechanical inelasticity", anything which "gives us, in a single combination, the illusion of life and the distinct impression of a mechanical arrangement" (Bergson 1984: 62-63), a definition suggesting that any act of mimicry, be it the Gothic mimicry of life in death (or of death in life), is by essence of a laughable nature. The staging of the fraud described here manifestly tends towards humour, since it stresses the incongruous endeavour to undo death, but it also pertains to Gothic, since "Gothic is fundamentally stagey and theatrical in its nature" (Spooner 2004: 1).

Now, if Gothic is so often associated with humour in neo-Victorian fiction, one may wonder whether the result can still be linked to the Gothic mode or whether it does not become a parody of the Gothic. In order to answer this interrogation a consideration of the definitions of parody is clearly necessary. Starting with Linda Hutcheon, the modern definitions dwell upon the importance of "trans-contextualization" (Hutcheon 1985: 8 and *passim*), as well as upon the paradox of a literary form that "both incorporates and challenges that which it parodies": parody, then, is "repetition with critical distance that allows ironic signalling of difference at the very heart of similarity" (Hutcheon 1988: 11, 26). The idea of a critical reprise is confirmed in a more recent study, according to which "parody is an intentional imitation – of a text, genre, or discourse – which includes an element of humour and which has an aim of interpreting its target in one way or another" (Korkut 2009: 21). Neo-Victorian fiction certainly "incorporates and challenges" Gothic texts and tropes (although I would contest the use of the notion of imitation in Korkut's definition, for imitation constitutes the principle of pastiche, not parody), and its aim is certainly to (re)interpret Gothic tenets. Likewise it evidently includes irony and humour, so it might be considered to resort to a parody of Gothic. But if parody is understood as mocking or ridiculing its source text or genre, then it cannot apply to neo-Victorianism for the Gothic constituents are transposed and remodelled, not dismissed as merely inadequate or ridiculous.

Rather than speak of a parody of Gothic, then, and so as to avoid the ambiguity linked to the concept of parody, I would prefer to evoke a hybridised mode in the case of neo-Victorian Gothic. It is the combination of humour and Victorian Gothic, fun and fear, which characterises neo-Victorianism, representing a new generic blend. It seems crucial to realise that the basic preoccupations of Gothic are not given up: humanity's capacity for evil, the persistence of the unknown, the unexplainable and the irrational, the blurred frontier between matter and spirit, natural and supernatural, life and death are all thoroughly explored in this strain of contemporary historical fiction. These preoccupations, dark as they may be, need not be dealt with in a tragic mode. Accordingly, neo-Victorianism makes an implicit claim that the fearful riddles of life can be exposed lightly and playfully – in particular through intertextual and metatextual games. In other words, it is not the matter but the manner, not the topic but the tonality of Gothic which is altered in neo-Victorian fiction. Fun does not cancel fear, it does not even alleviate it. Fun simply strikes a different attitude with greater self-consciousness and self-derision.

The playfulness inherent to the hybrid mode of humorous Gothic affects all the aspects of neo-Victorian novelistic art, starting with its very form. I have already mentioned Alasdair Gray's drawing of a naked woman in a skull, but there are many other etchings of bones, vertebras and anatomical parts which add to the fantasy of *Poor Things*' Gothic derision. Illustrations and caricatures are a common feature of neo-Victorian Gothic as can be seen in Byatt's or Jensen's novels.[11] Also ludic are the narrative forms and modes, not only because of their multiplicity and variety even within single works, but also because of the types of discourses used within the various narratives: from diaries to letters, from Victorian newspapers to contemporary emails, from quotations of poetry to quotations of critical reviews, from true historical documents to counterfeited testimonials, from transcriptions of Tennyson's thoughts to transcriptions of an illiterate prostitute's confessions, the discursive diversity of neo-Victorian fiction is the most ostentatious proof of its determination to play with the form of the novel – in spite of its frightful contents.

That the fanciful concern with the form of the text should also affect the words themselves can hardly come as a surprise. In the Gothic context, the quest for a new word stands always already for a quest for a new understanding of the unfamiliar. Thus, when *Utopia*'s

---

[11] Whereas Byatt includes both drawings of a dog and of a raven made especially for her novella and reproductions of drawings by Dante Gabriel Rossetti, Edward Burne-Jones and John Martin, Jensen inserts only caricaturish drawings illustrating scenes of her narrative. Such illustrative and playful drawings can be found in several other neo-Victorian Gothic novels such F.E. Higgins's *The Bone Magician* (2008) or Robert Frankin's *The Japanese Devil Fish Girl* (2010).

Victorian doctor imagines a "mentometer" (Miller 2010: 159), he is not merely coining a word; he is actually looking for a means of understanding the dark functioning of his patient's ill minds. In Jensen's novel, the heroine, who commutes between the Victorian present and the twenty-first-century future and tries to make sense of her schizophrenic experience, similarly fabricates a mixed language, sometimes directly inspired from Carroll's *Alice in Wonderland*'s composite lexis in the case of "galumphingly" for example, but more often than not creating her own idiosyncratic idiom with terms such as "bejozzled", "queasiatious", "disganglified", "thundacion", "hozzicky-wild", "thugaroos", "banjaxed" or "O fantabulosa" (Jensen 2007: 266, 79, 95, 182, 183, 189, 218, 265). What this eye-catching cult of the original signifier evinces is the simultaneously disorientating and fertile nature of the encounter with the unknown, that is, the coincidence of the Gothic and poetic functions of the uncanny. What these *neo*logisms also show, superficially but manifestly, is *neo*-Victorianism's ongoing quest for innovation.

So the playfulness derived from neo-Victorianism's humorous dispositions modifies the whole presentation of the Gothic novels: it is almost as if these brooding texts were clad in new fanciful attire, as if ghostly Gothic appeared in a festive form. Gothic fiction, then, is transformed and hybridised by this formal ludism – just as it is transformed by the self-conscious irony with which the troubling questions linked to the dark mysteries of life are raised. The result is a new, hybrid mode, an original novelistic species: the neo-Victorian novel of humorous Gothic. Humour grafted onto (neo-)Victorian Gothic has then mainly a function of regeneration and, as a process of hybridisation, can be considered as an illustration of the concept of heterosis, that is, "the energy or vitality produced by cross-breeding" (Knoepflmacher 2008: 752). This particular instance of miscegenation exemplifies neo-Victorianism's constant quest for new associations and blendings. It also illustrates the fact, as I have argued elsewhere, that "neo-Victorian fiction [is] an example of postmodernism which systematically hybridises the traditions, genres or works of the past with the contemporary aesthetic and ideological perspective" (Gutleben 2011: 60).

Admittedly, the innovative aspect of neo-Victorian humorous Gothic does not merely stem from the modal combination of humour and Gothic since, as Wolfreys has demonstrated, "comic-Gothic" was already a Dickensian speciality (Wolfreys 2002: 25-53), and, as Horner and Zlosnik have argued, "the comic turn in Gothic is [...] a key aspect of Gothic's essential hybridity" (Horner and Zlosnik 2005: 12). Unprecedented in this case, however, is the specifically Victorian dimension of Gothic that is ironically revisited. What is being reconsidered again and again through the dually distancing perspective of postmodernity and humour is the threat of an urban demonology and degeneracy. As much is evident in Max Duperray's reflections elsewhere in this collection on the innumerable revisions of the Jack the Ripper myth, or in neo-Victorian engagements with the fear of otherness and monstrosity, as seen in the numerous rewritings of *Jane Eyre*'s concern with madness and its repression,[12] with the self's troublesome duality and affinity with evil in re-visions of Stevenson's *The Strange Case of Dr Jekyll and Mr Hyde* (1886) such as Emma Tennant's *Two Women of London: The Strange Case of Ms. Jekyll and Mrs. Hyde* (1989) and Valerie Martin's *Mary Reilly* (1990), or with the Frankenstein-like exploration of the limits between the human and the non-human as recast in Alasdair Gray's *Poor Things* (1992), Anne Goonan's *Queen City Jazz* (1994) and Peter Ackroyd's *The Casebook of Victor Frankenstein* (2008). One could study the repercussions of several other aspects of the Gothic linked to Victorian urbanisation, industrialisation, imperialism or scientific discoveries, but what matters is that the emphasis on neo-Victorianism bears upon characteristically nineteenth-century anxieties – mirroring, of course, our own contemporary anxieties. Furthermore, what matters is that these anxieties are dealt with in a (post)modern form of irony, privileging intertextual and metatextual irony and clearly diverging from the traditional comic Gothic which relies on a comedy of characters or more or less deliberate black humour. It is this combinatory art associating humour and Gothic, irony and seriousness, playfulness and anxiety, a modern form and nineteenth-century interrogations, postmodernism and Victorianism, which distinguishes neo-Victorian humorous Gothic as a novelistic species perfectly adapted to its environment where hybridity has become the dominant trope.

---

[12] For an illustration of the number and diversity of adaptations of *Jane Eyre*, see Rubik and Mettinger-Schartman (2007).

To conclude, I would like to insist on the heterosis of neo-Victorian fiction. By grafting modern techniques, alternative perspectives or unexpected modes onto a Victorian support, neo-Victorianism constantly creates new sub-species. In the cases examined here, it is the cross-breeding of humour and Victorian Gothic that has proven fertile, but other hybrids, such as Gothic steampunk or the Gothic graphic novel, are similarly fascinating. And what is true of Gothic, of course, also holds true of neo-Victorian versions of the romance, the novel of adventure, the *Bildungsroman* or the detective novel. Neo-Victorianism's possibilities of procreation seem limitless, all the more so since any new artistic trend can immediately be mingled with the existing stock of neo-Victorian novels to engender yet another breed. Such unrestrained procreative potential and such extended possibilities of cross-breeding unmistakably have monstrous implications and the neo-Victorian undertaking thus deals with ontological monstrosity not only in its themes but also in its very generic constitution.

Perhaps most striking about the union of humour and Gothic is the two modes' common exploration of ambiguities, boundaries and indeterminacy, be they semantic or axiological. While humour and its extensive use of irony play on the plurality of meanings and interpretations, Gothic systematically substantiates the unclear frontiers between the animate and the inanimate or between the intelligible and the unintelligible. Consequently, the association of humour and Gothic necessarily strengthens the vacillation of the texts' decoding: as Wolfreys aptly remarks, humorous Gothic (which he calls comic-gothic) produces a "complication of reading" for "as with the gothic, the comic relies on the haunting installation of undecidability" (Wolfreys 2002: 27). Fundamentally open-ended, neo-Victorian Gothic opens several roads of interpretation, and this plurality is not the least of its attractions. Its challenging hermeneutic ambiguity constitutes neo-Victorianism's very essence, while also representing another source of fearful fun.

Bibliography
Ackroyd, Peter. 1998. *Dan Leno and the Limehouse Golem* [1994]. London: Vintage.
Arias, Rosario, and Patricia Pulham. 2010. 'Introduction', in Arias, Rosario, and Patricia Pulham (eds.), *Haunting and Spectrality in Neo-Victorian Fiction:*

Possessing the Past. Houndmills, Basingstoke: Palgrave Macmillan: xi-xxvi.
Bakhtin, Mikhail. 1973. *Problems of Dostoevsky's Poetics* [1963] (trans. R.W. Rotsel). Ann Arbor: Michigan University Press.
Barrett, Susan. 2005. *Fixing Shadows*. London: Review.
Bergson, Henri. 1984. *Laughter: an Essay on the Meaning of the Comic* [1900] (trans. Cloudesley Brereton and Fred Rothwell), in Palmer, D. J. (ed.), *Comedy: Developments in Criticism*. Houndmills, Basingstoke: Macmillan Education: 62-65.
Berthin, Christine. 2010. *Gothic Hauntings: Melancholy Crypts and Textual Ghosts*. Houndmills, Basingstoke: Palgrave Macmillan.
Botting, Fred. 1996. *Gothic*. London & New York: Routledge.
—. 2007. 'Gothic Culture'. In Spooner and McEvoy (2007): 199-214.
—. 2008. *Limits of Horror. Technology, Bodies, Gothic*. Manchester: Manchester University Press.
Byatt, A.S. 1990. *Possession: A Romance*. London: Chatto & Windus.
—. 1993. *Angels and Insects* [1992]. London: Vintage.
Carter, Angela. 1994. *Nights at the Circus* [1984]. London: Vintage.
Derrida, Jacques. 1994. *Specters of Marx: The State of the Debt, the Work of Mourning, and the New International* (trans. Peggy Kamuf; intro. Bernd Magnus and Stephen Cullenberg). London & New York: Routledge.
—. 1978. *Writing and Difference* (trans. Alan Bass). London & New York: Routledge.
Eco, Umberto. 1994. *Postscript to* The Name of the Rose (trans. William Weaver). London: Minerva.
Elliott, Kamilla. 2007. 'Gothic – Film – Parody'. In Spooner and McEvoy (2007): 223-232.
Gibson, Andrew. 1996. *Towards a Postmodern Theory of Narrative*. Edinburgh: Edinburgh University Press.
Gray, Alasdair. 1993. *Poor Things* [1992]. Harmondsworth: Penguin.
Gutleben, Christian. 2001. *Nostalgic Postmodernism: The Victorian Tradition and the Contemporary British Novel*. Amsterdam & New York: Rodopi.
—. 2011. 'Hybridity as oxymoron : An interpretation of the dual nature of neo-Victorian fiction', in Guignery, Vanessa, Catherine Pesso-Miquel and François Specq (eds.), *Hybridity: Forms and Figures in Literature and the Visual Arts*. Newcastle-upon-Tyne: Cambridge Scholars Publishing: 59-70.
Heilmann, Ann, and Mark Llewellyn. 2010. *Neo-Victorianism: The Victorians in the Twenty-First Century, 1999-2009*. Houndmills, Basingstoke & New York: Palgrave Macmillan.
Horner, Avril, and Zlosnik, Sue. 2005. *Gothic and the Comic Turn*. Houndmills, Basingstoke: Palgrave Macmillan.
Hurley, Kelly. 2007. 'Abject and Grotesque'. In Spooner and McEvoy (2007): 137-146.
Hutcheon, Linda. 1985. *A Theory of Parody: The Teachings of Twentieth-Century Art Forms*. New York & London: Methuen.
—. 1988. *A Poetics of Postmodernism: History, Theory, Fiction*. New York & London: Routledge.
Jensen, Liz. 1998. *Ark Baby*. London: Bloomsbury.

—. 2007. *My Dirty Little Book of Stolen Time* [2006]. London: Bloomsbury.
Knoepflmacher, U.C. 2008. 'Editor's Preface: Hybrid Forms and Cultural Anxiety', *Studies in English Literature, 1500-1900* 48(4) (Autumn): 745-753.
Korkut, Nil. 2009. *Kinds of Parody from the Medieval to the Postmodern.* Frankfurt am Rhein: Peter Lang.
Miller, Miranda. 2010. *Nina in Utopia*. London: Peter Owen.
Mitchell, Kate. 2010. *History and Cultural Memory in Neo-Victorian Fiction: Victorian Afterimages*. Houndmills, Basingstoke: Palgrave Macmillan.
Muecke, D.C. 1982. *Irony and the Ironic*. The Critical Idiom. London & New York: Methuen.
O'Gorman, Francis. 2010. 'What is Haunting Tennyson's Maud (1855)?'. On-line at: http://readperiodicals.com/201010/2202889071.html#ixzz1lgaxx2PU (consulted 12.02.2012).
Olsen, Lance. 1990. *Circus of the Mind in Motion: Postmodernism and the Comic Vision*. Detroit: Wayne State University Press.
Olson, Elder. 1968. *The Theory of Comedy*. Bloomington, Indiana: Indiana University Press.
Onega, Susana, and Christian Gutleben. 2004. 'Introduction', in Onega, Susana, and Christian Gutleben (eds.), *Refracting the Canon in Contemporary British Literature and Film*. Amsterdam & New York: Rodopi: 7-16.
O'Neil, Patrick. 1990. *The Comedy of Entropy: Humour, Narrative, Reading*. Toronto: University of Toronto Press.
Punter, David. 1980. *The Literature of Terror: A History of Gothic Fictions from 1765 to the Present Day*. London: Longman.
—. 2007. 'The Uncanny'. In Spooner and McEvoy (2007): 129-136.
Rubik, Margarete, and Elke Mettinger-Schartman (eds.). 2007. *A Breath of Fresh Eyre: Intertextual and Intermedial Reworkings of* Jane Eyre. Amsterdam & New York: Rodopi.
Simmons, Dan. 2009. *Drood*. London: Quercus.
Smith, Andrew. 2007. 'Hauntings'. In Spooner and McEvoy (2007): 147-154.
Spooner, Catherine. 2004. *Fashioning Gothic Bodies*. Manchester: Manchester University Press.
—. 2006. *Contemporary Gothic*. London: Reaktion Books.
—. 2007. 'Gothic in the Twentieth Century'. In Spooner and McEvoy (2007): 38-47.
Spooner, Catherine, and Emma McEvoy (eds.). 2007. *The Routledge Companion to Gothic*. London & New York: Routledge.
Wilson, A.N. 2006. *A Jealous Ghost* [2005]. London: Arrow Books.
Wolfreys, Julian. 2002. *Victorian Hauntings: Spectrality, Gothic, the Uncanny and Literature*. Houndmills, Basingstoke: Palgrave Macmillan.

Contributors

Kym Brindle is an Associate Lecturer at Edge Hill University, UK, where she teaches a range of courses including Victorian Literature, Gothic Fiction, and British Postmodern Fiction. She obtained her PhD from Lancaster University, for a study of epistolary strategies in neo-Victorian fiction, which was funded by the Arts and Humanities Research Council. She has published essays in *Neo Victorian Studies* and the edited collection *Histories and Heroines: The Female Historical Figure in Contemporary Fiction* (Palgrave Macmillan, 2012), and her book entitled *Epistolary Encounters in Neo-Victorian Fiction: Diaries and Letters* is due to appear with Palgrave Macmillan in 2013.

Sebastian Domsch teaches Anglophone literatures at the Ernst-Moritz-Arndt-University Greifswald, Germany. He has published a German-language monograph on Robert Coovers's work and is editor of a collection on American twenty-first-century-century fiction, *Amerikanisches Erzählen nach 2000: Eine Bestandsaufnahme* (edition text + kritik, 2008), contributing editor to the *Kritisches Lexikon zur fremdsprachigen Gegenwartsliteratur* (Anglophone literatures), and co-editor (with Cristoph Bode) of a collection on the formation of eighteenth-century literary criticism; two further books are forthcoming: *Cormac McCarthy* (edition text + kritik, 2012) and *Storyplaying – Agency and Narrative in Video Games* (de Gruyter, 2013). His major fields of interest are contemporary literature and culture, graphic novels, the history and theory of literary criticism, eighteenth-century and Romantic literature.

Max Duperray is Professor Emeritus at Aix-Marseille Université, France. He has published a number of essays and books on Gothic literature, covering writers from Ann Radcliffe, Mary Shelley, and Thomas De Quincey to Bram Stoker, as well as on the subjects of alienation in literature and on literary wanderings in/through London. A forthcoming book, *La lame et la plume: Jack l'Eventreur, échos littéraires d'une affaire et d'un mythe victoriens* (L' Harmattan, 2013) will complement his essay on the Jack the Ripper mythos in this volume.

Cheryl Edelson is Associate Professor of English at Chaminade University of Honolulu, Hawaii, USA. Her research and teaching interests include American Literature, the Literary Gothic, Film and Television Studies, Indigenous Literatures, and Popular Culture. Cheryl regularly presents her work at national conferences such as the annual meetings of the Modern Language Association, the American Studies Association, and the Popular Culture Association.

Jeanne Ellis lectures in English Literature at Stellenbosch University, South Africa. Her areas of research and teaching include Victorian, neo-Victorian and Gothic literature, especially in the context of nineteenth-century afterlives and/or historiographic metafictions. She is currently working on a comparative study of recent revisions of the nineteenth century in fiction, poetry, drama, film and visual art from or about former British settler colonial contexts.

Christian Gutleben is Professor at the University of Nice-Sophia Antipolis, France, where he teaches nineteenth- and twentieth-century British literature. His research focuses on the links between these two historical periods and traditions, and he is the author of one of the earliest critical surveys of neo-Victorian literature, *Nostalgic Postmodernism: The Victorian Tradition and the Contemporary British Novel* (Rodopi, 2001), as well as co-editor (with Susana Onega) of *Refracting the Canon in Contemporary British Literature and Film* (Rodopi, 2004). He has also published books on the English campus novel and Graham Greene, as well as numerous articles on postmodernism in British literature, and is co-editor (with Marie-Luise Kohlke) of Rodopi's Neo-Victorian Series, including *Neo-Victorian Tropes of Trauma: The Politics of Bearing After-Witness to Nineteenth-Century Suffering* (Rodopi, 2010) and *Neo-Victorian Families: Gender, Sexual and Cultural Politics* (Rodopi, 2011).

Marie-Luise Kohlke lectures in English Literature at Swansea University, UK, and is the General and Founding Editor of the peer-reviewed e-journal *Neo-Victorian* Studies. She is co-editor (with Luisa Orza) of *Negotiating Sexual Idioms: Image, Text, Performance* (Rodopi, 2008) and has published articles and book chapters on historical fiction, trauma literature, and women's writing. She is co-editor (with Christian Gutleben) of Rodopi's Neo-Victorian Series, including *Neo-Victorian Tropes of Trauma: The Politics of Bearing After-Witness to Nineteenth-Century Suffering* (Rodopi, 2010) and *Neo-Victorian Families: Gender, Sexual and Cultural Politics* (Rodopi, 2011).

Van Leavenworth is an Assistant Professor in English Literature at the Department of Language Studies at Umeå University, Sweden. He teaches undergraduate and graduate courses covering a wide array of literary and cultural studies topics. His research interests include neo-Victorian fiction, the Gothic (in diverse media forms), science fiction and conceptions of 'otherness' in various narrative contexts.

Sarah E. Maier is an Associate Professor in English and Comparative Literature at the University of New Brunswick, Canada, and recipient of her institution's Dr. Allan P. Stuart Memorial Award for Excellence in Teaching (2003). She has published on the work of James M. Barrie, Charlotte Brontë, Ella D'Arcy, George Eliot, Thomas Hardy, Mary Wollstonecraft and others, with scholarly editions of works by Louisa M. Alcott, Ella D'Arcy, Sarah Grand, and Bram Stoker forthcoming. Her research interests include decadents/ce and the 1880/90s, the New Woman, neo-Victorianism, and adaptations of Victorian texts to film, Jack the Ripper, vampires, and gothic fiction, as well as fictional representations of serial killers and forensic science in film/TV.

Patricia Pulham is Reader in Victorian Literature and Director of the Centre for Studies in Literature at the University of Portsmouth, UK. She is author of *Art and the Transitional Object in Vernon Lee's Supernatural Tales*, (Ashgate Press, 2008) and co-editor of *Hauntings and Other Fantastic Tales* (Broadview Press, 2006), *Vernon Lee: Decadence, Ethics, Aesthetics* (Palgrave Macmillan, 2006), *Haunting and Spectrality in Neo-Victorian Fiction: Possessing the Past*

(Palgrave Macmillan, 2010) and *Crime Culture: Figuring Criminality in Literature, Media and Film* (Continuum 2010).

Andrew Smith is Reader in Nineteenth Century English Literature at the University of Sheffield, UK. His extensive publications on the Gothic include *The Ghost Story 1840-1920: A Cultural History* (Manchester University Press, 2010) *Gothic Literature* (Edinburgh University Press 2007, with a new revised edition forthcoming 2013), *Victorian Demons: Medicine, Masculinity and the Gothic at the fin-de-siecle* (Manchester University Press, 2004) and *Gothic Radicalism: Literature, Philosophy and Psychoanalysis in the Nineteenth Century* (Macmillan, 2000). He is Co-President of the International Gothic Association, an elected Fellow of the Royal Society of Arts (2007), an elected Fellow of the English Association (2008), and an editorial board member of *Gothic Studies*. His research interests are in Gothic literature, literature and science, nineteenth-century literature, and critical theory, on which he regularly presents conference papers and keynote lectures in Europe and North America.

Index

Ackroyd, Peter, 27, 167, 180, 183-187, 309, 323
Adams, David, 138
Ahluwalia, Pal, 126-127
Akunin, Boris, 180
Alexander, Karl, 10
Altick, Richard D., 279, 285, 295
Andersen, Hendrick, 154
Arata, Stephen D., 30
Arias, Rosario, 5, 6, 150, 198, 269, 306, 311
Armitt, Lucie, 13, 26, 224
Armstrong, Anne, 288
Armstrong, Isobel, 162, 164
Atwood, Margaret, 13, 129, 139-140, 223, 225, 279-288, 291-296
Austen, Jane, 189
Babbage, Charles, 266
Bainbridge, Beryl, 279-296
Bakhtin, Mikhail, 307
Bardinelli, John, 265
Barker, Gus, 153
Barnes, Julian, 283
Barret, Susan, 319
Bartlett, Adelaide, 279
Baudelaire, Charles, 201
Baudrillard, Jean, 39
Bayard, Louis, 26
Beardsley, Aubrey, 174
Becker, Susanne, 221, 248, 285, 295
Beecham, George, 212
Bellop, Hilaire, 138
Belloq, Lowndes Marie, 167, 169, 177-179, 190
Belsey, Catherine, 138
Bentham, Jeremy, 257
Bergson, Henri, 319-320
Berthin, Christine, 3, 313
Best, Sue, 136
Beville, Maria, 39, 260, 296
Bidisha [aka ShonarKoli Mamata], 246-247
Birch, Carol, 18-19
Blake, Sarah, 5
Blake, William, 187, 205
Bloch, Robert, 183
Bloom, Clive, 198
Blumenberg, Hans, 137-138
Boas, Franz, 90
Boccardi, Mariadeli, 62,
Bolton, Linda, 77
Bonaparte, Napoléon, 173
Bond, T., 203
Borman, Daniel Candel, 75
Bosanquet, Theodora, 149
Botting, Fred, 1, 2, 4, 17, 40, 41, 114, 235, 242, 245, 286, 302, 312

Bowser, Rachel A., 20-21, 24, 109, 256
Brabon, Benjamin A., 240-241, 247, 248
Braddon, Mary Elizabeth, 28
Brantlinger, Patrick, 101, 106
Brewer, David A., 98, 105
Brewer, John Francis, 170
Brindle, Kym, 38, 129
Britten, Benjamin, 148
Brontë, Charlotte, 8-9, 13, 34, 130, 223, 233, 235, 237, 240, 289
Brontë, Emily, 223, 235
Brown, Charles Brockden, 191
Browning, Robert, 304, 305
Bucknill, Sir John Charles, 257
Burke, Edmund, 264
Bruhm, Steven, 20, 259
Burman, Carina, 28
Burne-Jones, Edward, 321
Burns, Robert, 173
Burstein, Miriam E., 242, 244-245
Busse, Kristina, 106
Butler, Octavia, 10
Byatt, A.S., 6, 10, 12, 14, 70, 83, 85, 304-308, 321
Byron, George Gordon, 31-32, 172, 173
Byron, Glennis, 76-77, 93, 280, 285
Caine, Michael, 193
Cameron, Deborah, 200
Campbell, Eddie, 29, 100, 112, 173, 197, 242
Canter, David, 206
Carew, Edith, 279
Carey, Peter, 26, 35, 127-128

Carr, Caleb, 13, 27, 197, 199, 206-213
Carriger, Gail, 24
Carroll, Lewis, 322
Carter, Angela, 141, 223, 232, 238, 296, 314-315
Castle, Terry, 155-156, 259
Castricano, Jodey, 125
Cavale, Jude, 21
Cave, Nick, 193
Cavendish, Margaret, 104
Cervantes, Miguel de, 107
Chaplin, Patrice, 191
Chapman, Alison, 269
Chapman, Annie, 202
Chappell, David A., 79
Charcot, Jean-Martin, 16, 182
Churchill, Winston, 22
Cixous, Hélène, 137
Clark, Clare, 6
Clark, Ronald W., 20
Clayton, Jay, 20
Coetzee, J.M., 140
Coleridge, Samuel Taylor, 6
Collela, Sylvana, 16
Collingwood-Whittick, Sheila, 126, 138
Collins, Wilkie, 28, 167, 172, 175, 177, 180, 235, 285, 318-319
Conan Doyle, Arthur, 99, 102, 105, 107, 175-176, 187, 188, 190-192, 201, 213, 217, 283, 285-286
Connor, Mick, 282
Conrad, Joseph, 53, 63, 68-69, 78, 79
Cook, Florence, 283

Cornwell, Patricia, 173, 189, 201
Cox, Michael, 11
Craft, Christopher, 290
Croxall, Brian, 20-21, 24, 109, 256
Dames, Nicholas, 130
Darwin, Charles, 269
Davison, Carol Margaret, 4, 44, 170
Dawson, Graham, 81
Day, Grove A., 84
de Certeau, Michel, 79-80, 82, 85, 92
Defoe, Daniel, 81
Degas, Edgar, 173
Depp, Johnny, 205
De Quincey, Thomas, 169, 171, 174-175, 185, 189, 199, 309
Derrida, Jacques, 55, 72, 271, 312, 313, 314
Desnos, Robert, 175
de Villiers, David, 141
D'Haen, Theo, 35-36
Dibdin, Michael, 172, 176, 197, 199, 213-218
Dickens, Charles, 8, 13, 20, 26, 35, 127-128, 167, 172, 176, 184, 186, 190, 246, 264, 318-319
Dickinson, Emily, 292
Di Filippo, Paul, 109
Di Rollo's, Elaine, 223
Domsch, Sebastian, 25, 32, 76, 173, 202, 256, 259
Dorsey, George, 90
Douglas, Carole Nelson, 172
Douglas, John, 201
Douglass, Jeremy, 254
Duda, Heather L., 98
Du Maurier, Daphne, 225
Duperray, Max, 29, 38, 100, 323
Dury, Japheth, 212
Eco, Umberto, 303, 311
Eddowes, Catherine, 192, 201-202
Edel, Leon, 147
Edelson, Cherryl D., 36, 131
Edmundson, Mark, 1, 19-20, 30
Edwards, Justin D., 125, 140
Elliott, Kamilla, 302
Ellis, Havelock, 155
Ellis, Jeanne, 37, 76, 316
Ellis, Markman, 3
Ellison, Harlan, 183
Engels, Friedrich, 72
Evans, Stuart P., 204
Faber, Michel, 13, 239, 266
Farber, Leora, 37, 76, 123-141, 316
Farjeon, Benjamin, 180
Farjeon, Clanash, 167, 180-182, 190
Faye, Lindsay, 176
Ferguson, Christine, 97, 200
Fiedler, Leslie, 247
Fish, Laura, 13
Flynn, Michael, 266
Foster, Hal, 34
Foster, Star C., 253, 265
Foucault, Michel, 15, 82, 87, 89, 246, 257
Fowles, John, 3
Frankin, Robert, 321
Franklin, Benjamin, 75, 89

Frenck, Joachim, 98, 111
Freud, Sigmund, 136-137, 150, 155, 246, 315
Freund, Karl, 92
Friedan, Betty, 234
Frisbie, Robert Dean, 79
Fritzl, Elizabeth, 28
Fritzl, Josef, 28
Fukuyama, Francis, 38
Fullerton, Morton, 149
Fuss, Diana, 206
Gamble, Sarah, 198
Gauguin, Paul, 77-79
Gavin, Adrienne E.,
Genette, Gérard, 291
Genz, Stéphanie, 248
Gibson, Andrew, 314
Gibson, Carlo, 128
Gibson, Matthew, 56-57
Gibson, William, 109, 256, 266
Gilbert, Sandra M., 8-9, 129, 235
Gilman, Charlotte Perkins, 229, 233, 240
Gissing, George, 185, 288
Glinoer, Anthony, 174
Godwin, William, 309
Goldie, Terry, 136
Gomel, Elana, 203
Goodman, Carol, 13, 313
Goonan, Anne, 323
Gosse, Edmund, 154, 155, 160, 163
Gray, Alasdair, 44, 308-309, 314, 321, 323
Gray, Drew D., 200
Greer, Germaine, 126, 140
Grimm (brothers), 176

Gubar, Susan, 8-9, 129, 235
Gull, William, 204
Guppy, Shusha, 284
Gutiérrez, Felix Martin, 192
Gutleben, Christian, 9, 39, 51, 125, 141, 202, 311, 317, 322
Guttman, Bertha, 125
Haggard, Rider H., 30, 99, 101, 103, 107, 110, 113
Haggerty, George E., 156-157
Halbwachs, Maurice, 58
Hall, Donald E., 270
Hallam, Arthur, 306-308
Halttunen, Karen, 162-163
Hannah, Daniel, 151, 156
Hantke, Steffen, 209, 260, 266
Harris, Joanne, 13, 313
Harrison, William, 293
Harter, Deborah A., 212
Hartlib, Samuel, 309
Harwood, John, 5, 148
Haste, Steve, 280
Hawksmoor, Nicholas, 184
Hayles, Catherine N., 254
Heawood, Jonathan, 42
Heiland, Donna, 231, 234
Heilmann, Ann, 5, 16, 42-43, 53, 57-58, 100, 125-126, 138, 164, 281, 283, 303-304
Hellekson, Karen, 106
Herenico, Vilsoni, 93-94
Hewit, Nicholas, 174
Heyns, Michael, 149
Higgins, F.E., 321
Hitchcock, Alfred, 177, 187, 193

Hoeveler, Diane Long, 223, 225
Hogle, Jerrold E., 40, 126, 264
Holland, Norman M., 239
Holland, Tom, 19-20, 30-32, 41
Hollinghurst, Alan, 149
Holman, Sheri, 12
Holmes, Oliver Wendell, 153
Homer, 106
Hood, Robin, 60
Hood, Thomas, 85-86, 88-89, 91
Horne, Philip, 160
Horner, Avril, 40, 259, 301-302, 318, 323
Howard, Jacqueline, 37
Howes, Craig, 89
Hughes, Albert, 205
Hughes, Allen, 205
Hughes, William, 42
Hume, David, 210
Hurley, Kelly, 23, 212, 238, 241, 269, 315
Hutcheon, Linda, 38, 296, 320
Hyams, Peter, 92
Hynes, James, 184
Ingersoll, Earl G., 294
Irigaray, Luce, 136
Irving, Henry, 170
Jack the Ripper, 27, 28, 29, 31, 32, 38, 100, 112, 167-193, 197-214, 216, 218, 242, 309, 323
Jacobs, W.W., 179
Jagoda, Patrick, 257
James, Henry, 13, 42, 147-165, 189-192, 310-312
James, P.D., 226

James, William, 189, 210, 211
Jensen, Liz, 10, 314, 316-317, 321-322
Jeremiah, Emily,
Johnson, Brian, 136
Jones, Amelia, 134
Jones, Jason B., 109, 111
Joukowsky, Paul, 163-164
Joyce, Simon, 59
Kaplan, Cora, 5, 147, 150-152, 224, 229, 234, 295
Keats, John, 306
Kelly, Gary, 222
Kelly, Mary, 202, 206
Kemp, Peter, 149
Khair, Tabish, 33
Khoury, George, 108
Killeen, Jarlath, 234
Kincaid, James R., 13, 14
Kinnear, Thomas, 282, 293
Kirchknopf, Andrea, 51
Kirtley, Becil F., 84
Kliś, Agnieszka, 206
Klopper, Sandra, 129-134, 136, 141
Kneale, Matthew, 6, 17-18
Kneubuhl, Nalani, 36, 75-77, 80, 88-93
Knight, Stephen, 100, 172-173
Knoch, Jessica, 267
Knoepflmacher, U.C., 124, 322
Knowles, Claire, 221
Kohlke, Marie-Luise, 9, 29, 58, 59, 141, 150, 198, 202, 216, 235, 294
Korkut, Nil, 320
Kostova, Elizabeth, 51-72
Kristeva, Julia, 228-229

Krueger, Christine L., 62
Krug, Christian, 98, 111
Kruger, Paul, 128
Kucich, John, 253
Laski, Marghanita, 10, 221-222, 226-234, 239
Law-Viljoen, Bronwyn, 142
Leatherdale, Clive, 60
Leavenworth, Van, 25, 32, 109, 268
Leder, Herbert J., 92
Lee, Christopher, 105
Lee, Vernon, 147, 174
Le Fanu, Sheridan, 174, 180, 190
Leno, Dan, 185-186
Lewis, Matthew Gregory, 174
Lincoln (President), 10
Llewelyn, Mark, 5, 16, 42-43, 53, 57-58, 76, 100, 125-126, 129, 138, 164, 217, 281, 283, 303-304
Locke, John, 210
Lodge, David, 149, 150, 152
Lombroso, Cesare, 216
Lonsdale, Kate, 205
Lord, Beth, 91
Lovecraft, H.P., 89, 92
Luckhurst, Roger, 16
Lugosi, Bela, 105
Lyne, Adrian, 31
Lyotard, Jean-François, 39
MacDonald, Dwight, 88-89, 91
Machen, Arthur, 171, 174
Machiavelli, Niccolò di Bernardo, 56
Mac Orlan, Pierre, 174-175
Maier, Sarah E., 27, 29, 31, 100, 242

Malchow, Howard, 101-102, 114
Manet, Edouard, 64, 77
Mann, George, 23-25
Mansfield, Richard, 170
Marantz-Cohen, Paula, 189, 191, 192
Marks, Bertha, 123, 128, 130, 136, 139
Marks, Grace, 13, 27, 129, 224, 279, 282, 283, 287, 288, 291
Marks, Sammy, 125, 128, 131
Marsh, Kelly A., 286
Marsh, Richard, 269
Martin, John, 321
Martin, Valerie, 28, 186, 323
Marx, Karl, 72, 185
Matheson, Neill, 156-157, 159-160
Maupassant, Guy de, 177
Maybrick, Florence, 279
McCarthy, Joseph, 60
McDermott, James, 224, 282, 293
McMaster, Juliet, 163
Mendelsohn, Richard, 128
Merivale, Patricia, 148
Merleau-Ponty, Maurice, 91
Merrick, Joseph John, 216
Mettinger-Schartman, Elke, 323
Meyers, Helene, 225, 226, 248
Michael, Magali Cornier, 287, 294
Mighall, Robert, 280, 286
Milburn, Colin, 198
Miles, Robert, 4
Miller, Frank, 104

Miller, Judy, 261
Miller, Kathleen A., 224
Miller, Miranda, 10, 316-317, 322
Milligan, Spike, 193
Mishra, Vijay, 260, 273
Mitchell, Kate, 5, 52, 58-59, 224, 306, 311
Mitchell, Margaret, 225
Moers, Ellen, 227
Montfort, Nick, 254
Montgomery, Nancy, 282
Moodie, Susanna, 129, 139-140, 283, 284, 287, 291-292
Moore, Alan, 29, 76, 97-98, 100-119, 173, 197, 200, 205, 212, 242, 256
Moorehead, Warren K., 90
Moretti, Franco, 9, 11, 15, 57
Morrison, Toni, 13, 313
Morrissey, Steven Patrick, 193
Muecke, D.C., 310
Mullan, John, 17
Muller, Nadine, 224
Murray, Jennifer, 294
Nevins, Jess, 97, 110, 117
Nichols, Mary Ann, 201-202
Nihipali, Hui Malama P'o Kunani, 87
Nodier, Charles, 174
Nora, Pierre, 58-59
O'Brien, Frank, 78
O'Gorman, Francis, 306
Oldfield, Pamela, 179, 191
Olsen, Lance, 315
Olson, Elder, 302
Onega, Susana, 317
O'Neil, Patrick, 40, 302

O'Neill, Kevin, 76, 97-98, 100, 104, 107, 110-119, 256
Onion, Rebecca, 21
Paley, William, 24
Palliser, Charles, 10, 239
Pater, Siemek, 128
Pater, Walter, 154
Payne, Sarah, 13
Pearl, Matthew, 26
Perschon, Mike, 98
Petschek, Willa, 290
Pick, Daniel, 268
Pietrzak-Franger, Monika, 100, 200
Pike, David L., 266
Plath, Sylvia, 134
Poe, Edgar Allan, 103, 169, 175, 182, 192, 201, 235, 306, 308
Pollidori, John William, 31
Porter, Brian, L., 177, 182-183, 191
Potter, Beatrix, 117
Power, Maggie, 40, 221-222, 234-241
Pratt, Marie-Louise, 265
Price, David, 16
Pulham, Patricia, 5, 42, 102, 150, 269, 306, 311, 312
Pullman, Philip, 20
Punter, David, 76-77, 93, 116, 280, 285, 304, 316
Pyrhönen, Heta, 224, 239
Rabaté, Jean-Michel, 150
Radcliffe, Ann, 17, 175, 180
Ravenhill, Mark, 246
Ravipinto, David, 253, 254, 265

Remington, Ted, 169
Reynolds, G.W.M., 172, 264
Rhys, Jean, 3, 34, 130, 226, 236
Ricoeur, Paul, 137
Riding In, James, 86-87
Rimbaud, Arthur, 187
Riquelme, Jean-Paul, 78
Roberts, Michèle, 283
Robertson, Fiona, 284
Robertson, Morgan, 111
Rohmer, Sax, 99
Roof, Judith, 258
Rossetti, Christina, 293
Rossetti, Dante Gabriel, 321
Rossington, Michael, 58
Royle, Nicholas, 124
Rubik, Margarete, 323
Rushdie, Salman, 37
Russell Perkin, James, 150
Saberhagen, Fred, 10
Sadoff, Dianne F., 35, 253
Sage, Victor, 10, 15, 25-26
Samuelson, Meg, 141
Sardou, Victorien, 246
Sargent, John Singer, 189
Scarfe, Alan, 180
Schmitt, Cannon, 101
Schopenhauer, Arthur, 210
Schwartz, Daniel R., 77
Scott, Walter, 318
Sedgwick, Eve Kosofsky, 152, 159, 263, 284
Self, Will, 42
Seltzer, Mark, 201
Seshagiri, Urmila, 98
Shakespeare, William, 309, 318
Sharpe, Jenny, 130

Sharrad, Paul, 80
Shelley, Mary, 174, 268, 308
Sherman, Cindy, 134
Sherman, Leona F., 239
Shiel, Matthew Phipps, 117
Shiller, Dana, 76, 127
Showalter, Elaine, 229
Sickert, Walter, 173, 189, 201, 205
Simmons, Dan, 26, 318-319
Sinclair, Iain, 102, 167, 176, 184, 187-188, 191-192
Skinner, Keith, 204
Smith, Allen Lloyd, 10, 15, 25-26, 28, 36, 40-41
Smith, Andrew, 3, 7, 29, 38, 42, 171, 177, 222, 227, 243, 281, 283, 313
Smith, Madeleine, 279
Southey, Robert, 86
Spencer, Herbert, 210
Spivak, Gayatri, 33
Spooner, Catherine, 1, 2, 4, 40, 42, 43, 52-53, 200, 217, 254, 280, 282, 296, 302, 312, 313, 320
Spurr, David, 257-258, 265
Stride, Elizabeth, 202
Stace, Wesley, 232
Staines, David, 139
Stalin, Iossif, 55, 56
Starling, Belinda, 13
Stead, W.T., 171
Stelard, 124
Sterling, Bruce, 109, 256, 266
Stern, Simon, 105, 106
Stevenson, Robert Louis, 88-89, 99, 110, 167, 172, 174, 188, 217, 227, 323

Stoker, Bram, 31, 53, 55-57, 60-62, 70, 83, 99, 101, 105, 108, 116, 167, 170, 172, 182, 189-191, 235, 290
Stoker, Dacre, 52, 71
Sugars, Cynthia, 127, 130
Summerscale, Kate, 283
Sussman, Herbert, 115
Swift, Jonathan, 104, 116
Symonds, John Addington, 154-155
Tabbi, Joseph, 274
Taylor, Don, 92
Tennant, Emma, 149, 323
Tennyson, Alfred, 291, 306, 308, 321
Thomas, D.M., 34, 239
Tillotson, Kathleen, 286
Todorov, Tzvetan, 217
Tóibín, Colm, 42, 147-165, 312
Torrey, Fuller E., 261
Trask, Haunani-Kay, 86-87
Trotter, David, 135
Tumblety, Francis, 177
Turcotte, Gerry, 127, 130
Turner, Frederick Jackson, 135
Tutu, Desmond, 123
Urquhart, David, 257
Van Rensburg, Willem, 129
Veracini, Lorenzo, 131, 138
Verlaine, Paul, 187
Victoria (Queen), 3, 23, 25, 204
Volk, Stephen, 193
Walkowitz, Judith R., 169, 172
Wallace, Diana, 222, 227
Walpole, Horace, 194, 281

Walshe, Eibhear, 151
Warwick, Alexandra, 10, 20, 26, 171, 191, 199, 201, 202, 206, 268, 296
Wasson, Richard, 60
Waters, Sarah, 13, 26, 28, 52, 71, 148, 154, 223, 225, 232, 238, 266
Watson, John Selby, 282
Waugh, Patricia, 283
Wells, H.G., 17, 99, 115, 117, 119, 171, 269
Wendt, Albert, 36, 75-77, 80-85, 92-93
West, Paul, 167-168, 172-174, 184, 191
Wharton, Edith, 149
Whistler, James Abbott McNeill, 173
Whitehead, Anne, 59, 61
Wiesenthal, Chris, 261
Wilde, Oscar, 154, 158-160, 164, 173
Wilke, Hannah, 134
Williams, Anne, 180, 226, 236
Williams, Kate, 13, 27, 221-222, 241-247
Williams, Rhynwick, 200
Wilson, A.N., 13, 148, 309-312
Wilson, Sharon R., 294
Winslow, Lyttleton S. Forbes, 180-181, 191, 208, 210
Wolf, Naomi, 224, 225
Wolfreys, Julian, 3, 7-8, 42, 149-150, 287, 311, 315, 322-323, 324
Womak, Kenneth, 9-10

Woolf, Virginia, 128, 131-132, 193, 229
Woolson, Constance Fenimore, 149, 154, 155, 164
Workman, Joseph, 292
Wright, Elizabeth A., 85
Yeats, W.B., 270, 273
Young, Robert J.C., 102, 130
Zlosnik, Sue, 40, 259, 301-302, 318, 323
Zylinska, Joanna, 17, 24

Figures de l'émigré russe en France au XIXe et XXe siècle

Fiction et réalité

Sous la direction de
Charlotte Krauss et
Tatiana Victoroff

Le présent ouvrage donne une vue d'ensemble des recherches actuelles consacrées à l'émigration russe en France. Il ose une approche nouvelle en confrontant les émigrés russes réels, dont de nombreux écrivains et poètes russes transitant par la France ou s'y installant, aux figures fictionnelles reflétant les retentissements de ces flux migratoires dans l'imaginaire du pays d'accueil. Le choix inhabituel d'une période très longue, du début du XIXe siècle à nos jours, permet de suivre les continuités et les évolutions, des migrations passagères et cas individuels sous le régime tsariste aux différentes vagues de l'émigration après la Révolution russe. Le recueil se compose d'une trentaine d'articles rédigés par des chercheurs internationaux, spécialistes de littératures russe, française et comparée. Leurs contributions, qui rendent compte de la complexité du phénomène, sont accompagnées de plusieurs témoignages ainsi que de nombreuses illustrations permettant de visualiser aussi bien la réalité que la fiction de l'émigration russe en France.

Amsterdam/New York, NY
2012. IV, 525 pp.
(Internationale
Forschungen zur
Allgemeinen und
Vergleichenden
Literaturwissenschaft 155)
Bound €105,-/US$142,-
E-Book €95,-/US$128,-
ISBN: 978-90-420-3477-8
ISBN: 978-94-012-0756-0

USA/Canada:
248 East 44th Street, 2nd floor,
New York, NY 10017, USA.
Call Toll-free (US only): T: 1-800-225-3998
F: 1-800-853-3881
All other countries:
Tijnmuiden 7, 1046 AK Amsterdam, The Netherlands
Tel. +31-20-611 48 21 Fax +31-20-447 29 79
Please note that the exchange rate is subject to fluctuations

Mapping Memory in Nineteenth-Century French Literature and Culture

Edited by
Susan Harrow and
Andrew Watts

Memory and memory studies have shaped a major site of humanities research over the last twenty years. Examined by ethnographers, archaeologists, social scientists, historians, economists, archivists, art historians, and literary scholars, the theme of memory – individual memory and memoir, collective memory, official memory and oral memory, cultural memory and popular memory – has informed academic discourse and formed institutional structures. Yet, the matter of memory is, paradoxically, under-explored in studies of the 'long nineteenth century' in France. *Mapping Memory in Nineteenth-Century French Literature and Culture* focuses critical attention on that neglected century when France was struggling to negotiate the serially renewed memory of revolutionary turmoil and socio-cultural redefinition. This volume explores the spaces that the memory process claims and shapes, and it works to identify the crosscurrents that connect those spaces. It asks how memory resists – or cedes to – colonisations by authority, by official discourse, by history, and by aesthetics. It asks how memory-work coincides with or morphs into the processes of the imagination. Eschewing diachronic approaches, the contributors to this volume explore *sites* around which memory is concentrated or which it shapes and informs: Memory on the Street; Sites of National Memory; Metamorphoses: Memory and Literary Practice; and Memory's Imaginary Spaces.

Amsterdam/New York, NY
2012. 331 pp.
(Faux Titre 369)
Paper €66,-/US$89,-
E-Book €60,-/US$81,-
ISBN: 978-90-420-3458-7
ISBN: 978-94-012-0742-3

USA/Canada:
248 East 44th Street, 2nd floor,
New York, NY 10017, USA.
Call Toll-free (US only): T: 1-800-225-3998
F: 1-800-853-3881

All other countries:
Tijnmuiden 7, 1046 AK Amsterdam, The Netherlands
Tel. +31-20-611 48 21 Fax +31-20-447 29 79
Please note that the exchange rate is subject to fluctuations

Aspects of Dostoevskii

Art, Ethics and Faith

Edited by
Robert Reid and
Joe Andrew

Perhaps more than any other nineteenth-century Russian writer, Dostoevskii's continuing popularity rests on his contemporary relevance. The prophetic streak in his creativity gives him the same lasting appeal as dystopian novelists such as Zamiatin and Orwell whom he influenced and whose ethical concerns he anticipated. Religious themes are prominent in his work, too, and, though he was a believer, his interest seems to lie in the tension between faith and unbelief, which was felt as keenly in the Russia of his time as in our own. The nature of Dostoevskii's art also continues to be debated. The older tendency to disparage his literary method has given way to a recognition of the originality of his techniques, without which his ideological concerns would not have emerged with such thought-provoking clarity. The chapters which comprise this volume address these issues in a range of Dostoevskii's works, from shorter classics, such as *House of the Dead* and *Notes from Underground* to great novels such as *Crime and Punishment* and *The Brothers Karamazov*. This work will be of use to scholars and students of Dostoevskii at all levels as well as to those with an interest in nineteenth-century literature more generally.

Amsterdam/New York, NY
2012. XIII, 306 pp.
(Studies in Slavic Literature
and Poetics 57)
Paper €66,-/US$89,-
E-Book €60,-/US$81,-
ISBN: 978-90-420-3514-0
ISBN: 978-94-012-0789-8

USA/Canada:
248 East 44th Street, 2nd floor,
New York, NY 10017, USA.
Call Toll-free (US only): T: 1-800-225-3998
F: 1-800-853-3881

All other countries:
Tijnmuiden 7, 1046 AK Amsterdam, The Netherlands
Tel. +31-20-611 48 21 Fax +31-20-447 29 79
Please note that the exchange rate is subject to fluctuations

Wagner and the Novel

Wagner's Operas and the European Realist Novel: An exploration of genre

Hugh Ridley

rodopi
Orders@rodopi.nl—www.rodopi.nl

This study bridges literature and music at an exciting and controversial point, offering the lover of music and literature and the specialist reader an insight into the relationship between Wagner's operas and the nineteenth century novel, including comparisons with *Rigoletto* and *Der Rosenkavalier* in their evolution from other forms. It discusses matters of genre and national tradition, placing Wagner's works in the heritage of the European Enlightenment.

Comparisons of Wagner's works with the novel have been fleeting, denoting only their length and complexity. Examining in principle and in detail the proximity of Wagner's themes and techniques to the practices of the Realist novel, this study sheds original light on major issues of Wagner's works and on opera as genre.

The book trawls extensively in two research fields. It looks to the established Wagner literature for understandings of the musical procedures which map his works onto the prose fiction, while reading Wagner's operas against the backdrop of the European novel, rather than against German Romantic fiction. It revisits Adorno's music sociology and his seminal study of Wagner, but repositions many elements of his argument. Unusually, this book adopts a critical stance to Nietzsche's view of Wagner. In marked contrast to Nietzsche, the study regards parallels between Wagner and Flaubert as an enrichment of our understanding of Wagner's achievement.

The book concludes with a major question of European cultural history: why it is that – in common with Italy, but in marked contrast to France or England – Germany's most representative works in the nineteenth century are operas rather than novels.

Amsterdam/New York, NY
2012. 235 pp.
(Internationale Forschungen
zur Allgemeinen und
Vergleichenden
Literaturwissenschaft 156)
Paper €50,-/US$65,-
E-Book €45,-/US$59,-
ISBN: 978-90-420-3521-8
ISBN: 978-94-012-0796-6

USA/Canada:
248 East 44th Street, 2nd floor,
New York, NY 10017, USA.
Call Toll-free (US only): T: 1-800-225-3998
F: 1-800-853-3881
All other countries:
Tijnmuiden 7, 1046 AK Amsterdam, The Netherlands
Tel. +31-20-611 48 21 Fax +31-20-447 29 79
Please note that the exchange rate is subject to fluctuations